Knowledge and Power in the Global Economy

Politics and the Rhetoric of School Reform

Sociocultural, Political, and Historical Studies in Education

Joel Spring, Editor

Spring • The Cultural Transformation of a Native American Family and Its Tribe 1763–1995

Reagan • Non-Western Educational Traditions: Alternative Approaches to Educational Thought and Practice

Peshkin • Places of Memory: Whiteman's Schools and Native American Communities

Spring • Political Agendas for Education: From the Christian Coalition to the Green Party

Nespor • Tangled Up in School: Politics, Space, Bodies, and Signs in the Educational Process

Weinberg • Asian American Education: Historical Background and Current Realities

Books • Invisible Children in the Society and Its Schools

Shapiro/Purpel, eds. • Critical Social Issues in American Education: Transformation of a Postmodern World, Second Edition

Lipka/Mohatt/The Ciulistet Group • Transforming the Culture of Schools: Yup'ik Eskimo Examples

Benham/Heck • Culture and Educational Policy in Hawa'ii: The Silencing of Native Voices

Spring • Education and the Rise of the Global Economy

Pugach • On the Border of Opportunity: Education, Community, and Language at the U.S.–Mexico Line

Hones/Cha • Educating New Americans: Immigrant Lives and Learning

Gabbard, ed. • Knowledge and Power in the Global Economy: Politics and the Rhetoric of School Reform

Glander • Origins of Mass Communications During the American Cold War: Educational Effects and Contemporary Implications

Knowledge and Power in the Global Economy

Politics and the Rhetoric of School Reform

Edited by

David A. Gabbard
East Carolina University

LEA LAWRENCE ERLBAUM ASSOCIATES, PUBLISHERS
2000 Mahwah, New Jersey London

Lawrence Erlbaum Associates, Inc., Publishers
10 Industrial Avenue
Mahwah, NJ 07430

Cover design by Kathryn Houghtaling Lacey

Library of Congress Cataloging-in-Publication Data
Gabbard, David A.
Knowledge and Power in the Global Economy: Politics and the Rhetoric of School Reform / edited by David A. Gabbard
p. cm.
Includes bibliographical references and index
ISBN 0-8058-2433-2 (hard : alk. paper) —ISBN 0-8058-2434-0 (pbk. : alk. paper)
1. Education—Economic Aspects—United States. 2. Politics and education—United States. 3. Educational change—United States. 4. Curriculum changes—United States. 5. Critical pedagogy—United States
LC66.G33 1999
370.11'—dc21 98-30956
CIP

Books published by Lawrence Erlbaum Associates are printed on acid-free paper, and their bindings are chosen for strength and durability.

Printed in the United States of America

10 9 8 7 6 5 4 3 2

Contents

Preface

This book advances a threefold political agenda:

1. It demonstrates how the meanings assigned to a whole vocabulary of words and phrases frequently used to discuss the role and reform of U.S. public schools reflect an essentially economic view of the world.
2. It contends that education or educational reform conducted under an economized worldview will only intensify the nefarious effects of the colonial relations of political, cultural, and economic domination that it breeds at home and abroad.
3. It offers a set of alternative concepts and meanings for reformulating the role of U.S. public schools and for considering the implications of such a reformulation more generally for the underlying premises of all human relationships and activities.

Toward these ends, the various entries comprising Part I of this volume critically examine many of the most commonly used terms within the rhetoric of educational reform since the early 1980s and before. Each of these entries expands our awareness of the *economized* worldview that pervades the contemporary educational reform movement and sensitizes us to the manner in which that worldview reduces the value of everything to a measure of economic utility. Accordingly, education is only valuable to the extent that it services an economic imperative.

The entries in Part II link the economized worldview to curricular and instructional issues. These entries are especially important for comprehending how the organization of school curriculum privileges those disciplines deemed most central to market expansion (e.g., math and science) and how the political centrality of the economic sphere influences the nature of the knowledge presented in specific content areas. In addition to critiquing the economic form of perception reproduced by these key concepts, the authors of the entries in Parts I and II also offer proposals for how the meaning of these words might be *de-economized* to reflect a different, more vernacular perception of reality, one that does not separate the economic from the cultural, political, spiritual, moral, and natural spheres of human experience. Given that language constrains as well as advances human thought, the twin tasks of *de-economizing* education and *decolonizing* society will require a vocabulary that transcends the familiar terminologies addressed in Parts I and II. Part III, then, provides space to cultivate the beginnings of such a vocabulary as the authors elucidate innovative concepts they view as central to the creation of truly alternative educational visions and practices. To paraphrase Wolfgang Sachs's (1992) description of his fine collection that inspired me to pursue this project, "this book is an invitation to review the economized model of reality and to recognize that we all wear not merely tinted, but tainted, glasses if we take part in the prevailing educational discourse" (Sachs, 1992, p. 5).

In addition to Maureen, Mark, Nate, and the other good people at The Percolator coffee shop who kept the java flowing while I edited this volume at my "office away from the office," I need to give special thanks to my wife, Astrid, for supporting me through many months of long evenings spent locked up in my "office at home." I gratefully acknowledge the institutional support of the Department of Foundations, Research and Reading in the School of Education at East Carolina University. I would also like to thank the many contributors to this volume, not only for their outstanding work but more important, for their patience and understanding while this project went through many too many unfortunate delays. Between the two of us, Astrid and I lost three parents and an older sibling while I carried out the editorial work on this collection. Losing them made an already daunting task that much more difficult. Finally, then, I want to thank Naomi Silverman and Joel Spring for their support. Their patience and compassion during this difficult time was most appreciated.

REFERENCE

Sachs, W. (1992) *The development dictionary: A guide to knowledge as power.* Atlantic Highlands, NJ: Zed Books.

Introduction

David A. Gabbard
East Carolina University

SPREADING THE SECULAR GOSPEL

To challenge the belief that a people's economic development proceeds in direct proportion to their level of educational achievement poses a threat of heresy against one of the most fundamental principles in modern secular theology. Precisely because education and development each implies a process resulting in some form of favorable change, we may properly speak of them as separate values. However, whereas education has a history of conceptual evolution separate from that of development, their evolutionary paths have since merged and congealed into one of the great and sacred certainties of our era. Nowhere, perhaps, has this belief taken stronger hold than in the United States, where the educational reform initiatives of the 1980s and 1990s have now elevated this belief to canonical status.

At least two approaches present themselves for casting doubt on this sacred truism. The first entails an inquiry into the truthfulness of the claim. Since the National Commission on Excellence in Education released "A Nation at Risk" in 1983, corporate elites and elected officials have orchestrated a massive propaganda campaign aimed at convincing the public that schools are, at once, the cause and the cure for their economic insecurity. In typical fashion, the media very obediently assisted in facilitating this fraud, helping to further entrench the belief that a people's economic development proceeds in direct proportion to their level of educational achievement. Not only has the media helped to spread this secular theology, it has also protected it from any serious public scrutiny by failing to report any of the most elementary facts that would call its presuppositions to question.

For example, current educational reform initiatives advanced under corporate sponsorship attribute the deterioration of U.S. competitiveness in world markets to the declining quality of U.S. education. They further attribute this decline to the "liberal" reforms of the 1960s and 1970s that sought to ameliorate the inequalities in educational opportunity that existed in years past, including the 1950s. The 1950s are an important decade to look at, because corporate-sponsored educational reforms portray this as the last decade in the golden era of American education. It was also in the late 1940s and 1950s that the United States emerged as the leading economic power in the world. According to the rhetoric of the most recent spate of educational reform initiatives, the United States ascended to this global supremacy in world markets because of the remarkable performance of its public schools. This conveniently ignores the fact that most of the United States workforce at the time had never graduated from high school. It also ignores the fact that the United States faced virtually no economic competition from any international rivals during this period. World War II left the economic and military infrastructures of Japan and the colonial powers of Europe in ruin. Therefore, the United States became the world's first truly global power almost by default, certainly not because of the educational credentials of its workforce.

The tremendous profits accruing from their supremacy in global markets made U.S. corporations more amenable toward making a few limited concessions to domestic pressures. Trade unions achieved better salaries, benefits, and working conditions for their members. Women and, especially, racial and ethnic minorities, won important battles in the ongoing struggle for civil rights. Federal and state governments created programs that built on the New Deal legislation aimed at improving the life conditions and economic opportunities of the poor, many of which focused on educational programs.

By the 1970s, precisely during that period in which the economic conditions of average U.S. citizens began to stagnate, the economies of Japan and the European nations had sufficiently recovered to threaten U.S. corporations with competition that they had not known since before WW II, when their power was largely limited to the Western hemisphere. This meant that U.S. corporations began losing part of their global market share, and consequently, their profit margins fell. By the end of the decade, it became obvious that they would have to make up for these shortfalls in other areas.

Since the 1980s, we have witnessed a increased tendency for large corporations to "shop" for the most favorable business climate in which to locate their domestic operations. Similar to the tactics historically used to control the political commitments of Third World governments, businesses have forced state and local governments into competition with one another to determine which can provide the most lucrative package of tax abatements and other forms of public subsidy to bring businesses into their communities. Compliance with the corporate vision of educational excellence, of course, is one characteristic of a favorable business climate, even though the government subsidies to private corporations place severe strain on state and local governments' ability to finance education and other social services that might benefit the general population.

At first glance, there would appear to be a glaring contradiction in corporations' demanding more from schools at the same time that they seek to contribute less to the schools' primary bases of financial support. I believe, however, that this contradiction is largely an illusion; it can only be taken seriously if we suppose that corporate leaders and elected officials are genuine in suggesting that increasing educational performance in U.S. schools will increase U.S. economic performance in the global economy and, thus, promote greater economic opportunities for more U.S. citizens. In order to believe this, we must believe that educational policy, and public policy more generally, is driven by an overriding concern for improving the living conditions of the great majority of U.S. citizens. In short, we must accept not only the pastoral image of the state as a benevolent shepherd who seeks to lead its flock to the 'promised land' but also a pastoral image of the corporate community at large. The state alone, we are to believe, has been unable to deliver the working poor and unemployed into a satisfactory state of *secular salvation*. And its failure to do so has damaged the ability of U.S. corporations to effectively compete in the global economy. The time has now come for those corporations to participate more directly in shaping educational policy in order to assure that U.S. workers will have "the right stuff" to provide economic security for themselves and their nation.

To dispel these illusions, we need only consider that U.S. corporations have relocated most manufacturing jobs to "undeveloped" regions of the world, where the U.S. government backs brutal military regimes whose chief function is to repress economic and political unrest that might threaten the quality of those regions' business climate for foreign investors. The U.S. government has also heavily subsidized (with taxpayers' dollars) high-tech industry's development of labor-saving technologies, which have displaced more U.S. workers than have plant relocations abroad (Rifkin,

1995). In light of these realities, the possibility that U.S. workers might benefit from even the grandest improvements in the performance of U.S. schools seems quite remote.

This leads me to conclude that the official line in educational discourse and educational reform rhetoric serves a dual function. First, it diverts public attention from the real issues behind the growing disparities between the haves and the have-nots in this country. Second, it manufactures a sense of false hope in people that increasing the nation's educational performance will enhance people's economic opportunities. But it is not my purpose in this book to challenge the feasibility of this proposition.

Again, at least two approaches present themselves for casting doubt upon the sacred truism that a people's level of economic development rises and falls with its level of educational achievement. The second approach, and the one that I wish to pursue in the remainder of this introduction, challenges not the truthfulness of the claim but the desirability of the values that it promotes.

DECOLONIZING SOCIETY

To paraphrase from Wolfgang Sachs' (1992) introduction to *The Development Dictionary*, I present this project "as an invitation to re-view the economized model of reality, as a call to recognize that we all wear not merely tinted, but tainted, glasses if we take part in the prevailing educational discourse." However, whereas Sachs claims to draw inspiration from his hope of disabling "development professionals by tearing apart the conceptual foundations of their routines," I do not want to overstate the parallels between his hopes and those that inspire this book. Indeed, my hopes of producing a broader understanding among educators of how the conceptual foundations of the prevailing educational discourse are linked to the conceptual foundations of the economic mode of human understanding and action inspired the idea for this book. I hope that this broadened understanding will disable the promulgation of educational discourses and practices that contribute toward and intensify the colonial relations that increasingly characterize our social life. So, my hope does not lie with disabling professional educators. To the contrary, my ultimate hope rests with inspiring them to enable themselves to forge dynamic grassroots initiatives within their schools and their local communities to deeconomize the public schools, thereby transforming them into sites for decolonizing society.

Economic interests, particularly those of the nation's corporate elite, have always dominated the formation of U.S. educational policy. Since the

National Commission on Excellence in Education released "A Nation at Risk" in 1983, however, U.S. educational reformers have consistently defined the purpose of the nation's schools in relation to the global economy. In some versions, the reformers hold the alleged failure of public schools accountable for the failure of the United States to maintain its economic dominance in world markets. Other reformers explain that as corporations have taken on a primarily transnational character, they have tended to view their potential labor markets in international terms. Thus, U.S. workers must learn that they are in competition with the workers of other industrialized nations to meet the labor demands of these transnational corporations (TNCs). Because the higher paying jobs in the new global economy require higher level skills, these reformers blame the steady decline in real wages in the United States on the failure of the public schools to provide people with the skills that would attract those jobs to U.S. shores. Regardless of the specific complaints against the schools, the demands of the global economy now drive U.S. educational discourse. Although my specific concerns are directed toward U.S. educational policy, the observations are generalizable to all modern industrial nations.

I demonstrate how the connections between the global economy and the U.S. system of mandatory schooling run much deeper than even the reform literature suggests. To reveal these connections, I compare U.S. educational discourse and international development discourse as elements of a larger historical process—global economization—that subordinates all other forms of social interaction to economic logic and transforms nonmaterial needs, such as education, into commodities.

To begin with, both education and international economic development have become synonymous with "progress." Although education has a history of conceptual evolution unto itself, its path has merged and congealed with that of development to produce one of the great and sacred certainties of our era. Namely, a people's economic development proceeds in direct proportion to their level of educational achievement. Both education and economic development imply a process that is required for, and leads inexorably to, favorable change related to the improvement of people's means to meet their needs. Education promises to effect this improvement by making the United States competitive in the global marketplace and by integrating U.S. workers into the global economy's international labor market, whereas development offers the poor, underdeveloped nations of the world the assistance that they need to join the more advanced nations in sharing the fruits of the international market system. When limited to this context, development discourse originated from President Harry Truman's inauguration speech of January 20, 1949, when he spelled out his Point Four Program for stabilizing international relations in the aftermath of World War II. "The old imperialism—exploitation for foreign profit—has no place in our plans," Truman (1949) explained. "What we envisage is a program of development based on the concepts of democratic fair dealing" (p. 19). At that particular moment in history, two thirds of the world's population became "needy," and Truman, at least rhetorically, committed the United States and the other developed nations to a system of world peace predicated on meeting the needs of that great majority so as to eliminate conflict among nations. Hence, the ultimate value of development rests in its allegedly benevolent intentions to satisfy the needs of the world's poor in order to integrate them into a system of peace keeping otherwise known as the global economy.

Through development discourse, the rich nations who already enjoy the fruits of development adopt a pastoral self-image for themselves and the international institutions that they have created to serve the needs of the undeveloped countries. As pastoral agents, the first need that the rich nations must satisfy on behalf of the poor is the need to be served by the rich, for their services are compensatory to the satisfaction of all other needs. Their services, and their services alone, will provide the poor nations with the means to achieve development and full integration into the peaceful kingdom of *pax œconomica*.

Ivan Illich (1992) detects a bitter irony in the emergence of development discourse as part of a program for world peace, associating this type of peace with the Roman notion of *pax*. "When the Roman governor raises the ensign of his legion to ram it into the soil of Palestine," Illich argues, "he does not look toward heaven. He faces a far-off city; he imposes *its* law and *its* order" (p. 16). Following a line of argumentation initiated by Polanyi in *The Great Transformation*, Illich identifies the peace offered under development as a *pax œconomica*, which amounts to little more than a formal peace between economic powers as they proceed to wage a war against subsistence for the purpose of expanding the global reach of the market.

However, development discourse did not begin its evolutionary path in this century. It began much earlier in medieval Europe. Gustavo Esteva points out that the social construction of the concept of development was wedded to a particular political design—economization—that sought to separate the economic sphere from society and culture, to liberate economic activity from the conservative effects of people's social and cultural patterns in order that an economy would emerge that could chart its own course in accordance with its own laws. As market capitalism evolved over the course of Western history, economic growth and development presupposed "overcoming symbolic and moral 'obstacles,' ... disposing of various inhibiting ideas and practices such as myths, ceremonies, rituals, mutual aid, networks of solidarity and the like" (Berthoud, 1992, p. 72). The Catholic Church, for example, forbid the practice of money lending on the grounds that it would lead borrowers to fall into a greater obligation to their debtors than to God. And to the extent that notions such as "myth," "ritual,"and "ceremony" sound archaic to our modern ears, we can "hear" economization's success in overcoming the constraints of traditional culture.

As archaic as such ideas and practices may sound to modern ears, these attributes of traditional cultures helped to maintain certain social conditions from which people in rich nations can learn in order to both diagnose and recover from the social and environmental illnesses generated by economization. Illich (1992), for example, contends that "all known traditional cultures," including those of premodern Europe, "can be conceived as meaningful configurations that have as their principal purpose the repression of those conditions under which scarcity could become dominant in social relations" (p. 117). To do so, these subsistence-oriented societies limit their notion of human "needs" to that which is necessary to their community's survival. A people's needs take shape in relation to what natural forms of abundance they find in the commons and in relation to the social availability of means for drawing on that abundance.

Illich adopts the notion of the "vernacular" to characterize such needs and the activities that people pursue toward satisfying them. He argues that this word best expresses the sense in which these activities can be viewed as concrete responses to concrete conditions. Also, he pointed out that the Indo-Germanic root for vernacular suggests "rootedness" and "abode," whereas, in the Latin usage, *vernaculum*, it referred to that which was *homebread, homespun, homegrown*, or *homemade*. Vernacular activities, Illich (1981) claims, "are not motivated by thoughts of exchange," but rather they imply "autonomous non-market related action through which people satisfy everyday needs—the actions that by their own true nature escape bureaucratic control, satisfying needs to which, in the very process, they give specific shape" (p. 57).

By the time that maintaining global economic hegemony required developed nations to rely on the rhetorical services of what we now know as development discourse, observers recognized that the

> economic development of an underdeveloped people by themselves [pre-modern Europeans included] is not compatible with the maintenance of their traditional customs and mores. A break with the latter is prerequisite to economic progress. What is needed is a revolution in the totality of social, cultural, and religious institutions and habits, and thus in their psychological attitude, their philosophy and way of life. What is, therefore, required amounts in reality to social disorganization. (Berthoud, 1992, pp. 72–73)

Illich and Esteva believe that what triggers this revolutionary social disorganization requisite to "economic progress" is the imposition of that which traditional cultures seek to repress—scarcity. Economization insists on scarcity as the defining characteristic of the human condition and, therefore, the universal condition of social life everywhere. Under the law of scarcity, human needs are no longer limited to the necessities for collective survival. This law transmogrifies limited needs into unlimited wants. Although vernacular activities enabled members of traditional cultures to obviate scarcity by providing for collective survival, economization places conceptual limits on them, defining such patterns of social behavior as incompatible with economic growth and development. Those conceptual limits manifest themselves most clearly in the law of scarcity, which proclaims that "[humanity's] wants are great, not to say infinite, whereas [its] means are limited though improvable" (Esteva, 1992, p. 19). Instead of limiting people's needs, economization limits their means to satisfy them.

It accomplishes this in a twofold sense. As just stated, the law of scarcity places conceptual limits on people's means to provide for their own needs. However, in presenting itself as the necessary path toward improving those means, economization also disvalues all other forms of social existence. Nonmarket directed activities become signs of "backwardness" and "underdevelopment." In producing this twofold scarcity of means, economization simultaneously awards itself supreme status in a hierarchy of universal human needs. Access to the market economy constitutes every people's most basic need. Without such access, their means for satisfying other needs remain forever limited. Economization, then, transmogrifies not only means into needs but needs into commodities and people into market-dependent consumers. And, as the law of scarcity helps to subordinate all other forms of social interaction to economic logic, it lends itself to the commodification of many nonmaterial needs, including education.

To people in the undeveloped nations, according to this logic, salvation requires development to improve their collective means previously limited by their "traditional customs and mores." Again, this form of salvation is incompatible with the maintenance of cultural traditions and other "moral 'obstacles.'" "Unhappiness and discontentment in the sense of wanting more than is obtainable at any moment is to be generated. The suffering and dislocation that may be caused in the process may be objectionable but it appears to be the price that has to be paid for economic development; the condition of economic progress" (Berthoud, 1992, p. 73). Especially to the suffering and dislocated populations of the United States, where economization has already effected a modernization of poverty that produces scarcity in the capacity of people to provide for their own needs, salvation requires the educational services of the state to improve their individual means for both contributing to and accessing the market on which they have become dependent.

Even though Truman announced that "the old imperialism" had no place in America's plans for a new system of world peace, he never suggested that the "concepts of democratic fair dealing" that were to provide the basis of this system included the recognition of any nation's right to refuse U.S. development initiatives. Esteva (1992) points out how the "the brutal and violent transformation" effected under economization, "first completed in Europe, was always associated with colonial domination in the rest of the world" where "economization and colonization were synonymous" (p. 17). Herein lies perhaps the most painful irony of development discourse. In associating favorable change with economization, development discourse has liberated "the economic sphere from the negative connotations it had accumulated for two centuries, delinking development from colonialism" (p. 17).

As many Native Americans and other indigenous peoples outside of western Europe could confirm from their own peoples' histories, development has never been an option for the colonized. It has been imposed on them by the "developed" nations who conquered them. Sadly, the discourses of multiculturalism seldom acknowledge that the numerous vernacular cultures in Europe were similarly subjugated under the weight of global economization. For economization originated and continues as a war against cultural and social heterogeneity, first in Europe and then throughout the rest of the world, where it has always been associated with colonial domination.

Like schooling, development constitutes a compulsory program for disciplining people in the habits and values of the market. The pastoral images of the institutions that deliver these programs merely seek to convince people that the programs being imposed on them are for their own good, to convince people that they need these programs, and to convince people that they should willingly and appreciatively go along with plans set down for them by others. Under vernacular conditions, people participate in fashioning the means by which their collective needs are met. However, the economization imposed under the pastoral guidance of development "experts" and educational "experts" alike fashions people to meet the needs of the market as the only legitimate means for satisfying their own individual needs.

Once the thin veneer of deceit is lifted from the various development schemes that have evolved over the course of the past 50 years, we recognize the familiar patterns of colonial domination. Development discourse is merely a polite way of informing the "undeveloped" nations that their people and their resources must be placed in the service of the global economy and the rich nations that manage and enforce it. Those people who might have other ideas about how the internal affairs of their countries should be arranged (e.g., Vietnam, Cuba, Guatemala, Honduras, El Salvador, Nicaragua, ...) invite stern retribution from the global masters for their lack of humility and understanding.

Other forms of retribution await poor people in the United States who lack the humility and understanding to seek the self-improvements that forced schooling promises them. In rejecting the opportunity to improve themselves, they remove themselves from compliant and productive service to the global economy and its corporate directors within the state apparatus. Without "market value," the "uneducated" condemn themselves to continued poverty, leading in many cases to eventual incarceration. But even those who sufficiently embrace the secular theology of schooling and tacitly agree to seek to maximize their utility within the global economy have no guarantee that their "investments" in their education will reap "dividends." As real wages continue to decline and jobs continue to dwindle in number, displaced U.S. workers are told to "go back to school" to update and upgrade their usefulness to the rich. (Where school cannot guarantee secular salvation in the global economy, it can offer infinite opportunities for redemption.)

In the final analysis, the economization of social space effected under official U.S. educational policy transposes the relations of colonial domination typically associated with the international arena to the domestic scene.

People have value only to the extent that they are useful and necessary to the market and the future goals of its directors. Those without such value are simply expendable.

REFERENCES

Berthoud, G. (1992). Market. In W. Sachs (Ed.), *The development dictionary: A guide to knowledge as power.* Atlantic Highlands, NJ: Zed Books.

Cayley, D. (1992). *Ivan Illich in conversation.* Concord, Ontario: House of Anansi Press Limited.

Esteva, G. (1992). Development. In W. Sachs (Ed.), *The development dictionary: A guide to knowledge as power.* Atlantic Highlands, NJ: Zed Books.

Illich, I. (1971) *Deschooling society.* New York: Harper & Row.

Illich, I. (1981). *Shadow work.* New York: Marion Boyers.

Illich, I. (1992). *In the mirror of the past.* New York: Marion Boyers.

Rifkin, J. (1995). *The end of work: The decline of the global labor force and the dawn of the post-market era.* New York: Putnam.

Sachs, W. (1992). *The development dictionary: A guide to knowledge as power.* Atlantic Highlands, NJ: Zed Books.

Shoup, L. H., & Minter, W. ( ). Shaping a new world order: The council on foreign relations' blueprint for world hegemony. In H. Sklar (Ed.), *Trilateralism: The trilateral commission and elite planning for world management* (pp.135–156). Boston: South End Press.

Truman, H. S. (1964). Inaugural address, January 20, 1949. In *Public papers of the presidents of the United States: Harry S. Truman: Containing the public messages, speeches, and statements of the president January 1 to December 31, 1949.* Washington, DC: Government Printing Office.

I

TERMS OF DEBATE

1

Global Economy*

Noam Chomsky
Massachusetts Institute of Technology

The South Commission (1990) study, *The Challenge to the South*, closes with a call for a "new world order" that will respond to "the South's plea for justice, equity, and democracy in the global society" (1990, p. 287). The rulers of that society, however, adhere to quite a different conception of world order, expressed by Winston Churchill (1951): "The government of the world must be entrusted to the satisfied nations," the "rich men dwelling at peace within their habitations" whose power places them "above the rest," not the "hungry nations" who "seek more" and hence endanger tranquility (p. 382). The global rulers can hardly be expected to heed the pleas of the South, any more than rights were granted to the general population, as a gift from above, within the rich societies themselves. Those assigned the status of spectators from below can afford no illusions on these matters.

The realities are illustrated in the South Commission's study. For instance, it observes that gestures to Third World concerns in the 1970s were "undoubtedly spurred" by worry about "the newly found assertiveness of the South after the rise in oil prices in 1973" (p. 216). As the threat abated, the rich lost interest and turned to "a new form of neo-colonialism," monopolizing control over the world economy, undermining the more democratic ele-

*This chapter is essentially a reprint of "World orders: Old and new," by N. Chomsky. In *Facing the challenge: Responses to the report of the south commission*. (pp. 139–151). Copyright © by ZED books. Reprinted with permission.

ments of the United Nations, and in general proceeding to institutionalize "the South's second-class status." The pattern is consistent; it would be remarkable if it were otherwise.

It is Churchill's vision that has always inspired the rich rulers, who, needless to say, did not achieve that status by "dwelling at peace within their habitations." Nor do they take lightly any threat to that status.

A few years before Churchill's forthright articulation of the vision of the powerful, a War Department study transmitted by Secretary Henry Stimson to the State Department warned of the "rising tide all over the world wherein the common man aspires to higher and wider horizons" (July, 1945).[1] It was in this context that a potential Soviet threat to the post-war order was perceived. There is no proof that Russia had "flirted with the thought" of supporting the rising tide of aspirations of the common man, the study observed, but it might do so. Taking no chances, the United States must therefore defend itself by surrounding the potential criminal with military force aimed at its heartland. The common man's aspirations posed a particularly severe threat, because as director of the Office of Strategic Services, William Donovan had informed the president, the United States had "no political or social philosophy equally dynamic or alluring" to counter the "strong drawing card in the proletarian philosophy of Communism," particularly attractive at that historical moment when empires were in disarray, the traditional conservative order was discredited by its fascist associations, and the resistance, popular based and exhibiting radical democratic tendencies, was enjoying much prestige. The threat was countered by a worldwide campaign to destroy the antifascist resistance and restore the conservative business-ruled order. This was chapter one of post-1945 history.

The threat, however, did not vanish. A decade later, President Eisenhower complained that unlike us, the communists could "appeal directly to the masses." His secretary of state, John Foster Dulles, deplored their "ability to get control of mass movements, ... something we have no capacity to duplicate.... The poor people are the ones they appeal to and they have always wanted to plunder the rich," he observed to his brother, CIA Director Allen Dulles, in 1958.[2] The "social philosophy" that the rich should plunder the poor lacks popular appeal, a public relations problem that the rich rulers

---

[1]Expanded draft of letter from SecWar to SecState, "U.S. Position re Soviet Proposals on Kiel Canal and Dardanelles," 8 July 1945. Cited by Melvyn Leffler, 1992, p. 78.

[2]Eisenhower to Harriman, quoted in Richard H. Immerman, "Confessions of an Eisenhower revisionist," *Diplomatic History* (Summer 1990). John Foster Dulles,"Telephone call to Allen Dulles, June 19, 1958," *Minutes of telephone conversations of John Foster Dulles and Christin Herter*, Eisenhower Library, Abilene, Kansas.

have never been able to overcome. The same concern extended to "the preferential option for the poor" of the Latin American bishops and other commitments to social justice or democracy in more than form. The basic threat is the possibility of loss of control. Accordingly, similar concerns extend to such traditional friends as Mussolini, Trujillo, or Saddam Hussein when they disobey orders.

Much the same was true of the relations of the United States with the U.S.S.R. It was not Stalin's crimes that troubled Western leaders. Truman noted in his diary that "I can deal with Stalin," agreeing with Eisenhower and others. What went on in Russia was not his concern, Truman declared. Stalin's death would be a "real catastrophe," he felt. But cooperation was contingent on the United States' getting its way 85% of the time, as Truman made clear. In a leading scholarly study of United States security planning in the early postwar period, Leffler observes that "rarely does a sense of real compassion and/or moral fervor emerge from the documents and diaries of high officials. These men were concerned primarily with power and self-interest, not with real people facing real problems in the world that had just gone through fifteen years of economic strife, Stalinist terror, and Nazi genocide" (Leffler, 1992, p. 15, 52).

The West's concerns were not with Stalin's enormous crimes but with the apparent successes in development and the appeal of the "proletarian philosophy" to the "common man" in the West and to subjugated and oppressed people everywhere. The failure of Eastern Europe to return to its traditional role as a supplier of food and raw materials to the West compounded these concerns. The West is not disturbed by crimes but by insubordination, as was shown once again in the case of Saddam Hussein, a favored friend and trading partner of the United States and its allies right through the period of his worst atrocities. As the Berlin Wall fell in 1989, the White House intervened directly, in a highly secret meeting, to ensure that Iraq would receive another 1 billion U.S. dollars in loan guarantees, overcoming the Treasury's and the Commerce Department's objections that Iraq was not credit worthy. The reason, the State Department explained, was that Iraq was "very important to U.S. interests in the Middle East;" it was "influential in the peace process" and was "a key to maintaining stability in the region, offering great trade opportunities for U.S. companies."[3] As in the case of Stalin, Saddam Hussein's crimes were of no account, until he committed the crime of disobedience on August 2, 1990.

---

[3]Lionel Barber and Alan Friedman, *Financial Times* (London), May 3, 1991. See also *Los Angeles Times*, Feb. 23, 25, 26, 1992.

Whatever its political color, an independent course is unacceptable; successes that might provide a model to others are still more so. The miscreant is then termed a "rotten apple" that is spoiling the barrel, a 'virus' that must be exterminated. It is a "threat to stability." When a successful CIA operation overturned the democratic capitalist government of Guatemala in 1954, an internal State Department report explained that Guatemala had "become an increasing threat to the stability of Honduras and El Salvador. Its agrarian reform is a powerful propaganda weapon; its broad social program of aiding the workers and peasants in a victorious struggle against the upper classes and foreign enterprises has a strong appeal to the populations of Central American neighbors where similar conditions prevail."[4] In the operative sense of the term, "stability" means security for the upper classes and large foreign enterprises," and it must naturally be preserved. These are crucial features of the old world order, well documented in the internal record, regularly illustrated in historical practice, bound to persist as contingencies change.

Writing on the world order in 1992, one can hardly ignore the approaching end of the first 500 years of a world order in which the major theme has been Europe's conquest of most of the world. The cast of characters has changed somewhat: A European-settled colony leads the crusade, and Japan, one of the few regions of the South to escape subjugation, was able to join the club of the rich. In contrast, parts of Western Europe that were colonized retain Third World features. One notable example is Ireland, violently conquered, then barred from development by the standard "free trade" doctrines selectively applied to ensure subordination of the South—today called "structural adjustment," "neo-liberalism," or "our noble ideals," from which the rich, to be sure, are exempt.

Throughout the Columbian era, the South has been assigned a service role: to provide resources, cheap labor, markets, opportunities for investment and for the export of pollution. For the past half-century, the United States has been the global enforcer, protecting the interests of the rich. Accordingly, the primary threat to U.S. interests is depicted in high-level planning documents as "radical and nationalistic regimes" that are responsive to popular pressures for "immediate improvement in the low living standards of the masses" and for diversification of the economies, tendencies that conflict with the need to protect U.S. control of raw materials and "a political and economic climate conducive to private investment." For more extensive citations and sources, see *On Power and Ideology* (Chomsky, 1987). The basic

[4]Internal State Department report of 1953 (prior to 1954 CIA-backed invasion). Burrows to Cabot (Assistant Secretary of State for Inter-American Affairs), 23 December 1953, cited by Piero Gleijeses, 1991, p. 365.

themes of internal planning sometimes reach the record, as when the editors of the *New York Times*, applauding the overthrow of the parliamentary Mossadegh regime in Iran, observed that "underdeveloped countries with rich resources now have an object lesson in the heavy cost that must be paid by one of their number which goes berserk with fanatical nationalism" (editorial, *New York Times*, Aug. 5, 1954). Most important, the historical record conforms to this understanding of the role of the South.

Within the rich men's club, order must also reign. The lesser members are to pursue their "regional interests" within the "overall framework of order" managed by the United States, the only power with "global interests and responsibilities," as Kissinger admonished Europe in 1973. In the early post-1945 years, a European third force could not be tolerated. Neutralism would be "a shortcut to suicide," Dean Acheson held. The formation of NATO was in large part motivated by the need "to integrate Western Europe and England into an orbit amenable to American leadership," Leffler observes. With U.S. economic domination in decline, those strictures might become harder to enforce. For the moment, they remain fairly valid in the loose framework of world government (Group of Seven, the IMF and World Bank, etc.).

Standard reasoning is developed in a secret February 1992 Pentagon draft of Defense Planning Guidance, which describes itself as "definitive guidance from the Secretary of Defense" for budgetary policy to the year 2000. The United States must hold "global power" and a monopoly of force. It will then "protect" the "new order" while allowing others to pursue "their legitimate interests," as the United States defines them. The United States "must account sufficiently for the interests of the advanced industrial nations to discourage them from challenging our leadership or seeking to overturn the established political and economic order" or even "aspiring to a larger regional or global role." There must be no independent European security system; rather, U.S.-dominated NATO must remain the "primary instrument of Western defense and security, as well as the channel for U.S. influence and participation in European security affairs.... We will retain the pre-eminent responsibility for addressing selectively those wrongs which threaten not only our interests, but also those of our allies or friends;" the United States alone will determine what are "wrongs"and when they are to be selectively "righted." As in the past, the Middle East is a particular concern. Here "our overall objective is to remain the predominant outside power in the region and preserve U.S. and Western access to the region's oil" while deterring aggression (selectively), and protecting "US nationals and property." In Latin America, a crucial threat is Cuban "military provocation against the U.S.[5] or an American ally"—the standard Orwellian reference to the escalating U.S. war against Cuban independence.

The case of Cuba well illustrates the persistence of traditional themes and the basic logic of the North–South conflict. One hundred and seventy years ago, the United States was unsympathetic to the liberation of Latin America, adopting Thomas Jefferson's precept that it is best for Spain to rule until "our population can be sufficiently advanced to gain it from them piece by piece." Opposition to Cuban independence was particularly strong. Secretary of State John Quincy Adams, the author of the Monroe Doctrine, described Cuba as "an object of transcendent importance to the commercial and political interests of our Union." Expressing the dominant elite view, he urged Spanish sovereignty until Cuba would fall into US hands by "the laws of political ... gravitation," a "ripe fruit" for harvest. One prime concern was the democratic tendencies in the Cuban independence movement, which advocated abolition of slavery and equal rights for all. In the rhetoric of contemporary planners, there was a threat that "the rot might spread," even to U.S. shores.

By the end of the 19th century, the British deterrent was gone, and the United States was powerful enough to conquer Cuba, just in time to prevent the success of the indigenous liberation struggle. Cuba was effectively placed under the rule of the White propertied classes and U.S. firms. In the 1930s, President Roosevelt revoked the so-called "good neighbor policy" to overturn a civilian government regarded as a threat to U.S. commercial interests. The Batista dictatorship served those interests loyally, thus enjoying full support.

Castro's overthrow of the dictatorship in January 1959 soon elicted U.S. hostility. By late 1959, Washington had concluded that Castro was unacceptable. One reason, State Department liberals explained, was that "our business interests in Cuba have been seriously affected." A second was the threat to "stability":

The United States cannot hope to encourage and support sound economic policies in other Latin American countries and to promote necessary private investments in Latin America if it is or appears to be simultaneously cooperating with the Castro program.

Studies of Cuban opinion provided to the White House concluded that most Cubans were optimistic about the future and supported Castro, while

[5]The draft of the 1992 Defense Planning Guide has never been released. The only information available is from press citations, which include leaked excerpts and comment; a sample is given in the *New York Times* (March 9, 1992) and Patrick Tyler, the *New York Times* (March 10, 1992). As indicated, text is from March 9 and commentary from March 10.

only 7% expressed concern about communism. The Soviet presence was nil. "The liberals, like the conservatives, saw Castro as a threat to the hemisphere," historian Jules Benjamin (1990) comments, "but without the world communist conspiracy component."

By October 1959, U.S.-based planes were attacking Cuba. CIA subversion included supply of arms to guerrilla bands and sabotage of sugar mills and other economic targets. In March 1960, the Eisenhower administration formally adopted a plan to overthrow Castro in favor of a regime "more devoted to the true interests of the Cuban people and more acceptable to the U.S.," though it must be done "in such a manner as to avoid any appearance of U.S. intervention." As always, the United States is the arbiter of "true interests."

Sabotage, terror, and aggression were escalated further by the Kennedy administration, along with the kind of economic warfare that no small country within the U.S. sphere can long endure. Kennedy also sought a cultural quarantine to block the free flow of ideas and information about Cuba to the Latin American countries, whose excessive liberalism was considered a problem, particularly their unwillingness to emulate U.S. controls on travel and cultural interchange and their legal systems, which insisted on evidence for crimes by alleged "subversives."

After the Bay of Pigs failure, Kennedy's international terrorist campaign escalated further, reaching quite remarkable dimensions. This is largely dismissed in the West, apart from some notice given to the assassination attempts, one of them carried out on the day of Kennedy's assassination. The operations were formally called off by President Lyndon Johnson. They continued, however, and escalated during the Nixon administration. Subsequent terrorist actions are attributed to renegades beyond CIA control, whether accurately or not; one high Pentagon official in the 1960s, Roswell Gilpatric, expressed his doubts. The Carter administration, with the support of U.S. courts, condoned hijacking of Cuban ships in violation of the antihijacking convention that Castro was respecting. The Reaganites rejected Cuban initiatives for diplomatic settlement and imposed new sanctions against Cuba on the most outlandish pretexts, a record reviewed by Wayne Smith, who resigned as head of U.S. Interests Section in Havana in protest.

The embargo against Cuba was tightened in the 1980s and again in mid-1991 while the United States resumed Caribbean military maneuvers, a standard technique of intimidation. As in the 1820s, such policies are supported across the spectrum of articulate opinion. Washington makes no effort to conceal that it is exploiting the disappearance of the Soviet deterrent and the decline of the Eastern bloc's economic relations with Cuba to achieve its longstanding aims, through economic warfare or other means. Similarly, throughout the 1980s, the liberal press scoffed at Gorbachev's "New Thinking," because he had not yet offered the United States a free hand to attain its objectives in Central America. The right of the United States to demolish those who stand in its way is beyond debate; ergo, those who attempt to defend themselves are criminals, and anyone else who assists them is engaged in a criminal conspiracy. The power and uniformity of these doctrines in a country that is unusually free, by world standards, constitute a most illuminating phenomenon.

The Cuban record demonstrates with great clarity that the Cold War framework was scarcely more than a pretext for concealing the standard refusal of the United States to tolerate Third World independence, whatever its political cast. From 1917 through the 1980s, virtually every U.S. act of subversion, violence, or economic warfare in the Third World was justified on the grounds of defense from the Russians. Woodrow Wilson needed other pretexts when he invaded Haiti and the Dominican Republic, just as George Bush needed to seek new ones. However, the basic realities do not change.

The Cold War itself had many of the features of North–South conflict. The Third World first appeared in Eastern Europe, which began to supply raw materials for workshops of the West as far back as the 14th century and then followed the (now-familiar) path toward underdevelopment, as trade and investment patterns took their natural course. For reasons of scale, Russia's economic subordination to the West was delayed, but by the 19th century the process was well under way. The Bolshevik takeover in October of 1917, which quickly aborted incipient socialist tendencies and destroyed any semblance of working-class or other popular organization, extricated the U.S.S.R. from the Western-dominated periphery, setting off the inevitable reaction, beginning with immediate military intervention. These were, from the outset, some of the basic contours of the Cold War.

The logic was not fundamentally different from the case of Grenada or Guatemala, but the scale of the problem was. It was enhanced after Russia's leading role in defeating Hitler enabled it to isolate Eastern and parts of Central Europe from Western control. A tiny departure from subordination is intolerable, a huge one far less so, particularly when it threatens "stability" through the "rotten apple" effect. No less ominous was the ability of the Soviet Union to lend support to targets of U.S. subversion or destruction, and its military capacity, so enormous as to deter U.S. intervention elsewhere. Under such circumstances, "coexistence" was even more out of the question than in the cases of Chile, Grenada, Guatemala, Nicaragua, etcetera.

Although far from the whole story of the Cold War, this was a major theme and a very familiar one.

The U.S.S.R. reached the peak of its power by the late 1950s, always far behind the West. The Cuban missile crisis, revealing extreme Soviet vulnerability, led to a huge increase in military spending, leveling off by the late 1970s. The economy was then stagnating and the autocracy unable to control internal dissidence. The command economy had carried out basic industrial development but was unable to proceed to more advanced stages and also suffered from the global recession that devastated much of the South. By the 1980s, the system had collapsed, and the core countries, always far richer and more powerful, "won the Cold War." Much of the Soviet empire will probably return to its traditional Third World status, and the ex-nomenklatura will be taking on the role of Third World élites linked to international business and financial interests. But the United States is deeply in debt at every level (federal, state, corporate, household) after a decade of Reagan–Bush economic mismanagement. It is not well placed, therefore, to compete with its rivals for domination of these restored Third World domains, one of the sources of tension within the rich men's club.

A further consequence of the Soviet collapse is that a new framework is needed for intervention. The problem arose through the 1980s, requiring a propaganda shift to international terrorists, Hispanic narco-trafficers, crazed Arabs, and other chimeras. Yet another consequence is that the collapse of the Soviet deterrent "makes military power more useful as a United States foreign policy instrument … against those who contemplate challenging important American interests (Dimitri Simes of the Carnegie Endowment for International Peace). This insight was echoed by Eliot Abrams, a Reaganite planner of policy toward Latin America, during the invasion of Panama and by commentators throughout the Gulf crisis, who noted that the United States and the United Kingdom could now use force without limit against a defenseless enemy.

Other factors, however, are likely to inhibit the U.S. recourse force to control the South. Among them are the successes of the past years in crushing popular nationalist and reform tendencies, the elimination of the "communist" appeal to those who hope to "plunder the rich," and the economic catastrophes of the last decade. In the light of these developments, limited forms of diversity and independence can be tolerated with less concern that they will lead to a challenge to ruling business interests. Control can be exercised by economic measures: structural adjustment, the IMF regimen, selective use of free-trade measures, and so forth. Needless to say, the successful industrial powers do not accept these rules for themselves and never have. But for the purposes of domination and exploitation, there is great merit in imposing them on the Third World. Quite generally, democratic forms are tolerable as long as "stability" is ensured. If this dominant value is threatened–by popular uprisings in Iraq, the electoral victory of a radical priest (Aristide) in Haiti, an Islamic movement in Algeria, or any uncontrolled popular force–then the iron fist must strike.

Another inhibiting factor in the United States is that the domestic base of support for foreign adventures has been eroded. A leaked fragment of a Bush administration national security review observes that "much weaker enemies" must be defeated "decisively and rapidly;" any other outcome might "undercut political support." The Reagan administration was compelled to resort to clandestine terror and proxy forces, because political support for violent intervention was so thin. And it has been necessary to whip up impressive propaganda campaigns to portray "much weaker enemies" as threats to the country's very existence, so as to mobilize a frightened population to give at least temporary support for decisive and rapid action.

Still another problem is that the other two centers of economic power–German-led Europe and Japan–have their own interests, though the Defense Planning study cited earlier is correct in noting that basic interests are shared, notably, the concern that the Third World should fulfill its service function. Furthermore, the internationalization of capital that has accelerated since Nixon dismantled the Bretton Woods system gives a somewhat new cast to competition among states. Merely to cite one indication, whereas the U.S. share in world manufactured exports declined by 3.5% from 1966 to 1984, the share of U.S.-based transnational corporations (TNCs) increased slightly. And international trade patterns yield a very different picture if imports from overseas subsidiaries are counted as domestic production. These are factors of growing importance in the new world order.

Furthermore, the United States no longer has the economic base for intervention. Recognition of this fact has led to proposals in the business press that the United States should become a "mercenary" state, using its "monopoly power" in the "security market" to maintain its "control over the world economic system," selling "protection" to other wealthy powers who will pay a war premium" (Neikirk, 1990). Foreign financing of Washington's war in the Gulf in 1991 provided the United States with "$33 billion more than the war cost, temporarily easing the budget deficit and balance of war payment," The *New York Times* economic analyst Leonard Silk concluded. Nearly half the substantial decline in the U.S. current account deficit for

1991 is attributed to foreign payments toward the cost of the Gulf war, much of the rest by exports to Middle East oil producers, including billions of dollars' worth of weapons exports.[6] The profits of Gulf oil production, in particular, must continue to be available to support the economies of the United States and its British associate, who are set to carry out the enforcer role. These events are foreshadowed in U.S.–U.K. internal documents after the Iraqi military coup of 1958, which emphasize that Kuwaiti oil and investment must be used to prop up the ailing British economy, a concern that extended to the United States by the 1970s and remains a significant factor in Middle East policy.

The use of force to control the Third World is a last resort. Economic weapons are more efficient. Some of the newer mechanisms can be seen in the GATT negotiations. One major U.S. concern relates to the "new themes:" guarantees for "intellectual property rights," such as patents and software, that will enable TNCs to monopolize new technology; and removal of constraints on services and investment, which will undermine national development programs in the Third World and effectively place investment decisions in the hands of TNCs and the financial institutions of the North. These are "issues of greater magnitude" than the more publicized conflict over agricultural subsidies, according to William Brock, head of the Multilateral Trade Negotiations Coalition of major U.S. corporations. In the latter sphere, the United States objects to a GATT provision that allows countries to restrict food exports in times of need, demanding that U.S. agribusiness must control raw material no matter what the human cost.[7] In general, each of the wealthy industrial powers advocates a mixture of liberalization and protection designed for the interests of dominant domestic forces, and particularly for the TNCs that are to dominate the world economy.

The effects would be to reduce the role of Third World governments to a police function, to control their own working classes and superfluous population, while TNCs gain free access to their resources and control new technology and global investment—and, of course, are granted the central planning and management functions denied to governments, which are unacceptable agents because they might fall under the influence of popular pressures reflecting domestic needs, the "radical nationalism" of the inter-

[6]Silk, *New York Times*, Sept. 22; *New York Times*, D21, March 18; Barry Schweid, AP, *Boston Globe*, Feb. 15, 1991.

[7]Khor Kok Peng, Martin. *The Uruguay Round and Third World Sovereignty* (Third World Network, Penang, 1990). Mark Ritchie, "GATT, Agriculture and the Environment, *The Ecologist*, Nov/Dec. 1990.

nal planning record. The outcome is called "free trade," but some have more accurately described it as a kind of "corporate mercantilism," with managed commercial interactions among corporate groupings and continuing state intervention in the North to subsidize and protect domestically based corporations and financial institutions.

The Latin Americanization of the East follows the familiar course. Poland, adopting the doctrines professed by the rich, liberalized its economy. In reaction, the European Community (EC) raised import barriers to protect its own industry and agriculture. EC chemical and steel industries warned that the "restructuring" must not harm Western industry. The World Bank estimates that the protectionist measures of the industrial countries—keeping pace with the free market bombast—reduce the national income of the "developing societies" by about twice the value of official "development assistance," much of it a form of export promotion.[8]

The situation is reminiscent of the 1920s, when Japan followed the rules officially proclaimed but so successfully that Britain abandoned its liberal doctrines and closed the empire to Japanese exports (as did the United Sates and the Netherlands, in their lesser domains). Similarly, the Reagan–Bush Caribbean Basin Initiative encourages open export-oriented economies while maintaining U.S. protectionist barriers. The patterns as a pervasive as they are understandable, on Churchillian grounds.

There are many familiar reasons why wealth and power tend to reproduce. It should, then, come as little surprise that the Third World continues to fall behind the North. United Nations statistics indicate that as a percentage of the GDP of the developed countries, Africa's GDP per capita (minus South Africa) declined by about 50% from 1960 to 1987. The decline was almost as great as in Latin America.[9] For similar reasons, within the rich societies themselves large sectors of the population are becoming superfluous by the reigning values and must be marginalized or suppressed, increasingly so in the past 20-year period of economic stagnation and pressures on corporate profit. Societies of the North—notably the United States—are taking on certain Third World aspects, as wealth and power are increasingly concentrated among investors and professionals who benefit from the internationalization of capital flows and communication.

Like the domestic poor in the developed societies, the South has little bargaining power in its dealings with the club of the rich. The prospects for

[8]World Bank Response to NGO Working Group Position Paper on the World Bank in Trócaire Development Review (Catholic Agency for World Development, Dublin 1990).

[9]*Monthly Review*, March 1992.

"justice, equity, and democracy" (in a meaningful sense) are not auspicious; but they are also not hopeless. The South Commission mentions several directions that should be pursued, though I think the analysis is too optimistic in expecting these to influence the policies and attitudes of the rulers. One direction is internal change leading to meaningful democracy, social justice and improvement of conditions of life, and popular control over capital and investment, so that such resources as are available will be used for constructive development rather than for investment abroad or enriching TNCs and small wealthy sectors linked to them. If, for example, Latin America could control its own wealthy classes, preventing capital flight, much of the region's foreign debt would be wiped out. A related need is South–South cooperation to address common economic, social, and cultural needs.

But the crucial factor can only be internal changes in the core countries. The possibility that such changes may take place is not to be dismissed. Throughout the North, notably in the United States, there have been significant changes in the past 30 years, at least at the cultural if not the institutional level. Had the quincentennial of the old world order occurred in 1962, it would have been celebrated as the liberation of the hemisphere. In 1992 large sectors will demand recognition of the fact that the "liberation" set off the two worst demographic catastrophes in human history, in the Western hemisphere and Africa. The domestic constraints on state violence, noted earlier, are another case in point. Perhaps the most striking example is the Third World solidarity movements that developed through the 1980s in the United States, to a large extent based in churches and with broad social roots. This process of democratization and concern for social justice threatens power and is therefore minimized or dismissed in the doctrinal system, but it has large significance, I believe.

Democratization and social reform in the South are values in themselves. But there is little reason to suppose that steps toward internal freedom and justice will appeal to elite opinion in the West; on the contrary, they will be no less frightening than the so-called "crisis of democracy" within the rich societies (that is, the efforts of large parts of the population, since the 1960s, to enter the political arena). But in this way, the South can move toward mutually supportive relations with liberatory tendencies within Western societies. Such developments will naturally be regarded by the powerful as dangerous and subversive. However, they offer the only real hope for the great mass of people, even for the survival of the human species, in an era of environmental and other global problems that cannot be dealt with by primitive social and cultural structures that are driven by short-term material gain and that consider human beings to be instrument, not ends.

REFERENCES

Benjamin, J. (1990) *The United States and the origins of the Cuban revolution*. Princeton: Princeton, NJ: Princeton University Press.

Churchill, W. (1951). *The second world war, vol. 5*. Boston: Houghton Mifflin.

Leffler, M. (1992). *A preponderance of power*. Stanford, CA: Stanford University Press.

Neikirk, W. (1990, September 9). We are the world's guardian angels. *Chicago Tribune*, (p.).

Piero Gleijeses, P. (1991). *Shattered hope: The Guatemalan revolution and the United States, 1944–1954* (p. 365). Princeton, NJ: Princeton University Press.

Simes, D. (1988). If the cold war is over, then what? *New York Times*, Dec. 27 (op. ed.).

South Commission. (1990). *The challenge to the South: The report of the South Commission*. New York: Oxford University Press.

2

Crisis

Karen A. Barnhardt
University of Montana

The United States can aptly be characterized as a "culture of crisis." It is a society that seems to nourish itself on the production, reproduction, and consumption of crises. Attending to the vast array of public discourses on any given day, one cannot help but be struck by the sense of apocalyptic doom they profess. From the breakdown of family values to the decline of economic stability, from the failure of the public schools to the collapse of public and personal ethics and morality, and from the uncontrollable spread of violence to the outbreak of increasingly alarming rates of drug use, the discourses of our day seek to remind us that we live in a sea of never-ending threat and turmoil. This chapter seeks to present a genealogical sketching of these "discourses of crisis" or what Linda Singer calls "crisis talk" (1993).

Throughout the last 350 years, European immigrants to North America have produced a vast genre of public crisis discourses called "jeremiads." A "jeremiad" derives its name from the Book of Jeremiah in the Hebrew Bible and from the Old Testament. It represents an ancient prophetic and ritualistic tradition of public lamentation that seeks to call a people back to faith, often in a time of great tribulation. In the mappings that follow, I will make visible the way in which the use of a jeremiad operates and functions as a "regime of truth"[1] (see Foucault, 1980) within US society. In this sense, the jeremiad functions as a truth that is made to prevail through a vast array of power arrangements that follow a certain grammar, semantics, and logic. Conformity to this logic, truth, or narrative is what makes its discursive practice necessary.

To illustrate, we can think of a regime of truth as a story of legitimation that is centered and central to a community or a people's understanding and expression of itself. It is the center to which all history and experience is compared, contrasted, and reproduced. It is a story that, in its construction of itself, denies its own historical or social situatedness. Mapping the terrains of "crisis" inherent in the jeremiad makes visible some of the faint outlines of power operating within and through its discursive practice; and it provides us with clues as to how these crisis discourses emerge as political and social commitments. It is my hope that a genealogy of "crisis talk" will also make visible other ways and means of negotiating the plethora of economic, political, social, and ecological problems that challenge our imagination, spirit, and energy.

ORIGINS? THE AMERICAN JEREMIAD

Emphasizing the spiritual and historical significance of their self-imposed exile to North America, New England Puritans reasoned that God had called them to perform an "errand;" they must build an ideal community in the wilderness, a "model of Christian Charity," "a shining city on a hill," which will serve as a beacon for all Christendom (see Carroll, 1969, p. 21; Miller & Johnson, 1963, pp. 198–199). Inextricably tied to their sense of mission was a firm belief that their efforts would ultimately lead to the manifestation of the promised millennium—a time of lasting peace and harmony. However, despite the excited anticipation regarding the potential of their mission, they were also mindful that "the eyes of all people are upon

---

[1]Michel Foucault (1980) explains the operation of a regime of truth as "'truth' ... linked in circular relation with systems of power which produce and sustain it, and to effects of power which it induces and which extend it"(p. 133). Foucault continues:

> Truth is a thing of this world: it is produced only by virtue of multiple forms of constraint. And it induces regular effects of power. Each society has its regime of truth, its "general politics" of truth: that is, the types of discourse which it accepts and makes function as true; the mechanisms and instances which enable one to distinguish true and false statements, the means by which each is sanctioned; the techniques and procedures accorded value in the acquisition of truth; and the status of those who are charged with saying what counts as true. (pp. 130–131)

us" (Miller & Johnson, 1963, p. 199). Should New England fail in its errand, the repercussions would be profound for both the community they build and the world as a whole.

Perry Miller (1984), in his *Errand into the Wilderness*, asserts that the New England jeremiads emerged from the peculiar circumstances of the people who crafted them. These circumstances were profoundly influenced by what Miller describes as the Puritans' inability to maintain the European audience required for their errand to unfold. Despite their careful preparations, the Puritan experiment with English rule under the Cromwell Protectorate proved to be unsuccessful. Further, with the restoration of the British monarchy, Puritan leaders in New England found themselves faced with the growing certainty that their triumphant return to England would not occur as foreseen. Amid a growing uneasiness, Miller argues that the errand itself was called into question, as Puritan leaders tried to make sense of their situation. With the loss of its witness (an England now busy with its own crises and affairs in Europe), New England Puritan leaders found it increasingly difficult to maintain the sense of imminent destiny associated with their errand. Miller concludes that the community had nowhere to turn for answers to resolve this dilemma but within itself (p. 3).

With the moral character and cohesion of their community in question, church leaders met in a Boston synod in 1679 to compile a long, detailed list of New England's most deplorable sins. This list, subsequently published under the title *The Necessity of Reformation*, and the numerous other New England jeremiads that emerged during that period shriek with the dismay of clergy who in their expectation of finding a "shining city on a hill," found nothing but a "sink of inequity." New England, they declared, indeed was in crisis. The external threats and hostilities of the wilderness, the Indians, the Spanish to the south, and the French to the north, paled in comparison to the menacing "moral wilderness" within the community itself. "God has a controversy with New England," the clergy boomed; "[it] was sent on an errand, and ... it has failed" (Miller, 1984, p. 2).

Miller (1984) claims that *The Necessity of Reformation* and similar dissertations ultimately served as a pseudo "handbook for preachers," providing an effective methodological ritual for public lament. In performing this ritual, the rhetor takes a verse from Jeremiah or Isaiah, for example, recites a long list of afflictions currently plaguing the community (ie., floods, famine, disease) as proof that God avenges, expounds on the community's most grievous sins, and finally issues a thunderous call for repentance. The jeremiads served to remind New England that if it persisted in its "evil" ways and failed to repent, the culmination of the end times would not be millennium but God's wrath visited on New England.

Miller argues that ultimately this period of crisis signaled a significant rupture in the errand and a profound crisis of identity in New England. When their religious errand failed to manifest in the historical sense they had expected, and no new social order worthy of the worlds devoted admiration materialized, Miller (1984) contends that the jeremiads precipitated a subsequent, albeit qualitative, change in the errand and ultimately in the story of America's divine origin. In this way, the errand could accommodate a changing communal identity that sought to legitimate its growing prosperity and opportunities, and the jeremiads could provide a release mechanism for any mounting apprehensions. Thus, the jeremiads served as a form of psychological release, an exorcism of sort, a ritual *mea culpa*. Members of the community could attend meetings and worship services, lament and tell each other how awful they all were, feel better for having confessed their ignominies, and then get on with the business of life in America. Miller concludes that "amidst the mounting wail of sinfulness, this incessant and never-ending cry for repentance, ... [New England] Puritans launched themselves upon the process of Americanization," and forging the identity of a newly emerging nation (p. 2).

Sacvan Bercovitch (1978) issues a serious challenge to Miller's thesis in his *The American Jeremiad*. Contrary to Miller, Bercovitch argues that the New England jeremiad did not emerge from the peculiar circumstances of New England; rather it was an import brought from the Old World by Puritan leaders. Bercovitch did acknowledge a difference in the New England jeremiad when compared to the more ancient jeremiads. Ancient jeremiads were crafted with "worldly" concerns in mind; they did not concern themselves with conversion, repentance, or reform but with moral obedience and the civic virtue of the community. New England jeremiads were directed toward both "worldly" and "heavenly" interests. They required the fusing together of the sacred and the secular in a clean, unified understanding of linear history. In this way, the jeremiads are subsumed under the much larger umbrella of a linear Christian understanding of a march toward salvation and an Enlightenment story of the forward march of progress. Furthermore, this fusion allowed the jeremiads to not only encourage moral obedience and civic virtue but also serve to direct an "imperiled people of God toward the fulfillment of their destiny, to guide them individually toward salvation and collectively toward an American city of God" (p. 9).

Thus, the jeremiads were not solely a lament, but an affirmation of a people's "unswerving faith in the errand" (Miller, 1984, p. 6). As the jeremiads increased in their passion and their ardor, so did the community's commitment to the errand. Within the texture of these texts, we can see the play of relationship between that which is "imperiled" and that which is "promised"—between the apocalyptic visions of crisis besetting a community and the millennialist imaginings that promise to set it free. Thus, Bercovitch (1978) claims that there was never a question of "Who are we?" but rather an enduring question of "When will our errand be fulfilled?" He contends that from the birth of Christianity to the New England sermons to the apocalyptics of present day, the errand stands as it always has, as a mission "to bring history itself to an end" (p. 21). In this way, the errand operates as an allusion to progress itself. It signifies the gradual conquest, battle, and victory over Satan and the redemption of the world for Christ (rightly or wrongly, often secularly defined as the apex of civilization.)

Within this understanding, each successive generation of God's "chosen people" exceeds the revelations of the preceding generation. For example, the revelations of Jeremiah were exulted and exceeded by those of Moses; and the revelations of Moses were exulted and exceeded by those of John the Baptist; and the revelations of John were exulted and exceeded by the Puritans; and so forth. In this sense, the Old Testament was an errand to the New Testament; "and all history after the Incarnation, an errand to Christ's Second Coming. It leads from promise to fulfillment: from Moses to John the Baptist to Samuel Danforth; from the Old World to the New World; from Israel in Canaan to New Israel in America; from Adam to Christ to the Second Adam of the Apocalypse" (Bercovitch, 1978, p. 14). In taking its place within this progressive unfolding of history, New England too became a harbinger of things to come. It was a signification of the unfolding of "America."

In making visible these progressive characteristics of the errand, Bercovitch (1978) claims we can begin to see the distinctive form and function of the jeremiad. In that they were a rebuke or a warning of divine retribution, God's punishments were not to be understood as destructive but as corrective. Thus, the admonitions and castigations were an exultation and affirmation of the promise of their future glory and success. The ancient jeremiads relied on fear and trembling as a way of making people accept fixed social norms. The New England jeremiads also relied on anxiety, but they made anxiety the ends as well as the means. Thus, their function was to inculcate "crisis" as the social norm, the modus operandi for propelling social and institutional mechanisms in the belief that this would release the "restless, progressivist, energies required for the success of their venture" (p. 22). Thus, the jeremiads are not merely a lament over that which is passing away; rather, they represent a "litany of hope" and affirmation in the "inviolability of the colonial cause"—a cause that in itself is defined as the cause of God (pp. 9–11).

The discourse of crisis or the apocalyptic terrain of the jeremiad, when placed in the service of a specific project or narrative, can be profoundly effective in eliciting and producing specific actions. The power that operates within and through the exercise of the jeremiad's discursive practices inscribes itself on the bodies and experiences of those who are colonized by its discourse. The jeremiad disciplines their thoughts, their hopes, and their actions to its logic and the logic of its projects.

EPIDEMIC LOGIC AND CRISIS TALK

Linda Singer (1993), in her book *Erotic Welfare*, presents a discussion of what she calls "epidemic logic" that I feel closely resembles an apocalyptic regime of truth inherent in the use of the jeremiad. Singer's work concentrates on the process through which specific phenomenon become transfigured by their "mediation through the construct of epidemic" (p. 27). Through this process of mediation, phenomena that have (through the workings of power) been named undesirable or in need of control, are presented as highly symbolic social signifiers representing sites of unregulated proliferation. In other words, Singer argues that "[in] order to represent a phenomenon as socially undesirable, ... one need only call it epidemic." She continues: "In doing so, one not only engages in a kind of rhetorical inflation, but also mobilizes a certain apparatus of logic, a particular way of producing and organizing bodies politically" (p. 27).

In looking at the regime of truth proliferated through the use of the jeremiad as a political construct, we must not assume or imply that there exists some true or unified origin or articulable intentionality behind its design. Further, we cannot assume or imply that the strategic apparatus it produces and utilized is consistent, unilateral, clean, or of one piece. On a similar note, Jana Sawicki (1988) reminds us that discourses that operate as a regime of truth (such as the jeremiad) are often ambiguous and circulate within the social field in ways that

> can attach to strategies of domination as well as to those of resistance. Neither wholly a source of domination nor of resistance, [the apocalyptic element of the jeremiad] is also neither outside power nor wholly circumscribed by it. Instead, it is itself an arena of struggle. There are no inherently liberating or repressive [apocalyptic] practices, for any practice is co-optable and is capable of becoming a source of resistance. (pp. 185–186)

As becomes visible through these analyses, the site of struggle within these discourses becomes inscribed on the bodies, events, and epochs mediated by the particular discourse itself. Singer (1993) suggests that these "regulatory encodings" may take the shape of race, class, gender, and so on (p. 27). To reiterate, these regulatory devices are not static; rather, they are constantly produced and reproduced by their administrations as well as by the conflict that results from competing theories, techniques, and the exercise of regulatory control. In this sense, bodies, events, and epochs are subjected to a continual construction, deconstruction, and reconstruction through regulatory mediations. In other words, often our attempts to control, constrain, and regulate a situation constructed as an epidemic results in a proliferation of the crisis. For example, when discourse is used as a regulating technique, as is the case with the use of crisis talk or the jeremiad, the rhetoric that ensues often signals a proliferation of the epidemic through the "communicability" of the threat—thus, simultaneously denouncing and affirming that which (at least on the surface) was originally targeted for mediation. Thus, by exercising the discursive practice of the jeremiad, we actually perpetuate that which we seek to regulate or abate.

No other available heuristic seems as sufficient as "regime of truth" or "epidemic logic" to enable a mapping or tracing of the power relations or operations at play in crisis discourses such as a jeremiad. Other analyses may assist in uncovering the ideological operations within structures or discourse. However, they use traditional liberal notions of power and knowledge that are legitimated within larger narratives to do so. Thus, these analyses are only helpful insofar as they locate power in macro social or political relations. They often ignore or bury the workings of power on the micro social or political level. When placed in the service of a specific project, crisis talk can be powerfully effective in eliciting and producing emotions that compel people to act in certain ways. Further, Singer (1993) suggests that epidemic or apocalyptic conditions tend to evoke a kind of panic logic that "seeks immediate and drastic responses to the situation at hand" (p. 28). She continues, "Under the logic incited by epidemics, forms of regulatory intervention into the lives of bodies and population which might, in other circumstances, appear excessive can now appear as justified forms of damage control ... " (p. 29).

Ivan Illich (1978), in his *History of Needs*, points out that the word "crisis" in the Greek meant "choice" or "turning point" (p. 4). In its modern usage, he maintains (as does Singer) that "crisis" now evokes the sense of threat or doom. It serves to define and identify a site in need of manipulation, isolation, or regulation. "Crisis understood in this way," states Illich, "is always good for executives and commissars, especially those scavengers who live on the side effects of yesterday's growth: educators who live on society's alienation, doctors who prosper on the work and leisure that have destroyed health, [and] politicians who thrive on the distribution of welfare...." (p. 4). But, as Illich points out, crisis need not mean this. It is possible for us to embrace the alternative meaning. Poised at the edge of what Albert Borgman (1992) calls the "postmodern divide," (1992) we must work to find ways in which to negotiate the apocalyptic dangers inherent in our crisis talk without necessarily abandoning the energy and spirit that embodies its accompanying millennialist imaginings. It is a negotiation of choice; it is a negotiation of crisis.

REFERENCES

Bercovitch, S. (1978). *The American jeremiad*. Madison, WI: University of Wisconsin Press.

Borgman, A. (1992). *Crossing the postmodern divide*. Chicago: University of Chicago Press.

Carroll, P. N. (1969). *Puritanism and the wilderness: The intellectual significance of the New England frontier, 1629–1700*, New York: Columbia University Press.

Foucault, M. (1980). Truth and power. In *Power/Knowledge: Selected interviews and other writings, 1972–1977*. New York: Pantheon.

Illich, I. (1978). *Toward a history of needs*. Berkeley, CA: Heyday Books.

Miller, P. (1984). *Errand into the wilderness*. Cambridge, MA: Belknap Press.

Miller, P., & Johnson, T. H. (1963). *The puritans*. New York: Harper & Row, 1963.

Sawicki, J. (1988). Identity politics and sexual freedom: Foucault and feminism. In I. Diamond & L. Quinby (Eds.), *Feminism and Foucault: Reflections on resistance* (pp.). Boston: Northeastern University Press.

Singer, L. (1993). *Erotic welfare: Sexual theory and politics in the age of epidemic*. New York: Routledge, Chapman & Hall.

3

Choice

Joel Spring
State University of New York at New Paltz

The word "choice" in education conjures up visions of democracy and freedom-loving parents happily selecting from many educational alternatives. How was this vision distorted into an antidemocratic plan to allow parents to choose among schools teaching the same centrally determined curriculum? How did choice plans calling for less bureaucratic control result in greater bureaucratic control of the ideologies taught in public schools?

To answer these questions, I begin with a discussion of Austrian economics and the reaction of Protestant fundamentalists to the secularization of public schools. In the 1970s, Austrian economists supported the demands of Protestant fundamentalists for the right of parents to choose between public and private schools. Christian fundamentalist organizations—the Moral Majority in the 1980s and the Christian Coalition in the 1990s—exerted political pressure on the Republican party to support choice in education. From the 1970s to the 1990s, conservative think tanks and foundations popularized Austrian economics which, in turn, influenced the Republican party, the movement to reinvent government and the schools, and President Bill Clinton's New Democrat doctrines. In addition, the sharp reaction of the teachers' unions influenced choice plans in the Democratic party.

Austrian economics is the best place to begin understanding the changing meaning of choice in education. Although originating in the 19th century, Austrian economics gained its foothold in the United States at the

University of Chicago in the 1950s. During that period, noted Austrian economist Friedrich Von Hayek helped create what was later called the Chicago School of Economics (Boettke, n.d.; Hayek, 1994; Rothbard, 1970).

Choice is a key concept in Austrian economics. Austrian economists argue that all centrally planned economies are doomed to failure because of the difficulty in determining the price of goods. Price represents the value of a product to a society. Creating prices requires balancing demand with manufacturing and the availability of resources. How can a centrally planned economy, for instance, determine the price of televisions without a knowledge of public demand? The answer for Austrian economists is that in a centrally planned economy the bureaucrats fix prices in their own self interest rather than in the interest of the public.

The solution, according to Austrian economists, is to have price determined by the workings of a free market. The assumption is that the "invisible hand of the marketplace" will establish prices and the production of goods that are more in line with the public interest as opposed to the interests of bureaucrats.

Austrian economists apply the same reasoning to ideas. A free market for ideas will allow the invisible hand of the marketplace to select ideas that are most compatible with the public interest. In a government dominated society, bureaucrats select the ideas placed in textbooks and disseminated through public schools. The ideas selected by bureaucrats, according to Austrian economists, are those that promote the self-interest of bureaucrats. For instance, bureaucrats might want to ensure their jobs by distributing ideas through public schools that support the continuing existence of a welfare state.

Therefore, Austrian economists see the major problem with education as the existence of a public school monopoly controlled in the self-interest of educational bureaucrats. In this context, educational choice means breaking up the public school monopoly, limiting the power of educational bureaucrats, and turning education over to the workings of the free market. It also means freedom of competition between ideologies in education.

In the 1960s, an influential member of the Chicago School, Milton Friedman, made the first proposal for a voucher system that would give parents a choice between public school districts. Friedman (1994) argues that school vouchers would allow children from some low-income families attending poor-quality city school systems to attend better schools in affluent suburbs. For Friedman, choice was a means of correcting the inequalities caused by the existence of rich and poor school districts. Based on similar arguments, Milwaukee and Cleveland in the 1990s initiated voucher plans to provide children from low-income families the choice of attending private schools. In these voucher programs, the purpose of choice was to allow low-income families to have the same choice of private schooling as high-income families (p. 89).

Christian fundamentalists and conservatives rejected the emphasis of Austrian economists on the freedom to choose between competing ideologies. In the 1970s, Austrian economists and their political counterparts, Libertarians, rushed to support Christian fundamentalists who demanded having the choice at public expense to send their children to private Christian academies. For both Austrian economists and Libertarians, the Christian revolt against public schools provided a chance to create competition between ideologies.[1]

Christian fundamentalists welcomed the support but rejected the concept of ideological competition among schools. From their standpoint, public schools traditionally taught Protestant values. With continuing secularization, they argued, schools were now teaching the religion of secular humanism. Consequently, from their perspective, choice between public and private schools would allow parents to choose traditional schools based on Protestant values. Because they believe that Christianity is the only true religion, Christian fundamentalists are not interested in a public choice plan that allows choice at public expense of Moslem or Afrocentric schools. Christian fundamentalists narrowed the meaning of choice in education from a free marketplace of ideas to the choice of a Christian alternative (see Buchanan, 1990; Delfatorre, 1992; Reed, 1996).

The meaning of choice was further narrowed by conservative foundations and think tanks, such as the Hudson Institute, the Heritage Foundation, the Olin Foundation, and the American Enterprise Institute and their scholars Diane Ravitch, Chester Finn, Denis Doyle, and William Bennett (see "Buying a Movement," n. d.; Ricci, 1993; Simon, 1978; & Smith, 1991). Traditionally, conservatives support government efforts to regulate social behavior through laws, police, and the schools. Conservatives sup-

[1]During the 1970s, I was an active member of the Libertarian movement and supporter of Austrian economics. While working for the Center for Independent Education, a Libertarian organization supporting Austrian economic ideas in education, I and other members of the institute provided legal and expert advice to the Christian movement. Since that time, I have abandoned libertarianism and Austrian economics because of a serious flaw in their ideology. This flaw is the almost mythical power that is given to the invisible hand of the marketplace to produce humane economic policies. I now believe that the end result of the invisible hand is to increase the wealth of the rich.

port a strong role for government in regulating education. For instance in the 1950s, President Dwight Eisenhower, a Republican and self-proclaimed progressive conservative, championed the National Defense Education Act, which greatly expanded the federal role in education (see Lind, 1996).

Therefore, it is not surprising that in the 1980s and 1990s, conservatives used Austrian economics to justify competition between schools while calling on the federal government to exert greater control over the curriculum of the nation's schools. The think-tank conservatives—Ravitch, Finn, Doyle, and Bennett—played active roles in the administrations of Republican conservatives Reagan and Bush in the 1980s and 1990s. The result was a combination of proposals for national standards and tests and plans for allowing parental choice between public and private schools (Finn & Ravitch, n. d.; Gerstner, Semerad, Doyle, & Johnston, 1994; Lawton, 1996).

The call for national academic standards eventually became part of President Bush's *America 2000* (1991). A major objective of *America 2000*, slightly revised and renamed before being passed into legislation by President Bill Clinton in April of 1994, was cooperation between state and federal governments in creating national academic standards and tests. In essence, these national standards, which were to be measured by national tests, would determine the content and curriculum in public schools. The resulting debate over history standards highlighted the issue of ideological control. What vision of American history should be represented in the history standards? Should the history curriculum emphasize Anglo-American traditions or a multicultural society? National standards would ensure the teaching of a common ideology (see Cody, Woodward, & Elliot, 1993; Cornbleth & Waugh, 1995; Diegmueller, 1995, 1996; Gluck, 1994;; "Plan to Teach," 1994; Schlesinger, 1991).

What does choice mean if all schools conform to the same national standards? What happened to the original Austrian economics idea that choice included a competition of ideologies in a free marketplace? Conservatives answered these questions by turning the idea of choice into a management technique. In this context, choice became a method for creating competition among schools over the best methods for imparting national standards to students. The invisible hand of the marketplace, conservatives hoped, would produce new forms of school organization and methods of instruction to more efficiently achieve national standards (see Cooper, 1991; Gerstner et al., 1994; Yang, 1991).

Of course, this conservative definition of choice denied the Christian fundamentalists' desire for parents to have the ideological choice of sending their children to Christian schools. Consequently, the influence of the Christian Coalition on the writing of the 1992 National Republican Platform forced Republican candidate Bush to withdraw support for national standards and simply advocate creating a plan to give parents a choice between public and private schools. In fact, the 1992 National Republican Platform not only abandoned support of national standards but also called for the demise of the Department of Education (Niebuhr, 1996).

In contrast to the Republicans, the New Democrats under the leadership of Bill Clinton were strongly influenced by the arguments of David Osborne and Ted Gaebler (1993) in *Reinventing Government: How the Entrepreneurial Spirit Is Transforming the Public Sector.* New Democrats argue that competition between government agencies results in more efficiency in the provision of services to the public. This means that competition between public schools would supposedly result in cheaper and better instruction of students. In addition, the two teachers' unions, who exercise major power within the Democratic party, oppose choice plans that include private schools. Therefore, the New Democrats advocated plans that would allow parents to make choices between public schools as opposed to choices among public and private schools. Similar to conservatives, the New Democrats advocated the establishment of national academic standards. Consequently, the New Democrats also reduced the idea of choice to a management tool to promote efficiency in achieving national standards (see Clinton, 1996; Clinton & Gore, 1992; Hale, n.d.; Riley, 1996; Smith, 1995; Weisberg, 1996).

In summary, major political groups have given the following meanings to choice in education:

- Choice to allow parental selection of a private Christian school.
- Choice between public and private schools to achieve more efficient attainment of national standards.
- Choice to promote competition among government agencies, such as choice among public schools to promote efficient attainment of national standards.
- Choice for low-income families in urban areas to attend private schools.

None of these various political uses of choice in education promote ideological freedom in public schools. The original Austrian economics idea of providing public choice of ideologies to be taught in school has disappeared from the debate. Conservatives and New Democrats have changed the meaning of choice into something antidemocratic. By reducing choice to a management tool for promoting efficiency in achieving national standards, Conservatives and New Democrats have rejected the notion of freedom of ideas in public schools. How can there be meaningful democratic politics if everyone is taught the same ideology? In fact, if schooling influences future choices, then schooling with national standards could result in everyone's making the same political choices. In other words, Conservative and New Democrat definitions of choice in education provide a new means of ideological control over the population.

Ironically, choice in education might mean the end of democratic choice of ideas. There is no meaningful freedom of thought if everyone thinks the same things. If choice combined with national standards results in uniformity of thinking in public schools, then democracy is dead. Interestingly, the Christian Coalition, acting from self-interest, is resisting this trend. Of course, the Christian Coalition would like to impose its own brand of uniformity on the schools. Therefore, the Christian Coalition, Conservatives, and the New Democrats have made choice an antidemocratic movement in education.

REFERENCES

America 2000: An education strategy. (1991). Washington, DC: United States Government Printing Office.

Boettke, P. (n.d.). Friedrich A. Hayeck (1899–1992). Department of Economics, New York University. www.econ.nyu.edu/user/boettke/hayek.htm.

Buchanan, P. J. (1990). *Right from the beginning.* Washington, DC: Regenry Gateway.

Clinton, W. J., & Gore, A. (1992). *Putting people first: How we can all change America.* New York: Times Books.

Clinton, W. J., (1996). *Between hope and history: Meeting America's challenges for the 21st century.* New York: Times Books.

Cody, C. B., Woodward, A., & Elliot, D. L. (1993). Race, ideology and the battle over the curriculum. In C. Marshall (Ed.), *The new politics of race and gender.* Washington, DC: Falmer Press.

Cooper, K. J. (1991, April 19). *National standards at core of Proposal: Model schools envisioned.* Compuserve Executive News Service Washington Post.

Cornbleth, C., & Waugh, D. (1995). *The great speckled bird: Multicultural politics and education policymaking.* Mahwah, NJ: Lawrence Erlbaum Associates.

Delfatorre, J. (1992). *What Johnny shouldn't read: Textbook censorship in America.* New Haven: Yale University Press.

Diegmueller, K. (1995, October 18). Revise history standards, two panels advise, *Education Week*, p. 11.

Diegmueller, K. (1996, April 10). History center shares new set of standards, *Education Week*.

Finn, C., Jr., & Ravitch, D. (n.d.). *Educational reform 1995–1996: Introduction* [On-line]. Available: www.edexcellence.net.

Friedman, M. (1994). *Capitalism and freedom.* Chicago: University of Chicago Press.

Gerstner, L., Jr., Semerad, R. D., Doyle, D. P., & Johnston, W. (1994). *Reinventing education: Entrepreneurship in America's public schools*. New York: Dutton.
Gluck, C. (1994, October 26) Let the debate continue, *The New York Times*, p. 23.
Hale, J. (n.d.). *The Making of the New Democrats*, Democratic Leadership Council Homepage [On-line]. Available: www.dlcppi.com.
Hayek, F. (1994). *The road to serfdom*. Chicago: University of Chicago Press.
Lawton, M. (1996). Summit accord calls for focus on standards, *Education Week* (3 April), pp. 1, 14–15.
Lind, M. (1996). *Up from conservatism: Why the right is wrong for America*. New York: The Free Press.
Niebuhr, G. (1996, September 16). Dole gets Christian Coalition's trust and prodding, *The New York Times* p. B8.
Osborne, G., & Gaebler, T. (1993). *Reinventing government: How the entrepreneurial spirit is transforming the public sector*. New York: Penguin.
People for the American Way. (n.d.). *Buying a movement: New report analyzes right-wing foundations* [On-line].
Plan to teach U.S. history is said to slight white males (1994, October 26). *The New York Times*, p. B12.
Reed, R. (1996). *Active faith: How Christians are changing the soul of American politics*. New York: The Free Press.
Ricci, D. M., (1993). *The transformation of American politics: The new Washington and the rise of think tanks*. New Haven: Yale University Press.
Riley, R. (1996, February 28). *State of American education address*, St. Louis, MO. Washington, DC: Office of the Secretary of Education.
Rothbard, M. N. (1970). *Man, economy, and state: A treatise of economic principles*. Los Angeles: Nash.
Schlesinger, A. M., Jr. (1991). *The disuniting of America*. Knoxville, TN: Whittle Direct Books.
Simon, W. (1978). *A time for truth*. New York: Readers Digest Press.
Smith, J. A. (1991). *The idea brokers: Think tanks and the rise of the new policy elite*. New York: The Free Press.
Smith, M. S. (1995). Education reform in America's public schools: The Clinton agenda, In D. Ravtich (Ed.), *Debating the future of American education: Do we need national standards and assessments?* Washington DC: Brookings Institute.
Weisberg, J. (1996). *In defense of government: The fall and rise of public trust*. New York: Scribner.
Yang, J. E. (1991, April 19). Bush unveils education plan: States, communities would play major role in proposed innovations, *Compuserve Executive News Service Washington Post*.

4

Reform

Thomas S. Popkewitz
University of Wisconsin–Madison

This chapter is about the study of educational reform. It is not to ask how can we engage in reform efforts but rather how can we think about reform as a governing practice. This governing is not one of governmental policy to set directions and principles for educational practices. Rather, the governing is concerned with linking political rationalities to subjectivities, that is, the governing principles through which people think, talk, speak, and act as self-responsible individuals. This governing is what Foucault (1979) calls *governmentality*.

Reform in the United States embodies efforts to administer change through the production of a self-governing individuality. We can excavate this idea of reform through recognizing that the word "reform"does not have constant meanings but embodies different concepts over time. In the beginning of the 19th century, reform was concerned with helping sinners find salvation. But by the mid-20th century, reform assumed its modern shape as state administrative projects to reorganize institutions and to change individuals in the name of liberty and freedom.

Reform as the administration of change embodies two overlaying discourses. One is "scientific" rational planning of social and individual life. The second is a millennial religious discourse about *progress*. This idea of progress is that the better world is to be produced through the administration of *the soul*. Policy and science are to change society through administering the inner capabilities of the individual who acts as a self-responsible and self-motivated citizen. Pedagogy was one meeting place that joined science with millennialism. Pedagogy was to administer (develop and nurture) the child's "soul."

This discussion about reform, then, moves against the grain. It does not assume schooling is a principled activity in which specific programs are measured against abstract social goals, such as those of justice, equity, the democratic citizen, or a more adjusted and competent worker. In contrast, I place reform within a particular problematic of governing the soul so the individual can be free to act. Further, that governing embodies strategies that both include and exclude. This irony and paradox of reform is one that is continually grappling with the problems of schooling.

REFORM AS SOCIAL CONSTRUCTION

If I retreat to history for a moment to understand the present, reform as the administration of social life is an invention of the 19th century. The Progressive Era in the United States (1880–1920), called the "Age of Reform," involved the formation of a state administration to regulate major segments of society, from coordinating transportation to forming a joint military command among the armed forces. Reform strategies were also concerned with "making" the individual who could participate in modern social and political institutions. Social welfare institutions were engaged in the pedagogical problems of how to make the new citizen a worker, a child, a parent. The governing function of reform, however, is lost in social policy and educational research. For many, the invention and measurement of reforms are the very markers of change and progress.

The Formation of the Modern State and the "Age of Reform": American Progressivism

By the late 1800s, tremendous social, cultural, and material change had become evident (see Bledstein, 1976; Hofstadter, 1955; Walters, 1978). Most discussions tend to focus on the physical changes brought by industrialization and urbanization, as well as the commercialization of farming. The narrative of reform of the Progressive Era makes these changes seem evolutionary and progressive as the modern U.S. state was constructed (for a discussion of state building, see, Skowronek, 1982). My concern here, however, is different because I am concerned with the "Age of Reform"as making apparent new administrative models for governing the individual (see Popkewitz, 1991). The state no longer only protected territories and ensured physical borders; the care of the state's territory shifted to include care for its population. The state was to shape the individual who mastered change through the application of rationality and reason (see, e.g., Hunter, 1994). New forms of participation, interpretation, social management, and amelioration appeared (see, e.g., Orloff & Skocpol, 1984).

Agencies of social welfare became responsible for child labor, health, education, and social planning. These agencies established a link between the macro programs of state governance and the micro organizations of the family and the school (Foucault, 1979).

The new practices of the state joined the register of social administration with the "register of freedom" (see Wagner, 1994). A disposition existed that change could be harnessed and progress produced through a reflexivity that made the person an object of scrutiny and the subject of self-scrutiny. Although not without contradictions, a belief was promoted that reform was a purposeful intervention to alter and improve social and personal life.

The construction of individuality became a problem of social administration. The individual could be produced who was a citizen of a nation who had certain obligations, responsibilities, and freedoms. Freedoms, however, involved a citizen who acted responsibly through a new sense of self-motivation and self-discipline.

The focus of the social administration was the soul, that is, the inner capabilities and dispositions through which individuals acted. Religious concerns with the saving of the soul were revisioned through placing individual salvation as produced through secular discourses of state planning and science. The "soul"derives from a specifically Western messianic tradition of redemption. Social administration of the "self" reenacted early church interests in rescuing the "soul"(Foucault, 1984; Rose, 1989). Previous church conceptions of revelation were transferred to strategies that were to administer personal development, self-reflection and the inner, self-guided moral growth of the individual (see, e.g., discussion about religious cosmologies and theories of social change and evaluation in Popkewitz, 1984, 1998 a, b; 1991). Modern pedagogy and the sciences of education embodied this belief in the administration of the "soul" (see Popkewitz & Brennan, 1998).

Why have I stressed this idea of the social administration of freedom with the problem of studying reform? There is a paradox (and irony) in the twin registers that I argue is still with us today. Reforms produced a national imaginary related to the Americanization of the immigrant, Native Americans, and former slaves. Reforms were also to produce the cosmopolitan subjectivities who can travel across multiple boundaries that form the worlds of business, politics, and culture. Reforms were to turn deviants into model citizens. At the same time, reforms produced new forms of exclusion that were related to poverty, race, and gender, among others. This social administration of the soul is embedded in current educational reforms, but I argue that the governing principles and exclusions today are articulated differently from those of the past. This last issue is one I believe is central to the study of education.

Reform and Governing the Soul: The Knowledge of the Social Sciences

The redemptive culture of the administration of freedom was embodied in the social and educational sciences (see Popkewitz, 1998a). The human sciences came to embody a radical assumption that human agency can produce its own improvement through rational means of control. Progress, inscribed in political theories of democracy, was made into an individual responsibility. The professionalization of knowledge became the crucial link in the transformations sought. The new social sciences were to be in service of the democratic ideals through providing objective, nonevaluative descriptions to guide social planning.[1] The authority of the expert, it was believed, was founded in evidence and dependent on the rules of logic and reference to the empirical rather than to the social status of the speaker or to the authority of God.

The social sciences replaced revelation with the administration of reflection in finding human progress. Social sciences were to interpret the more complex social relations and interdependence among communities and to reassert moral, social, and cultural authority through the processes of reform. The discourses of sociology, culture, and psychology would discipline and administer freedom in modernity: how the worker was to feel, see, think, and act in the new industrial relations; the dispositions and sensitivities of the mother, wife, and child in the new social relations of the home; the citizen who acted and participated through the problem-solving approaches of liberal democracies.

The discourses of psychology and sociology, for example, joined science with the ideas of progress and salvation. Religious confessional practices

---

[1]One can read the history of the social sciences as continually debating the pragmatics of research with the ideal of objectivity. See, for example, Novick, 1988. Also see Bazerman, 1987, for discussion of the rhetorical constructions of the idea of objectivity.

were transferred to the realm of personal self-reflection and self-criticism. Personal salvation and redemption were tied to personal "development"and "fulfillment,"words that signaled religious motifs but placed them in secular discourses of psychology. The confessional technologies in the methods of social and psychological sciences opened the thoughts and aspirations of the individual to inspection, scrutiny and regulation. American sociology, as well, maintained a millennial perspective (Greek, 1992). The theories and methods of the Chicago School of Sociology did not grow out of any pure science but from theology and social work. The research focused on issues of social control (in the sense of institutional planning) that were to not only to improve the life situation of the poor (Franklin, 1987), but also to remake the poor and immigrants who lived in the city in light of a millennial perspective.

It is here that we can return to Foucault's (1979) idea of governmentality. "The Age of Reform" melded a host of distinct and overlapping discourses about political philosophy (liberal democracy), progress, social administration, and salvation into strategies for constructing the new "citizen."

SCHOOL REFORM AND THE SOCIAL ADMINISTRATION OF THE CHILD

The paradox of the registers of administration and freedom provides a strategy to think about contemporary educational reforms. If the modern school is a governing practice, then contemporary pedagogical reform needs to be examined in relation to changes in its governing principles.

This social administration of freedom is most evident historically in the construction of pedagogy. Schooling and pedagogy made the soul as the object of scrutiny. Religious motifs of pastoral care and the confessional were brought into the curriculum through the discipline of psychology. *But the religious motifs about personal salvation and redemption had new points of reference.* It became possible to talk about children's inner sense of "self"as earlier religious discourses talked about the salvation of soul. The psychological vocabulary gave attention to seemingly secular concerns about personal development and "fulfillment." Categories about attitudes, learning, self-actualization, and self-esteem *signified religious motifs but placed them in secular discourses of science and rational progress.*

If we return to the 20th century, educational reforms, like other social projects, focused on the implementation of social, collective projects. The operative metaphors of progress and redemption were derived from social collective norms, common roles, and fixed identities. The child study movement, as well as competing curriculum theories, inscribed principles of progress and redemption in discourses about the self-governing child. From the pragmatism of John Dewey to the social utility theories of David Snedden and the child study movement of G. Stanley Hall, there was a concern with the "making"of a universal citizen who would participate in the collective projects of the new society.

Today's educational reforms reconstitute the image of governing the child (Popkewitz, 1998b). The social, collective identities and universal norms embodied in previous reforms are replaced with images of the local, communal, and flexible identity. Reforms inscribe a decentralized citizen who is active, self-motivated, participatory, and problem-solving (for comparative discussions of the child, see Hultqvist, 1998). The teacher and the child are constructed as having multiple identities, being oriented to collaboration, being part of a local "community,"and having a flexible problem-solving disposition. In recent policy discourses, the rhetoric of neoliberalism (e.g., markets, privatization, and community) embodies the local constructivist agent such as community health, community schools, community-based welfare systems (Rose, 1994).

Professional educational knowledge, as well, replaces the "social"with the new "local"researcher who speaks of "the personal knowledge of teachers,""the wisdom of teachers"and the relation of teachers to communities and parents. Whereas teacher education at the turn-of-the-century sought to remove communal and ethnic influences to create social collective identities, current discourses of teacher education reinsert the parent and ethnicity into pedagogical practices to administer social actions and participation.

The shifts in governing principles embodied in reforms are related to shifts of the past decades in the politics of social movements, state patterns of governing, and the economy of work (see Popkewitz, 1999). Whereas earlier political projects were concerned with the formation of a collective social identity and universal progress, today's politics demonstrate more localized trajectories. There is a new emphasis in the economy on the worker whose "being"emphasizes flexibility, problem-solving, and contingent, personal, or interactional communication.

In these reform practices, the governing of the individual is not effected through explicit procedures, but through the deployments of "reasoning," through which the teacher and child construct their capabilities and actions. In education, there is a "constructivist"pedagogy that makes the subjectivity of the child and the teacher as the locale for intervention. The site of change is the cognitive and moral comportment of the individual (see, e.g., Popkewitz, 1991).

Reforms as Systems of Inclusion/Exclusion

The new reforms produce new systems of inclusion/exclusion. I join the two terms to understand how each term embodies the other. Educational discourses produce "maps"; such maps provide a way to order the objects of the world for scrutiny and practice. When maps of the child are constructed, they are not only descriptive but normative. By that I mean the distinctions and differentiations of reform embody a continuum of norms that order and divide the capabilities of the child.

It is in the differentiating and dividing of the discourses of education that we can reapproach the problem of inclusion/exclusion. Pedagogy functions as "maps"whose principles of knowledge circulate norms about the "healthy"child who, for example, has problem-solving ability and high self-esteem. The norms about "health"and "development"appear as natural or universal to a productive childhood. But in constructing the norms of reason and thinking are also dividing practices because some people always lie outside the norms. One can look at state-sponsored reforms that focus on "urban"education and the "needy", for example, as rhetorically offering to deliver millennial promises but whose discursive constructions mobilize distinctions that divide the normal from the not-normal and sometimes the pathological. These norms are not about publicly declared ideal states that people should achieve. The dividing norms are inscribed in categories and distinctions of pedagogy to produce principles about qualities of the *being* of the child, no matter who that child is (Popkewitz, 1998b).

My argument sketched out here is that the new reform practices of participation embody ways of understanding, classifying, and acting on the subjects of government and create new relationships between the ways individuals are governed by others and the ways they govern themselves. The practices to democratize schools are governing strategies rather than searches for a normative ideal. The reform practices of the turn of the 20th century transferred *redemptive and pastoral motifs to the secular discourses of the science of personal administration*. Similarly, current reforms decentralize the individual by making specific attributes and dispositions the focus of change. The organization of reflection and "self" link the registers of social administration with the registers of freedom. These patterns of governing cannot be assumed but must be made problematic.

DISTINGUISHING BETWEEN CHANGE AND REFORM

Let me return for a moment to the distinction between the arguments about reform as a principled argument and one concerned with governing and governmentality. Research is not to argue that reforms are either good or bad but to inquire into its historical and social construction. But that inquiry has a certain problematic. It considers the rules and standards of "reason"that underlie the knowledge of schooling. It is to ask about the systems of reason that shape and fashion "our"thinking and acting in everyday life. It is to denaturalize thought and reason to understand them as historical constructions related to issues of power. That power, however, is not only to stop people from acting and participating but in fact is a productive power through generating the rules by which action and participation occur.

By focusing on the problematic of knowledge, I am suggesting that we eventualize reform, that is, to make it into the event that is studied as the data of research. Reform is an event that articulates the productive nature of power rather than a solution to solve problems of teaching or learning. Reform, then, becomes an event to understand the changes occurring, a monument that stands to "tell"of the power relations embodied in the construction of schools. But I have also sought to historicize knowledge, reason, and thought of the present. Throughout this discussion, I focused on the present as a break and rupture in the governing principles of pedagogy.

This focus on reason and knowledge brings to mind a conversation that Foucault (1980) had with a young student about social change. The student was deeply involved in the protests taking place in the French universities during 1968. The student came to Foucault and talked about how the protests were having important social results. There were "people's courts," the student said, that put many of the authorities in the university and the government on trial. Foucault asked the student to wait a minute. In putting the authorities on trial, Foucault asked, are they not using the rules and standards of reasoning that emerge from the very bourgeoisie courts that the students are trying to overcome? Foucault's argument is also one for the study of reform. Our task is to examine the rules of reason and the principles of action deployed as the effects of power. It is this type of historical interrogation of the present that is important if we are to consider the ethical, moral, and political issues that underlie the efforts for reform itself.

I am thus making a distinction between reform and the study of change. Research needs to consider how reforms provide a particular selectivity in organizing teaching, learning, classroom management, and curriculum. It is to examine the principles that are generated to qualify or disqualify children from participation. This qualifying or disqualifying occurs through differentiating the "being"of the child.

This argument about reform focused on the governing and governmentality of pedagogical practices. I argued that pedagogy creates new relationships between the ways in which individuals are governed by others and the ways in which they govern themselves. I related historically the organization of reform to the governing of the "soul."This relation links the registers of social administration and the registers of freedom. But I also raised the problem of the systems of inclusion as simultaneously systems of exclusion. This duality of reform requires a constant vigilance. All discourses are dangerous if not always bad. In research about schooling, the patterns of governing cannot be assumed but must be made problematic.

REFERENCES

Bazerman, C. (1987). Codifying the scientific style. In J. Nelson, A. Mogill, & D. McCloskey (Eds.), *The rhetoric of the human sciences* (pp. 125–144). Madison: University of Wisconsin Press.

Bledstein, B. (1976). *The culture of professionalism, the middle class and the development of higher education in America*. New York: Norton.

Foucault, M. (1979). Governmentality. *Ideology and consciousness*, 6, 5–22.

Foucault, M. (1980). On popular justice: A discussion with Maoists (C. Gordon, L. Marshall, J. Mepham, J. & K. Soper, Trans.). In C. Gordon (Ed.), *Power/knowledge: Selected interviews and other writings 1972–1977* (pp. 1–36). New York: Pantheon.

Foucault, M. (1984). What is enlightenment? In P. Rabinow (Ed.), *The Foucault Reader* (pp. 32–50). New York: Pantheon.

Franklin, B. (1987). The first crusade for learning disabilities: The movement for the education of backward children. In T. Popkewitz (Ed.), *The formation of school subjects: The struggle for creating an American institution* (pp. 190–209). New York: Falmer Press.

Greek, C. (1992). *The religious roots of American sociology*. New York: Garland.

Hofstadter, R. (1955). *The age of reform, from Bryan to F.D.R.* New York: Vintage.

Hultqvist, K. (1998). A history of the present on children's welfare in Sweden. In T. Popkewitz & M. Brennan (Eds.), *Foucault's challenge: Discourse, knowledge and power in education*. New York: Teachers College Press.

Hunter, I. (1994). *Rethinking the school: Subjectivity, bureaucracy, criticism*. New York: St. Martin's Press.

Novick, P. ( ). *That noble dream: The "objectivity question" and the American historical profession*. New York: Cambridge, UK: Cambridge University Press.

Orloff, A., & Skocpol, T. (1984). Why not equal protection? Spending in Britain, 1900–1911, and the United States, 1880s–1920. *American Sociological Review, 49,* 726–750.
Popkewitz, T. (1984). *Paradigm and ideology in educational research: Social functions of the intellectual.* London: Falmer Press.
Popkewitz, T. (1991). *A political sociology of educational reform: Power/knowledge in teaching, teacher education and research.* New York: Teachers College Press.
Popkewitz, T. (1999). The changing terrains of knowledge and power: A social epistemology of educational research. In T. Popkewitz & L. Fender (Eds.), *Critical theories in education: Changing terrains of knowledge and politics* (pp. 17–42). New York: Routledge
Popkewitz, T. (1998a). The culture of redemption and the administration of freedom in educational research. *Review of Educational Research,* 68(1), 1–34.
Popkewitz, T. (1998b). *Struggling for the soul: The politics of schooling and the construction of the teacher.* New York: Teachers' College Press.
Popkewitz, T., & Brennan, M. (Eds.). (1997). *Foucault's challenge: Discourse, knowledge and power in education.* New York: Teachers College Press.
Popkewitz, T., & Pitman, A. (1986). The idea of progress and the legitimation of state agendas: American proposals for school reform. *Curriculum and Teaching, 1,* 11–24.
Rose, N. (1989). *Governing the soul.* New York: Routledge.
Rose, N. (1996). The death of the social: Refiguring the territory of government. *Economy and Society, 25,* 327–356.
Rose, R. (1994). Expertise and the government of conduct. *Studies in law, politics and society, 14,* 359–397.
Skowronek, S. (1982). *Building a new American state: The expansion of national administrative capacities, 1877–1920.* New York: Cambridge University Press.
Wagner, P. (1994). *The sociology of modernity.* New York: Routledge.
Walters, R. (1978). *American reformers, 1815–1860.* New York: Hill & Wang.

5

Leadership

Wanda Pillow
University of Illinois at Urbana-Champaign

Who do you think of when you think of a leader: CEO, president, military figure, coach, parent, church official? Are there characteristics or qualities you think a leader must possess or not possess? More specifically, is this leader who comes to your mind male or female; what are her or his physical characteristics; how do you expect this leader to act? Perhaps more important who do you not think of when you think of a leader?

Our assumptions, images, and cultural understanding of who a leader is, who a leader should be, are embedded in the responses we give to these questions. Where do our images of leadership come from and why? This chapter traces some of the historical, cultural, and political tensions that have shaped how we think about educational leadership. It situates leadership within a political context—one influenced by cultural, political, moral, and economic needs. How has the development of schools as bureaucratic organizations affected educational leadership? How does the current reform movement characterize leadership? After considering these questions, I turn to the challenges and possibilities for transformational leadership offered by feminist interpretations of power, authority, and leadership.

From the time that school administration emerged as a profession in the mid-19th century, efforts to define the administrator's role have always been contentious. Is the school principal an administrator or a leader? The debate has centered around two competing purposes of education—management and training versus visionary citizenship—with recent reform movements paradoxically calling for school leaders to be *both* expert, efficient managers and creative, caring, responsive leaders. However the role of school principals is defined, it is accepted and expected that they use their leadership position to set or very strongly influence the overall tone and climate of the school. Deborah Jones (1997), for example, argues that "the principal plays a critical role in creating an environment that is conductive to learning, respect, and positive human relations"(p. 66). She and other researchers (Irvine, 1988, 1990; Lomotey, 1994; Turnage, 1972) have recently emphasized the impact that effective leadership (or lack thereof) can have on the educational experiences of African American students. Thus, the debate is not about the importance of the school principal but the role of the school principal as an educational leader.

Conventional theories of leadership embrace four main assumptions. First, they presuppose that leadership is synonymous with formal *positional authority*. Second, this authority is established through a *defined hierarchy*. Third, conventional theories associate leadership with two essential qualities: *technique* and *expertise*—qualities that, fourth, enable the leader to make *rational decisions based on technical evidence*. These four assumptions are deeply entrenched in our beliefs about leadership as evidenced by the prevalence of this model in a broad array of organizations and systems. The conventional theory of leadership also aligns with a bureaucratic business model of organization and leadership.

Although many assume education's linkages to and emulation of business models and practices to be a recent phenomenon, there is a long history of school's direct linkages and dependence upon the business corporate world. Schools have continually attempted to serve both human interest and corporate greed in everything from the conceptualization of what the purpose of schooling is to the organization and structure of the school board (Spring, 1994). By the late 19th century, schools had established themselves as bureaucratic organizations with a clear hierarchy of rank among teachers, administrators, and superintendents and a ranking of students by grade.

Several factors impacted and influenced the development of the organization of schools as we know them today. As America proceeded along the path of industrialization, schools responded to the need for and allure of systems of efficiency, rationality, order, and cost effectiveness (Spring, 1994). Educational policy makers equated schools with a training ground for providing individuals with an appropriate socialization experience—one that would discipline them in accordance with the values, behaviors, and skills necessary for the workplace. This remains one of the major stated purposes of schools today.

Education, from this point of view, is a commodity, an end to a means, and in this case a measurable end. In this sense standardized curriculum and test measures, and success measured in economic terms of "achievement up–costs down,"are designed as skillful management tools. Educational leadership departments have been influenced by and responded to this view of the scientific management of schools by creating training programs for school leaders that incorporate these beliefs and concepts. The use of standardized licensure and training programs for school administrators that exemplify these goals has proliferated.

The conventional model and view of leadership is dependent upon identifying some set of skills that we can feel assured represent best practice in school administration. Programs operate under the assumption of a positivistic belief that they can name and claim a definitive approach to leadership and that "a science of administrative behavior is achievable"(Foster, 1991, p. 127). As Kempner (1991) argues "all that is really needed from such a viewpoint is to discover the appropriate tools needed to control an organization and its people"(p. 113). A plethora of "handbooks"for "success-oriented schools"have been developed that lay out the "tools"for educational leadership. Citing "effective"strategies and "management"operations for "managing success"these handbooks come packaged in practical, easy to use exercises promising measurable achievement. In this sense, leadership is a "commodity"to be trained in and then "brokered for an administrative position"(Kempner, 1991, p. 111).

Site-based management, total quality management, continuous quality improvement are all business models of operation that have been adopted and have found their way into school reform talk. Kempner (1991) cites this "adoration of business by educators"as "a 'corporatism' mentality based upon a capitalistic orientation that separates the owners of the means of production from the laborers"(pp. 109–110). This thinking leads to a confusion for public education of what its purpose is and a conflation of the "social goals of education with the goals of industrial capitalism"(pp. 109–110). Kempner points out that this orientation also confuses "the role of administrators with capitalists and the role of teachers with laborers"(p. 110). Jill Blackmore argues that even those who espouse a humanist view of leadership that "softens"the assumptions of conventional leadership theory by discussing leadership as a "moral, political, and social activity ... still endows particular individuals with the innate or acquired capacity to make higher-level judgements based upon abstract and universal moral principals"(Blackmore, 1991, p. 20). As Kempner (1991) points out, "training programs, entry requirements, and the evaluation of administrators, however, are not primarily focused on the moral and democratic dimensions of educational administration. Instead, the focus is principally on the acquisition of the skills, techniques, and socialization that the keepers of the castle of educational administration deem appropriate for entry"(pp. 104–105).

Naming, analyzing, and coming up with alternative views of the characteristics of leaders and the goals of leadership is vital work, because it is these beliefs that influence and determine who we think can be an effective leader. For example, predominantly male experiences are repeatedly cited as the best preparation for leadership positions—e.g., football quarterback, participation in student government, military training, coach—all experiences that reinforce the characteristics of assertiveness, competitiveness, hierarchy, and individuality as necessary for effective leadership. Even the metaphors, case studies, and analogies used in educational leadership textbooks tend to incorporate sports terms and lingo. This discourse surrounding the field of educational leadership prevents many women from entering the profession "because they do not possess the appropriate traits and experiences needed to enter the castle [of administration]"(Kempner, 1991, p. 110).

As we have seen, this castle of administration is based on the development of schools as bureaucracies and education's historical and current linkages and alliances with the corporate economy. Additionally, feminist interpretations of school organizations, power, authority, and leadership situate educational leadership as entrenched within patriarchy. Schools, as bureaucracies, sustained and reinforced patriarchy through promotion of gender inequity.

Our schools today look amazingly similar to the bureaucratic system that evolved in the nineteenth century which deemed it natural that men should be in positions of power and management while women taught. During the late, 19th century, teaching was one of the few career opportunities available to women. As women moved into the teaching force, teaching became to be seen as women's work—the care taking of children (particularly young students) fit naturally with women's innate abilities and skills. By 1888, 63% of all teachers were women; by 1953, 93% of elementary teachers were women (Lerner, 1977, pp. 204–205).

With this resulting feminization of the teaching field came a decrease in teacher pay, so that historically all teachers, male and female, have been paid wages below their professional qualifications. The basis for this treatment in the 19th century was the widely held belief that women were naturally inferior to men. Although this belief may no longer be so widely held, we are experiencing the lingering effects of this history.

Feminist critiques of the "castle" of educational leadership have sought to interrogate conventional models of leadership and to point out the gender-specific characteristics embedded in this model. Although the number of women in educational administration training programs is now equal to the number of males (Shakeshaft, 1987), educational administration is still predominantly male, particularly the higher up in position one looks. Studies of women's leadership styles begun in the 1970s suggest that women have different leadership styles than male counterparts. Research on female administrators has found that, overall, women leaders make relationships central; create a school climate that is more conducive to learning; focus efforts on building a strong sense of community; work more collaboratively, emphasizing cooperation; use power to empower others; and in administration, exist marginally themselves (Shakeshaft, 1987).

These findings challenge conventional models of leadership by offering a rethinking of leadership that looks at "community and cooperation"not as weaknesses but as assets in leadership (Blackmore, 1991). This feminist interpretation of leadership is not necessarily hierarchical nor positional. It is not based on the ethics of competition of conventional corporate models but instead is based on transformative leadership as a resistance to social injustice.

Interestingly, analyses of women's leadership traits and feminist discussions of leadership highly correlate with research on "best practice"strategies (also begun in the 1970s) for schools. These strategies are not managerially driven but focus on the moral climate and cultural learning needs of a school. This research has moved discussions of leadership away from one of power, control, and domination to current school reform talk of the leader as visionary, as a facilitator, as an interactive leader. James Kouzes and Barry Posner (1987) incorporate these attributes into five successful practices for school principal: challenging the process, inspiring a shared vision, enabling others to act, modeling the way, encouraging the heart (pp. 8–14).

Consider also Irvine's (1990) characterization of an effective principal as:

> [A skilled communicator], energetic, active, and highly visible to students and teachers ... unthreatened by challenges or situations of high ambiguity and uncertainty....When well-conceived plans falter or unforeseen variables emerge, these principals enthusiastically rally their staff for renewed planning. They are attentive to the need to maintain and develop a strong school morale and healthy climate and often rely on their visionary leadership, optimism, and missionary zeal in unstable and uncertain circumstances. (p. 104)

These are attributes that are usually associated with women. Although this new participatory leadership uses terminology that is normally used to define female attributes—sensitivity to context; caring; hands on; less competitive, less driven—it has been mainly limited to "lower"levels of school leadership (i.e., the elementary school principalship) and in multiple ways reifies the gender inequities of a conventional model of leadership. Best practice research and strategies in leadership have borrowed from the critical insights of feminist analyses of power and packaged it into another more acceptable language—a softer language of feminist leadership. This allows the transformative and challenging structural critique of feminism to be ignored. One result is what Blackmore (1991) cites as a curious mix of "masculinist culture"with a corporate culture that "theoretically incorporates the 'feminine' skills"of leadership. In this way, masculinist corporatist practices continued to be maintained, reinforced, and replicated. Female administrators continue to state that it is men's opinions and practices that "still seem to count more"(p. 30).

Catherine Marshall and Edith Rusch (1996) describe the field of educational administration as "steeped in false consciousness"(p. 1) related to gender equity. They situate educational administration as an "untroubled profession"which sustains "a culture that effectively filters out conversations about equity, diversity, and gender issues both in university classrooms and in public schools"(p. 1). Thus, if a female administrator takes up a "woman's issue"she is seen as having interests that are too political, too particular. Women in leadership positions are caught in the dilemma of being too radical for some, too complicit with traditional ways for others. In this way, women are situated as " 'deficient' if they fail to fit the male model of leadership, and 'deviant' if they do"(Blackmore, 1991, p. 21).

Women leaders also continue to be held up to a higher level of scrutiny and different standards than their male counterparts. The emphasis on school administration as a caring profession means that as women they are being scrutinized on not only if they are a good administrator but if they are a good woman (as these traits are "natural"to women). The advent of participatory, "softer" forms of school leadership have become so equated with women as skills that are "natural"to women that they are then judged more harshly when they enact more traditional masculinist practices of leadership. Female administrators who demonstrate authority and power are often described as pushy, "bitchy," or oppositional, yet when they do not display authority, women administrators are often evaluated as weak or ineffective (Shakeshaft, 1987).

We may view the increased emphasis on dialogue, cooperation, and consultation in school leadership as positive, but it has also simultaneously incorporated but decentered gender issues. The incorporation of feminist research and "feminine"attributes into best practice strategies for school leadership without critical attention to the social inequities being replicated in this process has allowed the field of educational leadership to state that it is gender neutral and value free while reifying inequitable gender hierarchy. Similar to the feminization of teaching, we are now experiencing a feminization of the educational leadership profession, with the school principalship, particularly elementary school principals, being seen as a female role while higher levels of leadership (secondary schools, central office administration, superintendency) are thought of as male.

Carmen Luke (1997) suggests that "as good girl feminists we have replicated, perhaps unwittingly, all the classical 'school marm' virtues of selfless dedication to, nurturing and caring for our students" (p. 191). In other words, through a feminist attention to an ethics of collaboration, cooperation, and celebration of the skills women leaders possess, feminists have ignored, or not gotten their hands messy enough with, issues of power and authority in leadership. Helene Moglen (1983) comments that "the problem is neither how, as women, we disassociate ourselves from power nor how we can find ways to grasp it. Instead, we must determine the way in which power can be itself purged of its own crippling effects, destructive both of those who dominate and those who are subordinate"(p. 132).

Most recently, feminist interpretations of leadership acknowledge that attempts to deny power and authority of leadership masks inequitable practices. Other feminists have pointed out that attention to the need for caring in leadership without taking on critical structural change ignores existing power relations and conflicting interests in school organizations. In order to achieve the transformative change called for by feminist interpretations of leadership, we have to, as Carmen Luke (1997) suggests, make our power visible and political. This calls for an ethics of leadership that would be continuously grounded in a resistance to social injustice but that also interrogates the "assumptions and consequences of our critical practices"> (p. 207). Who is marginalized or silenced? Whose concerns are trivialized under the dominant system? How are my own transformative actions reifying inequitable power relations? A commitment to on-going reflective critique is necessary for transformational, collaborative leadership to exist in a system that values competitive individualism.

Viewing the historical entrenchment of school leadership with business needs, the development of a patriarchal bureaucracy, and the encapsulating of feminist critiques into current reform efforts that continue to promote inequitable structures, we can better understand how it is we have come to define and practice leadership in public schools. This knowledge yields the power to make changes in the way we think about and practice leadership. Feminist critiques and interpretations of power, authority, and leadership offer means to rethink leadership and to work toward democratic, transformative practices that promote social justice.

Yvonna Lincoln (1991) suggests that there are occurrences of transformative leadership occurring but that we are not hearing about them. Lincoln states a need for case studies, stories, and narratives of transformational leaders and struggles for empowerment. Lincoln further calls for the need and responsibility of transformational leadership to understand "the conflict and contradiction between its form of relations with the world, and the relations imposed by the dominant training mode utilized for both educational administration and higher education administration" (p. 177). In this way, perhaps, we can reorient how we think about, practice, and perform leadership.

REFERENCES

Blackmore, J. (1991). Changing from within: Feminist educators and administrative leadership. *Peabody Journal of Education*, 66 (3), 19–40.

Foster, W. (1991). Educational leadership and the struggle for mind. *Peabody Journal of Education*, 66(3), 124–137.

Irvine, J. J. (1988). Urban schools that work: A summary of relevant factors. *Journal of Negro Education*, 57(1), 236–242.

Irvine, J. J. (1990). *Black students and school failure: Policies, practices, and prescriptions*. New York: Greenwood.

Jones, D. (1997). The principal and African-American students in desegregated public schools. Unpublished doctoral dissertation. University of North Carolina at Greensboro.

Kempner, K. (1991). Getting into the castle of Educational Administration. *Peabody Journal of Education*, 66(3), 104–123.

Kouzes, J. M., & Posner, B. Z. (1987). *The leadership challenge: How to get extraordinary things done in organizations*. San Francisco: Jossey-Bass.

Lerner, G. (1977). *The female experience/An American documentary*. New York: Oxford University Press.

Lincoln, Y. (1991). Critical requisites for transformation leadership: Needed research and discourse. *Peabody Journal of Education*, 66(3), 176–181.

Lomotey, K. (1994). African-American principals: Bureaucrat/administrators and ethno-humanists. In M. J. Shujaa (Ed.), *Too much school, too little education: A paradox of Black life in White societies* (pp. 203–219). Trenton, NJ: Africa World Press.

Luke, C. (1997). Feminist pedagogy and the politics of authority, power, and desire. In C. Marshall (Ed.), *Feminist critical policy analysis II: A higher education schooling perspective* (pp. 189–210). London: Falmer Press.

Marshall, C., & Rusch, E. (1996). Troubled educational administration. Paper presented at the Annual Conference of the American Educational Research Association, New York.

Moglen, H. (1983). Power and empowerment. *Women's Studies International Forum*, 6(2), 131–134.

Shakeshaft, C. (1987). Theory in a changing reality. *Journal of Educational Equity and Leadership*, 7(1), 4–20.

Spring, J. (1994). *The American school 1642–1993* (3rd ed.). New York: McGraw-Hill.

Turnage, M. (1972). The principal: Change agent in desegregation. *Integrated Education: A Report on Race and Schools*, 10(2), 41–45.

6

Accountability

David A. Gabbard
East Carolina University

The notion of "accountability" resonates with the sound of authority and, therefore, the sound of power. It implies a state of being in which persons are obliged to answer to others. Accountability, then, also implies hierarchical institutional structures and a certain economy of power requisite to the maintenance and vitality of those structures. Individuals do not become accountable on their own. Accountability signifies a status that is only achieved through the delegation of authority. It assumes the existence of some person or group of persons who possess the authority to declare that something shall be done, but whose power to carry out that task is limited by their inability to be everywhere and do everything at the same time. Consequently, they must delegate their authority to others. Those who receive this authority, however, do not receive it in full. Delegation always implies a diminishment of authority. The aims of power have been previously determined. Those to whom authority has been delegated have no authority to determine what those aims should be. Power flows through them, not from them. Whoever is held accountable is an agent of power, a mere delegate of the authority who decides power's intended aims. At most, the authority of accountable persons is limited to establishing the means by which the ends of power shall be achieved. At the very least, their authority is limited to ensuring that previously established means are followed in pursuit of the desired ends. In either case, these delegates are accountable *to* some higher authority; they must answer to that authority. And they must answer *for* something.

For what must they answer? The obligation to "answer" – to speak—entails rendering an "account." Individuals must produce evidence testifying to the quality of their performance in exercising the authority delegated to them by or through those to whom they must answer. Are they exercising that authority in the expected manner? Are they satisfactorily pursuing the aims of power? Are their actions producing the intended results?

This obligation to answer to authority—to speak the truth regarding the performance of one's assigned responsibilities—stems from that authority's need to know. Authority needs to know if its will is being followed, if those responsible for pursuing its aims are performing their duties in a satisfactory fashion, and if those aims are being achieved. Moreover, authority needs to know its own strength. It needs to know how effective it has been in designing and implementing its strategies and tactics of power and how successful those strategies and tactics have proven in helping to strengthen the system of political economy that establishes and sustains authority.

Coupled with authority's demand to know, the delegate's obligation to "tell" precipitates an act of normalizing judgment that aids authority in controlling the behavior of its delegates. Under any system of accountability, delegates are granted the authority to do certain things but not others. This means that there are certain parameters or norms that must guide their behaviors. These norms, of course, are specific to the individual delegate's function as an agent of power.

At the moment that the delegate must render an account of his or her activities, the authority to whom he or she must answer will judge his or her performance in accordance with these norms and whether or not the delegate's behavior has produced the proscribed results. The delegate, of course, knows ahead of time that this judgement is pending. If only to maintain the privileges of his or her status as an ambassador of authority, the delegate wants to be judged as effective in fulfilling his or her function. Consequently, accountability systems expand not only the capacity of authority to intensify and diversity its strategies and tactics of power but also its ability to keep watch over those responsible for their deployment.

Authority is no more physically able to keep watch over everything than it is physically able to do everything. As authority increases the diversity of its strategies and tactics, as it undertakes to do more things, it requires greater cooperation from a greater diversity of functionaries and delegates—including their cooperation in watching over (governing) their own behavior. In assuming the responsibilities of delegated authorities, individuals know what is expected of them in terms of their behavior, attitudes, and values. They also know what is expected from them in terms of the intended outcomes of their actions. If delegates wish to maintain or increase the authority granted to them under the terms of accountability, they must learn to judge and direct themselves in accordance with the same norms that will be used to judge them at the moment when they must answer for their actions and the results they produce. Moreover, the formation of accountability systems aids authority in overcoming the physical limitations on its ability to watch over (govern) its delegates. For these systems establish conditions under which those delegates will govern themselves by keeping themselves under constant surveillance.

ACCOUNTABILITY AND THE REASON OF STATE

Again, accountability systems presuppose a delegation of authority that, in turn, allows for a greater dispersion of authority's power. Authority, of course, does not disperse its power arbitrarily. To the contrary, as we witness with the formation and evolution of the modern administrative state, authority disperses its power in accordance with a mode of rationality which dictates that any such dispersal must ultimately result in a subsequent strengthening of that power. Accountability systems necessarily function in accordance with this logic. They expand the scope of authority's power by enabling it to assume a greater variety of tasks that bring a greater number of things under authority's influence. And this influence, if authority's delegates are truly "accountable," must amount to an overall increase in authority's power.

Michel Foucault cites an extensive body of literature from the 16th, 17th, and 18th centuries that refers to this mode of rationality as the *reason of state*. One author from this period, Botero, defines the reason of state as "a perfect knowledge of the means through which states form, strengthen themselves, endure, and grow" (as cited in Foucault, 1988, p. 74). The reason of state, then, is linked to an "art of government" which, as Foucault (1991) explains,

> is essentially concerned with answering the question of how to introduce economy—that is to say, the correct manner of managing individuals, goods, and wealth within the family (which a good father is expected to do in relation to his wife, children, and servants) and of making the family fortunes prosper—how to introduce the meticulous attention of the father toward his family into the management of the state. (p. 92)

The emergence of the reason of state and the art of government signaled the *economization* of politics. Economization, however, meant much more than simply situating the wealth of the state as the primary aim of government. Previously, politics had followed the imperatives of sovereignty. The prince and his relationship to his territory and its inhabitants occupied the center of the political universe. Government operated through the imposition and enforcement of laws designed to preserve the order in which the prince maintained his position of sovereignty. This position granted the prince the authority to appropriate wealth from his subjects through a system of taxes and levies. The availability of wealth, of course, became increasingly important to the state as competition between rival nations intensified. And it was precisely in the context of this competition that many political theorists began to recognize that the survival of the state depended on much more than the preservation of the prince's sovereign relationship with his principality. Although his authority enabled the state to appropriate wealth from the inhabitants of his territory, the state could only draw upon whatever wealth was already present at the time. For these theorists, the state's survival hinged on its ability to intervene in the lives of individuals and play a more active role in what is now called "development"—the mobilization of the natural and human resources that a state has at its disposal in order to increase its material wealth and, hence, its strength as an economic and military competitor.

In order to mobilize these forces, the state needed to expand the scope of its power and concern itself with many more relationships other than the prince's to his principality. As Guillaume de La Peirre, another author from this period, wrote in his *Miroir Politique* (1567), "government is the right disposition of things, arranged so as to lead to a convenient end" (as cited in Foucault, 1991, p. 93). By "things," Foucault points out, La Peirre does not mean things as opposed to men, "but rather a sort of complex of men and things. The things with which in this sense government is to be concerned are in fact men, but men in their relations, their links, their imbrication with those other things" (p. 93). And those "other things" fall into three classes:

1. wealth, resources, means of subsistence, the territory with its specific qualities, climate, irrigation, fertility, etc.;
2. customs, habits, ways, of acting and thinking, etc.; and
3. accidents and misfortunes such as famine, epidemics, death. (Foucault, 1991, p. 93)

With all these relations between men and things with which government now had to concern itself, we can begin to appreciate the state's need to create the means by which it could disperse its power in a multitude of directions. Hence, we can begin to appreciate the significance of those systems of accountability that contribute to this greater economization of power. In accordance with the reason of state, the delegation of authority and the dispersal of power effected under any system of accountability signifies an investment of power on the part of the state. As a return on its investment, the state expects that this dispersal will lead to an increase in either its wealth or its capacity to procure more wealth—its strength. The state would not delegate its authority, it would not disperse its power, if accountability did not pay such dividends.

THE SCIENCE OF POLICE: LEGITIMATING THE ART OF GOVERNMENT

Under La Peirre's definition, government must promote the proper disposition of things so as to lead to "an end which is 'convenient' for each of the things that are to be governed" (Foucault, 1991, p. 95). The plurality of relationships between men and things dictated that the state disperse its power through the deployment of numerous tactics of intervention, and each of these tactics pursued its own specific set of aims. There was, however, a broader aim being pursued through each of these various strategies. Namely, power needed to be deployed in such a manner so as to "dispose" the population toward recognizing a continuity between their individual interests and those of the state:

> Interest at the level of the consciousness of each individual who goes to make up the population, and interest as the interest of the population regardless of what the particular interests and aspirations may be of the individuals who compose it, this is the new target and the fundamental instrument of the government of population. (Foucault, 1991, p. 100)

Manufacturing the "public interest"—"regardless of what the particular interests and aspirations may be of the individuals who compose it" (Foucault, 1991, p. 100)—required that the principles guiding the good government of the state be transmitted to individuals as the norms by which they conduct their lives. Hence, the economic imperatives of the state were passed on to "govern" individuals' interests and behaviors.

Those dispersions of power, those tactics and interventions designed to "help" individuals to develop and pursue the "public interest" and to equate that interest with their own interests proceeded in the name of the police.

As it relates to the reason of state and the art of government, the notion of "police" carries a meaning that radically differs from the one that we have learned to ascribe to it. Although we associate the police with the means to enforce the law and impose order, the original meaning signified the means through which the state intervened in individuals' lives so as to pursue the "public interest." Therefore, we find little reason to be surprised that this *science of police*, which " 'has as its general object the public interest' " (Duchesne, 1757, as cited in Pasquino, 1991, p. 109), was also called the *science of happiness*.

As a science of happiness, police made the population the target of political intervention. As one theorist of this new science put it, "The police sees to everything regulating society (social relations) carried on between men.... The sole purpose of police is to lead man to the utmost happiness to be enjoyed in this life" (Delamare, as cited in Foucault, 1988, pp. 80–81). Through the invention of the police, the state assumed a pastoral role in society that had previously been the exclusive function of the Church. While the Church concerned itself with leading individuals to salvation in the afterlife, the state used the police as a mechanism to lead them toward a condition of secular salvation. The state, of course, defined this condition in accordance with own economic imperatives; achieving secular salvation meant entering into a state of economic prosperity. And the state defined its relationship to the population under these terms. The role of the state is to help individuals prosper, while the proper role of individuals is to help the state prosper. In order for the state to full its role in "helping" individuals to prosper so as to increase its own level of prosperity and its own power to "help" them more effectively, it needed to follow the example of the Church and create its own cadre of pastoral workers.

TEACHERS AS POLICE

As early as 1611, theoreticians of police recognized that education is crucial to individuals' pursuit of happiness and the "public interest." In presenting his AristoDemocratic Monarchy (1611) to the Dutch States General, Turquet de Mayenne recommended that each province within the state establish a board that would "see to the positive, active, productive aspects of life. In other words, it was concerned with education; determining each one's tastes and aptitudes; the choosing of occupations—useful ones: each person over the age of 25 had to be enrolled on a register noting his occupation. Those not usefully employed were regarded as the dregs of society" (Foucault, 1988, p. 78).

In this obscure text from the early 17th century, we can recognize many of the same themes that we hear in contemporary educational reform discourse. The appearance of this text, and many others like it, helps to link education to the various police functions of the state and, consequently, to the reason of state and the art of government. Establishing these linkages helps us better understand how the various contemporary accountability measures effected under so many states' educational reform initiatives define the role of teachers and public school in accordance with the reason of state. And it is against this background that we can best determine the answers to two very important questions:

To Whom Are Teachers Accountable?

We could argue that teachers are accountable to the public. However, because schooling is a police function, the public is the target of its tactics. Certainly, public schools are charged with the task of pursuing the public interest, but remember that the "public interest," as we have seen, is itself a product of state intervention. As Foucault (1991) reminds us, "The population [public] now represents the end of government more than the power of the sovereign; the population [public] is the subject of needs, of aspirations, but it is also the object in the hands of the government, aware, vis-à-vis the government of what it wants, but ignorant of what is being done to it" (p. 100).

To be more accurate in our understanding of teacher accountability, we should consider the source of individuals' authority to teach. On this point, Bruce Beezer's (1991) explanation of why teachers do not enjoy the rights of academic freedom is especially illuminative. "The teacher," he quite correctly observes, "is legally an agent of the state and, therefore, the state has a legitimate interest in how the teacher exercises that authority" (p. 118). Since teachers derive their authority to teach from the state, we can reasonably conclude that they are accountable to the state.

For What Are Teachers Held Accountable?

If teachers are delegates of the state's authority, then the state must hold them accountable for performing their duties in accordance with the theory of police as it stems from the reason of state. The reason of state demands that teachers act in such a way so as to increase the wealth and the strength of the state. Through their actions, the state deploys those tactics aimed at properly disposing individuals to become what we have come to call "productive citizens." That is, the state holds schools and school teachers accountable for making individuals useful to the state.

CONCLUSION: POLICING TEACHERS

All this paints a very deterministic picture of the power relations between public school teachers and the state. As Foucault (1988) reminds us, however, power is never entirely deterministic. It is not the same as instrumental violence. Nevertheless, "the characteristic feature of power is that some men (sic) can more or less entirely determine other men's (sic) conduct—but never exhaustively or coercively....There is no power without potential refusal or revolt" (pp. 83–84).

In fact, we can best understand the the various "accountability measures" that are so central to recent state-mandated educational reforms as a "governmental" response to educational dimensions of the "crisis of democracy" that erupted in the 1960s and 1970s. This period signaled an important revitalization of educational debates dating back to the 1920s and before. As more people gained knowledge of how schools function to pursue the aims of power and the ends of government, the debate over the proper role of education in a democratic society increased in its intensity. The answers that they developed, however, contradicted the reason of state. Public schools, many people contended, should not function to strengthen the state; they should strengthen the powers of individuals to defend themselves from the state, to define and pursue their own interests (see Freire, 1970; Kozol, 1975/1990).

Recent accountability measures represent an effort to offset such "counterproductive" modes of rationality by tying teachers' salaries and continued employment to their compliance with the police functions that the state authorizes them to perform. In North Carolina, the extent to which teachers are judged accountable is determined not by a direct examination of *their* activities. Rather, teachers are judged in accordance with their students' performance on end-of-grade and competency tests. The scores that students receive on these exams provide the state with evidence as to whether or not teachers are properly exercising the authority that is delegated to them. Student testing becomes a police instrument, designed to properly dispose teachers to perform their duties and teach only those materials that the state deems essential to the formation of productive citizens.

The message of accountability is clear: Teachers' work must help the state achieve the ends of government (increased wealth and increased strength), or they must look for other work.[1] Or, again, they can refuse and resist!

REFERENCES

Beezer, B. G. (1991). *North Carolina teachers' professional competencies handbook.* Durham, NC: Carolina Academic Press.

Foucault, M. (1991). "Governmentality" In G. Burchell, C. Gordon, & P. Miller (Eds.), *The Foucault effect: Studies in governmentality* (pp. 87–104). Chicago: University of Chicago Press.

Foucault, M. (1988). "Politics and reason." In L. D. Kritzman (Ed.), *Michel Foucault: Politics, philosophy, culture* (pp. 57–84). New York: Routledge, Chapman & Hall.

Freire, P. (1970). *Pedagogy of the oppressed.* New York: Continuum.

Kozol, J. (1990). *The night is dark and I am far from home* (2nd ed.). New York: Touchstone Books. (Originally published 1975)

Pasquino, P. (1991). "Theatrum politicum: The genealogy of capital–police and the state of prosperity." In G. Burchell, C. Gordon, & P. Miller (Eds.), *The Foucault effect: Studies in governmentality* (pp. 105–118). Chicago: University of Chicago Press.

[1]Already, over 50% of those individuals who enter the teaching profession in North Carolina leave that profession by the end their 5th year. As accountability strips North Carolina teachers of what little professional autonomy they may have ever enjoyed, we should only expect these numbers to increase in the coming years.

7

Discipline

Felecia M. Briscoe
Concord College

It serves us well to remember that the public school has always been viewed as a mechanism for reforming the behavior of children and adolescents. It was the "sinful" behavior of colonial youth that prompted the first Massachusetts school law in 1642, and problems of "juvenile delinquency" triggered the urban school movement in the early 18th century. Discipline, then, is hardly a new concern in education. In tracing the genealogy of modern technologies of discipline, Michel Foucault (1977) describes a shift in the aims and strategies of power. Under the feudal system, the primary aim of sovereignty was chiefly concerned with protecting its power from domestic as well as foreign enemies. To protect his position, the sovereign could rely on force (punishment) or the threat of punishment to repress any behaviors that might endanger his authority. With the rise of the modern nation state, however, the aims of power shifted. It no longer sufficed to merely protect the sovereign authority of the state. The state now required the means to constantly expand and improve on its productive capacities in order to maximize its wealth and, thereby, its strength. As Foucault (1981) explains these new strategies of power exercised themselves

> through social production and social service. It becomes a matter of obtaining productive service from individuals in their concrete lives. And in consequence, a real and effective 'incorporation' of power was necessary, in the sense that power had to be able to gain access to the bodies of individuals, to their acts, atStitudes, and modes of everyday behavior. Hence the significance of methods like school discipline, which succeeded in making children's bodies the object of highly complex systems of manipulation and conditioning. (p. 125)

Recent discussions of school discipline in the United States have centered around two recurrent themes: increasing the domain of coherent intermeshing disciplinary regimes and increasing the international economic competitiveness of U.S. business. A high pitched anxiety about the nation's ability to compete in an international economic market, coupled with a reluctance to spend more money in schools, provides the rationale for attempting to create ever more efficient disciplinary technologies. As a means of increasing the effectiveness of school discipline programs, research and policies are recommending an expanded realm of seamless disciplinary processes.

INTENSIFYING DISCIPLINE

Contemporary educational discourse includes many proposed increases in both the breadth and the depth of disciplinary mechanisms. The demand for increased breadth is based on the claim that in order for students to be properly disciplined, their teachers and parents must also be properly trained and incorporated into the program. Proper parental and teacher training is necessary to ensure that the disciplinary techniques experienced by the student are consistent in the home and in each classroom throughout the school. Instead of just targeting the behavior of students for disciplinary purposes, programs now advocate a more systemic approach to discipline:

> It is our belief that successful school discipline is achieved through framing discipline as an organizational issue. Understanding teacher and student behavior as part of a larger organizational context provides better opportunity to identify causes of poor student discipline and to structure more effective means for dealing with the causes. (Short, Short, & Blanton, 1994, p. 9)

Ronald D. Stephens (1995), Director of the National School Safety Center agrees, "The best safe school plans integrally involve the entire community," (p. 32). Moles (1990), although listing the different types of strategies to be used in a disciplinary regime, emphasizes the importance of "nonstudent strategies concerned with school and classroom conditions thought to affect student conduct, such as improving teacher effectiveness" (p. 6). Robert Mahaffey (1995) director of the publications of National Association of Secondary School Principals writes, "We must remember, however, that the success of safe school strategies will depend on the commitment and cooperation of all members of the community. A safe school plan cannot be effectively implemented without extensive community involvement" (p. 7). Other policymakers strongly encourage gaining the cooperation of parents: "This guide offers suggestions on how to involve students, parents, law enforcement officials" (Stephens, 1995, p. 10); "Next to students, parents are the most important resource in promoting safe schools"(p. 51); and, America must ask the "question, 'How ready are parents to parent?'" (Kagan, 1990, p. 277). However, the involvement of parents, students, and teachers in school disciplinary programs need not and perhaps should not be democratic, as one writer explicitly questions, "Upon reflection, we find a question about how democratic our public schools can be" (Short et al., p. 93). Although new school disciplinary programs are calling for a broader, more seamless disciplinary regime involving teachers, parents, and the community, they are also seeking to more deeply infiltrate the student body. ·

School disciplinary programs of the 1990s seek a place in the heart of the student—similar to 19th-century Edward Ross's desire to place a policeman in the heart of every student. There are two aspects to the policing of the student's heart. The first aspect is to have a kinder, gentler form of discipline because it is more efficient. For example, one researcher asserts, "Teacher preparation programs now provide instruction for managing classrooms and for disciplining students in a much more systematic and psychologically oriented way" (Ryan, 1994, p. 76). Another wrote, "These program developers recognize the power of involving participants in the process of organizational change [for better discipline] to gain their commitment" and "raise the central question of whether punishment should be the central means of solving discipline problems. Punishment increases resentment, and does not emphasize desired behavior" (Moles, 1990, p. 7). Corporal punishment finds little favor in recent disciplinary discourse because of its relative inefficiency. Simmons (1991) summarizes the arguments for instituting a kinder, gentler method of discipline:

> Banning the hickory stick does not mean abandonment of school discipline. Without discipline there is chaos. Without orderliness, learning cannot occur. Spanking, however, confuses children about expectations and their own sense of personal well-being. Anyone who has ever had a public spanking can attest to feeling embarrassment, humiliation and personal violation. This dehumanizing treatment is not discipline....Such a [disciplinary] plan places responsibility where it should be—within the children. (p. 70)

The other latest technique for policing the heart of students is to build their self-esteem. On the surface, raising the self-esteem of students does not seem to be a method of discipline. In fact, it might even be counter to coercion as students may develop the self-esteem to question authorities rather than simply being obedient. However, school disciplinary programs are not seeking just any type of student self-esteem. These programs wish to engender student self-esteem that is based upon disciplinary criteria set by the school. Stephens emphasizes that schools should "create a climate of ownership and school pride [in students] ... every student and staff member should feel like a key part of the school community" (Stephens, 1995, p. 37). The desire to engender a specific type of self-esteem is clearly seen in the plethora of scholarly hand wringing about the high self-esteem of African American students that does not seem contingent on standards set by the schools (Covington, 1992; Steele, 1992). Recent disciplinary programs urge making student self-esteem dependent on school disciplinary standards.

School disciplinary programs recommend a more pervasive and invasive approach. Both a schoolwide commitment of teachers and a community-wide commitment of parents to a disciplinary program is advocated. These disciplinary programs seek to penetrate more deeply into students—seeking to be kinder and gentler because that is more likely to shape the student within and seeking to instill a sense of self-esteem that is dependent upon school standards. However, this increased pervasiveness and invasiveness must not cost more. As Denis Doyle (1991) writes, "The challenge is to do the job better with the same resources"(p. 190).

Many parents, teachers, and other citizens would not be adverse to better discipline in schools. However, they might balk at the notion that they too need to be properly "trained." But more important, they might question the ends of the improved disciplinary program. To what ends are these increasingly pervasive and invasive disciplinary techniques aimed? To answer this question, the rationale and the goals of the recent school disciplinary discourse should be examined.

U.S. ECONOMIC COMPETITIVENESS THROUGH BETTER SCHOOL DISCIPLINE

Historically one of the purposes of schools has been to socialize students as future workers. William Reese (1986) discusses the rationale for instituting bells and tardies in schools as a means of shaping the behavior and work habits of students appropriately as human capital for future factory work. Treating and understanding students as human capital has been a controversial issue since its inception. However, it is still an understanding used by many, if not most, who discuss education. During the 1990s, anxiety about the U.S. position in international trade has incited a sharper focus on students as human capital. A recent influential promoter is President Bill Clinton. President Clinton endorses the concept of students as human capital both in his speeches on the role of education in America and by signing his name to the amended Goals 2000 in 1994. According to Joel Spring (1996), "the overall goal of the Goals 2000 Educate America Act is improving the ability of the U.S. economy to compete in international trade by educating better workers " (p. 21). The standards endorsed by Goals 2000 were originally developed by the National Governors' Association in 1989. Signed by President George Bush in 1991, the sixth goal focused on discipline: "Every school will be free of drugs and violence and will offer a disciplined environment conducive to learning" (Bush, 1990). It is this goal that has provoked recent research and discussion about school discipline. Several authors who examine Goals 2000 have cited economic imperatives. Larry Cuban (1990), in describing the reasons for the development of Goals 2000, writes:

> Our onetime enemies, Japan and Germany, have now outstripped the U.S. on economic indicators and simple measures of wealth.... To corporate leaders and public officials who see public schools as engines of national economic progress, shortages of college graduates in science and engineering are a consequence of how poorly public schools teach ... [I]t becomes apparent that the schools are producing graduates armed with insufficient knowledge, inadequate basic skills, and poor work habits [emphasis added].... With schools being viewed as a first line of economic defense in the battle to remain internationally competitive, national and state leaders have become increasingly impatient with such shortcomings in school performances. (p. 269)

Denis Doyle (1991), in examining the merits of Goals 2000 writes,

> Modern economists have developed an arcane, but perfectly plausible explanation of most of the productivity gains of the past 50 years: an increase in human capital. What is human capital? It is what people know and are able to do. Human capital is knowledge, ability, skills, insights, dreams. It is the intellectual—and, yes, moral vision that transforms dumb matter into goods and services (p. 191).

Hence, one of the fundamental ends of the new efficient, pervasive, and invasive school disciplinary regimes is to form students whose knowledge, ability, skills, insights, dreams, and moral vision are shaped toward economic ends. These programs are designed to create students whose desires, habits, and abilities will make them better workers. How are "better workers" defined?—they are those who increase the international profits of U.S. business. Some might argue that more worthwhile desires and abilities to instill in our future citizens are the desire and ability to negotiate world peace (the United States is still a leader in the manufacture and sale of weapons), the desire and ability to raise the standard of living for all people, and the desire and ability to live with dignity in a free world.

REFERENCES

Bush, G. H. W., III, (1990). *State of the union address.*

Covington, M. V. (1992). *Making the grade: A self-worth perspective on motivation and school reform.* New York: Cambridge University Press.

Cuban, L. (1990, December). Four stories about national goals for American education. *Phi Delta Kappan, 72*, 265–271.

David, K. (1993). Pastoral care in the schools. In T. Charlton & K. David (Eds.), *Managing misbehavior in schools.* New York: Routledge, Chapman & Hall.

Doyle, D. P. (1991, November). America 2000. *Phi Delta Kappan, 73*, 184–191.

Foucault, M. (1977). *Discipline and punish: The birth of the prison.* A. Sheridan (Trans.). New York: Vintage.

Foucault, M. (1981). Truth and power. In C. Gordon (Ed.). *Power/knowledge: Selected interviews and other writings (1972–1977).* New York: Pantheon.

Hill. M. S., & Hill, F. W. (1994). *Creating safe schools: What principals can do.* Thousand Oaks, CA: A joint publication of The National Association of Secondary School Principals and Corwin Press.

Kagan, S. L. (1990, December). Readiness 2000: Rethinking rhetoric and responsibility. *Phi Delta Kappan, 72*, 272–279.

Mahaffey, R. (1995). Foreword. In R. D. Stephens (Ed.), *Safe schools: A handbook for violence prevention.* Bloomington, IN: National Education Service.

Moles, O. C. (1990). *Student discipline strategies.* Albany: State University New York Press.

Reese, W. J. (1986). *Power and the promise of school reform: Grass-roots movements during the progressive era.* Boston: Routledge & Kegan Paul.

Ryan, F. J. (1994, Winter). From rod to reason: Historical perspectives on corporal punishment in the public school, 1642–1994," *Educational Horizons, 72*, 70–77.

Short, P., Short, R. J., & Blanton, C. (Eds.). (1994). *Rethinking student discipline: Alternatives that work.* Thousand Oaks, CA: A joint publication of The National Association of Secondary School Principals and Corwin Press.

Simmons, B. J. (1991, Winter). Issues in Education: Ban the hickory stick. *Childhood Education, 62*,(2) 69–70.

Spring, J. (1996). *American education: An introduction to social and political aspects.* New York: McGraw-Hill.

Steele, C. M. (1992, April). Race and the schooling of black children. *Atlantic Monthly,* 269(4).

Stephens, R. D. (1995). *Safe schools: A handbook for violence prevention.* Bloomington, IN: National Education Service.

8

Classroom Management

William E. Doll, Jr.
Louisiana State University

Classroom management, indeed management in general, is usually not associated with disturbance. Disturbance is to be avoided, not advocated. Management has to do with control—centralized control—and disturbance dissipates that control; hence to be avoided. "Do not lose control of the classroom" is the number one fiat given beginning classroom teachers. The loss of control is the novice teacher's greatest fear. But what does this loss of control mean? What does *control* mean?

The dictionary I have at hand (*American Heritage*, 1969, pp. 290–291) says for control: (1) to exercise authority dominating influence over; direct; regulate. (2) to hold in restraint; to check. John Dewey devoted a whole chapter to control in his *Democracy and Education* (1916/1966). Presaging my dictionary definition, he says, "Control subordinates a person's natural impulses to another's end," and the term as thus used has "a flavor of coercion or compulsion about it" (p. 24). Indeed, if control—what I have elsewhere called "the ghost in the curriculum" (Doll, 1998, p. 295)—is exercising a dominating influence over, is holding in restraint, is subordinating a person's natural impulses, and has a flavor of coercion about it, then how can learning that is good, deep, meaningful take place in such an atmosphere? Wrestling with this question may well provide us with reason to rethink the whole notion of classroom management as centralized control. It may not be oxymoronic to think of a term like "dissipated control." Maybe a case can be made for a sense of control that is noncentralized; a sense of control based on "*just the right amount* of disturbance."

As I've argued elsewhere (Doll, 1998), the concept of control within the teaching framework is as old as is the use of curriculum as an educational term—back to the Protestant Reformation. However, its contemporary American roots are usually traced to the "scientific management" movement (Callahan, 1962; Doll, 1993; Kliebard, 1975; Rice 1914/1969; Taylor, 1911/1947), begun when Frederick Taylor (1911/1947) did his first time-and-motion studies at Bethlehem Steel in the 1890s. In this study, the concept of control is quite evident in the four principles that Taylor believed management and workers were to attend to: (1) a science for each element of a man's work to replace the old rule-of-thumb method, (2) a scientific selection and training of the men to do the work, lest these men be left to their own methods, (3) attention given to ensuring that all the work be done in accord with the scientific principles developed, and (4) an equal division of responsibility drawn between management and workers (pp. 36–39). This latter point Taylor considered the most important, one "requiring further explanation." Management is to plan out fully, "in writing and in detail," one day in advance, the work each man is to do. These orders are to specify "what is to be done, how it is to be done, and the exact time allowed for doing it" (p. 39). Workers are to follow, in exact detail, the orders given. Here then is Taylor's "equal division of responsibility"—one group is responsible for planning, the other group for following. That this dichotomous, planning-following model has strongly influenced American curriculum and instruction is an assertion that needs hardly be made. Nonetheless, the wording from a contemporary textbook, *Classroom Management Strategies: Gaining and Maintaining Student's Cooperation* (Cangelosi, 1993), is instructive:

> The *goals you establish for your students to achieve*; *how you plan*, prepare, and conduct [*their*] *learning activities*; *how you evaluate your students' achievements*; *how you organize*, and manage *the classroom setting*; and *the manner in which you communicate* with students and their parents *will* be major *influences* on how much of *your students'* time is spent cooperatively engaged in *learning activities*. Of course *other factors*, many of which *are out of your control*, will also influence how well your students cooperate.... *But dwelling on causes outside of your control* will *not be a productive* means *for you* to begin *increasing students' time on-task*. (p. 12; emphasis added)

The correlation between the 1911 statement and the 1993 statement is obvious. What may not be so obvious is that both statements emphasize a sense of cooperation. Taylor truly believed that his methods were those of shared and cooperative responsibility, the classroom management book uses the word cooperation in its title and does talk of the students being "cooperatively engaged in learning activities." What sort of cooperation, though, emerges when one person has a dominating influence over others? When one holds others in restraint?

Is there another way to deal with (or "manage") a classroom of learners? Indeed, is there another way to conceive of control? John Dewey said yes to both! In his chapter on control, Dewey (1916/1966, ch. 3), as one might expect, attacks the dualism of external and internal control. He finds both impositional, one directly, the other indirectly (as imitation of a pattern already set). Both require outside authority, neither develops a person's natural impulses. So Dewey mentions, but only mentions, a different form of control—one that is "more important," "permanent," "intellectual not personal" (pp. 27, 33). Today with our interest in and development of chaos or complexity theory, such control might well be called dissipative control, emergent control, self-organizing control. Dewey, a presager of such contemporary, postmodern thoughts and words, relied for himself on the concepts of interaction and development. He talks of this "other mode of control," as a "guiding of activity [by activity] to its own end" (p. 24). This guiding resides not unilaterally with the teacher or with the students but instead "resides in the nature of the situations" themselves (p. 39). That is, the control resides in the interactions (teacher–students, students–students, people–texts, history–present, present–future hopes, etc.) existent in the situations as they are. Again, in more contemporary, postmodern terms, the structure of control actually emerges from these interactions—interactions that need "just the right amount" of perturbations (Dewey called them problems) to be active and alive. For Dewey, the beginning of all learning starts with the "natural capacities of the individual," but these capacities need assisting, "assisting through cooperation," if they are to progress beyond mere impulses and undeveloped potentialities (p. 23). This, as well as I can phrase it, represents Dewey's concept of growth, a growth that develops over time through social interaction. Growth is a *reflective* process, subservient to no end beyond itself.

Can this same social–intellectual process model be applied to classroom management? Again, Dewey (1938/1963) said yes! In at least one place he uses the analogy of steering a boat:

> The teacher is a guide and director; he steers the boat, but the energy that propels it must come from those who are learning. The more a teacher is aware of the past experiences of students, of their hopes, desires, chief interests, the better will be understood the forces at work that need to be directed and utilized for the formation of reflective habits. (p. 36)

Two issues stand out here, I believe. One is that Dewey does propose a general goal or direction—that of reflective habits. Indeed, reflective habits are the primary goal Dewey posits for all education, these habits being necessary for our maintaining a democracy. The second issue is that this general goal achieves its specificity, its details, through a time-developmental process of cooperative interaction—the boatsperson steers, but the energy he or she steers comes from the boat itself, from the dynamic interaction of "the forces at work" in the present situation. There is a combinatory dynamic at work here. The teacher steers but does so by tapping into the creative energy existent in the classroom. Metaphorically, no one is merely taken for a ride, nor is anyone along just for the ride; the specific development of each situation—its own growth—is the result of the alive and dynamic interaction of "the forces at work" in the situation. Lest the boat sinks or capsizes, such a process-development, reflective-habit, social-interaction frame requires a very special form of community. Dewey chose to entitle his major educational work *Democracy and Education*.

Stuart Kauffman (1995), a leading complexity theorist, posits that such a "communitarian" frame (my word, not his)—one allowing for and indeed operating from a dynamic blend of stability and flexibility (p. 188)—can produce naturally all sorts of miracles: order, life, social justice. In simple terms, his argument is that under the right conditions order arises naturally from an interaction of forces. This order is neither through random chance nor imposed by a more superior force. It emerges as a consequence of an unpredictable interaction of forces, that which chaos mathematics refers to as deterministic but unpredictable (Crutchfield et al., 1986) and Gregory Bateson (1988) called the "Great Stochastic Process." We "see" this process (or at least the results of the process) in mathematical simulations of complex systems, in the formation of life itself, in the social arrangement we call democracy. The key to this emergence is the unique combination of constraining structural stability (mathematical equations, DNA codes, forms of society) and the liberating forces of flexibility operating within and challenging these structures. It is the dynamic interplay of these forces, not the exclusive dominance of any one, that produces the spontaneous emergence of order, growth, development, learning. For Dewey (1902/1990), the issue was not whether a child or a curriculum is dominant—he uses the phrase "child versus curriculum" to describe this unfortunate social frame—but how the child and the curriculum are interactive. "The child and the curriculum are simply two limits which define a single process" (p. 189).

Stuart Kauffman, as I've said, is the preeminent researcher in this field—variously called complexity theory, nonlinear dynamics, network systems—and draws the greatest attention today. The details of his work can be found in his two books, *The Origins of Order* (1993) and *At Home in the Universe* (1995), or in a short article, "Antichaos and Adaptation" (1991). Secondary sources of his work are in George Johnson's *Fire in the Mind* (1996) and Fritjof Capra's *The Web of Life* (1996). But Kauffman is not alone in this field, as a look at the bibliographies of any of these works shows. Business management theorists lead by Tom Peters (*Thriving on Chaos*, 1987; *Liberation Management*, 1992) have also picked up the concepts. David Parker and Ralph Stacey have a book on *Chaos, Management and Economics* (1994) as does Tony Watson, *In Search of Management: Culture, Chaos and Control in Managerial Work* (1994). In the field of educational administration, Spencer Maxcy (1995) has a book entitled: *Democracy, Chaos and the New School Order.* In short, the concept of a new sense of control, that which I am calling *dissipative*, is current. Is this new and "more permanent" sense of control worth considering for classroom management, which up to now has been extremely centralized in its conceptualization and application?

Whether one calls it *systems, networks*, or *communities*, the frame Kauffman and others are studying is that of a group, self-developing or self-organizing. The key to such organization —dissipative organization, if I may use such a phrase—is to set up (mathematically, socially) or find (biologically, ecologically, cosmologically) frames demonstrating "just the right amount of disturbance." As Piaget knew so well, in an equilibrium–disequilibrium–reequilibration frame, it is *just the right amount* of disequilibrium that "drives" the developmental process (Doll, 1983, 1993). Dewey knew this, too, with his continual insistence that school curricula be built around "problems," themselves the outgrowth of the "hopes, desires, and interests" of students. The development of experience into more experience, of unrefined experience into sophisticated, mature experience (Dewey, 1925/1958, 1938/1963), is the result of a process built around the notion of a *problematic*, that which is "asking" to be explored more than solved. Obviously the teacher (boatsperson) plays an important role here, but this role is not a dominating one; it is one of guiding, helping develop, suggesting a general direction for the creative energy that resides within the situation both to come forward and to be shaped (by all in the situation).

Stuart Kauffman (1995), not a Deweyan, a Piagetian, or an educator, but heuristic in his own right as a complexity theorist, posits that self-organizing systems develop or emerge when "just the right amount" includes (a) a critical, active mass, (b) only a few operating connections at any given time, and (c) a simple set of operating rules (ch. 4). Such a frame works as he experiments with mathematical iterations that produce order from randomness, is a hypothesis about the evolutionary origins of life on this planet, and is a speculation about the structure of social democratic groups. As a metaphor for the structure of classrooms, I see (a) [from previous list] as the collection of a viable, active group of learner-students, teacher included; (b) as the emergence of varying, interconnected, dynamic foci (the "aliveness" of situations as it were); and (c) as the few basic procedures needed for having the energy generated by these interactive situations iteratively or matrixically connected. Use of this frame does, of course, pretty well destroy the usual rubrics of classroom management—the centralizing of control with the teacher, the use of linear lesson plans, the detail of advanced organizers or syllabi, rules of conduct, and traditional evaluations. Control is dissipated into the group, community, network, system, and indeed frames itself. Lesson plans are nonlinear and (for me, recursive), depend on the interactions developing within the situations. Details dealing with organization, conduct, evaluation are all the result of reflections on real occurrences rather than on preset formulae or procedures to be followed.

As of this writing, I have tried implementing such a "management" system—akin somewhat to Lucent Technologies' "Mission from Above, Methods from Below" (Petzinger, 1997)—in university graduate and undergraduate classes. Work with schools in the K through 12 range is most informal and only beginning. Through the current students, future teachers in our Holmes teacher education program, and through the graduate teachers taking my elementary curriculum course, I hope in time to have some data on how this new sense of control works in their classes. In the meantime, the difference I see with these university students is amazing. The biggest change is that by my providing flexibility within a structured network, an in-depth study of issues emerges. A number of shifting and interconnected foci or attractors emerge from the group, and these are studies (recursively) over time from a number of varying perspectives. The "spirit" of the classes operating in this manner is truly exciting. Meaningful issues (in curriculum construction, in mathematics, in teaching, in the living of life) are raised, and their complexity studied. As I have argued elsewhere (Doll, 1998, ch. 14), a curriculum matrix, not a linear sequencing, is being built, and this construction is the result of our group interactions. As boatsperson, I steer or guide the creative energy we generate, an energy that propels our learning. 'Tis most fascinating to watch us navigate our way along the river of life and learning.

REFERENCES

American Heritage Dictionary. (1969). New York: Author.

Bateson, G. (1988). *Mind and nature*. New York: Bantam Books. (Original work published 1979)

Callahan, R. E. (1962). *Education and the cult of efficiency*. Chicago: University of Chicago Press.

Cangelosi, J. S. (1993). *Classroom management strategies: Gaining and maintaining students' cooperation* (2nd. ed.). New York: Longman.

Capra, F. (1996). *The web of life: A new scientific understanding of living systems*. New York: Doubleday.

Crutchfield, J. P., Farmer J. D., Packard N. H. & Shaw, R. S. (1986, December). Chaos. *Scientific American, 255*, 46–57.

Dewey, J. (1958). *Experience and nature*. New York: Dover. (Original work published 1925)

Dewey, J. (1963). *Experience and education*. New York: Collier. (Original work published 1938)

Dewey, J. (1966). *Democracy and education*. (New York: Free Press. (Original work published 1916)

Dewey, J. (1990) *The school and society and the child and the curriculum*. Chicago: University of Chicago Press. (Original works published in 1900 and 1902)

Doll, W. E., Jr. 1983). Curriculum and change: Piaget's organismic origins. *Journal of Curriculum Theorizing, 5*(2), 4–61.

Doll, W. E., Jr.(1993). *A post-modern perspective on curriculum*. New York: Teachers College Press.

Doll, W. E., Jr. (1997). Curriculum and concept of control. In W. Pinar (Ed.), *Curriculum identities: New visions for the field* (pp. 295–323). New York: Garland.

Johnson, G. (1996). *Fire in the mind: Science, faith and the search for order*. New York: Knopf.

Kauffman, S. A. (1993). *The origins of order*. New York: Oxford University Press.

Kauffman, S. A. (1995). *At home in the universe: The search for the laws of self-organization and complexity*. New York: Oxford University Press.

Kliebard, H. (1975). The rise of scientific curriculum making and its aftermath. *Curriculum Theory Network, 5*(1), 27–37.

Maxcy. S. J. (1995). *Democracy, chaos, and the new school order*: Corwin Press.

Parker, D., & Stacey, R. (1994). *Chaos, management and economics: The implications of non-linear thinking*. London: Institute of Economic Affairs.

Peters, T. (1987). *Thriving on chaos: Handbook for a management revolution*. New York: Alfred A. Knopf.

Peters, T. (1992). *Liberation management: Necessary disorganization for the nanosecond nineties*. New York: Knopf.

Petzinger, T., Jr. (1997, March 7) The front lines. *Wall Street Journal*, Section B., p. 1.

Rice, J. M. (1969) *Scientific management in education*. New York: Arno Press. (Original work published 1911)

Taylor, F. W. (1947). *Scientific management*. New York: Harper and Brothers. (Original work published in 1911)

Watson, T. J. (1994). *In search of management: Culture, chaos and control in managerial work*. London: Routledge & Kegan Paul.

9

Learning

Eleanor Blair Hilty
Western Carolina University

Learning. Isn't the concept of "learning" really the foundation of all discussions of school reform? It would seem that the aims and purposes of education and schooling are essentially linked to conceptualizations of learning. More important, discussions of these aims and purposes are integral to most critiques of public education and even to the reform recommendations that so often evolve from these critiques. Issues related to school improvement and school reform really focus on learning: *what* children should be learning, *why* children don't learn, and even *how* to be better parents and teachers so that we can *accelerate* learning and our children (and students) can achieve higher and higher test scores and be.... well, "successful."

Success in the 1990s has become synonymous with high test scores. The values and beliefs associated with using test scores as a measure of excellent academic programs and high achievement are unquestioned by a large percentage of the population. Perhaps more disturbing is the general acceptance and support of accountability measures among politicians and individuals in powerful positions who negotiate a vision of school reform that by necessity includes rewards and commendations for school systems that produce high test scores. For example, *site-based management*, one of the more popular school reform initiatives across the nation, merges issues of learning with accountability and autonomy. The following description is typical of most plans:

> Reasons for initiating site-based management run the gamut, yet virtually all are cloaked in the language of increasing student achievement. To some, site-based management is a governance reform designed to shift the balance of authority among schools, districts, and the state. This tends to be the rationale behind state efforts rather than district reforms, and it is often part of a larger reform agenda that claims to trade school autonomy for accountability to the state. (David, 1995/1996, pp. 5–6)

Rather than establishing a larger framework or vision that guides the teaching and learning act, site-based management and accountability—a focus on outcomes—now determine the "what" and "how" of classroom practice. This is a problem if one wants to seriously consider *learning* in a broader context; to really understand the phenomenon and its place in the educational process.

Ogbu (1990) warned social scientists that "in their eagerness to bring about change, they often design their studies not so much to understand the total situation as to discover *what is wrong* and how the situation should be changed...." (p. 398). His final caution is worthy of consideration: "This approach leads to the wrong kinds of questions, the wrong kinds of answers and the wrong kinds of solutions" (p. 398). In this chapter, I propose that we have lost sight of the *real* meaning of learning and that our attempts to address problems associated with learning are guided by the wrong kinds of questions, questions that ultimately produce the wrong kinds of answers.

WHAT IS LEARNING?

Since the early 1900s, schools have enthusiastically embraced scientific models of learning shaped by the industrial revolution, scientific efficiency, and behaviorism. Achievement and IQ tests in conjunction with behavioral theories of learning have "fit" nicely with the desire to make schools efficient and effective. Psychologists typically define "learning as all changes in behavior that result from experience, providing these changes are relatively permanent, do not result simply from growth or maturation, and are not the temporary effects of factors such as fatigue or drugs" (Lefrancois, 1991, p. 24). Although different conceptions of learning have evolved from various theories, schools still seem to be guided by notions of learning that emphasize a relationship between input and output: Children enter schools, teachers teach, children learn, and schools measure their learning through objective, standardized tests. High test scores equal success. End of story. Anything less than high test scores is interpreted as mediocre school performance, or at the worst, "bad" schools, "bad" teachers, "bad" students, and so forth. Thus, the goal of school reform becomes "fixing" schools and classrooms, teachers and students, so that everyone will be "successful."

The impetus for an increased emphasis on test scores and accountability came in 1983 when the National Commission on Excellence in Education (1983) published *A Nation at Risk*. The conclusions of this group were shocking to a nation that had grown complacent in its general acceptance of academic and educational superiority. The commission advised:

> If an unfriendly foreign power had attempted to impose on America the mediocre educational performance that exists today, we might well have viewed it as an act of war. As it stands, we have allowed this to happen to ourselves. We have even squandered the gains in student achievement made in the wake of the *Sputnik* challenge. Moreover, we have dismantled essential support systems which helped make those gains possible. We have, in effect, been committing an act of unthinking, unilateral educational disarmament. (p. 1)

Thus, with these words, Americans embraced school reform as higher standards and increased accountability. Few people questioned the findings of the commission or its assumptions about the aims and purposes of schools in this nation. Ignoring Ogbu's (1990) advice on defining "the problem," we accepted the findings of *A Nation at Risk* and allowed it to shape a reform movement that has affected the progress of education in this country for almost 25 years.

CONTEXTUALIZING THE CONVERSATION: LEARNING AS A POLITICAL ACT

> *"Never attribute to malice that which is adequately explained by stupidity."*
>
> —Ralph Lombreglia, "Somebody Up There Likes Me," The Atlantic Monthly, December 1994

When looking at school reform over the last 50 years, it is easy to see the shortcomings of many ideas that were once perceived as innovative. In fact, it is easy to make judgments about the values and beliefs that informed many of these innovations. However, one must be careful when attributing intent (or malice) to those individuals who assumed roles of responsibility and leadership in articulating a vision for school reform. In most instances, they were truly doing what they believed to be right and appropriate at a given time in history. Most reforms and innovations in education have been guided not by professional educators but rather by individuals who know very little about schools or teaching and learning. As such, efforts to address problems in schools today are being defined, funded, and led by individuals who seem to know very little about education but a lot about politics. The issues have been politically constructed and defined in such a way that political solutions do seem the most appropriate response by school districts that are too large, too diverse, and lacking resources in the form of new ideas and conceptualizations about schools and education. If we talk about learning and notions of school success strictly in terms of outcomes, we ignore the most fundamental and important aspects of the issue: the relationship between learning and issues of knowledge, power, and, yes, politics.

Discussions of "learning" ultimately lead us to questions concerning knowledge—whose knowledge, knowledge for what purpose, and the like. McLaren (1994) suggests that we must explore the social construction of knowledge as a phenomenon "rooted in a nexus of power relations." He argues:

> To claim that knowledge is socially constructed usually means that the world we live in is constructed symbolically by the mind through social interaction with others and is heavily dependent on culture, context, custom, and historical specificity.... some forms of knowledge have more power and legitimacy than others. (p. 178)

Thus, knowledge is power, and every powerful group in America has an agenda for the public schools, and that agenda is guided by strong beliefs about what children should learn. Regardless of how we define learning, ultimately we are talking about the acquisition of knowledge. Knowledge, whether it is experiential or factual, behavioral or cognitive is linked to power and politics. We seldom address the most disconcerting issue that lies just beneath the surface: school failure, or why large numbers of poor children, and most specifically, poor children of color simply do not learn in our schools, and yet our schools continue to function as if there was no problem.

There is a problem and critical discussions of learning within this context are important.

Our schools are not kind in their assessment of students who choose to place a low value on a curriculum that affirms and values high test scores and the authority of business and politics over the power of critical thinking and inquiry. The link among knowledge, power, and politics is self-evident in the repeated efforts of politicians to mandate educational reform through test scores, curricula, school management strategies, and so forth. These efforts to hold the schools "accountable" are grounded in a fundamental mistrust of educators and a general acceptance of the notion that learning (and knowledge) can be mandated and prescribed by individuals outside the educational process.

Fundamental to questions regarding an essential knowledge base, if there is such a thing, are issues related to "knowledge for what purpose?" As I read recommendations for educational reform, and as I listen to parents and teachers talking, it seems that the primary purpose for education today is for economic prosperity, both personally and nationally. Discussions of school reform are often critical of the multifaceted responsibilities assumed by the school, and yet, at what point in our history did we accept the proposition that the schools were responsible for maintaining the economic well-being of the nation? And, if a country's dominance and supremacy in the world market is waning, then is it a necessary assumption that the schools are failing?

We're preparing children for jobs; thus, to a great extent the marketplace defines for us the nature of good learning; that is, good learning equals good workers. The raison d'être for school success seems to be "getting more and getting better:" more and better schools, more and better jobs. Of course, "more and better" is the ideal, but then would it be naive to assume that if every child was sufficiently motivated and endowed with intellectual prowess, there would be opportunities for everyone to attend the best school, receive advanced educational degrees, and enter white-collar jobs with status, prestige, and sufficiently high wages to ensure a middle-class lifestyle? These are not realistic goals for any nation. And therein lies a fundamental problem with linking educational achievement to economic development. By necessity, it forces schools to assume the role of "sorting" children for future economic roles and positions, a goal that seems to contradict the most fundamental principles of equality of educational opportunity.

There is strong evidence that a people's level of economic development rises and falls with its level of educational achievement. However, the desirability of promoting these values is seldom explored. How do we define learning for "productive citizenship?" "Productive citizenship" for whom? Whose needs are being met? These are political issues, issues that emphasize why discussions of learning cannot ignore politics or issues related to race, class, and gender. Discussions that ignore these issues are meaningless. And thus, I might add, most contemporary discussions of learning are meaningless. They ignore the most difficult issues, issues that can only be addressed by a serious consideration of the morals and values of a country in which White middle-class children thrive, and poor children of color see their futures compromised and marginalized by people with power and status but little inclination to challenge the status quo by asking hard questions with hard answers. The most important questions, of course, are what are the *real* reasons that some children do not learn, and what can we do about it?

DIFFERENTIATING WANTS AND NEEDS IN LEARNING

Everyone learns. We begin to learn at birth, and it is necessary for our survival that we be good learners. The most significant point of this discussion, however, is that we all learn, regardless of race, class, gender, or educational interventions. What we learn varies, but we learn. Learning is not simply the product of planned intervention; it is ongoing, and it is driven by human desire and need. Perhaps that is where we get into trouble in the schools. Who *wants* or *needs* what we offer on a daily basis? For what purposes do "we" articulate a curriculum or program of study, and does this curriculum have anything to do with the lives of the children we teach? And perhaps, more important, what group of people consistently benefit from the educational efforts of our teachers and schools? Psychologists argue that "much of our intellectual potential has already been developed by age 6" (Lefrancois, 1991, p. 161). Similarly, most children have learned to speak and comprehend the language with some level of fluency by this same age. Thus it would seem that this level of development and skill acquisition is, perhaps, far more advanced than any task we teach in school, and yet, most children do come to school fluent in their native tongue, and then we "fail:" We fail to teach large numbers of children to read and write at the most basic levels of literacy. Narrow conceptualizations of learning cause our discussions of learning to be misguided and often useless. If we only talk about learning in traditional institutionally prescribed ways, it predetermines notions of success and failure and leads us to ignore issues related to situating teaching and learning issues in cultural contexts that are fluid and dynamic, and thus resistant to simple solutions.

If school achievement and success are essential to one's survival in this society, what does one do with the specter of school failure—defined as a "failure" to learn—in our discussions of equity and excellence in the public schools? Or, how do you answer the most frequently asked questions in these discussions, "Who do we blame for this problem?" Is this a social problem or an educational problem? How can it be that in a country devoted to the ideals of equal educational opportunity, so many children who come from less advantaged backgrounds fail to succeed? Erickson (1984) attempts to answer this question in the following way:

> Given that for approximately 5 million years human societies have managed to rear their young so that almost every one in the society was able to master the knowledge and skills necessary for survival, why does this not happen in modern societies with schools? Or does it happen—do schools teach what is necessary, but define and measure achievement in such ways that it looks as if large proportions of the school population fail? (p. 527)

Have public schools simply lost touch with the "knowledge and skills necessary for survival," or have we simply accepted the myths perpetuated by *A Nation at Risk*? The education provided by many schools may lack relevance to the lives of children who come from diverse sociocultural backgrounds. In most contemporary school environments, the strict regulation of curricula requirements and the use of standardized measures of achievement often shift the focus from "teaching the child" to "teaching the test." In this way, students are denied access to the knowledge and skills necessary for survival in a variety of contexts.

Unfortunately, the public schools are forced to regularly address the contradictions inherent in discussions of "equality of educational opportunity." Not surprisingly, McLaren (1994) argues that "[o]ne of the greatest determinants of academic success is parental income.... [T]he myth of equal opportunity therefore masks an ugly truth: the educational system is really a loaded social lottery, in which each student gets as many chances as his or her parents have dollars" (pp. 220–221). Does "equality of educational opportunity" mean an "equal chance" or an "equal share?" Is it possible to do both, provide equitable educational experience and promote excellence in the schools? More simply, is it enough to provide all children equal access to an education regardless of quality, or must we consider issues related to giving all children an equal chance: an equal chance to learn, an equal chance to be successful in a myriad of ways. The competing tensions between the pursuit of equity and excellence in public schools have characterized most discussions of failure and, subsequently, more recommendations for reform. These discussions often focus on raising academic standards in pursuit of higher test scores, and yet, we ignore the plight of children who couldn't meet previous academic standards, standards that were supposedly lower, unchallenging, and out of sync with the needs of society. Once again, do the schools serve the needs of society or the needs of the individual? What about individual desires? Individual actions? Does everyone support this notion that the needs of individuals are subordinated to a perceived sense of what is good for society? Is a lack of learning or a lack of school success indicative of large groups of students who are not willing to accept this proposition and are thus asserting the power of individual desire and action?

As I talk to teachers working on the "front-lines" of our schools and classrooms, I am discouraged by their cynicism and abject disappointment with public education. Too often, top-down decision making aimed at increasing learning in our schools focuses on "whipping into line" teachers who are obviously perceived as recalcitrant and unprofessional. Thus, the strategies employed involve accountability translated as increased test scores. Is this learning? How many people believe that "teaching the test" is learning? Well, perhaps people believe that this is all that we can expect from schools and classrooms as they presently exist. But, once again, these decisions and the subsequent outcomes are political and focus on the wants and needs of one group taking precedence over the wants and needs of less powerful groups, for example, students, teachers, and parents. Children from wealthy, better-educated backgrounds will abandon public schools and attend private schools, where learning is not necessarily defined more broadly but at least gives them access to the more traditionally defined canons of knowledge that have typically had more status and prestige in our culture, for example, the education of leaders.

REFERENCES

David, J. (1995/1996). The who, what and why of site-based management. *Educational Leadership*, *53*(4), 4–9.

Erickson, F. (1984). School literacy, reasoning, and civility: An anthropologist's perspective. *Review of Educational Research*, *54*,(4), 525–546.

Lefrancois, G. (1991). *Psychology for teaching* (7th ed). Belmont, CA: Wadsworth.

McLaren, P. (1994). *Life in schools: An introduction to critical pedagogy in the foundations of education*. New York: Longman.

National Commission on Excellence in Education (1983). *A nation at risk: The imperative for education reform*. Washington, DC: U.S. Government Printing Office.

Ogbu, J. (1990). Social stratification and the socialization of competence. In K. Dougherty & F. Hammack (Eds.), *Education and society: A reader*, (390–401). Fort Worth, TX: Harcourt Brace Jovanovich.

10

Literacy

Colin Lankshear
Central Queensland University

Educational reform discourse emphasizes four broad types of literacy. These may be construed as the "lingering basics," the "new basics," the "elite literacies," and "foreign language literacy." There is an overarching emphasis on standard English literacy, presupposed in the first three types.

At the school level, "lingering basics" refers to mastery of generalizable techniques and concepts for decoding and encoding print, presumed to be building blocks for subsequent education: content and "higher order skills." At the adult level, it refers to functional capacities with everyday texts enabling citizens to meet basic print needs for being incorporated into the economic and civic "mainstream." These conceptions "linger" from an earlier period.

The "new basics" reflects recognition that major shifts have occurred in social practices with the transitions from an agro-industrial economy to a postindustrial information–services economy; "Fordism" to "post-Fordism;" personal face-to-face communities to impersonal metropolitan and "virtual" communities; a paternal (welfare) state to a more devolved state requiring greater self-sufficiency. These shifts are seen to demand on the part of all individuals qualitatively more sophisticated ("smart"), abstract, symbolic–logical capacities than were needed in the past. Hence, "the percentage of all students who demonstrate ability to reason, solve problems, apply knowledge, and write and communicate effectively will increase substantially" (Goals 2000, Goal 3 B [ii]).

"Elite literacies" refers to higher order scientific, technological, and symbolic practices grounded in excellence in academic learning. Here "literacy" denotes advanced understanding of the logics and processes of inquiry within disciplinary fields, together with command of state of the art work in these fields. This allegedly permits high level critique, innovation, diversification, refinement, and so on, through application of theory and research. The focus here is "knowledge work," (see Drucker, 1993) construed as the real "value-adding" work (see Reich, 1992) within modern economies.

"Foreign language literacy" is seen ultimately in terms of proficiency with visual and spoken texts integral to global dealings within the new economic and strategic world order, thereby serving "the Nation's needs in commerce, diplomacy, defense, and education" (NCEE, 1983, p. 26)—genuflections toward more "humanist" rationales notwithstanding. This calls, minimally, for communicative competence allowing functional cross-cultural access to a range of discursive practices and, optimally, for levels of fluency and cultural awareness equal to being persuasive, diplomatic, and strategically effective within sensitive high-risk–high-gain contexts.

CHARACTERISTICS OF LITERACIES IN EDUCATIONAL REFORM DISCOURSE

The Functional Symmetry of Literacies With New Conditions and Types of Work

A clear functional symmetry exists between these broad literacy types and trends within "the new work order." Increasingly, work is becoming polarized between providing "symbolic analytic services" at one extreme and "routine production" and "in-person" services at the other (Gee, Hull, & Lankshear, 1996). At the same time, modern enterprises seek to infuse a sense of responsibility for the success of the enterprise throughout the entire organization, and to push decision making, problem solving, and productive innovation as far down toward "front-line" workers as possible.

Symbolic analytic work is seen as "substantial value-adding" work and is well paid (Reich, 1992, p. 177). It provides services delivering data, words, visual and nonvisual representations. This is the work of research scientists, all manner of engineers (from civil to sound), management consultants, investment bankers, systems analysts, authors, editors, art directors, video and film producers, and the like. It involves high level problem-identifying, problem-solving, and strategic brokering activities.

Routine production and in-person service work, by comparison, are construed as "low value-adding," and are poorly paid. Beyond demands for basic numeracy and the ability to read, "routine" work often calls primarily for reliability, loyalty, and the capacity to take direction, and, in the case of in-person service workers, "a pleasant demeanor." The gulf between this and symbolic analytic work marks the difference between "elite literacies" and the "lingering basics."

Between these extremes, work is affected by the "changed rules of manufacturing and competition," whereby front-line workers must increasingly solve problems as they arise, operate self-directed work teams, understand and apply concepts and procedures of quality assurance and control, and assume responsibility for many tasks previously performed by lower-level management (Wiggenhorn, 1990). Such work is agreed to require a "higher-level basics" than previously. Yet, this work also is often not well paid. To this extent, both the "lingering basics" and the "new basics" underwrite systematic exploitation in the workforce.

The Emphasis on Standard English

Educational reform discourse makes explicit that with the one exception noted in the previous section, "literacy" means "standard English literacy" (*Goals 2000*, 1994; Kearns & Doyle, 1991; NCEE, 1983). At formal and official institutional levels of economic, business, commercial, and civic life, Standard English dominates. Mastery of Standard English literacy is seen to be necessary for individuals to participate in, benefit from, and advance personally through these institutionalized spheres of social practice. More to the point, mastery of standard English is necessary for individuals to be regulated and constituted "effectively" and "efficiently" as workers and citizens. The stronger the presence of persons from non-English-speaking backgrounds within our populations, the greater the "need" to define literacy in Standard English terms-so far as maintaining dominant discourses (Gee, 1996) and established elite interests are concerned.

Furthermore, Standard English has thus far emerged as the international language of the information age. Even if this is not yet a fait accompli, it is not for nothing that there are currently more Chinese studying English than there are U.S. citizens! (Kearns & Doyle, 1991, p. 86). In times when maintaining competitive edge requires fine-tuning human resources for value-adding service in the information economy, maximizing the Standard English proficiency of our nonstandard English-speaking citizens becomes an urgent capitalist instrumentality.

The Clamor to Technologize Literacy

The many and prominent references to technological literacy and technologized curricula in educational reform discourse reflects escalating dependence of work and other daily routines on computer-mediated texts. "The whole task set by contemporary education policy is to keep up with rapidly shifting developments in technology" (Aronowitz & Giroux, 1993, p. 63). Toch (1991) cites claims that "alarming numbers of young Americans are ill equipped to work in, contribute to, profit from, and enjoy our increasingly technological society" (p. 16). The "Technology Literacy Challenge" package of February 1996 voted US$2 billion over 5 years to mobilize "the private sector, schools, teachers, parents, students, community groups, state and local governments, and the federal government" to meet the goal of making all U.S. children "technologically literate" by "the dawn of the 21st century" (Winters, 1996).

Labor market needs are clearly a large part of the story. In addition, however, new technologies directly and indirectly constitute key products of new capitalist economies for which worldwide markets need to be generated and sustained. Educational reform agendas serve crucially here as a means to creating and maintaining enlarged markets for the hardware, software, and burgeoning service products (from repair to Internet access provision and Web site design) of the information economy. Besides exhorting educators to integrate new technologies into curriculum and pedagogy, reform discourse advocates extensive use of new technologies within administrative tasks of restructured schools (Kearns & Doyle, 1991).

Literacy as "Standardized and Homogenized"

Educational reform standardizes literacy practices against "benchmarks" and accountability criteria predicated on broad goals of economic competitiveness, cultural cohesion, and national allegiance (see Popkewitz, 1991). Although details vary from place to place, the general trend and underlying purpose are clear. Standardization provides close guidelines for teaching and evaluation. As Popkewitz (1991) notes, a key rationale here relates to labor demands outside the school, "in which work patterns are conceived as flexible but require greater inner discipline to produce standardized outcomes" of uniform high quality within a context where international quality assurance standards have been defined and agreed (p. 46).

Despite increased emphasis within work and civic domains on team work and participation in communities of practice, literacy is seen to consist in the measured capacities of the individual learner. This "literacy" is then compiled into personal portfolios. At a time when individuals must be prepared to move around to find employment, "portable certified literacy competence" assumes functional significance.

This is a facet of "possessive individualism," a key operating principle of current reform discourse grounded in a liberal conception of people and society, according to which: "Society is composed of free, equal individuals who are related to each other as proprietors of their own capabilities. Their successes and acquisitions are the products of their own initiatives, and it is the role of institutions to foster and support their personal development," not least because national revitalization—economic, cultural, and civic—will "result from the good works of individuals" (Popkewitz, 1991, p. 150).

At the same time, literacy has become profoundly commodified under the current reform agenda. Literacy "packages," "recipes," and "quick fixes" are being produced on an unprecedented scale. They cover literacy assessment; evaluation and validation; remediation; instructional texts and other literacy support resources; teacher professional development and in-servicing; adult and workplace literacy provision; requirements for translating curriculum frameworks and syllabus guidelines into classroom programs; and so on. Individuals' assessed literacy "competencies" have varying exchange values and are increasingly perceived and valued in these terms. Commodified literacy is, perhaps, most clearly evident in workplace programs in which workplace tasks and "needs" are analyzed and translated into units and elements of competence. On this basis, vocational education and training "providers" can design and "deliver" courses, modules, materials, and resources for teaching and assessing literacy as components of competency-based training initiatives.

"Incorporated" Critique

Although educational reform discourse emphasizes critical forms of literate practice, couched in terms of a "critical thinking" component of effective literacy or as text-mediated acts of problem solving, it is important to recognize the nature and limits of the critical literacies proposed. They are typically practices that permit subjecting means to critique but take ends as given. References to critical literacy, critical analysis, critical thinking, problem solving, and the like, have "in the current climate ... a mixture of references to functional or useful knowledge that relates to demands of the economy and labor formation, as well as more general claims about social inquiry and innovation" (Popkewitz, 1991, p. 128). The nearer that literacy approaches the world beyond school, the more functional and instrumental critique becomes, with emphasis on finding new and better ways of meeting institutional targets (of quality, productivity, innovation, improvement) but where these targets are themselves beyond question. The logic here parallels that described by Delgado-Gaitan (1990) as operating in notions of empowerment construed as "the act of showing people how to work within a system from the perspective of people in power" (p. 2). The fact that standards are specified so tightly and rigidly within the current reform agenda reveals that the ends driving these standards are to be taken as beyond critique.

LITERACY FROM A DIFFERENT POINT OF VIEW

What should those committed to a social ideal that lies beyond economization be struggling for in the name of literacy? This question presupposes its own answer: Literacy should engage us in critique of practices that regulate who and what we become individually and collectively. The following ideal of powerful (or "liberatory") literacy is framed by Gee (1996). It builds on Gee's distinctive account of discourses and a distinction between "acquisition" and "learning". It also presumes that discursive constructions of the good life are provisional, that to be educated is to be capable of critiquing discourses, and that it is the right of every person to be educated in this sense.

Discourses are construed in terms of playing socially meaningful "roles" and being identifiable as a member of some recognizable group, class, or network (Gee, 1996, p. 131). We have primary and secondary discourses. Our primary discourse is how we learn to do and be within our intimate group during our early years. It comprises our first notions of who "people like us" are, and what "people like us" do, think, value, say, and so on (Gee, 1996, p. 137). Our secondary discourses are those we are recruited to through participation in "outside" groups and institutions, such as schools, clubs, workplaces, churches, and community groups. Gee defines literacy as control of a secondary discourse. Since there are many secondary discourses there are many literacies, and most of us are multiliterate.

Familiarity and competence with discourses generally involves some mix of acquisition and learning. Acquisition involves exposure to models within natural and functional settings. It is an essentially subconscious process, exemplified in the way humans master speech and get (acquire) their first language. Fluent performance is overwhelmingly a function of acquisition. By contrast, learning is a conscious process involving either instruction or reflection or both. When we learn something, we get some "meta-knowledge" about it, as well as getting the "it" itself (Gee, 1996, p. 137). Language learning yields, say, knowledge of verbs or sentence structure along with new capacities to conjugate verbs and frame good sentences. Learning is good for analysis and critique.

The more a context of recruitment to a discourse is one of pure acquisition, the more our recruitment is a matter of being "colonized" (Gee, 1996, p. 145). A literacy (control of a secondary discourse) can be seen as powerful, or liberating, when we can use it to get beyond colonization. This involves using a literacy as "a meta-language or a meta-Discourse (a set of meta-words, meta-values, meta-beliefs) for the critique of other literacies and the way they constitute us as persons and situate us in society" (Gee, 1996, p. 144).

To get beyond colonized recruitment and incorporated critique, we need access to perspectives from which we can seriously critique that discourse and adopt others from an informed and principled base. This presupposes meta-level knowledge about the discourse to be critiqued, together with experience and meta-level knowledge of the other discourse(s) on the basis of which it will be critiqued (Gee, 1996, p. 145). Hence, powerful literacy presupposes learning and a commitment to exposing learners to diverse discourses. The meta-level knowledge of discourses that can become available through learning is knowledge about what is involved in recruitment to those discourses. It is more than (merely) knowing how to perform them with fluent control. Beyond this knowing how, meta-level knowledge is knowing about the nature of a discourse, its constitutive values and beliefs, its meaning and significance, how it relates to other discourses, what it is about successful performance that makes it successful, and what some of the significant consequences are of that discourse operating the way it does within the larger universe and hierarchy of discourses.

Contrary to literacy ideals enshrined in educational reform discourse, the ideal of powerful literacy presupposes discursive diversity and commitment to keeping options and critique open, as preconditions for any genuinely open pursuit of the good life. A complex of dominant discourses, educational reform is an elaborate strategy for maintaining hierarchies, shoring up selective interests, and reproducing familiar patterns of advantage and disadvantage in increasingly polarized forms. The ideal of powerful literacy presupposes an agenda of radical democracy, in which possibilities for future ways of doing and being are wilfully kept open and in which commitment to hearing voices on an equal basis is genuine. Educational reform discourse(s) should be among the first objects of critique within any such agenda and the call to powerful literacy it will foreground. This essay is a modest attempt to call us to such an agenda.

REFERENCES

Aronowitz, S., & Giroux, H. (1993). *Education still under siege.* Westport, CT: Bergin & Garvey.

Delgado-Gaitan, C. (1990). *Literacy for empowerment.* London: Falmer Press.

Drucker, P. (1993). *Post-capitalist society.* New York: Harper & Row.

Gee, J. P. (1996). *Social linguistics and literacies: Ideology in discourses* (2nd ed.). London: Taylor & Francis.

Gee, J. P., Hull, G., & Lankshear, C. (1996). *The new work order: Behind the language of the new capitalism.* Boulder, CO.: Allen & Unwin & Westview Press.

Goals 2000: Educate America act. (1994). Washington, DC: U.S. Government Printing Office.

Kearns, D., & Doyle, D. (1991). *Winning the brain race: A bold plan to make our schools competitive.* San Francisco: ICS Press.

National Commission on Excellence in Education (NCEE). (1983). *A nation at risk: The imperative for educational reform.* Washington DC: U.S. Department of Education.

Popkewitz, T. (1991). *A political sociology of educational reform: Power/knowledge in teaching, teacher education, and research.* New York: Teachers College Press.

Reich, R. (1992). *The work of nations.* New York: Vintage Books.

Toch, T. (1991). *In the name of excellence.* New York: Oxford University Press.

Wiggenhorn, W. (1990, July–August). Motorola U: When training becomes an education. *Harvard Business Review,* 71-83.

Winters, K. (1996). *America's technology literacy challenge.* Washington, DC. U.S. Department of Education. Posted on <acw-1@unicorn.acs.ttu.edu> 17 Febuary 1996

11

Ideology

Michael A. Weinstein
Purdue University

"Ideology" and "Education" are radically polysemic signifiers. The definition of ideology varies according to each ideology, and there is no non-ideological ("scientific" or "objective") definition that provides a standard for judging all other ideologies definitively. Then what does this chapter mean by *ideology*? This discourse is about educational ideologies and the ideology of education ("education" as the supreme signifier) from the viewpoint of a radically individualizing pedagogy. It is ideological according to the definition of ideology that is interior to it.

Education is a practical philosophy; it considers all human practices from the viewpoint of how they are to be taught, which means that education must understand those practices in order to transmit them. The entire structure of knowledge is present in a different way—as a structure of transmission—in education than it is in philosophy, which entertains knowledge through the reflective judgement. There are at least as many definitions of *education* as there are philosophical positions. This chapter has already defined education in terms of practices and their transmission, which invokes an agent–patient relation rather than, for example, mutuality and is biased in favor of behavior over personal experience. For the critical side of individualizing pedagogy, education in contemporary capitalist societies is predominantly a system of transmitting practices and co-constituting subjects who are fit to perform those practices. The co-constitution of those fit subjects is the ideological phase or component of education in the capitalist apparatus.

For the affirmative side of individualizing pedagogy, education means the cultivation of individuals through a process of voluntary mutual learning. That is the utopia of individualizing pedagogy, which can only be imperfectly approximated within contemporary educational institutions. The co-constitution of individualized subjects is the ideological phase or component of individualizing pedagogy.

The theoretical vocabulary and the rhetoric of this chapter are grounded in an approximation and modification of Louis Althusser's theory of the ideological state apparatus and the interpellation of subjects into the capitalist system of production crossed with a vitalist discourse that appropriates Miguel de Unamuno's notion that each human being is a unique species rather than a species being; that is, the human is not defined by some common quality but by the particularity of individuals, each of whom is formed from within a community and a succession of selves: The human personality is a tribe of selves. From the sociological viewpoint of Althusser, humans are raw material fashioned by social structures into functions of production and sites of consumption in the capitalist system. For the existentialist position of Unamuno (1954), humans constitute worlds unto themselves that potentially can be shared and enhanced by "mutual imposition" and "invasive charity." The harsh counterpoint between humans as factors of production and as unique species structures the discourse of individualizing pedagogy, which is a critique of the ideologies composing contemporary pan-capitalist political–educational discourse and a call to mutual learning and individuation in the education sector of the ideological state apparatus (ISA).

Although Althusser's structuralism and Unamuno's vitalism are crossed in the present text, they are not mutually implicated: One need not make a vitalist response to the structuralist critique, though one is likely to credit the structuralist position in macrosociology if one is a vitalistic individualist.

Althusser's definition of ideology breaks with the modern discourses on ideology and of ideology critique by conceiving of ideology in practical rather than in theoretical terms. In the Marxist tradition, which has dominated the study of ideology, an "ideology" is a distorted expression of a structural position that can be decoded in terms of a science of society that is not itself ideological. Marx's decoding instrument was his class theory of society. Liberal and conservative theorists of ideology succeeding Marx changed the key from class to interest group or biological drive, but ideology retained its formal status as distorted knowledge. Althusser does not deny that ideology has a cognitive component that does not accurately represent social conditions, but he is not interested in exploring the truth value of ideologies; instead, he is concerned with their function.

"All ideology is the function [which defines it] of 'constituting' concrete individuals as subjects" (Althusser, 1971, p. 160). The major extension that Althusser effects in the definition of ideology is to make it the form by which human subjects are constituted. For Althusser, subjects (selves) come into being through being called forth by social institutions. Think of the newborn infant who comes into the world already gifted or burdened with a name and a host of imposed expectations. For Althusser, one's definitions of oneself as parent, spouse, professional, employee, believer, and, indeed, human being are all the results of being called forth (interpellated) by the ideological state apparatus (including family, religion, the media, and education) to perform and to be processed in prescribed ways. Humans become selves, for Althusser, through their institutional performances. Ideologies are the discourses by which humans orient themselves to their functions within the capitalist system. The self is constituted by the discourses that explain and justify the practices that capitalism requires human organisms to perform. The ideological state apparatus produces selves. The human organism is raw material to be worked up as both labor and consumption by providing it with skills and definitions of itself that fit it to perform in the system.

The implication of Althusser's definition of ideology as the constitution of subjects through their interpellation by the ideological state apparatus is that selfhood is exhausted by interpellations into discourses and practices. Althusser does not recognize personal selfhood in his theorization of ideology. That limitation does not affect the applicability of his critique to contemporary pan-capitalism, which is a system of production that militates against individualization. That is, the critical side of a radically individualizing pedagogy appropriates Althusser's theory of ideology as a description of how the institutions and organizations of pan-capitalism operate, not as an ontology of the self. That pan-capitalism deindividualizes and tries to foreclose individualization does not mean that individualization is impossible or nonsensical, just that it is achieved only through resistance to the ideological state apparatus.

Pan-capitalism refers to the situation since the fall of the Soviet Union, in which capitalism for the first time in history stands alone without any competitor and, thus, without any structurally based external critic. The aristocracy competed with and criticized capitalism, as well as collaborating with it, until the mid-19th century, when the rising worker's movement took over the role of competitor and critic. Today, the only critic of globalized and globalist capitalism is capitalism's defensive form, fascism, which attempts to limit the damage that global capitalism does to particular classes and societies by controlling it under the signs of nation, race, religion, or ethnicity. The current political situation pits global capitalism against exclusivist movements aiming at purified communities that resist globalization but do not break with the capitalist system of property relations.

The 1996 presidential campaign in the United States illustrates the current situation. Both the Democratic candidate, Bill Clinton, and the Republican candidate, Bob Dole, supported global capitalism. The only large-scale opposition to the pan-capitalist hegemon were Ross Perot's and Pat Buchanan's national–capitalist candidacies. There was no major candidate from the left, though Ralph Nader's Green Party made a left option of anticorporatism and radical democracy available. One would expect that in the United States, the heart of pan-capitalism, retro-fascism would be weak. Where historical conjunctures disadvantage a group or a nation, retro-fascism can become the dominant political formula, as the Serb republic of Bosnia.

Now that capitalism has undisputed sovereignty as the global economic system, its ideology becomes the dominant interpellation. Here the Althusserian ideology critique joins with the critique of global economization inspired by Ivan Illich. From the viewpoint of the economization critique, pan-capitalism not only has to interpellate organisms into the specialized functions of a technological life-order, but it must also perform the more general and comprehensive operation of interpellating human organisms as subjects of capitalism in the double sense of selves who are psychologically subjected to capitalist labor and consumption disciplines, and selves who find their meaning in life by transforming the demands that the system makes of them into values that form the core of their identities. The interpellation of economic subjects (personalities) is the ideological dimension of economization.

The two dominant educational ideologies in contemporary American society are the global-capitalist neoliberal interpellation of the human organism as a "human resource" and the cultural conservative interpellation of the human organism as member in good standing of Western civilization, Christian America, or White Christian America, depending on how the exclusive community is defined. These ideologies are the expressions, for the particular conjuncture of American politics and education in the mid-1990s, of the contradiction between global capitalism and retro-fascism. The Clinton administration has been identified with the neoliberal perspective, and recent Republican administrations have championed cultural conservative views. Robert Reich, secretary of labor under Clinton, and William Bennett, secretary of education under Ronald Reagan, epitomize, respectively, the two positions.

The neoliberal view that education is a process of enhancing "human resources" so that they will be more efficient factors of production and, therefore, will help the United States win the trade wars in the global marketplace is radically economistic. There are many forms of economism, and their appearance varies according to the condition of each national capitalism in relation to global capitalism in each historical period: In times of prosperity, economization often means interpellation as consumer; in times of struggle, economization means interpellation as producer. A radical productionism reduces the human organism to, as Martin Heidegger (1977) states in "The Question Concerning Technology," a part of the "standing reserve" of means and materials to be "challenged forth" to perform and to be processed. Labor here is no longer a separate factor of production but is treated no differently from raw and semiprocessed materials.

To be interpellated as human resources means to see oneself as a set of potentials to be worked up through the educational system so that one can compete effectively in the employment market. It means acquiring the skills for which the system of production and social reproduction calls and gaining one's self-esteem through the exercise of those skills. From the viewpoint of the interpellated organism, it is only common sense to see oneself as a resource. How else does one survive than by fitting oneself to the system's demands? Meanwhile, the system gets the functionaries it needs and renders waste products the organisms it cannot use.

For radical productionism, education is the supreme signifier, because the educational ISA is the site where skills and practices are transmitted. It is where human resources are worked up for the trade wars.

Cultural conservatism does nothing to challenge the basic economistic interpellation of contemporary American education but only attempts to restrict individuals' freedom to vary in ways that are not directly related to their role as producers. To the inculcation of skills and the interpellation of human resources, the cultural conservatives add to the educational agenda the indoctrination of certain values and virtues that they believe are superior, native to the nation or race, and graced with absolute truth. Indeed, they argue that their program of moral education will produce better—more "responsible" (docile)—human resources than will the purely technocratic policies of the neoliberals who leave the cultural sphere to mass entertainments and the schools prey to multiculturalism and egalitarian secular humanism.

In the present American public situation, all other educational ideologies are marginal to neoliberalism and cultural conservatism. Operatives in the educational ISA (teachers) who do not interpellate their students as human resources are positioned as interstitial resisters. Educational resistance, when it is feasible within the apparatus, can take many forms, including teaching anticapitalist content of various sorts, experimenting with democratic educational situations, or facilitating self-interpellation.

The possibility of self-interpellation is the ground of individualizing pedagogy, which aims to help students cultivate a discourse through which they can deliberate their interpellations and eventually construct a discourse unique to each of them, which will, as it continually mutates, constitute their ideology(ies). The practices of individualization are numerous, and different ones are appropriate to different temperaments. Nevertheless, they share the common presupposition that the human self is formed by discourse, and that it is possible, at least in some cases, under present conditions, for people to individualize themselves through a discourse that emerges from reflection on the discourses that have always already interpellated them.

Individualization does not transcend ideology; rather, it personalizes it. Self-interpellation does not reveal one "authentic" self waiting for the language to express it, nor does it replicate one type, such as the civilized Western individual; it continually constitutes a self from the shards of criticized interpellations and whatever new meanings that imagination provides. It is a resistance to the dominant pan-capitalist ideologies and, perhaps, the ground of the possibility of any alternative to pan-capitalism that incorporates mutuality rather than the agent–patient duality.

By virtue of promoting a discourse that coconstitutes a subject, individualizing pedagogy is an ideological practice. It differs from other ideological practices in the education ISA only because it cannot by definition control the contents of the self-interpellations that it promotes but is restricted to showing and cultivating the possibility of a self founded on critical reflection on interpellations. For individualizing pedagogy, the final discourse is that which individuals conduct with themselves, the discourse in which they call themselves forth into the apparatus and/or into opposition to it or separation from it (dropping out), for whatever reason and in whatever ways they have determined. To hail oneself forth is to learn to talk to oneself about whom one is being called to be by the different sectors of the apparatus and to formulate a life-strategy of one's own under an emergent and mutating table of values.

Learning to talk to oneself as a strong ego (what Unamuno called an "auto-dialogue") can be aided by teachers in every part of the curriculum by encouraging students to reflect on who they are being called to be by the apparatus in this particular educational situation and in the work of civic situations to which the former refers. It is learning to keep one's own counsel through the din of the siren songs of the apparatus.

REFERENCES

Althusser, L. (1971). *Lenin and philosophy and other essays*. London: New Left Books.

Heidegger, M. (1977). *The question concerning technology, and other essays*. New York: Harper & Row.

Unamuno, M. (1954). *The tragic sense of life*. New York: Dover.

12

Empowerment

H. Svi Shapiro
University of North Carolina–Greensboro

Several languages of power frame schooling and education in the United States; the most salient of these is what is sometimes referred to as "possessive individualism." It is a concept of power or empowerment that reflects a marriage of liberal individualism and the constitutive social context of the capitalist market. In this, power is a personal attribute—a set of skills, capabilities, and knowledge that promise an individual the possibility of successfully negotiating the hazards of a competitive and predatory culture. To be without such skills and capabilities is to make oneself vulnerable to economic disenfranchisement and to social stigmatization. School is the principal agency for the allocation of this knowledge. More than this, school is the social institution that most strongly articulates this language of personal empowerment and the possibility of acquiring those traits that can, at the very least, ensure the capacity for survival in an uncertain and dangerous world.

I have written earlier that this notion of education, understood as the medium for the acquisition of certain minimum competencies that might ensure an individual a degree of agency in the pursuit of one's livelihood, forms a potent focus for the public discourse around education (Shapiro, 1993). Its resonance is associated with the way in which school is viewed by much of the population as crucial to the possibilities for individual self-sufficiency and self-reliance. To be "minimally competent" comes to imply some capacity to make one's way in the world. It suggests that the appropriately schooled graduate is the proprietor of capacities that might insulate him or her from the hazardous nature of market influences in our society and protect him or her from the insecurity of our social and economic environment. More positively, educational success means that the individual possesses those things (knowledge, credentials, "cultural capital") that raise one's market value and provide the means to empower one as a consumer. This is the power to choose and acquire commodities, certainly the most visible and seductive face of "possessive individualism." In the hyperconsuming societies of late capitalism such so-called "empowerment" is (or promises to be) the royal road to status and pleasure. The capacity to endlessly admire and choose commodities becomes the apotheosis of self-fulfillment and self-determination. Of course, here is not the space to examine the neurotic aspects of such desire, its moral aimlessness, or the destructive consequences of compulsive work and production on human life and the environment.

In seeing the individual as the sole proprietor of one's own person or capacities, the lone and self-sufficient agent of one's economic success or survival, education mediates the ideology of the marketplace. Personal struggle, competitiveness, atomization, and scarcity of success or well-being are the constitutive elements of both the social and educational world. Failure to achieve at school marks one as incapable or undeserving of economic well-being, a state that destines one to live a life of cultural, material, and social subordination. It is, of course, precisely from this thinking that poverty, joblessness, homelessness, and the like. become understood as the consequence of personal failure and moral deficiency rather than as the result of the structural inequities of a class-divided (and racist and sexist) society.

School's meritocratic emphasis on personal ability and achievement obfuscates the deep structures of power—and lack of power—that are constitutive of United States society. Of course, this emphasis on personal achievement and effort, with its strong concern for the moral disposition of individuals, is resonant with the individualistic mythology of American Protestantism—the "frontier," Horatio Alger, the depraved nature of welfare dependents, and so forth ... (Slater, 1991; Shor, 1992). Systemically reproduced structures of social inequality are converted into individual deficiencies of intellect, effort, or moral fortitude. Unemployment is no longer understood as the consequence of deliberate policies formulated by those wielding immense economic and political power to weaken workers' ability to press for higher wages or to increase corporate profits through downsizing and workforce "rationalization." It is understood instead as the failure of individuals to achieve the levels of education necessary to their viability in the job market. Poverty is not the product of policies promulgated by economic and political elites that have produce urban disintegration, "capital flight," "redlining," and discrimination against women and people of color. It is the result instead of a failure of commitment and effort among those who have recklessly neglected the opportunities afforded through schooling. Not surprisingly, in the public discourse it is increasingly not poverty but the poor who are made the subject of our indignation (Derber, 1996).

This obfuscation of social and economic power is manifest in the usual professional discourse of educational practice, in which the focus on individual 'learning styles', cognitive development, and intellectual ability, ensures that the integration of schools into a society stratified along the lines of race, class, and gender will escape the attention of citizens and educators alike. Only a very limited awareness exists of the way that schools act as a transmission belt for the reproduction of social and economic privilege. They are far from objective or disinterested judges of students' capabilities or intelligence (Kincheloe, 1993). The contours of academic success closely mirror the contours of the larger structures of social hierarchy. It is abundantly clear, for example, that urban schools are part of a cultural and economic system that maintains the widespread impoverishment and marginalization of racial minorities in this country (Kanpol & McLaren, 1995).

HEGEMONY AND THE STATE: CONTESTED TERRAIN OF POWER

This is not to suggest a conspiratorial system of power and control. Only a very crude form of Marxist analysis would suggest a simple, single locus of power in contemporary capitalist societies, one in which there is clear consensus on class interests and needs. Certainly in a society of the complexity and scale of the United States this is far from the case. There is, for example, a significant disarticulation between and among elements of the society; culture, economy, state, civil society, and so forth are far from neatly interlocking pieces of a puzzle. Although a dominant social class certainly exists, it is far from a uniform or monolithic entity. Within it are factions divided by often distinct regional, industrial, cultural, and political interests. It is more than a matter of cynicism to describe the Democratic and Republican parties as opposing wings of the same—*ruling*—class. So, for example, the New Deal tradition within the Democratic party seeks not to abolish corporate power or the free market, but to protect the long-term profitability of corporate enterprise by intervening in the economy to offset the most disastrous social consequences of the market. After all, the legitimacy of the state rests not on the sheer brute control of money and markets but on its claim to embody the popular will of a democratic citizenry (e.g., averting the "most disastrous consequences of the market"). And in any attempt to make sense of issues of power and education the peculiar nature of the state in capitalist society must be engaged (Shapiro, 1990).

As a number of important commentators have noted, the state is the central source of organized violence in society. This coercive power is deployed principally against those who would attempt to resist or subvert the existing hierarchy of privilege and opportunity. In this sense, the state's power is deployed most commonly to defend and extend the prerogatives of capital—that class that owns and controls the principal means of production. Yet, as we have already noted, the state is more than what Marx called "the executive of the bourgeoisie." As we have learned form Gramsci, Poulantzas, and others, the state in capitalist society is also the site of social struggle. In a democratic (or partially democratic) society, the state can only assure its own legitimacy by acceding, or appearing to accede, to some of the demands and concerns of subaltern groups. This is the real meaning of Gramsci's concept of hegemony (Brosio, 1994). The state assures the fundamental dominance of the ruling social, economic, and political groups by conceding and absorbing some of the demands that well up from the bottom end of the society—of course, never so much that it would really upturn the apple cart. In this sense, hegemony is always a tense and unfinished process in which the state's power is tested, confronted, and reconstituted. Indeed within the complex structures of the state, departments are shaped in way that reflect varying forms of hegemonic settlement, for example, human services with its links to the poor, minorities, women, or the Department of Commerce, which is essentially an agency connected by a revolving door with the board rooms of big business.

In grasping the complexity of hegemony, one may come to a much more sophisticated understanding of the relationship of education to power. As an agency of the state, schools, especially public schools, are janus faced, They must, on the one hand, assist in the reproduction of social, cultural, and economic hierarchies, and they must socialize the young into appropriate forms of control and discipline. On the other hand, however, schools create a focus for various forms of popular empowerment and social justice. They mediate concrete struggles for increased democracy and opportunity and challenges to sedimented forms of inequality and hierarchical control (Apple, 1983; Carnoy & Levin, 1993). Examples of the latter include the struggle to abolish segregation and racism in schools; inclusion of handicapped children in public education; redistribution of funding for public education; financial support and open admissions for students in higher education; challenges to tracking and other forms of educational discrimination. Such struggles are sometimes faulted for foregrounding educational concerns instead of the more significant social and economic context. Certainly, they are no substitute for broader struggles for democratic empowerment or social justice. Nonetheless, education has been an important and emotional catalyst for galvanizing poor and working people to question and challenge the structures of state power. Even the stress in recent times on the key role of education in improving the competitiveness of business with a crude reductionism of education to work skills and the enhancement of human capital reaffirms the state's responsibility for ensuring jobs and livelihoods for working people. In this time of downsizing, surplus populations, and growing poverty, maintaining issues of work and income as a public responsibility is of no small importance.

SCHOOL AS A REGIME OF POWER AND KNOWLEDGE

Despite the often highly visible nature of these political conflicts, school remains a vehicle unquestionably concerned with issues of socialization into a world of discipline and control—an institution that mediates what Foucault terms a "regime of power/knowledge" (Ball, 1990). A large number of writers and observers have made clear the nature and form of this regime as it exists in schools. Some of these (e.g., Henry Giroux, Peter McLaren, Ira Shor, and Donaldo Macedo) have followed the Brazilian educator Paulo Freire in describing the forms of pedagogy typically found in schools that emphasize an uncritical, unquestioning educational process. Such pedagogy is profoundly disempowering in its reification of the knowledge and the social reality that are presented in classrooms and in texts. Students are taught to accept without serious challenge the injustices and the dehumanization of their world. Others in this volume describe this process in greater depth. This disempowerment of students is much more than a merely cognitive phenomenon. There is a deep process of control and discipline mediated through the regulations of space, time, and the physical body. As we have learned from Foucault and subsequent commentators, the surveillance and regulation of the body is fundamental to the "micro-physics of power" (Bordo, 1993). Anyone who has spent any time observing children in school is easily made aware of this process. Disempowerment is also, profoundly, a matter of the spirit. It is a commonplace of those who observe schools (especially high schools) to note the stultifying boredom and emotional blandness that are characteristic of such institutions—places where students are emotionally and intellectually alienated and where schoolwork becomes, at best, a crude search for grades. The alienation is compounded by the exclusion of so much of students' experience and their life-world. Particularly, the process serves to marginalize and silence students who, by virtue of their race, gender, sexuality, or social class, do not recognize their lives in school narratives. Much powerful writing has documented the debilitating effect of this exclusion on students' interest or success in school.

The typically bureaucratic and hierarchic nature of school organization is disenfranchising for the clients of this institution providing little real opportunity for meaningful decision making or choice. The absence of any sense of significant democratic community among students raises only very limited public concern. This, however, is not quite so true concerning the role of teachers. The legitimation crisis of public institutions, with its demand for greater accountability among public employees, has opened the door to the call for more decentralized power in school systems and greater institutional empowerment for teachers. Unfortunately, this comes at a time when more and more significant decisions about curriculum and testing are being made by central governmental or quasi private agencies. This has meant a situation in which, as Tom Popkewitz observed, teachers have more and more power to decide fewer and fewer matters (Popkewitz, 1991).

CONCLUSIONS: TOWARD A PEDAGOGY OF EMPOWERMENT

The danger in all this analysis is that schools come to be seen in ways in which the powers of control and discipline are overwhelming and unopposed in their practice. This is far from the reality. Critical ethnographers have vividly described how schools need to be understood as a "terrain of cultural struggle"(Willis, 1977, p.). Students (and sometimes teachers) frequently resist the alienation and disempowerment of educational life.

There is a constant contest over what meaning is to be attached to the experience and knowledge that form the matrix of pedagogy and curriculum, what sense and what importance is given to the official story transmitted by school authorities. Classrooms are often battlefields where time, space, bodies, and meaning are matters of conflict and contestation. And away from the classroom, resistance is carried on in the form of truancy, vandalism of school property, and increasingly violent rejection of school authority. Not surprisingly, this is most apparent in and around schools located in those urban areas where economic and social disenfranchisement are high.

Although such resistance points to the incomplete nature of domination and control, this is not to be confused with a significant transformation in the relations of power in our class-structured, racist, and patriarchal society. In this sense, real empowerment is inseparable from the project of radical democracy. This is the multifaceted struggle to restructure relationships of power throughout the institutions and informal sites of social life—in the workplace, the media, the political arena, domestic relations, and so on. It challenges relationships that are racist, sexist, ageist, homophobic, and class determined. It is a struggle impelled by the moral criteria of social justice and a communal solidarity rooted in the values of human dignity and cultural difference. Of course, in the quest for a more deeply democratic society, education is an important focus of concern. In the institutional sense, there are the important struggles around issues of access, the distribution of resources, the influence and control of the testing industry, and the bureaucratic power of educational managers. In a deeper sense, radical democracy means challenging and transforming the forms of pedagogy that seek to reify intellectual and cultural hierarchy and that stifle and silence the critical capacities of students to seriously question the dehumanizing nature of modern society. Such a "critical pedagogy" will require not only this ability to seriously interrogate our world but also, perhaps even more importantly, the capacity to imagine and re-envision a world free from the pain and disfigurement of domination and exploitation.

REFERENCES

Apple, M. (1983). *Education and power.* London: Routledge & Kegan Paul.

Carnoy, M., & Levin, H. M. (1993). *Schooling and work in the democratic state.* Stanford, CA: Stanford University Press.

Ball, S. J. (Ed.). (1990). *Foucault and education: Disciplines and knowledge.* New York: Routledge, Chapman & Hall.

Bordo, S. (1993) *Unbearable weight.* Berkeley, CA: University of California Press.

Brosio, R. A. (1994). *A radical democratic critique of capitalist education*. New York: Peter Lang.
Derber, C. (1996). *The wilding of America*. New York: St. Martin's Press.
Kanpol, B., & McLaren, P. (Eds.). (1995). *Critical multiculturalism*. Westport, CT: Bergin & Garvey.
Kincheloe, J. L. (1993). *Towards a critical politics of teacher thinking*. Westport, CT: Greenwood.
Popkewitz T. (1991). *A political sociology of educational reform*. New York: Teachers College Press.
Shapiro, S. (1990). *Between capitalism and democracy*. Westport, CT: Greenwood.
Shapiro, S. (1993). Curriculum alternatives in a survivalist culture: Basic skills and the minimal self. In S. Shapiro & D. Purpel (Eds.), *Critical social issues in American education*. New York: Longman. 288–304.
Shor, J. (1992). *The overworked American*. New York: Basic Books.
Slater, P. (1991). *A dream deferred*. Boston: Beacon Press.
Willis, P. (1977). *Learning to labor*. Farnborough, England: Saxon House.

13

Inclusive Education

Linda Ware
University of Rochester

In this chapter I present a genealogy on special education informed by the experiences of 12 high school students with whom I conducted research on inclusion. The students participated in a series of four critical dialogues—a research method designed to engage research participants and researchers in open-ended dialogue specific to an identified research problem (Ware, 1994a, 1995a, 1997; Ware & Gee, 1995). With an emphasis on meaning making at the local level, critical dialogues take shape over time (repeated sessions) and build on the belief that from birth on, humans construct webs of belief, desires, and attitudes that ground their view of self and reality and that these webs allow us to interpret and thus to act in the contexts in which we find ourselves (Rorty, 1982, 1991). Critical dialogues were also conducted with teachers who supported the inclusion program; however, moving the microphone from the teachers to the students framed inclusion in a more politicized context informed by struggle, resistance, and conflict.

The students recounted prior experiences in traditional pullout special education programs as well as in their present experiences with inclusion, describing their lives in the *space between* the binary divisions of exclusion and inclusion. Their histories spanned 5-to-10 years of special education placement in which their local accounts of the examinations, the judgments, and the uninterrupted observations paralleled the "techniques of surveillance" described by Foucault (1978). In their tales of what has been done to them as the subjects of the disciplinary power of special education, their accounts confirm that power is everywhere and so, too, is resistance:

> These points of resistance are present everywhere in the power network. Hence there is no locus of great Refusal, no soul of revolt, source of all rebellions, or pure law of the revolutionary. Instead there is a plurality of resistance, each of them a special case: resistances that are possible, necessary, improbable; others that are spontaneous, savage, solitary, concerted, rampant, violent; still others that are quick to compromise, interested, or sacrificial; by definition, they can only exist in the strategic field of power relations. (Foucault, 1978, p. 96)

The experiential knowledge of the students represented "a whole set of knowledge that have been disqualified as inadequate to their task or insufficiently elaborated: naive knowledge, located low down on the hierarchy, beneath the required level of cognition or scientificity" (Foucault, 1980, p. 82). This "popular knowledge" albeit, far from everyday common knowledge, is nonetheless

> a particular, local, regional knowledge ... which owes its force only to the harshness with which it is opposed by everything surrounding it [and] that it is through the reappearance of this knowledge ... that criticism performs its work. (Foucault, 1980, p. 82)

The students' resistance took many forms over the years they spent in special education, an experience many likened to imprisonment, in that prior to inclusion there was "no way out" of special classes. Their analysis resonates with Foucault's view that the prison "shuts the prisoner up (in both senses), and the resulting silence allows the professionals to make what claims they like as to the curative process being enacted" (Philip, 1985, p. 77). This chapter, as a genealogy on special education practice (curative processes), is similar to Foucault's genealogy on madness, prisons, and the dangerous individual, in that it is not intended to

> denounce us for what we have done to them, but to show us what we have done to ourselves by doing these things to them. To show, that is, that we have made ourselves mad, sick and delinquent by seeking to treat the madness, sickness and delinquencies of others. (Philip, 1985, p. 77)

Special education has not worked as intended for many reasons (discussed later in this chapter); however, it is argued here that chief among its failures is its refusal to "open the prison doors so as to allow the prisoner to speak" (Philip, 1985, p. 77). These voices are critical to reform through inclusion, because as Foucault (1981) suggests:

> If prisons and punitive mechanisms are transformed, it won't be because a plan of reform has found its way into the heads of the social workers; it will be when those who have to do with that penal reality, all those people, have come into collision with each other and with themselves, run into dead ends, problems and impossibilities, been through conflicts and confrontations; when critique has been played out in the real, not when reformers have realized their ideals ... Critique does not have to be the premise of a deduction which concludes: this then is what needs to be done. It should be an instrument for those who fight, those who refuse and resist what is. Its use should be in processes of conflict and confrontation, essays in refusal. (p. 13)

Readers Note. All of the participants had been, or were currently students of Valerie, one of the pro-inclusion teachers who cofacilitated the student dialogues with me (L). The students had been in the high school inclusion block since their freshmen year, moving from previous placement in a self-contained resource room in middle school. The teachers involved in this research were in general agreement that the students were more successful because of inclusion. Yet, much of what the students described surprised the teachers, and as one teacher summarized in our final member check of the data, caught them "off guard." This data could easily stand alone as a genealogy of special education as it is rich with interpretation, only a small portion of the data collected for this research has been included in this chapter.

Silenced by years of meaningless work assignments, banished to classrooms that separated these students from their friends, and with no clear path to challenge this subjectification, it is no surprise that students recalled feelings of inadequacy. Years of surveillance marked these students and yet, for the most part, they succeeded in their resistance and evidenced clear intelligence and confidence. Had all the years of special education research conducted to serve the needs of researchers instead been targeted to determine how these students persevered in the face of such oppression, their counternarratives would rival the "official" hegemonic narrative of special education. Opening the prison door that has silenced the voices of students who possess incredibly harsh first-hand accounts of the madness, sickness, and delinquent behavior inherent in the "curative process" of special education practice would inform the long overdue critique of the profession. For example, consider Lena's experience on escape from special education.

"I was bored with it. I was getting straight A's on everything. The work was just too easy. I didn't like it because it was too easy. I'd get my work done everyday and then just have to sit there till class was over looking at magazines."

"But earlier you said you were afraid to go to general ed classes." (L)

"I was, but see, the teachers would always tell me that I'd really have to work hard in those classes and that I'd have to be more prepared than I was. When I think about it now, I really believe the just told me that because they wanted to keep me there."

"Meaning?" (L)

"My teachers always told me in grade school and mid school, 'I don't want you leaving special ed, you're the best student we have in here'—you know—because I made straight A's. And so it just scared me, the idea of getting out. I'd go to my IEP meetings hoping[1] they wouldn't move me. I'd even start crying so they wouldn't move me."

Although Lena ultimately left special education and succeeded in the high school inclusion block, her struggle to shed an identity framed by incapacity, incompetence, and insecurity supports Tomlinson's (1982, 1995) critique of the "benevolent humanitarianism" frequently disguised as intervention in special education's professional practices. That this unchecked compassion led Lena's teachers to overtly manipulate her identity for fear of losing "their best student" seems unconscionable. And yet, in this research, a similar benevolent humanitarianism occluded the teachers' awareness of the need for confrontation of the conflict their students described. Their professional gaze ensured that the teachers were always one step removed from the experiences their students described. Although there was clear discomfort on the part of the teachers when initially considering the students' description of the madness, sickness, and the delinquencies of the profession, they possessed no tools with which to intervene. As a consequence, the teachers were generally unable to help the students recognize and name their acts of resistance and even less able to encourage resistance as a means to inform inclusion and broaden the agenda. Had the teachers' professional preparation included consideration of a knowledge set other than that which is officially sanctioned, they might have ventured forth in

[1]Individual Education Plan (IEP) a meeting convened yearly to discuss student progress in special education, which then becomes the IEP document that is drafted and signed by all participants (e.g., parents, teachers, administration).

support of the students. However, student accounts of special education remain outside the knowledge tradition of special education. Although parent accounts have been invited, they are often rejected when they transgress the limits of the reigning discourse (Ware, 1994b; 1999). Best and Kellner (1991) suggest that genealogies are attempts to "foreground the material context of subject construction, to draw out the political consequences of 'subjectification,' and to help form resistances to subjectifying practices" (p. 47). In this genealogy, the material context was challenged by these student voices whose first-hand narratives serve as "essays in refusal" (Foucault, 1981), essays that could greatly inform the special and general education professions.

Because this chapter was invited to address "Inclusion," some background is necessary to ground the reader in the official transcript of this reform effort and its "professional claims." The educational meaning of "inclusion" is so wrapped up on the macro-politics of integration within society and warped by micropolitics within the professions of general and special education, definition is often framed by the conventional binarism of inclusion and exclusion. At the macro level, inclusion, as a goal for society, gains in meaning when explicitly connected to issues of human rights and social justice. At the 1994 UNESCO World Conference on Special Needs Education, representatives from 92 governments and 25 international organizations adopted *The Salmanca Statement and Framework for Action on Special Needs Education* (1994), and declared that

> [t]he trend in social policy during the past two decades has been to promote integration and participation and to combat exclusion. Inclusion and participation are essential to human dignity and to the enjoyment and exercise of human rights. Within the field of education, this is reflected in the development of strategies that seek to bring about a genuine equalization of opportunity. (p. 11)

In this pact, the participants also addressed inclusive schooling, which they acknowledged "provides the most effective means for building solidarity between children with special needs and their peers" (p. 12). To characterize inclusion as action toward the promotion of solidarity among children widens the impact of inclusion, and more important, it attempts to make an explicit connection between the purposes of schooling today and its impact on society in the future. However, as inclusion is defined in practice in schools, the micropolitical issues remain unchanged—determining whether special education is a service or a place.

According to the National Center on Educational Restructuring and Inclusion (NCERI), inclusion is underway in over 900 school districts in the United States (National Study, 1995). Although the actual definition of inclusion remains ambiguous across these sites, the NCERI defined inclusion as

> the provision of services to students with disabilities, including those with severe impairments, in the neighborhood school, in age-appropriate general education classes, with the necessary support services and supplementary aids (for the child and the teacher) both to assure the child's success—academic, behavioral, and social—and to prepare the child to participate as a full and contributing member of society. (p. 3)

With an emphasis on the "where" and the "what" of inclusion, this definition characterizes the "service delivery" approach, which has as its focus instructional techniques and special education *program* change. Although this definition has served to launch inclusion in many schools, it restricts understanding as "service–place" becomes another item in the growing list of conventional binary oppositions that have characterized the lexicon of special education (e.g. ordinary–special; integrated–segregated; inclusion–exclusion). The limitations of such analysis lead educators to proclaim with ease, "We do inclusion in our school," or "I'm the inclusion teacher," or "We don't really have any inclusion kids in our school—so we don't do inclusion" (Ware, Keefe, & Blalock, 1998). This conceptualization of inclusion is further endorsed by so-called "professional" literature focused on the "nuts and bolts" of implementation in which practical guides to inclusion offer strategies for success, 12-step plans, and contrived reward systems for teachers and schools. This rational–technical approach to the implementation of inclusion through perfected practices is a well-intentioned response to this highly complex reform, but it is a short-sighted approach given the many moral challenges inclusion poses for schools and for society.

Nonetheless, inclusion has served to interrupt the once singular official discourse on disability that has, over the past 3 decades, legitimized policies, practices, and perspectives grounded in a functionalist tradition. Inclusion all but ensures that students previously identified "in need of special education services" will no longer be placed in segregated settings supported by a separate system of schooling. The large-scale return of students to classrooms from which they have been excluded to engage in instruction for which they have not been readied and to the end goal of successful interaction with peers and teachers who may *initially* lack the critical commitment to create classrooms as caring communities suggests nothing short of a wildly complex process.

Thus special education, as a consequence of inclusion, is now situated in the space between changing "regimes" of power and truth, periods marked by shifting discourses, new forms of knowledge, and discontinuity (Foucault, 1980). Whether the profession will seize the moment and engage in a theoretical discourse to examine the "unconscious assumptions" (Skrtic, 1988, p. 480) that drive traditional special education remains to be seen. Although, theoretical criticism of special education made by social science dates back to the 1960s, this critique was all but ignored by the profession because it was judged "external" to the field (e.g. Farber, 1968; Goffman, 1961, 1963; Lemert, 1967; Scott, 1969; Szaz, 1961). Today, as inclusion is underway in schools both nationally and internationally, there exists both the aforementioned external critique, and an ever-widening internal critique by its own members (e.g. Bogdon & Knoll, 1995; Bogdon & Kuglemass, 1984; D. Ferguson, 1995; P. Ferguson, 1987; Heshusius, 1986, 1995; Iano, 1986, 1987; Poplin, 1984; 1987; Skrtic, 1986, 1988, 1991a, 1991b, 1995; Ware, 1994b). Taken together, these critiques could provide an opening for the field to reshape the discourse on special education and to employ new forms of knowledge toward progress as a profession. However, Skrtic (1995) warns, this may prove to be the greatest challenge to inclusion:

> When special education professionals are confronted with theoretical criticism, they ordinarily have difficulty accepting and using it. Theoretical criticism is difficult for special educators to accept because it questions their taken-for-granted assumptions about themselves, their clients, and their practices and discourses. It is difficult for them to use because it is presented in theoretical languages that fall outside the logic of special education's functionalist knowledge tradition. (p. 82)

At the micropolitical level there exists great fear of change and a defensiveness about the goals of inclusion as political struggle not for individuals with disabilities but rather the struggle to preserve the existing regime of power lodged within the traditional special education discourse. For example, at a recent faculty meeting to consider possible programmatic change for inclusion, emotions ran high as one faculty member charged, "In your zeal to promote inclusion, don't forget that these kids need our voices." As the target of this indictment, I concede that I transgress the limits imposed by a narrowly conceived university program for the training of undergraduate and graduate special education majors and that by exploiting my own privileged position as a university researcher and professor, I seek to interrupt the social relations of research reproduction by engaging with individuals in the struggle against social oppression. However, the zeal with which I promote inclusion is informed by the voices of the students and parents with whom I research the meaning of special education as they live the experience (Ware, 1994b, 1995; 1997; 1999). In this process, I seek to mine the resistance and struggle buried within the "local, discontinuous, disqualified, illegitimate knowledge [and to work] against the claims of a unitary body of theory which would filter, hierarchise and order them in the name of some truth of knowledge" (Foucault, 1980, p. 83).

In previous research, high school students, over the course of a semester, abandoned their unconscious reliance on the "techniques of surveillance" (Foucault, 1980) and, instead, came to know Josh, a fellow student with profound disabilities (Ware, 1997; Ware & Gee, 1995). Josh, who had infrequent access to a speech communication board (read frequent technical malfunction), and thus, limited speech, nonetheless maintained meaningful interaction with his peers. Among the many dialogues that informed the research, students analyzed whether "acting as if an actor" is the same as "being an actor." They grappled not only with Josh's "real" capacity to be in a theater arts class but their own assumed entitlement to the class simply because they possessed speech and so-called "normal" communication. Intensive observations in classrooms, campuswide interactions, and interviews with various individuals close to Josh revealed a changing perspective on disability that was far more progressive than state and local policies could support. Similar research with parents (Ware, 1994b; 1999) has focused on probing the "ruptural effects of conflict and struggle that the order imposed by functionalist thought is designed to mask" (Foucault, 1980, p. 82). In sum, my research seeks to unmask functionalism by exposing the harshness of the accounts of struggle, resistance, and conflict by those who have lived the experience and, further, to present these accounts as viable teaching instruments for those who fight, refuse, and resist what is—for those who opt to play out the critique in the real.

REFERENCES

Beegle, G., Counts, J., Ware, L., & Gee, K. (1995). *Evaluation report for Supported Education in Kansas (SEIK): Statewide Severe Disabilities Systems Change Project.*

Best, S., & Kellner, D. (1991). *Postmodern theory: Critical interrogations.* New York: Guilford.

Bogdon, R., & Knoll, J. (1995). The sociology of disability. In E. L. Meyen & T. M. Skrtic (Eds.), *Special education and student disability*. (675–711), Denver, CO: Love.

Bogdon, R., & Kuglemass, J. (1984). Case studies of mainstreaming: A symbolic interactionist approach to special schooling. In L. Barton & S. Tomlinson (Eds.), *Special education and social interests* (173–191). New York: Nichols.

Farber, B. (1968). *Mental retardation: Its social context and social consequences*. Boston: Houghton Mifflin.

Ferguson, D. L. (1995) The real challenge of inclusion: Confessions of a "rabid inclusionist." *Phi Delta Kappan, 77*,(4) 281–287.

Ferguson, P. M. (1987). The social construction of mental retardation. *Social Policy, 18*(1), 51–56.

Foucault, M. (1978). *The history of sexuality*. New York: Random House.

Foucault, M. (1980). Two lectures. In C. Gordon, (Ed.), M. *Foucault, power/knowledge: Selected interviews and other writings, 1971–1977* (pp. 78–108). (C. Gordon, L. Marshall, J. Mepham, & K. Soper, Trans.). New York: Pantheon.

Foucault, M. (1981, Spring). Questions of method: An interview with Michel Foucault, *Ideology and Consciousness*, 8 (pp. 3–14).

Goffman, E. (1961). *Asylums: Essays on the social situation of mental patients and other inmates*. Garden City, NY: Doubleday/Anchor Books.

Goffman, E. (1963). *Stigma: Notes on the management of spoiled identity*. New York: Simon & Schuster.

Heshusius, L. (1986). Paradigm shifts and special education: A response to Ulman and Rosenberg. *Exceptional Children, 53*(5), 461–465.

Heshusius, L. (1995). Holism and special education: There is no substitute for real life purposes and processes. In T. M. Skrtic (Ed.), *Disability and democracy: Reconstructing (special) education for postmodernity* (pp. 166–189). New York: Teachers College Press.

Iano, R. P. (1986). The study and development of teaching: With implications for the advancement of special education. *Remedial and Special Education, 7*(5), 50–61.

Iano, R. P. (1987). Rebuttal: Neither the absolute certainty of prescriptive law nor a surrender to mysticism. *Remedial and Special Education, 18*.(1), 51–56.

Lemert, E. (1967). *Human deviance and social problems, and social control*. Englewood Cliffs, NJ: Prentice-Hall.

National Study of Inclusive Education. (1995). New York: National Center on Educational Restructuring and Inclusion.

Philip, M. (1985). Michel Foucault. In Quentin Skinner (Ed.), *The return of grand theory in the human sciences*. Cambridge, England: Cambridge University Press.

Poplin, M. S. (1984). Toward a holistic view of persons with learning disabilities. *Learning Disabilities Quarterly, 7*(4), 290–294.

Poplin, M. S. (1987). Self-imposed blindness: The scientific method in education. *Remedial and Special Education, 8*(6), 31–37.

Rorty, R. (1982). *Consequences of pragmatism*. Minneapolis: University of Minnesota Press.

Rorty, R. (1991). Inquiry as recontextualization: An anti-dualist account of interpretation. In D. Hiley, J. Bonham, & R. Shusterman (Eds), *The interpretive turn: Philosophy, science, culture* (pp. 59–80). Ithaca, NY: Cornell University Press.

The Salmanca statement and framework for action on special needs education. (1994). World conference on special needs education: Access and equality. New York: UNESCO.

Scott, R. (1969). *The making of blind men*. New York: Russell Sage Foundation.

Skrtic, T. M. (1986). The crisis in special education knowledge: A perspective on perspective. *Focus on Exceptional Children, 18*(7), 1–16.

Skrtic, T. M. (1987). An organizational analysis of special education reform. *Counterpoint, 8*(2), 5–19.

Skrtic, T. M. (1988). The organizational context of special education. In E. L. Meyen & T.M. Skrtic (Eds.), *Exceptional children and youth: An introduction* (pp. 415–447), Denver, CO: Love.

Skrtic, T. M. (1991a). *Behind special education: A critical analysis of professional culture and school organization.* Denver, CO: Love.

Skrtric, T. M. (1991b). The special education paradox: Equity as the way to excellence. *Harvard Educational Review, 61*,(2), 148–206.

Skrtic, T. M. (1995). *Disability and democracy: Reconstructing (special) Education for Postmodernity.* New York: Teachers College Press.

Szaz, T. S. (1961). *The myth of mental illness.* New York: Hoeber-Harper.

Tomlinson, S. (1982). *A sociology of special education.* Boston: Routledge & Kegan Paul.

Tomlinson, S. (1995). The radical structuralist view of special education and disability: Unpopular perspectives on their origins and development. In T. Skritic (Ed), *Disability and democracy: Reconstructing (special) education for postmodernity.* New York: Teacher College Press.

Ware, L. (1994a). *Innovative instructional practices: A naturalistic study of the structural and cultural conditions of change* Unpublished doctoral dissertation. University of Kansas, Lawrence.

Ware, L. (1994b). Contextual barriers to collaboration. *Journal of Educational and Psychological Consultation,* 5(4), 339–357.

Ware, L. (1995a) The aftermath of the articulate debate: The invention of inclusive education. In C. Clark, A. Dyson, & A. Millward (Eds), *Towards inclusive schools?* New York: Teachers College Press.

Ware, L. (1995b, November). Reconstructing welfare policy: Voice and empowerment in evaluation research. Paper presented at Evaluation '95: An International Evaluation Conference co-sponsored by the Canadian Evaluation Society and the American Evaluation Society, Vancouver, British Columbia.

Ware L. (1997). Sometimes I wonder if we're fooling ourselves In T. Booth & M. Ainscow (Eds.), *From them to us: An international study of inclusion in education.* London: Routledge, & Kegan Paul.

Ware, L., & Gee, L. (1995, December). Listening to teenagers: What they're saying about what's happening in their schools. Paper presented at the Annual Meeting of the Association for Severe Handicaps (TASH), San Francisco.

Ware, L. (1999). Kids like mine and kids kinda like him. In K. Ballard & T. McDonald (Eds.), *Inclusive Education: International voices on disability and Justice*, pp. 43–66. Falmer Press.

Ware, L. Keefe, L., & Blalock, G. (1998). *Inclusion Practices in New Mexico: A Final Report to the New Mexico Sate Board of Education.* University of New Mexico: Department of Special Education.

14

Gifted Education

Mara Sapon-Shevin
Syracuse University

Gifted education consists of programs, courses, and opportunities that are provided for a small group of students who are identified as "gifted" or "talented." Admission to a gifted program is generally obtained by scoring well on a standardized IQ test, which must often then be supported by teacher recommendations. Students identified as "gifted" sometimes attend pullout enrichment programs for part of the day or week, or they may be served in segregated all-gifted classrooms or attend completely separate schools, to which they must apply and are admitted competitively.

Why do some students get certain educational benefits whereas others are denied them? I examine here the reasons that gifted education systems are promoted and maintained, the implications of those constructions, and then the ways in which the discourse about gifted education impedes a more critical stance.

The need and importance of providing discrete, specialized services for students identified as "gifted" is generally justified in three ways: educational need, social justice, and political and economic necessity. Those who argue from an educational perspective assert that providing different educational opportunities for students with accelerated skills is simply a way of meeting the individual (and different) needs of different students. In other words, it's just "good teaching" to treat different kids differently. The social justice perspective argues that it's only fair to treat different kids differently, and since schools already provide differentiated programming for students identified as "learning disabled," "bilingual," or "mentally retarded," they should further pursue their commitment to equity by providing specialized programs for students identified as "gifted." Political and economic exigencies constitute the third major form of support for gifted programs: Our nation can ill afford not to develop the "best and the brightest" lest we lose our standing as a major world power or cease to be on the cutting edge of technology, medicine, and science.

Each of these arguments can be analyzed in terms of both explicit and hidden agendas, intended and unintended outcomes, and the ways in which gifted education becomes linked to and embedded in broader political and economic ideologies. One way to explore this is to critically examine the underlying assumptions that undergird the stated justifications for gifted education:

- There is such a thing as "giftedness"; some children "have it," we can test for it, and once we have identified it, respond to it educationally.
- A "gifted child" is one who can be objectively identified and confidently discriminated from a "ungifted" child.
- Gifted children represent a "class" of children, that is, we can speak of programming or education for "the gifted" in generic or group ways.
- What is good for gifted students is not beneficial for everyone else (the Shakespeare in the Park program, the Young Philosophers' Club, the great book programs, and community mentorships are not advisable or appropriate for other students).
- General educational reform can never be structured broadly enough to meet the needs of gifted students, that is, curricular and pedagogical reforms such as whole language, portfolio assessment, a focus on multiple intelligences, thematic instruction, or multilevel teaching is insufficient to address the discrete educational needs of students identified as "gifted."
- Some curricular and pedagogical "best practices" are actually detrimental to students identified as gifted; cooperative learning, for example, with its focus on heterogeneous grouping, deprives gifted students of opportunities to match minds with others who work at their level and forces accelerated students into the inappropriate role of junior teacher or peer support.

What are the consequences of the acceptance of these arguments and assumptions, and how else might we talk about and respond to interindividual differences, educational goals, and social justice imperatives?

I argue that giftedness, rather than representing an objective reality, is a social construct, a way of thinking and describing that exists in the eyes of the definer (Sapon-Shevin, 1987). Children do differ in many dimensions. But decisions about how to define a category, where to make "cut-off" points, and how to discriminate between those in the category and those outside it are ethical and political decisions that are highly influenced by values, beliefs about children, intelligence and education, and the surrounding cultural and economic context. Failing to acknowledge the socially constructed nature of the category makes it easier to ignore the political and economic consequences of its usage.

It is also a mistake to issue blanket statements about "what gifted students need" as though they are, in fact, a coherent, homogeneous group with a unified set of educational needs. Providing a "generic" gifted program both fails as responsive pedagogy and homogenizes some of the more blatant inequities in who gets what that might be more apparent if we compared programming for specific students.

There is no research to support the contention that the educational opportunities currently being provided for students identified as "gifted" would not also be positive for unidentified students, or that specialized services cannot be provided within a broader context. Nor should one assume that the worksheets that dominate many classrooms are indeed appropriate to "typical" children either—changing conceptions of best educational practice confirm that many of the tasks that frustrate and vex children with exceptionally high skills are also not the best for teaching students with more typical skills. A dramatic play activity, for example, could easily include all the students in a school, involving them in different ways in a wide range of learning experiences. This does not mean that all students would be doing the same thing: researching the background of the play, writing the play, designing scenery, organizing rehearsal schedules, designing and sewing costumes, helping others to learn their lines, composing and performing music—the list of many-layered tasks and opportunities is endless and could engage a whole range of student skills, interests, and performance levels. Arguing in support of gifted education that differentiation is the key and that "one size doesn't fit all" Gallagher (1997, p. 281) implies that all children will be "fitted" with equal care and attention and masks the fact that most children will get baggy, unfitted rags while a few get personalized tailoring or designer clothes.

Gifted education proponents argue that the regular classroom as currently organized and the curriculum as implemented is largely not amenable to change and that many teachers and students are hostile to gifted students, thus necessitating the removal of gifted students to a safe haven in which they can be with other students like themselves. I agree with the characterization of many (most?) classrooms as boring, uninspiring places filled with irrelevant curricula, unimaginative teaching, and a singular lack of community. But I find these classrooms unacceptable for all children, not just those identified as "gifted."

Deciding to remove some children from that setting in order to meet their putative educational needs elsewhere has significant implications. First, it communicates a sense of hopelessness and despair about the ability of teachers to change—about the possibilities of ever structuring our classrooms as inclusive, stimulating, multilevel, diverse learning communities that meet the needs of a wide range of students within a unified setting. Second, removing those children whose needs are not being met in the typical classroom makes it painfully clear that some parents (because of wealth, information, connections or power) have the possibility of removing their children (whose scores are used to justify that removal) whereas others do not. Most significantly, however, the removal of gifted children in order to provide them with an "appropriate" education leaves untouched the nature and quality of the regular education classroom. Arguing that school reform is hopeless justifies a mass exodus from public school education and intensifies support for privatized and semiprivatized education (charter schools, magnets, voucher programs, and segregated gifted programs).

By making a case for the ways in which gifted students are neglected, poorly served, often ridiculed and isolated, gifted education advocates argue that gifted programs are not inequitable at all but simply a way of providing the differential education that different students need and that to deny a specialized education to gifted students is no more just than denying such an education to students identified as "disabled" or "handicapped" (Marland, 1971).

Justifying the validity of the educational needs of gifted students by referencing the ways in which schools have been willing to or forced to meet the needs of students with disabilities (quite common among gifted educators) fails to take into account that models of special education are changing dramatically in this country and that segregated special education classrooms and even pullout programs are increasingly being replaced by more inclusive, push-in models of service provision (Stainback & Stainback, 1990; Villa, Thousand, Stainback, & Stainback, 1992). Declaring that "it's only fair" to provide services to gifted students doesn't tell us how those services should be provided, by whom, where, or in what relation to the services provided to other students. It is impossible to argue for justice for any particular group without discussing what constitutes justice for the majority. There are no absolute standards of justice; we must always know the context (political and economic) within which demands for justice are issued.

Justice arguments often fail to discriminate among the goals of equality of access, equality of services, and equality of outcome. The problem lies in determining which differences should be attended to and how. What is the difference between appropriate differentiation based on a valid difference and elitism or prejudicial treatment based on an assumed difference, a value-laden description of that difference, or assumptions about who can and cannot profit from such different treatment? Perhaps an argument for "equal treatment" should be recast as a need for "equally good treatment"or "equally responsive treatment." Arguing that gifted programs are "fair" is irrelevant and leads us away from a careful examination of the context in which such programs occur and the effects of gifted programs on children, teachers, parents, schools, and society.

Political and economic arguments for gifted programs are advanced at both local and national levels and are often coupled with justice arguments:

> For several years now, the term elitism has been used to undercut efforts to support young musicians and scholars who are gifted (somehow, though, we are able to support, often royally, elite athletes). Perhaps this common spirit goes back to a misreading of our nations's political credo, "All men are created equal." If so, it is not only a misreading of the intent of our Founders but a danger to the nation they brought into being. A nation that does not develop its gifted children is a nation that eats its seed corn. (Harris, 1995, p. 307)

Buttressing support for gifted programs in the name of democracy is an interesting twist; perhaps, as in Orwell's *Animal Farm*, some animals are simply "more equal than others." And although eating one's seed corn is admittedly foolhardy and short sighted, what about noticing that the majority of the population is already going hungry and that the crop, even if planted and harvested, will not be distributed equally to all?

Within large urban districts, particularly those characterized by impoverished, struggling schools and large, ethnically diverse populations, gifted programs (including gifted magnet programs) have served and have sometimes been promoted) as a way of stemming White flight; by providing segregated gifted programming, some White parents whose children are in a gifted program will remain within the district and the tax assessment area. Parental demand or an increased interest in gifted programming can be traced directly to the increasing racial integration of many schools and communities. Gifted programs often result in the resegregation of schools; White students in gifted programs and students of color in the "mainstream." The benefits provided by such programs—smaller classes, more enthusiastic teachers, a rich curriculum, more individualization—are all changes that would benefit all students. How could we look, instead, at the problems of poor urban schools and inadequate funding for education without resorting to resegregation in the name of quality education? What kinds of programs (schools within schools, multilevel curricula, mentorship programs) could be implemented that would meet the needs of a wide range of learners? What kind of nonexclusive, quality educational programming would keep parents of privilege within city limits?

In order for an inequitable system to maintain itself over time, several things are necessary. First, the system must be designed so that it is self-sustaining; that is, that it must perpetuate itself. The second requirement is that the discourse surrounding the system be controlled in such a way that people are socialized to accept the rightness or inevitability of the inequality.

Gifted education meets both these criteria. First, "giftedness" is defined as a percentage of the population, often the top 3% to 5%. Without standard criteria or external references, inevitably, 95% to 97% of the population is "not gifted"—and not entitled to the services provided to those who are labeled "gifted"—a tautological relationship. Second, gifted education is perhaps the most blatant example of the sorting and selection function schools serve within a capitalist society. Access to gifted programs controls access to elite colleges, which controls access to high-level, lucrative jobs. If everyone did well in school and everyone were on the honor roll, how would we know who the really worthy and deserving students are? How would we decide which students who would reap the benefits of advanced educational opportunities and increased earning potential? Because within our current economic system access and distribution are controlled so there isn't enough (time, money, resources) to go around, we must make a decision about who should receive these things, and identifying a small group of students as "gifted" allows us to do this without accusations of fairness or elitism.

And, in order to maintain such a system of inequality, we must socialize the participants—students, teachers, parents, community members—to accept such differentiation as inevitable, desirable or, at the minimum, not subject to discussion.

Consider these remarks from inside schools:

- A teacher is asked what she says to students who inquire, "When will I be going to that special program Michael goes to?" She responds, "Oh, they're good. They never ask."
- Another teacher, of sixth graders, responds, "Oh, by this age, they've stopped asking. They already know who's smart and who isn't."
- A new child in an elementary school stops the principal in the hall and says, "I heard about this thing some kids go to—how can I do that?" The principal confides to me, "I didn't know what to say. How could I tell him that he'll probably never go." A fourth-grade teacher who tries to honor multiple gifts and talents in her inclusive, highly diverse classroom shares with me, "I made the school psychologist come in and explain why only some children were going to the gifted program—I didn't want to be the one to have to explain it to them."
- Third graders are having a discussion. One girl makes a clever comment; her classmate turns on her, "You're not so smart. You don't go to [the gifted program]."

We witness in these comments how gifted education formalizes a system of meritocracy training. As the result of this training, students learn two things: who is smart and worthy of exciting opportunities and who is not, and when apparent unfairness or inconsistencies are noted, it is better not to ask. Not asking is "good"; making teachers uncomfortable with such questions is not good.

Because gifted education is putatively "fair"—anyone who tests high enough can get in—the differential treatment must also be fair. It would be poor sportsmanship, ungenerous, and petty to find fault with one's exclusion from a game from which one was eliminated "fairly." The damage of meritocratic thinking—people who are worthy deserve what they get and get what they deserve—is that it has the weight and power of educational objectivity and "fairness" to silence any protest or objection.

But in recent months, the public silencing of the discourse on giftedness has been broken. Within a two month period, *The Washington Post* did a special issue on education with a feature called, "The Best for the Brightest" (Kaufman, 1997); the *New York Daily News*' front-page story was entitled, "Gift Rap: Bright Kids, Big City Rift" (Sugarman & Chang, 1997), and the *Congressional Quarterly* devoted an entire issue to "Educating Gifted Students" (Jost, 1997). No longer the province of only educational theorists (Oakes, 1985; Wheelock, 1992), the discussion of gifted education and its fairness has taken to the streets. In the *New York Daily News*, a mother describes how one of her twins was admitted to the gifted program and the other denied and her agonizing decision, "Should I hold Jordan back and not sacrifice his brother's feelings or allow him to do the gifted program and get a much better education than Ari?" She laments, "They [the gifted class] get more money to spend and learn in classrooms with half as many students. Doesn't Ari deserve the same individual attention as his brother?" (Chang & Sugarman, 1997, p. 6).

The debate is impassioned and intense, and raises some of the most basic questions of racial and social class representation. At Johns' Hopkins Center for Talented Youth, a study of its class of 1992 revealed that of the 3,453 teenagers who completed summer camp sessions, only 1.4 percent were African Americans, and there were even fewer Hispanics. And yet the center refuses to change the rules of entry to the program. "Some have wanted us to use different or wider criteria for qualifications, but our experience with the SATs has been very good. That test has been an accurate predictor of which students can do the work and which cannot," says talent search director Linda Barnett (Kaufman, 1997, p. 35).

I believe that gifted education can be conceptualized as a form of educational triage—a decision about how different children will be treated that results in sacrificing and abandoning those considered less capable or less worthy of investment (Sapon-Shevin, 1994, 1996). Charles Derber (1995), in an article entitled "The Politics of Triage: The Contract with America's Surplus Populations," argues that

> economic triage can be seen in the withdrawal of viable employment or livable wages from sectors of the labor force, creating surplus populations with no economic prospects. Cultural triage is manifest in intellectuals' embrace of ideologies that explicitly justify the abandonment or elimination of surplus populations Political triage involves the explicit decision-making by government leaders to stop assisting—with money, housing, or other services—the abandoned groups. (p. 37)

Viewing the intersection between these other forms of triage and educational triage makes it imperative that we not conceptualize excellence and equity as competing agendas. If we do, we will all lose. We cannot withdraw resources from the most needy. Trickle-down economics has not worked, and neither has the belief that providing a good education to some children will somehow transform the education of all children. Rather, we must explore excellence within the context of equity. How can we achieve success for *all* students? Derber warns: "Triage, like war, perversely offers the promise of solidarity based on mobilizing against a common enemy, in this case the enemy within.... Until we respond to our needs for both economic security and moral awakening with a positive vision of community, the politics of triage will loom as a barbaric surrogate" (p. 88).

Certainly from a moral or ethical stance, such educational triage is indefensible. If we really believe in high-quality democratic public schooling, we must guarantee first-class educational nutrition for all students, not haute cuisine to the chosen few and stale peanut butter sandwiches to the majority.

REFERENCES

Chang, D., & Sugarman, R. (1997, March 23). Test scores split up twins. *New York Daily News*, p. 6.

Derber, C. (1995). The politics of triage: The contract with America's surplus population. *Tikkun, 10*(3), 37–43; 86–88.

Gallagher, J. J. (1997, March 28). Should public schools devote more resources to special programs for gifted students? Yes. In K. Jost, (Ed.), *The CQ Researcher, 7*(12), p. 281.

Harris, C. R. (1995). Wing and flame: Ability grouping and the gifted. In K. Ryan, & J. Cooper (Eds.), *Kaleidoscope: Readings in education* (7th ed. pp. 301–307) Boston: Houghton Mifflin.

Jost, K. (1997, March 28). Educating gifted students. *The CQ Researcher, 7*(12), 265–288.

Kaufman, M. (1997, February 2). The best for the brightest. *The Washington Post Magazine*, pp. 18–20; 32–35.

Marland, S. P., Jr. (1971). *Education of the gifted and talented* (2 Vols.). Washington, DC: U.S. Government Printing Office.

Oakes, J. (1985). *Keeping track: How schools structure inequality*. New Haven, CT: Yale University Press.

Sapon-Shevin, M. (1987). Giftedness as a social construct. *Teachers College Record*, 89(1), 39–53.

Sapon-Shevin, M. (1994). *Playing favorites: Gifted education and the disruption of community*. Albany: State University New York Press.

Sapon-Shevin, M. (1996). Beyond gifted education: Building a shared agenda for school reform. *Journal for the Education of the Gifted, 19*(2), 194–214.

Stainback, W., & Stainback, S. (1990). *Support networks for inclusive schooling: Interdependent integrated education*. Baltimore, MD: Paul H. Brookes.

Sugarman, R., & Chang, D. (1997, March 23). Gift rap: Bright kids—big city rift. *New York Daily News*, pp. 6–7. Villa, R. A., Thousand, J. S., Stainback, W., & Stainback, S. (Eds.), (1992). *Restructuring for caring and effective education*. Baltimore, MD: Paul H. Brookes.

Wheelock, A. (1992). *Crossing the tracks: How "untracking" can save America's schools*. [For the Massachusetts Advocacy Center]. New York: The New Press.

15

Desegregation

Marvin J. Berlowitz
Ivan Watts
University of Cincinnati

Although neoliberalism has its origins outside the United States, its basic premises support the traditional doctrines of laissez faire capitalism (also see Joel Spring on the notion of "choice," this vol.). In essence, neoliberal policies seek to advance the 'natural rights' of private corporations to freely pursue their rational interests—to maximize profit and market share. To protect and defend that freedom, corporations must negate whatever rights that the general public might claim to protection from the consequences of their pursuits. The public's exercise of those rights, as manifested in the labor movement, the civil rights movement, the environmental movement, and the women's movement, resulted in the same governmental regulations and social programs now under heavy attack in the era of neoliberalism. Programs ranging from Reaganomics to the Contract with America, buttressed by President Clinton's peculiar brand of accommodation, are dismantling the gains of the civil rights movement and even the New Deal. This chapter focuses on the undermining of the landmark *Brown* decision of 1954 by means of racist offensives in educational reform that use magnet schools as mechanisms for restoring a camouflaged dual school system. This dual school system functions to reproduce the division of labor in this "neoliberal" stage of capitalist development.

In more advanced nations such as the United States, neoliberal policies manifest themselves in an increasing polarization of living standards and wealth. The 1950s "Ozzie-and-Harriet icon of the White middle-class family living in racially segregated suburbia provided a reassuring image of stability and social cohesion that could support the liberal reform of the 1960s. Earlier generations of unskilled blue collar youth were able to drop out of school and find a safety net in the labor market of an industrialized economy insulated from the advances of the Scientific and Technological Revolution (STR) and unscathed by global competition. However, the 1970s ushered in the "deindustrialization" of the United States that restructured our nation's economy. Transnational corporations engaged in a massive export of industrial jobs to underdeveloped nations in the Pacific Rim, Taiwan, and the southern hemisphere, conspicuously excluding most of Africa. The U.S. economy was dramatically transformed from an industrial economy to primarily a service economy, with drastically reduced wages, benefits, and job security in all but the most privileged sectors of the society (Bluestone, 1984).

Education reformers attempted to explain away the massive loss of jobs by the formulation of an "economic imperative." According to this construct, declining educational standards resulted in our nation's losing its competitive edge in the global marketplace. The reality is that the export of finance capital by transnational corporations resulted in the permanent loss of large numbers of jobs constituting a form of "structural unemployment." If we set hourly wages and benefits for General Motors workers at 100%, the percentages for affiliates abroad are as follows: Brazil, 15%, Argentina, 16%, South Africa, 20%, Mexico, 35%, and even in Britain, 37%, Australia, 44%, and West Germany, 65%. Average hourly wages in assembly plants in electronics are 14 cents in Taiwan, 27 cents in Hong Kong, and 53 cents in Mexico (Astopovich, 1983). The utilization of prison labor in China is an even more enticing source of increased rates of profit. Thus it is more likely that lower wages and an elimination of benefits and the regulation of working conditions rather than a more highly educated workforce were the real incentives.

The result has been a general polarization of wealth and a specific "shrinking of the middle class"—the fall of the Ozzie-and-Harriet icon. A study of the period 1960 to 1987, appropriately entitled *Toward Two Societies*, comparing the wealthiest .5% of our population with the least wealthy 90% reveals significant disparities, including ratios of net worth of 125:1 and of mean incomes of 15:1. When wealth is restricted to stocks, bonds, and business assets, the ratio is an astounding 566:1 (Winnick, 1989). As for the middle class specifically, whether it is defined as having a family income ranging from $15,000 to $40,000 or $20,000 to $50,000, individuals in this group have been experiencing a steady decline in social mobility since 1973. The incomes of families in the United States rose fairly steadily in real terms from at least 1949 to 1973, pausing only briefly during recessions and reaching new heights during each expansion. Since 1973, however, the ground lost in recessions has not been recovered in the ensuing expansions. Thus the fraction of families with middle class incomes did indeed decline between 1973 and 1984, from 53% to less than 48% (Bradbury, 1986).

In light of the impact on families, the "family-values" rhetoric associated with champions of neoliberalism like Patrick Buchanan and his moral majority legions has a particularly ironic ring. Many families have been unable to achieve the living standards they had expected to attain at their current stage in life. The median income of 35- to 44-year-old husband and wife families with two children declined by 7.4% in real terms during the period 1973 to 1984, from $34,200 to $31,600. The stress on these middle class families also increased, because this decline would have been even greater if many of these families had not made the transition to dual income. Spouses were working or looking for work in 42% of husband and wife families in 1974 and 54% in 1985. The additional stress of job insecurity in the context of structural unemployment is an additional subjective factor (Bradbury, 1986).

The polarization of living standards and wealth among African Americans has been even more dramatic. "Race specific" reforms such as affirmative action have significantly increased the proportion of African Americans achieving middle class status in contrast to the vast legions of the "underclass" isolated in inner city ghettos. In several areas, African Americans have not only improved their social and economic positions in recent years but have made those improvements at a relatively faster rate than the reported progress of comparable Whites. The most notable gains have occurred in professional employment, income of married couple families, higher education, and home ownership. The number of African Americans in professional, managerial, technical, and administrative positions increased by 57% (from 974,000 to 1,533,000) from 1973 to 1982, whereas the number of Whites in such positions increased by only 36%. The fraction of African American families earning $25,000 or more (in 1982 dollars) increased from 10.4% in 1960 to 24.5% in 1982. Meanwhile, the number of African Americans enrolled full time at American colleges and universities nearly doubled between 1970 and 1980 (going from 522,000 to over 1 million). African Americans recorded a 47% increase in home ownership during the 1970s (from 2.57 million to 3.7 million), compared to a 30% increase for Whites (Wilson, 1996).

One of the ironies of the progress of the civil rights movement against discrimination in housing is that the polarization of living standards and wealth in the African American community is compounded by a social isolation of the underclass as a function of the migration of middle- and working class families from ghetto neighborhoods. Like most of the nation, the African American middle class is increasingly isolated from a vast "underclass" that has come into being as a function of structural unemployment.

The progress of middle class African Americans must be put into perspective by the realization that the vast majority of African Americans are locked into urban ghettos and excluded from the mainstream of the U.S. occupational system. For many decades, the structural violence imposed by centuries of cumulative institutional racism excluded much of the African American community from the safety net of industrial jobs available to many unskilled whites. As African Americans finally began to establish a foothold in the realm of industrial production, they were disproportionately affected by the "deindustrialization of America." Our current service-oriented economy that favors the educated professional, skilled, and technical worker with middle-class status abandons the majority of those remaining in urban ghettos to a life of hopelessness and a living standard and lifestyle more comparable to the masses in underdeveloped nations. In order to describe their plight, sociologists needed to develop a construct more precise than "lower class," hence the advent of the "underclass." Those included in this designation are "individuals who lack training and skills and either experience long-term unemployment or are not members of the labor force [sic], individuals who are engaged in street crime and other forms of aberrant behavior, and families that experience long-term spells of poverty and/or welfare dependency" (Wilson, 1996).

Despite the controversy surrounding the development of the construct of the underclass, explanations of its origins have nothing in common with various racist reactionary theories associated with eugenics, cultural deficiency, or pathology. Rather, the origins of the underclass are grounded in the structural economic transformations discussed throughout this chapter.

Declining wages and increasing unemployment are a growing problem for the entire nation. Although the growing wage inequality has hurt both low-skilled men and women, the problem of declining employment has been concentrated among low-skilled men. From 1987 to 1989, a low-skilled male worker was jobless 8 ½ and a half weeks longer than he in 1967 to 1969. Moreover, the proportion of men who "permanently" dropped out of the labor force was more than twice as high the late 1980s as it had been in the late 1960s. A precipitous drop in real wages—that is, wages adjusted for inflation—has accompanied the increases in joblessness among low-income workers. If you arrange all wages into five groups according to wage percentiles (from highest to lowest), you see that men in the bottom fifth of this income distribution experienced a 30% drop in real wages between 1970 and 1989 (Wilson, 1996).

The problem with unemployment figures is that they under-represent the plight of the underclass, because they represent only the proportion of workers in the labor force —that is, those who are actively seeking work. A better measure is the employment-to-population ratio, which corresponds to the percentage of adults 16 years old and older who are working. For example, whereas the unemployment rate for African American youth 16 years old and older was 34.6% in December 1994, compared with a White youth unemployment rate of 14.7%. Only 23.9% of all African American youth was actually working, compared with 48.5% of White youth.

In the context of the current structural unemployment, with prolonged periods of recession and shorter boom periods, tighter labor markets are of insufficient duration to draw significant numbers of underclass youth back into the labor force. In addition, urban underclass youth are geographically isolated from the large proportion of jobs that have permanently relocated from the central business district to the suburbs (Wilson, 1996).

Thus, the internal colony theory that has often been applied as a metaphor to African Americans is taking on new forms as the structural economic transformation manifests itself with a particularly racist cutting edge. The modest race-specific reforms that have proliferated the African American middle class provide the same tenuous stability and social cohesion as they do in a classic colonial situation.

Furthermore, it is the advent of the underclass that provides the United States with significant advantages in an intensifying global competition. Neoliberal policies that emphasize draconian cuts in welfare benefits along with the "workfare" program combine to provide the potential for an unprecedented depression of wages and the most vicious offensive against a trade union movement that is making dramatic attempts to revive itself. The move toward privatization of prisons and the subcontracting of prison labor in a nation that has the largest prison population among advanced nations even holds forth the promise of competition with prison labor around the globe. This prison population is so overwhelmingly drawn from the ranks of the African American underclass that it approaches the scale of genocide (Madhubuti, 1990; & Miller, 1992).

The works of the "new historical revisionists," such as Clarence Karier, Paul Violas, and Joel Spring, along with neo-Marxists, most notably Samuel Bowles and Herbert Gintis, all emphasize that public schools function to reproduce the capitalist social division of labor. Specifically, neoliberal policies in educational reform manifest themselves by reinforcing the oppression of the urban underclass. Thus, as magnet schools have functioned to dismantle the gains of the landmark *Brown* decision of 1954, they create a new camouflaged dual school system. This system consists of magnet schools that emphasize quality education juxtaposed to neighborhood schools that not only tend to remain racially and socioeconomically segregated but serve to further isolate the urban African American underclass.

It was Ronald Reagan, one of the pioneers of neoliberal policymaking, who successfully established the dominance of magnet schools in the realm of desegregation reforms. In 1984, the Reagan administration, along with the Magnet Schools Assistance Program (MSAP), began using magnet schools as a strategy for effecting out of court settlements for desegregation. Reagan's assistant attorney general for the civil rights division of the U.S. Department of Justice, Bradford Reynolds, provided reactionaries with the following assurances:

1. The *Brown* decision assuring desegregation as a means of assuring equality of opportunity would no longer carry with it the force of the Constitution but would become voluntary. Reynolds declared that, "the magnet school program can be an educationally sound program if you resort to magnet schools which enhance the curriculum of the educational program, as opposed to just putting a school in place as a magnet school device, if you will, to desegregate. Instead of doing that, if you use magnet schools which are educationally sound and do enhance the curriculum, then that kind of a voluntary program works" (Cited in Bryant, 1987, p. 3).
2. Reynolds provided further assurance by disassociating magnet schools from the letter and spirit of the *Brown* decision by saying, "Schools should not be utilized for the achievement of racial balance; they should be utilized for the development of educational purposes rather than exclusively for desegregation purposes".

The assurances of Reynolds were legitimated by the endorsement of magnet schools by the Task Force for Economic Growth along with the recommendations of the nation's governors, both associated with the National Commission on Excellence in Education (Bryant, 1987, p. 3).

The adoption of magnet school programs also received significant financial incentives from the Reagan administration through the Emergency School Aid Act (ESAA). In the first year of the ESAA's magnet school funding in 1976, only 14 districts applied. By 1980, over 100 district applications were received by the Department of Education, and 65 programs were funded at a total of approximately $30 million per year. By 1982, the number of urban school districts implementing magnet schools had grown to over 140, encompassing more than 1200 schools and programs (Blank & Messler, 1987). At a time when public education in general and urban school systems in particular are in financial crisis, the funding available for magnet school programs is a significant incentive.

The critics of magnet schools voiced a concern that they will contribute to the further isolation and oppression of the underclass. If magnet schools are to be showcases that attract students by means of superior facilities, higher achievement, and quality programs, then they are likely to do so at the expense of neighborhood schools.

Critics have expressed concerns about processes of "skimming" and "creaming" that will establish two classes of schools—one that demonstrates improvement and educational quality and another destined for neglect and decline. Magnet schools are attracting or "creaming" the best students and neglecting those with the highest concentration of disadvantaged and unmotivated students. The process is explicitly exacerbated by screening processes such as admissions requirements including standardized testing, interviews, and auditions. Complicated brochures describing the programs and eligibility requirements also favor middle class students (Hale & Maynard, 1987). Evan Clinchy makes the following prediction: "What we would almost inevitably end up with are two quite separate, thoroughly unequal, and de facto racially and economically segregated school systems" (Clinchy, 1991, p. 211).

This prediction was confirmed in a case study of the Cincinnati public schools during the academic year 1991—1992 (Watts, 1994). Cincinnati was one of those school systems that used a magnet school program in an out-of-court desegregation settlement. Ironically, those schools that were not included in the magnet school program were referred to as the Coalition of Innovative Schools (CIS). The result of Watts's study are summarized in Tables 15.1 and 15.2. Table 15.1 illustrates the function of the Cincinnati Public Schools in maintaining the isolation and oppression of the urban underclass in a camouflaged dual school system.

TABLE 15.1
Disparities in Race, Income, and Achievement Expressed in Percentages in CIS Schools Versus Magnet Schools

	CIS Schools	*Magnet Schools*
Low-income students (average for system) 68%	98.7%	55.9%
African American students (average for system) 62.5%	82%	54.5%
Students performing below the national average	88%	15%

Note. Statistics from Watts, 1994

Earlier in this chapter, it was pointed out that U.S. capitalists could improve their position in global competition by maintaining an internal colony of underclass youth whose exclusion from the labor market could serve to depress wages and threaten unions; and furthermore, that an underclass that is disproportionately channeled into the prison system could facilitate competition with nations such as China, which rely heavily on prison labor in the manufacture of exports.

Pushing students out of school could contribute to both of these objectives. Previous studies have demonstrated that suspension, expulsion, and mobility all contribute to a dynamic of structural violence that systematically pushes students out of school (Berlowitz & Durand, 1980; Garibaldi & Bartley, 1988). Table 15.2 illustrates that urban underclass youth in the CIS schools were the victims of the pushout syndrome.

In Table 15.2, it is interesting to note that African American males suffer disproportionate rates of suspension and expulsion in both CIS schools as well as magnet schools. It should be recalled that this same group is also victimized by much higher rates of unemployment and incarceration.

There was no significant disparity between the per pupil expenditures in CIS schools versus magnet schools. However, this measure is confounded by the fact that CIS schools were generally housed in older buildings that often required more repairs. Thus, some funds counted in the per pupil expenditure may have gone for repairs rather than for instructional purposes. However, it is significant that when the federal funds received from the Magnet Schools Assistance Program were calculated into the per pupil expenditure for the magnet schools, the per pupil expenditure was then 1.53%

higher than that of the CIS schools. Although this may not seem significant, these funds were earmarked for the implementation and equipping of innovative programs (Watts, 1994).

The implementation of neoliberal policies in the United States has generally manifested itself in an intensification of the polarization of wealth, living standards, and class stratification, including the shrinking of the middle class. The impact on the African American community has been even more dramatic. It has given rise to an intensely polarized internal colony in which the middle class has expanded whereas a vast urban underclass has come into being.

TABLE 15.2

Disparities in Rates of Suspension, Expulsion, and Mobility in CIS Schools Versus Magnet Schools Expressed in Percentages

	CIS Schools	*Magnet Schools*
In-school suspensions		
Total	43.5%	16.2%
African American/White males	28.6/5.1	9.7/1.7
African American/White females	8.6/1.1	4.2/.77
Out-of-school suspensions		
Total	14.8%	6.2%
African American/White males	9/2.4	3.9/.70
African American/White females	3/.38	1.6/0
Expulsions		
Total	2.25%	.23%
African American/White males	1/.25	.08/0
African American/White females	.75/.25	.15/0
Mobility*		
Total (average for the system) 10%	17.5%	4.5%

Note. *Mobility is defined as the proportion of students who transfer into and out of schools within the system. Statistics from Watts, 1994.

This new capitalist social division of labor is reproduced, in part, by neoliberal policies in educational reform that have served to undermine the progress toward equal opportunity central to the landmark Brown decision of 1954. As predicted by national critics and confirmed by the case study of the Cincinnati public schools, the proliferation of magnet school programs as a means of effectuating the settlement of desegregation cases facilitates the new social division of labor by creating camouflaged dual school systems.

REFERENCES

Astopovich, A. Z. (1983). *The strategy of transnational corporations*. Moscow: Progress.

Berlowitz, M. J., & Durnad, H. (1980). Beyond court ordered desegregation: School dropouts or student pushouts? In M. J. Berlowitz & F. Chapman (Eds.), *The United States educational system: Marxist approaches* (pp. 37–53). Minneapolis, MN: Marxist Educational Press.

Blank, R. K., & Messler, P. R. (1987). *Planning and developing magnet schools: Experience and observation*. Washington DC: Office of Educational Research and Improvement.

Bluestaone, B. (1984). *The deindustrialization of America: Plan closing, community displacement, and the dismantling of basic industry*. New York: Basic Books.

Bradbury, C. L. (1986, September–October) The shrinking middle class. *New England Economic Review*, 41–55.

Bryant, F. B. (1987). *Components of successful magnet schools*. Washington DC: Office of Educational Research and Improvement.

Clinchy, E. (1991). America 2000: Reform, revolution, or just more smoke and mirrors? *Phi Delta Kappan, 73*(3), 210–218.

Garibaldi, A. M., & Bartley, M. (1988). Black school pushouts and dropouts: Strategies for reduction. *Urban League Review*, 11, 227–235.

Hale, P. D., & Maynard, L. O. (1987). *Effective information dissemination and recruitment strategies for magnet schools*. Washington DC: Office of Educational Research and Improvement.

Madhubuti, H. R. (1990). *Black men: Obsolete, single, dangerous? The Afrikan American family in transition*. Chicago: Third World Press.

Miller, J. G. (1992). *Hobbling a generation: Young African American men in the criminal justice system in American cities*. Arlington, VA: National Center on Institutions and Alternatives.

Watts, I. (1994). *Desegregation and the rise of the camouflaged dual school system*. Cincinnati, OH: Masters degree project, University of Cincinnati.

Wilson, W. J. (1996). *When work disappears*. Chicago: University of Chicago Press.

Winnick, A. J. (1989). *Toward two societies: The changing distribution of income and wealth in the U.S. since 1960*. New York: Praeger.

16

Race

Joyce E. King
Medgar Evers College

> By conservative estimate, upward of fourteen million Africans were imported into the Atlantic slave trade. For every African that reached these shores alive, four died in the machinery of slavery at one end or the other of the traffic or in the dreadful Middle Passage. That's at least sixty million people lost from West Africa in less than four hundred years—genocide on a scale unmatched in recorded history. (Walker, 1979, pp. 43–44)

> ... *Everybody talking 'bout heaven ain't goin' there.*
>
> —African American Spiritual

Although anthropologists have called race "man's most dangerous myth" (Montagu, 1974), this societal discourse continues to function as the metanarrative of our times. Acknowledging that race is a "tricky social construction," Scheurich and Young (1997) observe that "to use it is to reinforce it as 'real', to naturalize it ... ; to not use it is to act as if race were no longer a significant differentiating variable in social life ... or in education and research" (p. 12, note 1). This chapter discusses this dominant metanarrative from an *altercentric* perspective, that is, from the liminal perspective; of "alterity" that results from the alter-ego status of conceptual blackness in relation to conceptual whiteness (S. Wynter, personal communication, March 18, 1994). Such a perspective locates the origins of the ideological belief system of race and current usages of this construct in the encounter of "Red," "Black" and "White" peoples during the founding of the Americas and the colonization of Africa, Asia, and other parts of the so-called non-White world (Drake, 1987). Emphasizing alterity in this way does not essentialize race as a reductive, fixed biological essence nor reify the mode of thought being critiqued. Rather, it provides a *perspective advantage* on race that deciphers how blackness matters in more specific and detailed ways. For example, Prager (1982) explains how this socially constructed dialectic, as cultural imagery, prescribes the status and identity of African Americans beyond the bounds of the normative (Eurocentric) conception of self and other:

> It is not the mere fact that blacks hold a dual identity in this country which has constrained achievement, to one degree or another, every ethnic group and racial group has faced a similar challenge. The black experience in America is distinguished by the fact that the qualities attributed to blackness are in opposition to the qualities rewarded in society. The specific features of blackness as cultural imagery are, almost by definition, those which the dominant society has attempted to deny in itself, and it is this difference between blackness and whiteness that defines, in many respects, American cultural self-understanding. For blacks, then, the effort to reconcile into one personality images which are diametrically opposed poses an extraordinarily difficult challenge. (p. 111)

According to Omi and Winant (1986), race is a "pre-eminently *socio-historical* concept" that has been "rigidly defined and enforced" (p. 60). "Much racial theory," Omi and Winant argue, "treats race as a manifestation or epiphenomenon of other supposedly more fundamental categories of sociopolitical identity," that is, "ethnicity, class and nation" (p. 66). Moreover, neoconservatives are appropriating the language of racial equality to avoid racial collectivity (Omi & Winant, 1986). Neoliberals, on the other hand, expect the "melting pot" ethnic paradigm of social amalgamation to resolve "the Negro problem." Liberals and progressives alike point to cross-group alliances and other forms of social "integration" (such as interracial marriage) as signs that Black culturalist or nationalist "separation" and "racial-thinking" are outmoded. The radical postmodernist paradigm rejects such "essences" in favor of hybridity and multiple identities and subjectivities.

Achieving cultural, not just racial, democracy, however, is not a dualistic choice between either integration or separation; it requires overcoming "blocked cultural pluralism" (Cruse, 1967). As Woodford (1993) notes regarding "the multicultural debate": "We are witnessing a strong attempt by White establishment figures (including 'non-whites') on both the left and the right to eradicate the distinction between Black group-consciousness, or nationalism and Black separatism" (p. 38). Semmes (1992) also observes that "the label 'segregation' is incorrectly applied to any group-focused effort by African Americans ... to rectify the past and current effects of White supremacist oppression and structured inequality" (p. 105). Because apparent social and political "progress," like affirmative action, encourages the belief that focusing on race, or "race-thinking" is obsolete, "paranoia about the threat of perceived essentialism" among theorists contributes to this evasion (Fuss, 1989, p. 1). Unexamined and untheorized, such notions of supposed "progress" prioritize a social ethic of integration that permits no understanding of the culture-systemic character and mode of functioning of "Race" as ideology. Since the invention of race and the mythology of White superiority that condoned four centuries of enslavement, people of African descent continue to experience racial oppression in genocidal proportions. Furthermore, America's urban gang wars, and Africa's so-called "tribal wars," such as those slave hunters fomented in earlier times, are rooted in the mythology and structures of White supremacy.

DuBois (1920) observes that the "discovery of personal whiteness" is a "very modern thing" (p. 20). Wynter's (1992b) analysis of the belief system of race draws attention to the medieval Judeo-Christian cultural model that preceded it. This cultural model was based on a binary opposition between the "Fallen Flesh" and "Redeemed Spirit" of the feudal laity and the clergy. The hegemonic scholastic order of knowledge that prevailed then normatively defined the laity (men and women enslaved to original sin and therefore excluded from "grace") outside the bounds of redemptive value. Within our present cultural model, conceptual blackness is to conceptual whiteness what the feudal laity was to the clergy. Like the laity, we cannot be saved by ameliorative educational reforms or declarations that race does not exist. Rather, the "specific value terms of the opposition" between blackness and whiteness must be transformed (Wynter 1992a). To find freedom the lay humanists broke with their hegemonic episteme and transformed the premises that "narratively instituted" their status in the feudal social order (Wynter, 1992a). This revolution of humanism brought in a new *secularized* order of knowledge that remains in our humanities and scientific disciplines. Unfortunately, this new episteme that permitted "Man" to be perceived in biological not theological terms, also made it possible, during the era of colonization and the slave trade, for instance, to perceive humans—indeed whole groups of people—as *naturally* inferior or superior races according to their genetic traits. Hacker (1994) comments on the persistence of this belief:

> The ascription of inbred incapacity is the ultimate expression of racism, the one hardest to eradicate, not least because most people will deny they hold this view. It is a shackle that Americans of African origin have had to bear since they were first brought here as slaves. Could there have been something, whites wondered, that rendered the black race suitable for bondage? This suspicion has by no means disappeared, even among those who wish they could rid themselves of it. (p. 459)

Educators and scholars along the political spectrum evade the culture-systemic premises of this metanarrative of race within our present order of knowledge and on which the social framework is founded. Academic scholarship and textbooks that purport to offer a "history of multicultural America" bear close scrutiny, because the strategy of "ethnicizing" the experience of all groups does not address fundamentally the problem of "Race." Likewise, ethnic studies and women's studies curricula that focus narrowly on group-specific knowledge and experiences or simply multiculturalize the curriculum without "an account of racialization processes" linked to the larger struggle for social change are inadequate to the urgent task we are facing (Omi & Winant, 1986, p. 64). Rather, as Morrison (1993) suggests, education should involve a rereading of U.S. national fiction to decipher the ways that race, in the form of invented "Africanism," functions dialectically in literature and in the social imagination of White writers and readers. Wynter (1992a; 1992b) suggests that a new theoretical synthesis is needed to rewrite knowledge in the academic disciplines to replace the status-organizing principle of "the gene" that is manifested in our narratively instituted biologistic conception of the human. This anachronism, which permits us to talk about "mixed" people and "African blood," must be replaced with a recuperation of "the Word," that is, sociogeny instead of ontogeny. Human freedom requires a new perception or conception of the human as an "always already" socialized subject instead of "Man" perceived as a genetically inferior or superior "natural organism."

The racial signifiers that have been used to mark the (natural) difference between "Blacks" and "non-Blacks" have advantaged European ethnic immigrants in the United States (but perhaps not the Gypsies in Europe). Thus, although Europeans have not always been perceived as one race,

Irish, Italians, and Jewish Americans are among those who have become "White" through specific historical and sociocultural processes (Banks, 1995). (Asians and Hispanics are deemed "honorary Whites.") The history of blackface minstrelsy, a form of popular entertainment during the last century, is illustrative. Native Whites widely equated the immigrant Irish with "blacks as an alien, subhuman, and brutal species" (Lott, 1993, p. 71). Minstrelsy, as the performance and institutionalization of racial difference, assisted a generation of Irish immigrants to develop a working class (White) consciousness and, by becoming "White," to escape their degraded status. It produced both psychic and pecuniary rewards for Irish immigrant "delineators," who blackened their faces, danced "Jim Crow," and sang in Black dialect, imitating Black people 's supposed imitation of Whites. Antagonistic socioeconomic class relations were thus "soothed" at the expense of the further degradation of Black people. Variations of such impersonation and cultural appropriation have continued—from Jewish jazz singer Al Jolson in the 1920s, Elvis Presley in the 1950s, to today's White rappers and "wiggers"—"White kids" in the suburbs "with Black attitude" (Rogers, 1994) who are the major consumers of hip-hop music. Part of the problem is that education does not prepare teachers or students to perceive the hegemonic interests involved in the appropriation of Black cultural forms—or the marginalization and invisibilization of Black people's historical contributions that have been absolutely essential to development of U.S. society. A student teacher's journal entry typifies the dysconsciousness (King, 1991) and miseducation of educators:

> I believe that people should vote if they are employed because there are so many people who are not employed and living off the tax dollars of those who are employed. So many people have the system all figured out with living on welfare and receiving more money with the more children they have.... Do they do anything to help our country become a better place to live? No. So why should these people who contribute nothing and actually milk the system for everything it's worth be allowed to vote?

An op ed letter to the *San Francisco Chronicle* (1994) opposing a bill concerning reparations for African Americans further illustrates the ignorance, cultural arrogance, and "counter-egalitarian" sentiments in the general population that reject "minority demands for 'group rights ' " (Omi & Winant, 1986, p. 127) to redress historical wrongs:

> [This is yet] another attempt by underachieving, separatist blacks to obtain by legal fiat what they are incapable of achieving through honest, hard work, persistent personal effort and willful assimilation.... Still another attempt to arrogate unto themselves the respect and benefits the rest of us have had to work generations for. HR 40 is nothing but societal extortion.... Now they want a cash payoff? How much tax money has been dumped down the rat-hole of social programs since LBJ's signing of the civil rights bill? ... Someone had better explain to them that when the internal parasite becomes too greedy, it kills its host and thereby commits suicide.... When in God's name, is enough, finally enough? (p. A–18)

The question these comments suggest is, "What is *wrong* with their education?" (Institute N.H.I., 1994). The belief structure these comments exemplify fails to connect four centuries of stolen Black labor and genocide with continuing societal injustice, including the disproportionate number of Black people who are unemployed and imprisoned. Also ignored are the corporate commercialization and exploitation of "blackness" that continue the contradictory historical pattern of "love and theft" (Lott, 1993) involved in the appropriation of Black cultural style in the media, sports, and other cultural industries. One highly visible example of this contradiction is the "be like Mike" breakfast cereal commercial targeted at White children that featured the megastar celebrity basketball player Michael Jordan. A national fascination with Black culture and style in America (Europe and Asia) coexists with a visceral, media-manipulated fear of young urban Black males, in particular, who are emulated and impersonated but also envied, criminalized, and jailed, if not beaten or killed (as if "no humans are involved").

The West has yet to come to grips with the holocaust of African enslavement and the enduring significance of race. Between 1884 and 1900, more than 2,500 people, of whom most were African American, were lynched in the United States (Banks, 1995). Woodson (1933) observed that such lynchings were made possible by forms of psycholgical lynching in the classroom, or miseducation, that elevated Whites and denigrated Blacks. The abduction of millions of people to feed the slave economy has been replaced by the abduction of consciousness in order to sustain the globalized market economy. What remains to be abolished is the belief system of race.

Myrdal (1972) concludes (quite incorrectly) that "Negro thinking is almost completely determined by white opinion—negatively and positively ..." (p. 474). As I have written elsewhere, "our ancestors confronted the slave system that denied their humanity" with the autochthonous knowledge that what the master was "talking 'bout" did not represent reality (truthfully or accurately), but instead represented the interests of the social category to which the master belonged. "Heaven" in the wisdom spirituals that enslaved African Americans created "represented an expanded universe and vision of equitableness that was also a moral and spiritual critique of the existing order" (King, 1990, p. 4). This phrase is taken from the spiritual that includes the line, "When I get to heaven, gonna put on my shoes and walk all over God's heaven." Like this perspective advantage illustrated by the spirituals, the music of politically oriented, progressive rap groups like Public Enemy—whose leader, Chuck D, helped to create an organization called Human Education Against Lies (HEAL)—indicates a critical awareness of social injustice and the miseducation that sustains it. A student think tank at Stanford University, Institute NHI. ("No Humans Involved"), "offers a *new vision* to ameliorate the systemic pathologies of racism, poverty, joblessness, and environmental degradation that plague us while also threatening the viability of the human species as well" (The acronym, "NHI," is used by judicial officials of Los Angeles in referring to cases of intrahomicide among young Black males of the inner cities [see Institute NHI, 1994].) A statement from their "Reader" is worth quoting at length:

> Given the contemporary global crises which confront the human species as a whole, the question that we pose is, "what is the connection between these crises and our system of education?" For, unlike present-day discourse on education which focuses on the type of education that our present world-system needs—i.e., a "multicultural" education for a "multicultural" world, or the "back-to-basics" approach to prepare a workforce to compete in the technological age—the question that we pose is not "what type of education our world needs," but more profoundly, *what type of world does our education* (including the 'multicultural' and 'back-to-basics' approach) *create?*" (Institute NHI, 1994)

In conclusion, a new vision of education is needed to address the origins and the social consequences of the belief that some "races" are biologically (e.g., genetically) superior to others (and more deserving of the planetary resources). Undeniably, there is only one race, the human race. However, the culture-systemic premises of value opposition in the metanarrative of Race must be abolished or blackness will remain as the conceptual other to the category of whiteness.

REFERENCES

Banks, J. A. (1995). The historical reconstruction of knowledge about race: implications for transforming teaching. *Educational Researcher, vol. 24*, (2), 15–25.

Cruse, H. (1967). *The crisis of the Negro intellectual: From its origin to present*. New York: Morrow.

Drake, S. C. (1987). *Black folk here and there* (Vol. I). Los Angeles: UCLA Center for Afro–American Studies.

DuBois, W. E. B. (1920). *Darkwater: Voices from within the veil*. New York: Harcourt, Brace & Howe.

Fuss, D. (1989). *Essentially speaking: Feminism, nature and difference*. New York: Routledge, Chapman & Hall.

Hacker, A. (1994, April 4). The delusion of equality. *The Nation* (13), 457–459.

Institute N.H.I. (1994). What is wrong with our education? Unpublished Manuscript.

Johnson, A. C. (1993). *Wade in the water: The wisdom of the spirituals*. Maryknoll, NY: Orbis.

King, J. E. (1991). Dysconscious racism: Ideology, identity, and the miseducation of teachers. *Journal of Negro Education*, 6(2), 1–14.

King, J. E. (1990). Introduction: Toward African liberation pedagogy. *Journal of Education, 122*(2), 3–4.

Lott, E. (1993) *Love and theft: Blackface minstrelsy and the American working class*. New York: Oxford University Press.

Montagu, A. (1974). *Man's most dangerous myth: The fallacy of race*. New York: Oxford University Press.

Morrison, T. (1992). *Playing in the dark: Whiteness in the literary imagination*. Cambridge, MA: Harvard University Press.

Myrdal, G. (1972). *An American dilemma: The Negro problem and modern democracy*. New York: Pantheon.

Omi, M., & Winant, H. (1986). *Racial formation in the United States: From the 1960s to the 1980s*. Boston: Routledge & Kegan Paul.

Prager, J. (1982). American racial ideology as collective representation. *Ethnic and Racial Studies*, 5, 99–119.

Rogers, P. (1994, January 10). White B-Boys in the burbs, or: Up against the mall. *Newsweek*, p. 49.

Scheurich, J. J., & Young, M. D. (1997). Coloring epistemologies: Are our research epistemologies racially biased? *Educational Researcher*, 26, 4–16.

Semmes, C. E. (1992). *Cultural hegemony and African American development*. Westport, CT: Praeger.

Walker, W. T. (1979). *Somebody's calling my name: Black sacred music and social change*. Valley Forge, PA: Judson Press.

Woodford, J. (1993). The Malcolmized moment: En-gendering and re-politicizing the X man. *The Black Scholar*, 23(3/4), 24–38.

Woodson, C. G. (1933). *The mis-education of the Negro*. Washington, DC: Associated Publishers.

Wynter, S. (1992a). *Do not call us 'Negros': How multicultural textbooks perpetuate racism*. San Francisco: Aspire Books.

Wynter, S. (1992b). Rethinking "aesthetics": Notes towards a deciphering practice. In M. Cham (Ed.), *Exiles: Essays on Caribbean cinema* (pp. 237–279), Trenton, NJ: Africa World Press.

17

Class

Steve Tozer
University of Illinois, Chicago

A major premise underlying this volume is that the agenda of educational reform in this country has been driven not primarily by a commitment to the development of human capacities but instead by the language and concerns of economics. The case of "class" presents something of a paradox. Here we have a social construct that is centrally economic in its origins, but one that has been nearly omitted from the educational conversation altogether. At best, class is admitted to the discussion only in a modified form—usually as a notion of "socioeconomic status" or SES. Socioeconomic status shifts the educational analysis away from the role of society's economic structure toward family backgrounds and practices, such as parents' education and numbers of books in the household. For the educator who understands its multiple meanings, however, the notion of class not only explains a great deal about why so many students and teachers struggle to achieve learning in the classroom; it also challenges the particular economic world-view underlying the contemporary school reform movement.

It is not surprising that economic class structure in the United States is not a part of the language of contemporary school reform. Serious discussion of class—or even its mention—is uncommon in the United States generally, where the popular myth is sustained that "we don't live in a nation of classes" (Fussell, 1992, p. 15). Americans readily recognize, of course, the existence of extremes of wealth and poverty, as they are portrayed in enduringly popular literature, film, and musicals such as *Les Miserables*, *The*

Grapes of Wrath, and *Oliver Twist*. There is even a popular syndicated newspaper cartoon, Pluggers, devoted to the working class experience in America. Yet the language of class analysis and class consciousness is missing from the mainstream media, the speeches of political leaders, school textbooks, educational policy making, and most scholarly treatments of education in the United States. Although it may be too strong to say that class is "America's forbidden thought," its range of use is certainly limited (Blumberg, cited in Fussell, 1992, p. 15).

The division of societies into classes of people by economic standing and social function extends far back into recorded history. In classical Athens, Plato recommended the division of society into the ruling, warrior, and laboring classes—but at the same time warned that the ruling classes should have no private economic interests to influence them. In Medieval Europe, the feudal economic and social structure were characterized by the divisions among nobility, clergy, and serfs, status divisions known as "estates." By the 1770's, before the industrial revolution in Europe, the language of "estates" gave way to the notion of "classes," and British economist Adam Smith had by 1776 identified three basic elements of the economic class structure: capital, landed property, and wage labor. At this same time, Benjamin Franklin sought to recruit European craftsmen to the United States by advertising that nearly all Americans were of the "middling sort," rather than sharply divided into classes. By the 1830s, self-consciousness of economic class and class interests was evident among laborers in both England and France. Soon thereafter, in 1848, Karl Marx and Friedrich Engels published the *Manifesto of the Communist Party* in London, in which they declared, "The history of all hitherto existing society is the history of class struggle," which has since become perhaps the best known single statement in the history of the social sciences.

Marx had a distinct notion of class as an economic construct that expressed the opposing economic interests of wage labor and capital—everything else, including the social relations of production, political power, and social status, followed from that fundamental economic class distinction. For Marx, the concept of class was partly defined by the power of one class over another, specifically the exploitive relations between the ownership and the laboring classes, thus "the history of class struggle." However, the language of *social status* and of *economic class* were often interchangeably used throughout the 19th century, and economist Max Weber sought to sort out differences between status and economic class in the early 20th century. Weber's efforts to keep these ideas separate and distinct were of limited influence, and mainstream American sociology has generally conflated these two terms.

A classic and influential example of this is W. Lloyd Warner's 1949 book *Social Class in America*, subtitled *A Manual of Procedure for the Measurement of Social Status*. Warner's analysis replaces Marx's two opposing classes with multiple status gradations: upper class, upper-middle class, lower-middle class, upper-lower, and lower-lower class. These gradations are based on family income, educational attainment, occupation, house type, and dwelling area. Warner's work contributed to the shift away from thinking about class as an economic concept emphasizing the exploitation of one class by another toward a notion of class as social status, one that we now often characterize in educational literature as SES. That important shift came about after the organized labor movement in the United States had peaked in the 1930s, and the American Socialist Party had dissipated, before World War II. After the war, legislation continued to contain social class conflict in the United States effectively, and high-wage blue-collar jobs helped shift the concerns for inequality away from class divisions to divisions marked by ethnicity and gender (Aronowitz, 1997, p. 194).

The Marxian notion of class was based on division of people into two classes according to their different places in the *production* of goods—either owning the means of production or working for those owners. The SES concept is based more on the idea of people as *consumers* of goods, defined by their incomes, their possessions, and their ability to buy social goods, such as education (Scott, 1996, p. 15). As the 21st century approaches, not only has the economic concept of class been replaced by attention to social status, even the attention to SES often has been replaced by attention to ethnicity, gender, sexual orientation, and other sources of inequality and identity formation.

Just as Marx's concept of class differs from today's notion of SES, so it is important to recognize that these two terms differ from income or wealth, though again, all of these terms are often used as if they meant the same thing. The "middle class" is often defined by income level, for example, rather than by a more complex understanding of differences between white-collar and blue collar labor in the economic system of capitalism.[1] Differences in income and wealth are not unimportant, of course. It is clear

[1]For an illustration of these different uses, see the discussion of the Black middle class defined by income in Sam Roberts' *Who We Are: A Portrait of America Based on the Last U.S. Census* (1995) versus the Marxist analysis of the middle class throughout Erik Olin Wright's (1997) *Class Counts*.

that families of different income levels have different access to good neighborhood schools. When differences in educational achievement are reported for different ethnic groups, as they often are in the current reporting on school reform, it is often differences in income and wealth that lie behind those ethnic differences. In the mid 1990s, for example, over 39% of all White families, but only 20% of Black families and 19% of Hispanic families, earned over $50,000 annual income, modestly above the national median of $38,782. This means that over 23 million White families earn over $50,000 annually, whereas just over a million Black families and under a million Hispanic families earned above this figure. At the other end of the income range, 13% of all White households earned below $15,000, whereas a third of all Black families and 30% of all Hispanic families fall into this low-income category, barely above poverty level (*American Almanac*, 1997, p. 466). Just as disturbing is that fact that 47% of all family income earned is earned by the top 20% of families—leaving the remaining 80% of the population to share the remaining 53% of family income—with the lion's share going to the next quintile (*American Almanac*, 1997, p. 467). Because family income corresponds closely with educational attainment—more closely, in fact, than ethnicity does—these figures begin to explain differences in different ethnic groups' educational attainment. Even Warner in 1949 recognized that high school dropout rates correspond so closely with family income as to be essentially SES determined (Warner, 1949, p. 29; see also Brantlinger, 1993, p. 41). However, these relationships between family income and educational attainment are not addressed in the current school reform language.

Family wealth is distributed even more unequally in the United States than family income. Family wealth refers to the net dollar value of the assets less liabilities held by a household at one point in time (Wolff, 1995, p. 5). Inequality in U.S. wealth distribution is, in the 1990s, at its highest point since the stock market crash of 1929, with the top 1% of wealth holders today controlling 39% of household wealth and 49% of financial wealth. *Financial wealth* is the wealth held by a household apart from marketable goods, such as house and auto, and the top quintile of U.S. society holds 94% of the total financial wealth, the second quintile nearly all the rest. In the 1920s, wealth inequality was lower in United States than in Great Britain and comparable to Sweden. By the late 1980s, however, the situation had reversed, with the inequality in the United States exceeding both those nations. Europe, once regarded as highly stratified in comparison to the United States, now appears to be a land of equality in contrast to the United

States, which is marked by "a widening fissure separating the strata within our society" (Wolff, 1995, pp. 7, 10, 21, 27). The "widening fissure" is divided unequally along lines of race and ethnicity as well. The Federal Reserve Bulletin reports that in the early 1990s, White families had a mean net worth of $58,500 and half of all White families had a net worth over $203,000. Non-White mean family wealth was $4,000, with half exceeding $45,000 (Tozer, Violas, & Senese, 1998, p. 372).

Although it is tempting to attribute these massive inequalities of income and wealth to educational differences among different population groups, the data do not support this interpretation. For example, the high school graduation gap between Blacks and Whites has narrowed dramatically since the 1960s, but poverty levels for Blacks have remained two to two-and-a-half times the poverty levels for Whites. Explaining the persistence of these income and wealth disparities between different population groups requires an understand of how class stratification works in America and how race discrimination serves to place people of color into lower economic strata. Two authors working on this project in the late 1990s are Stanley Aronowitz (1997) and Erik Olin Wright (1997).

Thus far, this chapter has treated differing but intertwined conceptions of economic class and social status, with attention to related concepts such as wealth and income. These differing conceptions draw attention to different features of contemporary society. Attention to wealth versus income differences, for example, reveals much greater inequality in society than attention to income alone. Emphasis on a Marxist conception of economic class draws attention not to how income is distributed but, more fundamentally, to how production is structured in the hands of an ownership and a working class. Such a focus also draws attention to opposition between these two classes and how power is exercised through the government, the economy, and schools to maintain the class structure. Emphasis on SES, on the other hand, focuses on how children from different backgrounds have different life chances in the educational and economic system. High SES tends to ensure good educational opportunities culminating in at least a college education, whereas low SES tends to make such outcomes unlikely. But attention to SES or to income or wealth does not provide much *explanation* for why these educational outcomes should differ so greatly. For that, a deeper analysis of class is necessary.

PROBLEMS WITH THE PREVAILING VIEW

The prevailing stance toward the discussion of class in educational reform is to ignore the concept in favor of other social groupings that do not challenge the basic power relations of capital versus laboring classes. These other groupings include gender, SES or race, or ethnicity—all of which are used to indicate how well or poorly different segments of the population are achieving various educational goals. Thus, the *National Educational Goals Report*, distributed nationwide, presents tables on disparities in Children's Health Index by race and ethnicity; high school completion rates by race and ethnicity; disparities in achievement levels in math, reading, science, history, and geography by race or ethnicity and sex; but nothing on the economic conditions that would help us understand why some groups perform better than others. Similarly, in explaining the reasons for the gap between U.S. students' achievement and the achievement of students from other industrialized nations, the primary reasons given in the report are the less advanced U.S. curriculum, weaker instruction, and inadequate teacher preparation in the United States (National Educational Goals Panel, 1997a, pp. 35–50).

Here again, attention to economic stratification, greater in the United States than in virtually any other industrialized nation, would shift the discussion significantly. Although the report does not provide the necessary information, high-income children in the United States are already achieving the educational goals of Goals 2000, whereas low-income students are not, and limiting the data to race or ethnicity and gender obscures this. For example, compared to White non-Hispanics, Asian Americans drop out of high school somewhat less, African Americans drop out slightly more, and Hispanic students drop out twice as often as the White comparison group. Girls drop out slightly less than boys. Much greater disparities appear, however, when SES is examined. Taking all ethnic groups and both genders together, low-SES students drop out *six times as often* as high SES students and almost three times as often as middle-SES students. Similarly, Whites are more than twice as likely to complete college as Blacks, but high-SES students, regardless of ethnicity, are more than six times as likely to complete college as low-SES students and more than twice as likely as middle SES students (*Chronicle of Higher Education*, 1997, p. 14).

The efforts of educators, social scientists, and the public to understand the educational system are severely truncated by the reluctance of the school reform establishment to recognize the importance of economic stratification in shaping educational experiences and outcomes for people of different ethnic groups. *This does not diminish the importance of ethnicity and gender in explaining school outcomes.* But to discuss these variables without showing how economic inequality interacts with them is to miss a much more penetrating analysis.

Focusing on the economic origins of educational problems, however, leads in directions that legislators and the business community in our society are not prepared to take: addressing the economic inequalities that underlie our educational shortcomings. It is much more attractive for those who benefit most from economic inequality to engage in school reform efforts rather than in efforts that would address economic inequality itself.[2]

One of the most important efforts to understand schooling through class analysis was Bowles and Gintis' (1976), *Schooling in Capitalist America: Educational Reform and the Contradictions of Economic Life*. Bowles and Gintis argued that the schools produce unequal learning outcomes primarily because schools are structured to serve an economic system marked by unequal property and power relationships. The hierarchical social relations of the capitalist workplace are reproduced in the school, and children are prepared for the unequal social relations of the workplace by the unequal social relations of the school, in which children early learn that some children are more deserving of reward. Although schools legitimate inequality and prepare people for governing and governed roles in society, Bowles and Gintis continued, they also can help produce a certain amount of resistance and rebelliousness to that social order (p. 13). Other researchers have demonstrated that tracking practices, curriculum choices, and instructional approaches all vary with economic class and SES in public schools, and that resistance to schooling is heavily influenced by class. The result is that, in general, working- and poverty-class children experience very different education from that which the propertied classes receive (see for example Anyon, 1981; McLaren, 1998; Spring 1989; Willis, 1977).

TOWARD A MORE USEFUL UNDERSTANDING OF CLASS

"In recent years," writes historian Patrick Joyce (1995), "the concept of class has come under increasing scrutiny as a means of explaining both the past and the present" (p. 3). The influences that have led to the reconsider-

---

[2]This point has often been made. See for example Ellen A. Brantlinger's (1993) *The Politics of Social Class in Secondary School* (p. 41).

ation of class include the erosion of the laboring classes in postindustrial society; expansion of work for women, largely in parttime service economy jobs; increasing under- and unemployment; the shift from production to consumption as bases for collective and personal identity (you are connected to others by what you buy, not what you do for a living); and a postmodern decentering of power and authority, including Foucault's notion that power is omnipresent, located in all sorts of social relations, and that power creates knowledge, not knowledge power (Joyce, 1995, pp. 3–8). In the face of these challenges to the traditional Marxist conception of class, it appears that the historical moment for class analysis has passed. Yet the concept of class as an economic category that identifies competing interests in an unequal social order is one that helps us come to distinctive insights that are not readily available without class as a conceptual tool.

It has become almost axiomatic, for example, that teachers need to understand or at least try to take into account the cultural backgrounds of their students if they wish to teach effectively. By "cultural backgrounds" we typically mean such things as a particular ethnic group's cultural values, language, practices, ways of interacting, and perhaps learning styles. We might even mean socioeconomic status, though usually only in conjunction with ethnic differences. We rarely mean class as Marx meant it, as a way of understanding relations of domination and subordination in the economic structure and therefore the social and political structure as well. Without that attention to relations of domination and subordination as they reside in economic class, the attention to "cultural backgrounds" of students is inadequate on two counts. First, culture is importantly influenced by economic class in contemporary society, and second, school cultures devalue the knowledge and practices of the working and poverty classes while privileging the knowledge and practices of the propertied classes (and the middle class that ties its fortunes to the propertied class).[3]

Educators must acknowledge the impact of economic class on culture—the manner in which one's class experience significantly shapes a person's cultural knowledge and practices, regardless of ethnicity. One's cultural experiences *are* shaped by gender and ethnicity, of course, but also by the ways of knowing, speaking, and valuing that are sharply chiseled by class stratification. Working-class African American children, in general, are exposed to very different life experiences, and sustain very different life

[3]For a detailed treatment of the placement of the middle class in contemporary cultural analysis, see Erik Olin Wright's (1997) *Class Counts* (p. 41).

aspirations, from their propertied-class African American peers, who are almost guaranteed to grow up in different neighborhoods, attend different schools, speak with different linguistic patterns, and so on.

Not only do students—White, Black, Hispanic, or Asian—from different economic classes have different cultural backgrounds, but they are perceived by dominant institutions such as schools in different ways. That is, the knowledge, behavior, and language patterns of the middle- and upper-middle class child, regardless of ethnicity, tend to be valued by the school, whereas the language and practices of the working-class child tend to be devalued. "Standard English," for example, is a middle- and propertied-class linguistic system into which some of us are born and some of us are not and that the school values at the expense of other linguistic systems.

This points to an important theoretical difference between the "multiple gradations" or SES approach to social class as opposed to the notion of economic classes in opposition to one another. The SES approach is easily compatible with a "cultural-deficit" understanding of low-income students. In this explanation, low-income children do poorly in school because their "cultural backgrounds" ill-prepare them to succeed, and the source of the problem lies therefore in the home, an environment deficient in the language and practices necessary to support school success.

An oppositional economic class analysis, however, reminds us of a different way of understanding the experience of working-class children and youth in schools, one in which their cultural practices and language are subordinated to the dominant class that governs the schools. This is the second major problem, then, of looking at "cultural backgrounds" without taking class seriously: The knowledge, language, and practices of one class are dominant and valued; those of the other classes are subordinate and devalued. Instead of a cultural deficit explanation for persistent school failure of low SES children, we can see the possibility of a cultural subordination explanation that is grounded in relations of domination and subordination in the economic and political order of society.

Origins of differences in student learning are found not simply in family backgrounds, understood as different income levels or different ethnic origins, but in an unequal social and economic structure that is rooted in economic class differences as well as in differences of race or ethnicity and gender. These economic origins of learning differences remain unchallenged by school reform measures that focus on the symptoms, but not the causes, of educational inequality. Thus, when the National Educational Goals Panel emphasizes young children's readiness to learn, school completion, student academic achievement, and adult literacy, it should be remembered that all of these (and others as well) are issues that cannot be adequately understood without an understanding of how economic class conditions them.

Because the logic of public education in a democratic society demands a fundamental commitment to equality of education, the professional ethics of teaching are grounded partly in democratic ideals. Teachers and other educators need to understand class if they are to serve the ethical ideals of their profession well. Class relations constitute a distinctive source of unequal power relations—a distinctive source of inequality. Coupled with the influences of other sources of power relations, such as ethnicity, race, and gender, the power relations of class become more complicated and influential in the lives of students. Even ownership-class Black students experience discrimination in school and society, for example, and working-class White students experience discrimination of different kinds. For working class Black students, these sources of power relations interact.

The concept of class can therefore be an empowering one for teachers and students, because they can learn how class operates in the classroom to enable some students and disable others. It reminds teachers and students that problems in learning often may not reside in some deficiency in the student or in the student's background but in the interaction between a class-based school culture and the class-conditioned cultures from which students come. So understood, teachers can pursue ways of teaching that respond to the class differences among their students and that recognize and mediate the conflicts between the school's class-based norms and the students' values, knowledge, and practices.[4]

REFERENCES

American almanac, Statistical abstract of the United States 1996–97. (1997). Austin, TX: Hoover's.

Anyon, J. (1981). Social class and school knowledge. *Curriculum Inquiry, 2*(1), 3–42.

Aronowitz, S. (1997, Summer). Between nationality and class. *Harvard Educational Review, 67*(2).

Bigelow, W. (1990). *The power in our hands*. New York: Monthly Review Press.

Bowles, S., & Gintis, H. (1976). *Schooling in capitalist America: Educational reform and the contradictions of economic life*. New York: Basic Books.

Brantlinger, E. A. (1993). *The politics of social class in secondary school*. New York: Teachers College Press.

---

[4]One intersting effort to develop curriculum around recognition of the significance of class is William Bigelow's (1990) *The Power in Our Hands*.

Chronicle of Higher Education 1997–1998 Almanac Issue. (1997, August 29) 44(1).
Fussell, P. (1992). *Class: A guide through the American status system*. New York: Touchstone.
Joyce, P. (1995). *Class*. New York: Oxford University Press.
McLaren, P. (1998). *Life in schools* (3rd ed). New York: Longman.
National Educational Goals Panel. (1997a). *The national educational goals report: Building a nation of learners*. Washington, DC: U.S. Government Printing Office.
National Educational Goals Panel. (1997b). *The national educational goals report summary: Mathematics and science achievement for the 21st century*. Washington, DC: U.S. Government Printing Office.
Roberts, S. (1995). *Who we are: A portrait of America based on the last U.S. census*. New York: Times Books.
Scott, J. (1996). *Stratification and power*. Cambridge, England: Polity Press.
Spring, J. (1989). *The sorting machine revisted*. New York: Longman.
Tozer, S. E., Violas, P. C., & Senese, G. (1998). *School and society: Historical and contemporary perspectives* (3rd. ed.). New York: McGraw Hill.
Warner, W. L. (1949). *Social class in America: A manual of procedure for the measurement of social status*. New York: Harper & Brothers.
Willis, P. (1977). *Learning to labour*. Lexington, MA: D.C. Heath
Wolff, E. N. (1995). *Top heavy: The increasing inequality of wealth in America and what can be done about it*. New York: New Press.
Wright, E. O. (1997). *Class counts*. Cambridge, England: Cambridge University Press.

18

Gender

Kathleen Bennett deMarrais
University of Georgia

What do we mean by gender? How do we construct gendered identities? What role do family and friends play in this construction? How do our cultural institutions and practices, particularly schools, shape our gendered identities? What roles do schools play in this process? This chapter addresses these questions through the story of Lauren (a pseudonym) and her experiences of identity construction. Following Lauren's story, I explore gender in relation to the realities of educational reform in today's schools. I conclude with suggestions for ways we might transform current notions of gender in school sites to work toward collectively constructing lives that are more truly free of current capitalist dictates.

First, a clarification of terms. The words *sex* and *gender* do not carry the same meaning; they are not interchangeable. *Sex*, a visible and usually permanent identifying attribute acquired at birth, refers to the physical characteristics associated with being male or female. *Gender* is a more inclusive term that refers not only to physiological characteristics but to learned cultural behaviors and understandings. Joan Wallach Scott (1988) reminds us that the word "gender"

> becomes a way of denoting 'cultural constructions'—the entirely social creation of ideas about appropriate roles for women and men. It is a way of referring to the exclusively social origins of the subjective identities of men and

> women. Gender is, in this definition, a social category imposed on a sexed body. (pp. 31–32)

Recently, the term *gender* has been used to refer to women or women's issues. However, it is important to remember that gender refers to social categories for both men and women.

Children's gender is shaped as they are socialized by families, friends, educators, and other cultural and market forces as they learn what constitutes "culturally appropriate" gender roles. Girls and boys learn different patterns of behaviors. By 6 or 7 years of age, children have a clear idea about gender roles, prefer sex-segregated play, and tend to strive to conform with stereotypic gender roles. Corporate America continues to provide sex-role stereotyped toys and clothing that reinforce traditional notions of gender and limit children's explorations into alternative roles for themselves. Not only are the manufactured toys stereotypic, they tend to be at the extremes of gender socialization so that "boys' toys" are primarily vehicles and toys of destruction such as weapons and action figures whereas "girls' toys" are dolls, stuffed animals, and accessories that encourage caregiving and homemaking.

Children watch television and movies, listen to popular music, and are confronted daily with advertisements—in magazines, in newspapers, on TV, on buses, and in school. Popular culture transmits messages about the values, behaviors, and communication styles of men and women, generally in stereotyped and often derogatory forms. We need only flip through the pages of popular magazines to see the gender models offered to young people. Young girls learn early in life that their bodies define who they are as individuals. The most highly valued bodies, both male and female, in this patriarchal culture are tall, able-bodied, lithe, and usually adorned with blue eyes and blond hair. This European American notion of what constitutes beauty is consistently sold to young people through the media and is often reinforced by families and peers. Unfortunately, children and young adults who do not fit into these models struggle to develop their identities within these racist, restrictive, and usually impossible frames.

Although there is certainly human agency in ways people develop and define themselves within their social circles, there is overwhelming pressure from the marketplace shaping our gendered notions of ourselves. We can easily see how this capitalist, patriarchal culture colonizes individuals as they construct their gendered identities. I illustrate this process through the story of Lauren, whose experiences reflect some of the central struggles of young women in U.S. culture today. Her story is interesting because it has evolved over the past 2 decades after the women's movement and passage of Title IX and during an era of educational reform in the United States. In some ways Lauren has benefitted from these events; in others she is the recipient of mixed messages and capitalist mythology. Although Lauren certainly does not represent all young women, she does provide a personal story through which we might reflect on the construction of gender in late 20th century American culture, where patriarchy and capitalism reach deep into individual lives.

LAUREN'S STORY

The Myth of Educational Equality for Women

Lauren is a 20-year-old college student from a White, working-class background. She grew up in a family in which she received mixed messages about her educational opportunities and goals. A major message was that she needed to get a "good education" in order to be able to be independent and a consumer of all the material goods society has to offer. School reinforced these messages; she came to understand she had an equal opportunity to be successful if she worked hard in school. The more education, the higher status she might be able to achieve in the economic hierarchy. Her school experiences reinforced an ideology that women are equal and can achieve anything they want in life. She describes her beliefs about education:

> My philosophy is that an education is the most important thing you can have and this doesn't just mean from school. I want to be a "human sponge" and learn as much as possible from EVERYONE! ... Honestly, just having the word "Dr." in front of my name is one of my ultimate goals.

Lauren's parents believe that an expensive private school education is worth their sacrifices. They want a safe, conservative environment that supports their values so sent her to a college that is White, upper-middle class, and Republican. During her first year at this school, Lauren found that she was quite different from her wealthier peers in both political and social perspectives. She found she was one of a handful of Democrats who openly critiqued the lack of diversity in the student body. She became heavily involved in women's issues through a leadership role in a campus sexual assault response team. Her responsibilities include giving presentations about date rape, dating violence, sexual assault, and harassment. Despite the limitations of her college social environment, she is able to focus her energies on social and political issues that are important to her.

The Beauty Myth[1] and Self-Esteem

While she was being socialized in the myth of educational equality for women, she was also being socialized into the implicit cultural understanding that women's bodies are of primary importance. Through her family, peers, and all forms of media, she learned that unless she was slim and attractive, she'd face major barriers in her personal life. After a childhood of playing with Barbie dolls, she entered her teen years concerned with staying thin and keeping up with the latest clothing fashions. During high school she ran with the preppy crowd and earned extra money by working at a clothing store catering to young people, a job that required her to maintain a look that would help to sell clothes. As a senior in high school she was popular with the "right" crowd, had a boyfriend on the football team, and conformed to the dictates of the youth culture around her—a culture largely controlled by marketing. Her social life was central to her concerns.

As a college freshman, Lauren gained 15 pounds, changing her appearance from very thin to healthy. With this weight gain, coupled with difficulties in relationships, her self esteem began to falter. She describes an incident that happened at the completion of her second year of college that illustrates the fragility of her self-esteem within the context of assaults to her appearance:

> When I was at school, I was having some serious stomach problems (I think I have an ulcer). Anyway when I came home, I went to my family doctor (the same one who called me FAT a year earlier). Without even hearing what I had to say, he yelled at me and told me that I was gaining yet more weight and diagnosed me within 2 minutes. Whenever I tried to talk, he cut me off and played me off like I was some meaningless person. But instead of speaking up when I had the chance and telling him to stuff his fucking attitude, I just shut up, and later when I went home I cried my eyes out for 2 hours. Granted, I did switch doctors and now have a female doctor who is treating me excellently, and I am planning on filing a complaint with my insurance company. There's no satisfaction there because I am not standing up for myself by standing up to him. Not kidding, this shit really takes a toll on my self-esteem.

---

[1]Borrowed from the title of Naomi Wolfe's (1987) book of the same name.

Lauren recently confronted the very issue she worked on through the sexual assault response team—sexual harassment. She describes this incident:

> To make money this summer, I was working at a small cafe. At first it was cool; I learned how to make a killer cafe mocha. But then I started taking some serious shit from my boss. He was working me 13-hour days everyday and worse than that, he was getting "fresh" with me as my mom would say. At first he would rub my hands and arms, then he kept trying to massage my shoulders and the last straw was that he slapped my ass. I hate it. I hate it so much.... This was, unfortunately, not my first experience with sexual harassment and most definitely won't be my last, and what I hate more than these shitheads is ME. The way I act when put in the situation. I mean, I can talk a good talk, but when it comes down to it, I don't say anything when put in the situation. I just smile. I smile this ridiculous, flaky, unintelligent smile. I really hate me sometimes. I have all these ideas and goals but a person, usually a man, can knock me down to a 5-year-old little kid in about 5 seconds.

Here we see Lauren beginning to experience the type of harassment that many women in this culture face in work environments. She lives in a patriarchal world where men in positions of power intrude on her body as well as her sense of self. At this point in her life she feels unable to defend herself and simply quits the job for a safer work environment.

The Myth of the Perfect Family, or Living Happily Ever After

Related to the beauty myth, Lauren was socialized into the cultural "norm" that she would grow up to want a heterosexual marriage and a suburban home complete with children. During high school, interest in and talk about males dominated her relationships. Although she had good relationships with girlfriends, these friendships often centered around discussions about "boys." A series of relationships with young men in high school and college turned out to be unsuccessful in that the young men viewed her as the caregiver or placed themselves in power positions to instruct her as to what she should be doing. She reflects on these relationships:

> You know, sometimes, I think I'm going through a bit of an identity crisis. Mostly when it comes to guys. My first "real" boyfriend was a major league asshole who got off on talking down to me, and my next boyfriend was an

> abusive drug addict who has now dropped out of college. And every guy in between was just a jerk. I don't know, what does this say about me?

Clearly, Lauren blames herself for what she considers poor choices of partners. Currently, Lauren believes she must choose between herself and getting a good education or working at a relationship with a man. She has made a commitment to concentrate on herself and let relationships with men wait. As we see in the following quote, she seems satisfied with her choice and is questioning the cultural myth of the perfect family as a possibility for her own life:

> I have been totally single for about a year now, and honestly I like it. I'm not really lonely, because I keep so busy and its cool not having some dopey guy around acting like he's better than me. I even think I'm beginning to like myself better—maybe because I'm concentrating on me and not we. I get strength from doing things for myself like taking long trips alone or walking around the city or anything. I'm beginning to realize that I'm not going to have the "normal" life like [my brother]. I'm not going to meet my mate in college and marry as soon as I have a secure job and then start a family soon after. I'm not going to have the "perfect" house and car and kid. And you know what? I'm fine with that....So what if I don't meet Mr. Right. Who makes the rules, who says I have to get married or have kids?

Although Lauren is attempting to create her life on the belief that a good education will enable her to achieve her professional goals, she is also caught within a culture in which women are treated as sexual objects, property, or second-class citizens. She's resisting these latter messages but with little support from the people, institutions, or culture around her.

Implication of Lauren's Story for Schooling

Schools are sites in which conservative economic and sociocultural patterns continue to thrive. Like Lauren, young people learn to participate in a capitalist system in gendered ways. Men as well as women participate in social experiences in which restricted notions of gender are modeled and learned. Schools provide little critique of the ways capitalism and patriarchy play out in individual lives. Ironically, the women's movement of the 1960s and the federal gender equity legislation has led educators to believe and promulgate the myth of gender equality. Women are taught that they can strive for a profession and are led to believe that there will be no barriers obstructing their personal and professional goals. Many young women believe that gender discrimination is ancient history, their own personal desires and experiences will be free from such inequities. They are promised equality of educational opportunities in all aspects of their schooling and believe that a good education will lead them toward independence, economic success, and a share in the material goods U.S. society has to offer. However, as we know from current research, women are still underpaid and their jobs concentrated in the traditional service industries. In 1990, more than two-thirds of working women were in service sector industries, in wholesale and retail trade, and in protective service fields such as teaching and nursing (Ries & Stone 1992). In the same year, 46% of female workers were in low-paying service and administrative-support occupations such as health aide, secretary, and waitress. Overall, most jobs tend to be gender segregated along traditional lines, with women's earnings continuing to lag far behind men's.

Gender and Educational Reform

Despite federal legislation and a growing body of literature detailing sexist practices in schools, gender is a sorely neglected category in recent reform literature calling for equity and excellence in schooling. Tetreault and Schmuck (1985) reported that gender is virtually ignored as an equity issue in schooling by at least eight of the major commission reports. They argue:

> Gender is not a relevant category in the analysis of excellence in schools. When gender was considered, it appears to merely embellish the traditional—and male—portrait of the school. The proposed vision for excellence in the schools is of education for the male student in the public and productive sphere. Because gender, as a relevant concept, is absent, even Title IX is ignored. Issues of gender in relation to policy, students, curricula, and faculty are not identified nor treated as educational problems to be solved. The goal of excellence does not even have the female student in mind. (p. 63)

When educational reformers talk about equality of educational opportunity for males and females, they are referring to providing the same educational opportunities, support, and expectations regardless of gender. The implication that school programs will provide for females what they have been providing for males means that women's progress and the excellence of programs for them has been judged in terms of what is considered good practice for men. Reform efforts fail to examine the unique experiences of boys and girls in order to provide equitable programs, structures, and practices that are geared toward the differing needs of both genders. This is certainly a beginning but not nearly enough. The term *gender equity* goes beyond equality of educational opportunity. Maxine Greene (1985) argues:

> To work for sex equity in education and the social order as a whole is to move to alter the oppressiveness that makes individual autonomy antithetical to social concern. It is to rediscover what it signifies to be a person and a woman, while discovering what it signifies to transform. (p. 42)

Transformative Possibilities for Schooling

How might schools prepare young people like Lauren to construct their lives in ways that are not in response to gendered stereotypes and marketplace forces? School structures and practices must be transformed so that students can engage in active, democratic practices. Current school structures are based on hierarchical patriarchal models. We need to develop more democratic school structures in which teachers and students can participate fully in decision making regarding school policies, curriculum, and practices that affect their daily lives. Problem-posing education (cf. Freire, 1970; Shor & Freire, 1987) that openly critiques sociocultural and political agendas while inviting collaborative approaches to reform is a process that enables students to critique the forces on their lives and create alternative ways to direct their experiences. Gender, a category largely ignored in school policies and practices, needs to be moved to the center of educators' and students' concerns. We might provide curricular forums for groups within schools to examine the ways capitalism and patriarchy shape the ways we construct our gendered identities. Students can learn to critique what it means to be a man or woman in this culture and to explore alternative ways of constructing collaborative social relationships.

REFERENCES

Freire, P. (1970). *A pedagogy for the oppressed*. New York: Seabury Press.

Greene, M. (1985). Sex equity as a philosophical problem. In S. Klein (Ed.), *Handbook for achieving sex equity through education* (pp. 29–43). Baltimore, MD: The Johns Hopkins University Press.

Ries, P., & Stone, A. J. (1992). *The American woman 1992–93: A status report*. New York: Norton.

Shor, I., & Freire, P. (1987). A *Pedagogy for liberation: Dialogues on transforming education.* Westport, MA: Bergin & Garvey.
Scott, J. W. (1988). *Gender and the politics of history.* New York: Columbia University Press.
Tetreault, M. K. & Schmuck, P. (1985). Equity, educational reform and gender. *Issues in Education, 3* (10), 45–67.
Wolfe, N. (1987). *The beauty myth.* New York: Anchor Books.

II

TERMS OF POWER/KNOWLEDGE

19

Curriculum

Brent Davis
Dennis J. Sumara
York University

John Ralston Saul (1995) describes ours as "a civilization ... in the embrace of a dominant ideology: corporatism" (p. 2). And, as with any successful ideology, the corporatist mind-set spreads a transparent web of metaphors and assertions that support particular manners of perceiving "reality" and of acting toward it.

Having settled into the invisibility of common sense, it is not surprising that corporatist notions infuse conventional curriculum projects. Most obviously, the manner of thinking and acting that corporatism sponsors is revealed in the uncritical rhetoric and activity that characterize the modern schooling project, made evident in desires to specify outcomes, establish standards, increase efficiency, ensure accountability, maintain competitiveness, and so on.

The profound intertwinings of corporatism and curriculum are perhaps most clearly articulated in the work of Ralph Tyler (1949), wherein curriculum making is reduced to set of prescribed directives and decisions. In essence, as articulated by Tyler (and as pervasively taken up by today's curriculum authorities), the process of assembling a curriculum is not unlike any project of construction. It begins with the determination of the end product—in this case, the desired learning outcomes that, following Tyler, are commonsensically defined to be the sorts of things that one needs to know in order to function as an adult in a democratic society. Once specified, and in a manner not dissembling the modern assembly line, such objectively determined and commodified knowings are sliced into discrete subject areas and sequenced in logical learning trajectories.

This approach is, of course, associated with what has been depricatingly called the "factory model" of schooling. However, in spite of countless critiques and numerous initiatives to alter such structures, virtually all current curriculum-making efforts (and most of the critiques) rest on the assumption that outcomes not only can be but must be specified. Moreover, once collected, such outcomes can be tidily and unambiguously arranged in the project of transforming perceived-to-be deficient children into desired-to-be functional adults.

The import of this point should not be lost, as it has serious ramifications for efforts toward classroom change. Throughout this century, considerable effort has been given to exploring alternative modes of teaching. However, in comparison to such efforts, there has been very little consideration of alternative conceptions of curriculum. This attempt to reconfigure formal education by focusing on the teacher's activities without adequately considering the backdrop of prespecified learning objectives—or, put differently, this tendency to separate how one teaches from what one teaches—is at the root of many frustrated pedagogical efforts.

The concept of "curriculum" that is implicit here merits examination. In contrast to uses of the term outside of schooling contexts (e.g., a "curriculum vitae," which is written after the fact to describe a path that has unfolded), the formal educational use of "curriculum" implies a pre-specified route toward a future that is held to be knowable. It is thus that the terms "curriculum" and "program (of studies)" have become interchangeable. The logical, mechanical, predetermined character of the latter, which has long been used to refer to a prestated sequence of events (e.g., performance programs and, more recently, computer programs), has been mapped onto the former.

There are, of course, important historical and cultural reasons for this equating of programs and curricula. However, such details are not easily (and perhaps not entirely wisely) extricated from one another, for this sort of effort risks falling into the same linearizing and reductionist mode of thinking that is implicit in a corporatist ideology and that, à la Tyler, explicitly informs modern curriculum making. Nevertheless, there is something to be gained by attempting to explore the tacit ground of our curriculum acting rather than focusing on its explicit figure.

In the Western context, the modern school arose alongside—and, notably, largely in the service of—the industrial complex. The development of the modern school also coincided with the emergence of a mathematized science as the culturally privileged means of establishing knowledge claims. The simultaneous appearance of formal education, corporatist interests, and scientized thinking was hardly coincidental. But neither was their shared emergence a matter of cause-and-effect mechanics. Rather, they arose codependently, each affecting the other.

This is not to say, however, that there have not been direct and traceable causal influences of corporatism on curriculum. One need only consider the businessman's need for a competent and specialized, but complacent, workforce in the early days of the industrial revolution. Or the sudden change in curriculum content that was prompted by a perceived Soviet superiority in the early days of the space program. Or the transmutation of concerns and corresponding projects of curriculum revision that began when politicians diverted the public's attention away from their own near-sighted economic decisions and onto the (suggested to be causal) correlation between the performance of Japanese students on standardized mathematics tests and a booming Japanese economy. To construe the relationship between corporatism and curriculum in such unidirectional terms, however, is to miss the manner in which formal schooling is complicit in the creation and the maintenance of the very structures that direct its course. It is thus that we argue that what is interesting is not so much the relative influence of corporatism (or scientism) on curriculum making but the worldview that is shared and maintained by these projects.

Consider the common desire for progress, for example. Corporatism and modern curricula are premised on a conception of relationship (among individuals, businesses, and societies; or between humanity and the nonhuman world) as fundamentally competitive in nature. The consequent purposes of existence are to outperform and to dominate one's rivals, and success is measured according to one's progress toward such domination. Modern curricula are implicated in this project not only through their linear sequential structures (through which one is compelled to progress) but through the persistent evaluations of each learner's progress and the constant comparison of learners to one another. Prescriptive curricula and their regimes of testing do not merely prepare one for the dog-eat-dog world projected by the corporatist mind-set. Nor are they simple reflections or consequences of the corporatist agenda. Rather, the straightforward curriculum asserts and participates in the perpetuation of a competitive, self-seeking, future-oriented, progress-based world. It is as much the instigator as the unfortunate product of a corporatist worldview.

Implicit in this pervasive desire for progress is a faith that the world is fixed—or at least unfolding according to deterministic rules—and, hence, the project of preparing a citizenry for an as-yet unrealized future is deemed to be a viable one. This conception of the clockwork universe rests on a troublesome overgeneralization of Newtonian mechanics. Designed to describe simple macroscopic movements, the power of Newton's laws to predict planetary positions and missile trajectories has been extended to all facets of existence, instilling a pervasive and linear cause-and-effect mentality. Historically, corporatism has relied heavily on this mode of thinking, seeking to translate complex social and economic movements into simple linear equations, and, from there, articulating growth programs and strategic plans. The stunning ineffectiveness of such programs has not prevented the same notion from being applied to other endeavors, and curriculum making is no exception. Not bothering to wonder about the accelerating pace of cultural change, curriculum makers have tended to cling to false comfort offered by the misapplication of Newton's laws—to the point that conventional programs of study are often pathetically out of step with current circumstances, let alone with the unrealized future.

There are other important consequences of the unquestioned adherence to corporatist and scientistic mind-sets, among them, the maintenance of arbitrary subject area boundaries and the perpetuation of the tacit belief that the knowledge bits that fill the pages of curriculum documents have little or no moral significance. The net effect is a model of curriculum that is unable to acknowledge its history, its relevance, or its own complicity in our culture. The pedagogies that accompany this mode of curriculum are similarly unconscious: unaware of the source of their concerns for management (of time and resources) and control (of persons and futures), oblivious to their dehumanizing reductions of learners (to clients and consumers) and knowledge (to capital and products).

Despite the pervasiveness of such attitudes, they have long been subject to criticism. John Dewey (1902/1956), for example, argued that curriculum had to do with the dynamic and complex relationships among children, teachers, and culture. He thus sought to erase the rigid boundaries that had been drawn between the learner and the curriculum, contending that the two were not distinct but intertwined. For him, the same fluid and coemergent relationship existed between established knowledge (that is, the focus or figure of conventional curricula) and the character of society (that is, the uninterrogated ground of our acting).

Unfortunately, Dewey's contributions were eclipsed by the mode of thinking represented in Tyler's writings, and it is only recently that this trend has been seriously challenged. In the mid-1970s, William Pinar (1975) introduced the term "reconceptualist" to the field of curriculum inquiry through an edited volume of essays from theorists who had begun to question the field's underlying instrumental rationality. Arriving from backgrounds in literary, existentialist, critical, feminist, and phenomenological thinking, these scholars called for a greater awareness of the ecologies of existence, the agency of the learner, the interconnections and interdependencies of knowledge areas, and the value of diversity, thus opening the door to a new form of curriculum study. They did so not merely by offering an effective critique of conventional practices but by reminding us that education is never merely concerned with matters of established knowledge. All curriculum events, rather, were shown to be simultaneously transformative of the individual and collective character.

Put differently, curriculum reconceptualists trouble the common sense separations of what one knows and who one is, suggesting instead that identity is inseparable from knowledge. Identity is not a fixed phenomenon but unfolds from culturally embedded experiences. The static nature of curricula and the presumed-to-be-neutral ethical status of the educational project are thus questioned by reconceptualist thinkers. Far from being on a moral high ground, or even in neutral territory, a schooling that is not conscious of the ground of its actions is a troubled and a troublesome project.

Curriculum reconceptualists also challenge the very possibility of predetermining what is to be learned. A complex and poorly understood phenomenon, human learning has proven itself to be tremendously adept (but wildly unpredictable) at fitting into the flow of life's contingencies: One never knows exactly what one will learn, just as, on a broader level, one can never predict the directions in which collective knowledge might evolve. Curriculum makers, it seems, have disregarded these commonplace understandings, electing to work from the maxim that what is to be learned can be controlled through careful articulation. The reconceptualist movement, in contrast, might be understood as a return to an acknowledgment of the ambiguities and uncertainties of life. Curriculum is thus not conceived of in terms of distinct knowledge bits but as having to do with the existential qualities of life in schools.

Not surprisingly, then, part of the reconceptualist project has involved an effort to "free" the notion of curriculum from its corporatist frame. To this end, William Pinar and Madeleine Grumet (1976) have reminded us of the verb *currere* from which *curriculum* (along with a host of other terms, including *course* and *current*) is derived. *Currere* refers to "the running of the course" rather than "the course to be run, or the artifacts employed in the running of the course" (p. 18), and Pinar and Grumet use the term to refocus attention away from the impersonal goals of conventional curriculum projects and onto the meaning-making process of moving through the melée of present events. In rendering experience meaningful, one recovers and recreates one's history and simultaneously creates new possibilities for one's future. Such sense making is understood to be both enabled and constrained by language and, as such, fundamentally social and relational. In brief, "curriculum"—far from popular conceptions—is conceived as the interpretation of lived experience and is thus valued for its transformative rather than its transmissive potential. Implicit in the notion of *currere* are an acknowledgment of the relational basis of knowledge (and being) and a recognition of the happenstantial, continuously negotiated nature of existence.

Stated more directly, reconceptualist thinkers problematize the monologic and totalizing discourses of corporatism and scientism. Rejecting defining imageries of linear equations and assembly lines, and troubling the notion that schooling is at the service of the economy, reconceptualist thinkers embrace a vision of existence that is better represented by fractal geometry and nonlinear dynamics, an imagery that presents constant surprise and ever-mounting complexity and that refuses simplistic separations of any part from the whole. Further, the language of Newtonian physics, with its deterministic functions and its inevitable reductions, is supplanted by a metaphoric web that is drawn more from biology. The desire to specify trajectories thus gives way to a need to prompt and to attend to complex, organic, and intertwined unfoldings. The causal model of teaching is replaced by a pedagogy that is aware of its complicity in cultural forms and that seeks to participate with learners in the recognition and the re-cognition of such forms.

This is not to say, however, that the complexified conception of curriculum recommends that efforts to establish standardized programs be abandoned in favor of more local, idiosyncratic, and spontaneous courses of study. On the contrary, pervasive cultural forms (which are already well represented in conventional programs of study, albeit on an unconscious level) might serve as the subject matter for a broad set of interests. What is challenged, however, is the notion that a program of studies can be written today that can be read in the same way in diverse settings or that will maintain its relevance many years hence. In particular, what is troubled is the manner in which curricula have been founded on an attitude of preparing for the future—to the detriment and ignorance of the immediate present. The vital point is that formal curriculum documents should no longer be regarded as programs to guide the acquisition of cultural capital but as possible occasions for the interpretation of cultural forms.

For more than 2 decades, reconceptualist curriculum scholars have focused their efforts on explicating the implications of this assertion. By way of example, we have sought in our own work to rethink English and mathematics curricula as occasions for invoking the literary imagination (Sumara, 1996) and for embarking on mathematical anthropologies (Davis, 1996). Although acknowledging conventional subject area boundaries, such emphases do not embrace such distinctions as essential. And, although gathering around significant texts and theorems, such approaches seek to unearth personal and collective engagements with such "canonical ideas," rather than ignoring such engagements in favor of mining themes and mastering procedures.

Such notions, of course, are not readily embraced in the current context. A large part of the reason is that they push against a long-standing (but, we believe, waning) common sense that refuses the complexities and contingencies of existence. But another more deliberate and more insidious reason is suggested by Lynn Margulis (1995), a biologist and evolutionary theorist whose work has helped to prompt cross-disciplinary rethinkings of the very nature of existence. In reviewing some of the barriers that her ideas have met through her distinguished career, Margulis comments, "Accepting the shifting boundaries and new alliances is strange and costly. It is far easier to stay with obsolete intellectual categories." (p. 136)

And so we end this discussion of "curriculum"—what it is and what it might be—with a dose of conventional (corporatist) reality. The matter of corporate investment in curriculum presents a twofold problem. First, as a collective, Westerners are deeply invested in the corporatist ideology. That conceptual investment is manifested in a common sense that is not easily interrupted, especially in the academic world where subject area boundaries, research, status, and capital are knotted together. Second, and more pragmatically, textbook publishers, computer manufacturers, and other aspects of the corporate matrix have a huge financial investment in current models of schooling. Conventional curriculum is a multimillion dollar industry, and although there seems to be an increasing willingness to consider alternative ways of thinking differently about what happens in classrooms, it would be foolish to ignore the interests of industry in maintaining the status quo.

However, even though no one should be deceived into thinking that the transformation of modern schooling is a simple matter of thinking differently, it must be borne in mind that education is about learning. For us, that demands a willingness to question the transparent notions, corporatist and otherwise, that give shape to our interpreted existence.

REFERENCES

Davis, B. (1996). *Teaching mathematics: Toward a sound alternative*. New York: Garland.

Dewey, J. (1956). *The child and the curriculum*. Chicago: University of Chicago Press. (Original published 1902)

Margulis, L. (1995). Gaia is a tough bitch. In J. Brockman (Ed.), *The third culture* (pp. 129–146). New York: Simon & Schuster.

Pinar, W. F. (Ed.). (1975). *Curriculum theorizing: The reconceptualists*. Berkeley, CA: McCutchan.

Pinar, W. F., & Grumet, M. R. (1976). *Toward a poor curriculum*. Dubuque, IA: Kendall/Hunt.

Saul, J. R. (1995). *The unconscious civilization*. Concord, ON: Anansi.

Sumara, D. J. (1996). *Private readings in public: Schooling the literary imagination*. New York: Peter Lang.

Tyler, R. W. (1949). *Basic principles of curriculum and instruction*. Chicago: University of Chicago Press.

20

Arts Education

Leila Villaverde
The Pennsylvania State University

Art has been designated as "art" only with the advent of modern times, never before considered outside the necessary or the way of life. Art has thus been mystified allowing only those that are "talented," innately creative or artistic, to belong in that world. As Kincheloe and Steinberg (1993) state, "Intelligence and creativity are thought of as fixed and innate, while at the same time mysterious qualities found only in the privileged few" (p. 298). This only perpetuates the alienation of art from one's life.

Artists are left somewhat vulnerable to the external definitions of art, given exclusive designations of who is and isn't an artist. These definitions are constructed by a modernist ideology of art that is hegemonic in its perpetuation of a singular view in defining art and artist and acquiring a wide consensus of these definitions. The modernist ideological perspective judges art on its pleasing aesthetics, assigning aesthetics the standards to demarcate the boundaries between high and low art, as well as inscribing a superficially removed quality to experiencing art. Yet contemporary art has changed modernism's perspectives to some extent, redefining what art is and where it is. Giroux (1992) proposes:

> As an antiaesthetic, postmodernism rejects the modernist notion of privileged culture or art; it renounces "official" centers for "housing" and displaying art and culture along with their interests in origins, periodization, and authenticity. Moreover, postmodernism's challenge to the boundaries of modernist art and culture has, in part, resulted in new forms of art, writing, film-making, and various types of aesthetic and social criticism. (p. 58)

How art and artists are regarded in the society will determine to what extent the arts will suffer in its economic regime. Capitalism is a major influence over the construction of the art world, the divide between high and low art, and art education. Art is maintained at the periphery of economic development, regarded as luxury, therefore superfluous to necessary funding in the schools. Artistic development is rarely recognized for its positive influence on language acquisition and cognitive processes. The development of visual symbolization, that is the ability to create images, aides the development of language organization, because language is also a symbolic process (Wilson, 1985, p. 88).

Through countless educational reform attempts, the arts are either ignored or transformed into technocratic skills and requirements, completely eradicating any space for creativity and expression. The language used by educational reformers leaves little room for any other behavior that does not fit into an industrial mode of production and outcome. The arts have suffered substantially in education and subsequently in their ability to influence students' development. As a result of obsessive concerns with global economization, education becomes the operative factor in a positive correlation to economic achievement. In order to succeed economically, one must adhere to those disciplines that will guarantee a secure future, a monetary security. Success is even streamlined into a linear cause-and-effect expectation devoid of any semblance to a holistic definition of success including progress or development in emotional, intellectual, physical, cultural, or social realms. Individuals are deskilled and fragmented into windows of productivity for economic gains. Every other discipline or cultural practice that falls outside the ladder of economic success is marked expendable, therefore limiting the ways individuals and groups must interact to maintain that success. The power constructed through the dissemination of this ideology convinces individuals to reject anything other than what is going to make them succeed. This systemic ideology permeates as if by default into education and the construction of school curricula.

In an attempt to compete with social powers and to create individuals who are prepared to work within these powers, schools have tailored their educational philosophies to the mainstream. Rarely are schools challenging the mainstream for the betterment of their students. The close marriage between corporations and schools makes any deviation from the mainstream almost impossible. Schools then become subservient to corporate moguls in the hopes of securing funding for their schools, yet inadvertently sacrificing the overall educational development of their students. This marriage also delineates the discipline hierarchy that will ultimately shape the curriculum. The arts, of course, are hardly ever a priority since careers in the arts are not a staple of the economy at-large. The only exception is Disney products and, in that case, Disney can set up its own schools centered around graphic design and animation to later recruit "la creme de la creme" into its own corporate kingdom. But in ordinary schools around America, the arts are being cut *out* of the curriculum, art rooms are made dispensable or relocated to trailers outside the schools so deemed more important classes can occupy their spaces. Art teachers are displaced or spread thin throughout an entire school, carrying their supplies in carts. This marginalization of the arts obstructs its teaching and extinguishes its creativity, reducing "art" to crafts or activities that cater to stereotypes and holiday artifacts approved by the mainstream.

Education must be radically transformed (and not merely reformed) to accomplish Dewey's aspirations of making education encompass all facets of society rooted in the familiar democratic vision of a reflective and productive citizen who enjoys thinking, working, and living (Simpson & Jackson, 1997, p. xxiv). The insertion of a radical democracy into educational discourses is imperative to the reinstatement of a well-rounded curriculum in which the arts are not minimized, but rather deemed necessary to the development and success of student life. Efland (1996) states:

> The arts and humanities are important precisely because they cultivate the capacity to reflect on issues that open a vision of human possibility that may question the morality of social, economic or military priorities.... The case for the arts in education is not merely that it can encourage thinking but that it can permeate such thinking with feelings which help give rise to a moral sense.... Art educators need to remind the public that man [sic] does not live by bread alone, that the arts maintain the viability of human culture. Human beings survive humanly only through their efforts to make culture. (pp. 51, 53, 54)

In order to deeconomize the curriculum, schools need to reconfigure their relationship with corporations, to renounce its prostitution to the capitalist ideologies that convert the schools into cultural commodities. By re-emphasizing and centralizing the arts in the curriculum, students' educational experiences are deeconomized by recasting student positionality within the web of receiving, interpreting, and expressing information with a critical awareness of the school's function as a cultural industry. The arts with their multiplicity of media, genre, and process can reconfigure students' ways of knowing, how they search for that knowledge, what they consider knowledge, and how they apply it. In essence, this is how learning becomes a life-long process and not a means to an economic end.

In incorporating the study of the arts into a postmodern pedagogical paradigm, the possibilities for an individual to seek and experience expand almost instantaneously. Art requires a deeper involvement with the self, forcing one to interrogate the why and how of the phenomena that surround the self to further knowledge and expression. Franklin (1992) states, "When creating art one cannot help but look inward and participate in decision making that is targeted at the resolution of various emotional and cognitive processes" (p. 79). Art is paramount in influencing self-formation and consciousness. McNiff (1995) discusses the need for an inverted perspective, which he attributes to Adolf Arheim: "The creative process thrives on the inversion of habitual thoughts. When I reverse a fixed point of view ... I'm open to alternate ways of looking, and I see how custom and bias can hinder a more comprehensive interpretation of a particular situation" (p. 163).

He also contends a singular vantage point distorts rather than clarifies and believes education has been afflicted by this "illusion of linear reality." An inverted perspective yields a space replete with freedom where an individual can assume different roles as well as grapple with the coalescence of intangible and tangible realms, concepts, and experiences. In a society of visual, intellectual, physical, affective, and kinesthetic multiplicity, yet one obsessed with cultural and economic capital and exchange values, there needs to be a flexibility that both students and teachers can use in order to resist and counterbalance the industrialization of school and life. This can help in navigating through a variety of disciplines and planes that our socialized actions and thoughts are bound by. In the process of socialization, subtle controlling agents permeate our thinking and acting, hence an understanding of the power dynamics that shape our identity and sense of agency is imperative.

Schools geared by curriculum kits seldom bridge the gap between learning and "real life", thus tailoring student life to specific desired outcomes and not to the student's needs. The arts can provide an outlet for students to explore the void and, consequently, provide a place where they may find validation and ownership of their voice, whether its through sketchbooks, paintings, sculptures, performances, songs, dances, or writings. The arts should not be the only venue through which students can exert their creativity; neither should they be deemed unnecessary in the curriculum. The inclusion of the arts ironically affords a freedom that helps students to cope with the regiment of other subjects.

Greene (1988) states, " Education for freedom must clearly focus on the range of human intelligences, the multiple languages and symbol systems available for ordering experience and making sense of the lived world" (p. 125). Schools should be concerned with providing opportunities for meaning-making processes, so that students readily apply what they learn to their lives. Both students and teachers need to combat the meaninglessness and alienation produced in schools and explore the dynamics behind the nature in which they learn, what constructs and produces knowledge, what they internalize, and how it influences their subjectivity. Judith Rubin (1984) describes a "framework for freedom" in which an amiable existence of extremes provides the freedom and structure necessary for creative growth. So the structure becomes critical awareness of the contextual circumstance instead of a confining boundary. Rubin believes art does this naturally: "Art itself offers a kind of protective framework, a boundary between reality and make-believe, which enables the [individual] to more daringly test [him or herself] and more openly state [his or her] fantasies than is possible without its aesthetic and 'psychic' distance (p. 28). It is her belief, as well as mine and many others, that we have an "inner creative potential," and it is this that will afford us the possibility of deeconomizing the schools' curricula.

How can we integrate the importance and necessity of the aesthetic into pedagogical interventions? How do we water the seed of creativity? What this requires is a rearticulated curricula, emphasizing art's pivotal position in the production, reception, and construction of knowledge and in self-formation. These elements also call forth a responsibility in substantiating one's creations, thoughts, and actions. Art is an arena for this type of critical work largely due to its nature, its multiplicity and inclusivity.

One, of course, questions, "what is the nature of art" or even, "what is art"? There isn't just one answer but rather a synthesis of the artist, agenda, project, philosophy, emotions, media, genre, society, politics, class, race, and so forth. What it elucidates is the complexity that resides in one site, whatever that site may be, particularly an individual's historicity, meaning-making processes, and agency. Art may provide the struggle necessary for pedagogy, pushing and challenging the development of an idea or process against its own grain. Lewis and Simon (1986) discuss the basic conditions for a process of pedagogy as "a struggle over assigned meaning, a struggle over discourse as the expression of both form and content, a struggle over interpretation of experience, and a struggle over self" (p. 469). Michael Franklin (1992) eloquently describes the parallels between the art-making process and life's processes:

> The unformed materials, much like the notion of *tabula rasa*, begin to take shape as the artist engages in a decision-making process that documents change. To work with art materials is to transform their physical and symbolic potential. Thus, art may be considered a simultaneous process of reformulating the self through the active formation of an object. (p. 79)

The anxiety about and defense against change is something that must be considered in an attempt to revamp anything radically. In order to initiate the deeconomization of schooling, we need to make accessible to help reconfigure various disciplines within the curriculum, enriching, politicizing, and questioning existing paradigms. The possibilities this entails, particularly for the schools, to reinstate the hope, meaning, purpose, and motivation that many students have lost or never experienced, are invaluable. Art classes can nurture this hope making the curriculum applicable to a student's interests. There are many spaces across the curriculum in which art can be the vehicle to meta-awareness and critical perspectives on the production of knowledge, power dynamics, self-formation, and consciousness construction. Neither the theoretical nor practical dimensions of art have to be confined to art classes but rather should be infused throughout the curriculum. Art should not be considered a separate, foreign element but as central to the conception and deployment of any subject matter.

It is paramount that students acquire a critical consciousness that is political, democratic, passionate, subversive, informed, and informative—all of which can be encouraged through engaging with and producing art. bell hooks (1995) discusses the notion of using art as a space to exercise one's freedom:

> Art should be, then, a place where boundaries can be transgressed, where visionary insights can be revealed within the context of the everyday, the familiar, the mundane. Art is and remains such an uninhibited, unrestrained, cultural terrain only if *all* artists see their work as inherently challenging to those institutionalized systems of domination (imperialism, racism, sexism, class elitism, etc.) that seek to limit, coopt, exploit, or shut down possibilities for individual creative self-actualization. Regardless of the subject matter, form, or content, whether art is overtly political or not, artistic work that emerges from an unfettered imagination affirms the primacy of art as that space of cultural production where we can find the deepest, most intimate understanding of what it means to be free. (p. 138)

Here, hooks delineates not only what art is but its potential in encouraging a critical discourse to understand and create freely. Art can serve as part of a counternarrative of emancipation in which new visions, spaces, desires, and discourses can be developed that offer students the opportunity for rewriting their own histories differently within rather than outside the discourse of critical citizenship and cultural democracy. Ultimately this leads to a desire to perform *good work*,[1] with a sense of responsibility, initiative, and creativity, engaging with learning through art to find a purpose in what we are taught and to use it to critically transform our existence.

I believe art is inherently political, ethnographic, and interdisciplinary, always expanding and challenging the stasis of reality. Art facilitates an examination of how images construct realities that perpetuate power relationships, questioning references conveyed by the image and its form; the cultural values placed on the materials and methods of production of the art; and the aura created by the context or use of the art, critically exploring cultural myths, social structures, and rituals as the media of power in society, none of which is ideologically neutral (Day, 1961/1991, p. 12). A literacy of power would then facilitate deconstructing art as phenomena and necessity.

Trend (1992) discusses:

> ... how artists, educators, and cultural workers are recognizing their responsibilities as active agents, that this is largely a pedagogical process that takes place as individuals come to know the means through which they are ideologically constituted. This activates human agency, as it begins to tell people that their actions can make a difference, that their voices can be heard. It means deconstructing the repressive myths that would objectify individuals into faceless masses of "the public." (p.149)

Struggling with art, its concepts, process, and materials, provides a space for individuals to reconfigure the particular way they fit into their lives and society. Engaging in this struggle is tantamount to a struggle with one's own identity, in which persons make their resistance productive through an interrogation of norms, mores, cultural practices, power relations, and the entire notion of knowledge production. A pedagogical intervention through art facilitates self-expression and critical commentaries on culture, social stratifications, class, gender, age, race, sexual orientation, ideologies, and so

---

[1]See Joe L. Kincheloe's notion of "good work,"in his *Toil and Trouble: Good Work, Smart Workers, and the Integration of Academic and Vocational Education* (New York: Peter Lang, 1995, p. 30).

forth. Yet one must comprehend pedagogy as a configuration of textual, verbal, and visual practices that seek to engage the process through which people understand themselves and the ways in which they engage others and their environment (Giroux, 1992, p. 3).

The multiplicity within art fosters its own problematic hierarchies that parallel those for the larger society. The art world is not free from the things that plague society, nor will art miraculously solve the interpersonal and intrapersonal problems individuals or groups face. Nevertheless, engaging in the arts, struggling through the process of creating art, amalgamating ideologies, concepts, feelings, the body, desire, politics, and such can provide the flexibility to accommodate the interchangibility of these things. Such engagement also challenges Art's expression, redefinition, or rearticulation, inadvertently fostering insight as one produces or thinks out what is internal, informed externally, and therefore reexternalized with residual traces of history gathered from its trajectory through the mind, and body. Art, therefore, provides the conditions to meet, understand, work through, and enact radical democracy and critical citizenry. This is possible through the art-making process, whether individual or collective, requiring individuals to involve themselves with a project on a number of levels, such as intellectual, emotional, and physical. The unconscious and conscious internalizations and expressions of art force reflections and intuitive reactions that are hard to ignore. Art allows for a personal involvement in school, helping to alleviate the alienation and meaninglessness many students feel. When art, critical pedagogy, power, and youth intersect, possibilities expand, differences can be pursued, and a pedagogy of hope and imagination can emerge.

REFERENCES

Day, H. T. (1991). The nature of power. *Power: Its myths and mores in American art*. Originally published 1961) Indianapolis: Indiana Press.

Efland, A. (1996, September). The threefold curriculum and the arts. *Arts Education, 49*(5), 49–56.

Franklin, M. (1992). Art therapy and self-esteem. *Art Therapy Journal of the American Art Therapy Association, 9*(2), 78–84.

Giroux, H. A. (1992). *Border crossings: Cultural workers and the politics of education*. New York: Routledge, Chapman & Hall.

Giroux, H. A. (1993). Living dangerously: Identity politics and the new cultural racism. In H. A. Giroux & P. McLaren (Eds.), *Between borders: Pedagogy and the politics of cultural studies*. (P. 51). New York: Routledge, Chapman & Hall.

Greene, M. (1988). *The dialectic of freedom*. New York: Teachers College Press.

hooks, B. (1995). *Art on my mind: Visual politics*. New York: New Press.

Kincheloe, J. L., & Steinberg, S. R. (1993). A tentative description of post-formal thinking: The critical confrontation with cognitive theory. *Harvard Educational Review, 63*(3), 296–320.

Lewis, M., & Simon, R. I. (1986). A discourse not intended for her: Learning and teaching within patriarchy. *Harvard Educational Review, 56*(4), 457–472.

McNiff, S. (1995). *Earth angels: Engaging the sacred in everyday things*. Boston: Shambhala.

Rubin, J. A. (1984). *Child art therapy: Understanding and helping children grow through art.* (2nd ed.). New York: Van Nostrand Reinhold.

Simpson, D. J., & Jackson, M. J. B. (1997). Preface. *Educational reform: A Deweyan perspective* (pp. Xix–xxix). New York: Garland.

Trend, D. (1992). *Cultural pedagogy: Art/ education/ politics*. New York: Bergin & Garvey.

Wilson, L. (1985, February). Symbolism and art therapy: Symbolism's role in the development of ego functions. *American Journal of Art Therapy, 23*, 79–88.

21

Language Arts Education

Alan A. Block
University of Wisconsin, Stout

But there is no "p" in literacy, you may note. And perhaps that is the problem with issues of literacy as they are discussed in public circles in the United States today. I argue that unless we situate the "p" in literacy—acknowledge its basis in politics—all our discussions and efforts produce what might be conceptualized as an educational black hole. Now, as I understand the concept of a black hole, it is an object in which the atoms have collapsed for some reason—probably under the weight of gravity—and whose resultant density is so great that the object absorbs everything, even light. Reflecting no light, black holes cannot be seen; unapparent to perception, a black hole's density is nevertheless so great that it may weigh more than the sun, thoroughly invisible yet impenetrable, obstructionist, and highly destructive. Black holes consume everything and emit nothing.

Such is the case of literacy considered without the "p." Any discussion that fails to acknowledge the political basis of literacy collapses the concept into a veritable black hole that not only emits no light but whose energy is so great that it absorbs everything around it. With literacy so apolitically formulated, it becomes possible to talk about "a thousand points of light" without emitting any, or to be the "education president" without being able to illuminate what that could possibly mean. Such discourse admits of "building a bridge to the future" but offers no vision of that future nor any material means for its construction. Finally, as physicists tell us, black holes are dangerous, threatening to destroy everything that comes within their gravitational pull. And an apolitical and ahistorical notion of literacy threatens to devour the very idea of education.

Now, to situate the "p" is to impart volume to it by acknowledging the social setting that is constitutive of the concept of literacy. Such situation locates literacy within a specific space and time and permits it to be visible within a distinctive and material community and its culture. To acknowledge the "p" in literacy is to permit education to occur; to deny it is to create an entity invisible and engulfing, endangering the existences of the very population that literacy was meant to enhance. Today, I hold with Dewey (1916/1966) who argued decades ago that "the democratic ideal of education is a farcical yet tragic delusion except as the ideal more and more dominates our public system of education (p. 98). Across broad ranges of the political spectrum, this absence of the ideal is acknowledged. I assert that the quest for the ideal is only possible by first situating the "p" in literacy.

Through yet another metaphor, let me again explore the necessity of situating the "p" in literacy. Recall with me Shakespeare's political tragedy, *Macbeth*. In Act 1, scene 5, Macbeth, returning from victorious battle in the service of the king, meets the three weird sisters who, to his amazement, hail him Thane of Cawdor and king hereafter, titles to which Macbeth has, he believes, no access and little hope. Yet on meeting King Duncan, Macbeth learns that for his efforts on the king's behalf during a recent rebellion involving the traitorous Cawdor, he (Macbeth) has been awarded the rites and privileges of that perfidious Thane. Devoted and loving husband that he is, Macbeth writes to his wife of this good news, of the realization of the first part of what he now considers the weird sisters' prophecy, and of his hopes that, indeed, the promise to be king hereafter will also be fulfilled. On reading his letter, Lady Macbeth acknowledges her husband's ambition and admits that she harbors the same desire for her husband's ascendancy to the kingship. In considering his character, however, she fears that Macbeth's good nature will frustrate the prophecy's fulfillment. Despite his towering ambition, she characterizes her husband as

> ... too full o' th' milk of human kindness
> To catch the nearest way (I, v, 15–17).

Note first her acknowledgment that his ambition is lofty and high achieving; note next that her priority is for the achievement of his ambition, and that, initially and paradoxically, Macbeth understands that catching the nearest way—the quickest means of achieving that ambition—in essence, will produce an education that must ultimately destroy Macbeth:

> In these cases [of murder]
> We still have judgement here, that [in our actions] we but teach Bloody instruction, which, being taught, return
> to plague the inventor" (I, vii, 7–10).

The quickest way of which Macbeth speaks, of course, is the murder of the good King Duncan.

And so, in her soliloquy, Lady Macbeth concedes of her husband:

> Thou wouldst be great;
> Art not without ambition, but without
> The illness should attend it. What thou wouldst highly,
> That wouldst thou holily; ... (I, v, 17–20).

Now what does she mean here? Lady Macbeth acknowledges her husband's lofty ambition, but she concedes that this supreme position to which he aspires—*what thou wouldst most highly*—he would accede to only in a way most righteous—*that wouldst he holily*. I would like to pursue this metaphor for a little while and see if I might make some connection, albeit by a somewhat circuitous route, to the issues of literacy and literacy instruction in the schools of the twenty-first century and to situating the 'p' in it. The play, *Macbeth*, is above all concerned with politics, its practice and its products. By ignoring the politics of his actions, Macbeth prepares his own demise: He know that his actions teach others the practice of murder, but he disregards this knowledge for the desire of possessing the throne. He pretends that politics is only a singular assertion of power and not the continuous exercise of it. As his wife knows, he is too full of the milk of human kindness to wholly understand—or admit to—the relationship. As his wife knows, Macbeth has much to learn. For what Macbeth wouldst most holily must not be tainted by political motives; this is, as he tragically must learn, impossible. I am certain that Macbeth intended his rule to be a good one once the messy business of killing Duncan was completed. Macbeth's eventual discovery of the politics denies the wholeness or holiness of his intended enterprise; it is an inclusion he should have earlier known. Denying the politics implicit in his acts denies both what he wouldst most highly and holily. Finally, he must fail altogether.

I suggest that literacy, of which reading and writing are primary modes, is what we educators 'wouldst most highly,' the lofty end to which we all seek. It is a towering goal—what we 'wouldst most holily'—for literacy offers power and agency to those who attain it. Hence literacy's exalted, but heavily contested, position: As knowledge is power, literacy is both means and ends to power, to knowledge, to knowledge as power. Literacy is, finally, political. The conservative arguments posit literacy merely in its functional perspective, tied to narrowly conceived economic interests—getting a job—or to an ideology designed to initiate the poor, the underprivileged, and minorities into the logic of the dominant cultural tradition. At present, much of our instruction in literacy is based on these ends. Literacy is associated with the transmission and mastery of a unitary Western tradition, and schooling is conceived as a site for character development. The essential political character of literacy is obfuscated. In this sense, literacy provides little opportunity for acquisition of power except within narrowly defined socially organized structures that are posited beyond politics. Reading and writing in schools, indeed, all literacy learning—learning to read and write—is organized by the canonical texts and textbooks and our belief that therein lies truth, that we have only to pore assiduously over the text—basal reader or Shakespeare—and we may become enlightened. Meaning is embedded in texts, and our skills are developed and practiced to mine those meanings to reveal Truth, which is always beyond politics. "Only in schools," Madeleine Grumet (1988) tells us, "are we so stupid. Only in schools does the text become a spectacle, and we the dazed spectators, eyes glazed, sit in mute recognition for something to appear" (p. 144). Language learning in schools is for the most part premised on the belief that meaning may be, in fact, discovered, that it exists out there, and that there are skills that may be taught which facilitate meaning discovery. These skills are ahistorical constructs. "Outside-in theories," Frank Smith (1983) tells us, "are characterized by the notion that everything on a page of text is 'processed' and that reading is primarily a hierarchical series of decisions—first letters are discriminated, then they are synthesized into words (usually but not always through 'decoding' into a phonological or 'underlying' level of spoken language), as a consequence of which comprehension takes place" (p. 59). According to outside–in theories, we have but to activate the machine, and meaning appears. Outside-in theories also posit the learner as an object of learning rather than a subject of it and assume a power relation based on knowledge that denies agency to the learner. The effect of this system, which is a "fixation of social activity, this consolidation of what we ourselves produce into an objective power above us, growing out of our control, thwarting our expectations, bringing to naught our calculations" (cited in Marx, 1988, p. 53), usurps the learners' identity and robs them of not only the entitlements due their position but the very position itself. But, in order to better situate the "p" in literacy, I would rather define literacy as the ability to produce or assign meaning in a world where meaning can be assigned to phenomena (Hall, 1987, p. 8). A concept of literacy must include, then, an awareness of the socially and politically constructed origin of meaning production and a creation or situating of the self in that society in which meaning has been produced. Literacy assumes an agency; "Man's consciousness of the necessity of associating with the individuals around him," Marx argues, "is the beginning of the consciousness that he is living at all" (cited in Marx, 1988, p. 51). The breadth and depth of that life is dependent on the quality of associations and must be acknowledged as productive: "In a real community, the individuals obtain their freedom in and through their association" (p. 83). The nature of those associations is a product of and produces the educational system and the idea of literacy in a society. Literacy events, of which reading and writing are primary modes, must then be acknowledged as productive activities.

It is important to see that the ability to assign meaning—to produce knowledge—and the range of meanings assigned, even in writing and reading, are social constructs, and therefore are implicitly political. Meaning evolves only in a social context, and these contexts are not skill bound. How I may produce meaning, what meaning I produce, depends on the social and political context in which I do it: A cross burning in a church afire is different from a cross afire in an open field. So, too, with words. The Supreme Court tells me that I may not yell "fire" in a crowded theatre unless, indeed, there is a fire. Meaning is, John Gee (1990) declares,

> a choice about which other words and phrases a word is used in relation to, what other words and phrases it will be taken as excluding or as not applicable, and what the operative and relevant context will be taken (assumed) to be. The production of meaning (what speakers and writers do) is concerned with the choices about exclusions (and inclusions) and assumptions about contexts made on a certain basis. (p. 85)

Those choices are always socially constrained, as Marx (1984) tells us: "Men make their own history, but they do not make it just as they please; they do not make it under circumstances chosen by themselves, but under circumstances directly encountered, given and transmitted from the past"

(p. 15). We enter a field already constructed and in which our choices are thereby limited. We enter what Stanley Fish (1980) calls "interpretive communities". We have all heard a child emit what we would believe is an irrelevant statement during a story telling session. But we must consider that child's statement in terms of decisions and understandings and relations of power before we deny it meaning, or rather, before we, as teachers, assume the assignation of meaning while denying that same privilege to the expressive child. What the child produced and what we might comprehend must be understood in light of contents, contexts, and processes by which the statement was constructed and spoken and received. The limits of meaning are social and not individual, and this knowledge is fundamental to literacy and language arts education.

This belabored point is that meaning is socially constructed and that literacy is a socially embedded event. It is a concept steeped in politics. Literacy development is the situating of self within society, even as the child does so in discourse, quite naturally I might add, within the environment of the family. But, unlike in school and other social environments, the acquisition of language is not a prerequisite for membership in the family; rather, it is developed naturally within the family structures and grows from real, meaningful, and active engagement in that environment. Michael Halliday says that

> The child is learning to be and do, to act and to interact in meaningful ways. He is learning a system of meaningful behavior; in other words, he is learning a semiotic system. Part of his meaningful action is linguistic. But none of it takes place in isolation; it is always within some social context. So the context of the utterance is the meaning that it has with respect to a given function, to one another of the things that the child is making language do for him. (cited in Goodman, 1987, p. 39)

Children do not learn to talk so that they can find a place within their families; their talk produces and determines that place. Literacy is, ultimately, the construction of one's voice, the construction of identity.

Literacy, then, what we "wouldst most highly," I repeat, is the practice and reflection on meaning making in a world where meaning may be assigned to phenomena. It is not merely discovering an already embedded meaning but is an active process occurring in a social situation that is determinant of a range of meanings. Part of that situation is embedded within the individual identity of the participant in the event, itself a product of a social process, and must be recognized in discussions of literacy. And part of that situation is located in a social setting into which the individual identity enters and that he or she can transform in a literacy event. The opportunity for transformation is dependent on the political atmosphere in which the event occurs and, hence, any discussion of literacy must first situate politics in that discourse. Literacy offers power only when it is capable of situating meaning, a process I will shortly argue is natural within a social context.

I am arguing here that literacy itself is a political issue: Who defines literacy defines power and how it can be maintained. Theories of literacy, J. Elspeth Stuckey (1991) says in her book, *The Violence of Literacy*, are theories of society. And of course, the aim of literacy, which is power, defines the means for either attaining or maintaining power or both. What we wouldst highly—to give power to students, to offer the ability to produce identity—is the function of literacy development and language arts education. And discussions of politics are and ought to be inseparable from politics.

And so, what we wouldst highly, that wouldst we holily. Whole language is more than a pedagogical technique; not the most recent educational bandwagon: It is a political philosophy that assumes a literacy and intends its development.[1] This is to say, whole-language practitioners approach both the child and language as already whole. Children are from very early in their lives—indeed, are from birth—already producers and comprehenders of meaning. These original practices of meaning making are not first taught so that they can later be used but are developed in the course of daily life naturally:

> Children learn language because they are predisposed to do so. How they set about the task is largely determined by the way they are: seekers after meaning who try to find the underlying principles that will account for the patterns that they recognize in their experiences. At each successive stage ... they are capable of dealing with new evidence of a certain degree of complexity, and they are able to incorporate it into their developing language system. (Wells, 1986, p. 43)

Children learn language from the outset, and regardless of social class, children are part of a literate community into which they would be initiated, and which makes room for them, and which organizes means and practices for that initiation. We must remember that *every* child has capabilities and competencies and that they are embedded within each child's own organically experienced and meaning-filled language. Gee (1990) says:

> All humans, barring a serious disorder, become members of one Discourse free.... This is our socioculturally determined ways of thinking, feeling, valu-

[1]I have argued elsewhere (Block, 1995) that whole language by any other name has a long and glorious pedigree and tradition in the United States but a powerful political opponent.

> ing, and using our native language in face-to-face communication with intimates which we achieve in our initial socialization within the "family" as this is defined within a given culture. (p. 150)[2]

Almost all children are already literate long before they arrive in our classrooms, long before they even hear the word school or teacher. Children are meaning seekers from birth. As early as 48 hours after birth, an infant will show a preference for pattern, (e.g., a drawing of a face is preferred to concentric circles), and after 2 months, dimensional objects are preferred to flat ones (Grumet, 1988, p. 948). As young as 3 months of age, infants respond to the mother's gestures; these responses are sometimes accompanied by vocalizations; by 6 months babies and caregivers have established the basis for communication: a relationship of mutual attention. "I know that you are attending to me, and you know that I am attending to you, and we both know that we both know that that is so" (Wells, 1986, p. 35). Within this relationship, children may develop both a sense of identity and a sense of community as they discover how their particular behavior elicits certain responses in others and how particular types of behaviors in others produce specific types of responses in themselves. From this basis of intersubjectivity, all communication derives and, I would argue, all sense of self. Identity is a product of the relations established: "Identity," says Bertell Ollman (1988), "is the relation between entities whose role as necessary elements in one another is appreciated for what it is" (p. 68). Parents respond to children's behavior as if they had intention. Thus, in time, babies come to have intentions, discovering in the process that their behavior can affect their environment, that they can communicate, producing as well an identity whose behavior is meaningful within the contexts in which that behavior can have meaning. The end of communication, after all, is to have power to affect the environment. Of course, parents do not respond to all the child's behavior, only those behaviors that have meaning, and these behaviors are never isolated but are always culturally situated. Parents attribute meaning first to actions, and then to language; but these are always cultural meanings and therefore initiate the child into the culture. Literacy is always already cultural.

Thus, naturally, in the course of natural living, children must first learn that there is a code, a relationship between sounds and meanings. This learning begins in the home. Children learn that what people do is make meaning. Then the child must learn how the code works—the particular

---

[2]Gee (1990) defines Discourse "as a way of being in the world ... forms of life which integrate words, acts, values, beliefs, attitudes, social identities, as well as gestures, glances, body positions, and clothes (p. 42).

language used in the particular community. As Gordon Wells (1986) says, "A lot of children's learning ... is dependent on making connections between what they know and what they are able to understand in the speech that they hear" (p. 39). Thus, literacy is not something we give children, but rather, something we promote. The phrase *emerging literacy* assumes something always already present. This places teachers in a new role in the classroom and, not incidentally, also reorders social relations, relations of power. "When supporting—not directing—their growth," Jean Ann Clyde recounts of her whole-language classroom, "we used our observations to keep ourselves informed—to help us determine the kinds of experiences and demonstrations that we should provide next in order to challenge their current understandings and help them refine their current notions of literacy" (Mills & Clyde, 1990, p, 41). Children in whole language classrooms often direct and organize their curriculum. Says one whole-language teacher:

> I have learned how valuable it is to follow the children's lead in creating a learning environment that is exciting and interesting. This, of course, does not imply throwing up my hands and allowing the children to do whatever they want. By planning open-ended invitations and questions, using strategy-sharing sessions, allowing meaningful choices, and instilling in children the notion that they are competent learners with much to share, we can help children go easily and comfortably beyond what they already know. (Mills & Clyde, 1990, p. 92)

This treats children not as empty vessels who must be filled with information and knowledge but as already active producers whose growth is premised on facilitation and not direct instruction. This is a political decision that offers power to the child by recognizing the power of the child. To treat the child wholly it is necessary to foster the sense of developing self that derives from literacy. Whole language means just that: that language is experienced as a process of social and personal invention from the outset and that it is originally learned from whole to parts. Form and function must develop together, or ought to in language learning. Children do not begin speaking words solely and then develop to the production of sentences. What we hear with the baby's first words are holophrastic phrases, whole sentences packed into single words. It is we who teach children in our interactions with them to extend their language. But this must occur in a meaningful situation. Language must have meaning. And it must take place in a real context. What we wouldst highly—to enable literacy—can only be done by promoting it and not by teaching it. "The strategies that children have developed for actively making sense of their experience have served them well (before school); they should now be extended and developed, not suppressed by the imposition of routine learning tasks for which they can see neither a purpose nor a connection with what they already know and can do" (Wells, 1986, p. 68). What we wouldst highly, that wouldst we holily, treating a child and his or her language as one and as intrinsically meaningful.

Language must, then, in our schools, be experienced in ways that reflect the everyday use of language. In this sense, whole-language classrooms develop a community of language users. This community is a functional one: It plans, evaluates, and self-evaluates. It is a community where teachers are learners and learners are teachers and where an atmosphere of mutual trust is evident.

If we are to promote literacy, curriculum decisions in language arts education ought to be a community effort, though there must be the possibility of access for all students to pursue individual interests. Hence, literacy learning—the practice of assigning meanings in a world where meaning can be assigned to phenomena—occurs in conversation, not monologue. Conversation—dialogue—is the basis of learning and democracy. "And when you hear all these different voices," Jerry Harste exclaims, "*new* conversations begin. That's the foundation of strong communities—difference, not like-mindedness. If everybody thinks the same, then there's no basis for a conversation. ... It's the differences that transform our thinking" (Mills & Clyde, 1990, p. 303). Transformation of thinking is learning; it is the goal of education. This thinking, "in which the existing knowledge base and those cognitive processes that operate on that knowledge base are altered structurally," Marzano (1991) reminds us, is higher order thinking, is the goal of education, and is how I have defined literacy here.

I want to return briefly to *Macbeth* for my conclusion. For Macbeth chooses a way less holy and acquires the kingdom by murdering the rightful king. And yes, he becomes King, but from the moment of his ascension, he understand that he is ultimately illegitimate and that his claim to royalty is fraudulent. In foregoing means most holy, by ignoring the politics in his politics acts, Macbeth has forfeited what was also most high. And as the forces gather against him in revolt, he discovers how powerless he truly is. He cries:

> My way of life
> Is fallen into the sere, the yellow leaf;
> And that which should accompany my old age,
> As honour, love, obedience, troops of friends,
> I must not look to have; but in their stead,
> Curses not loud but deep, mouth-honour, breath
> Which the poor heart would fain deny, and dare not. (v, iv, 23–29)

We would not have this for our students. Having gained the kingship not holily, Macbeth has achieved nothing highly. If we would have our students aspire to what is highly valued—literacy—it must be done only in a whole-language classroom. Only there can a true partnership in learning take place, where we as teachers may participate with children in meaning making that is embedded in an openly acknowledged politics.

REFERENCES

Block, A. (1995). *Occupied reading: Foundations toward an ecological theory*. New York: Garland.

Dewey, J. (1966). *Democracy and education*. New York: The Free Press. (Originally published 1916)

Fish, S. (1980). *Is there a text in this class?* Cambridge, MA: Harvard University Press.

Fishman, A. (1988). *Amish literacy*. Portsmouth, NH: Heinemann.

Freire, P., & Macedo, D. (1987). Introduction. In *Literacy: Reading the word and the world* (pp.). Boston: Bergin & Garvey.

Gee, J. (1990). *Social linguistics and literacies: Ideology in discourses*. New York: Falmer Press.

Goodman, K. (1986). *What's whole in whole language*. Portsmouth, NH: Heinemann.

Goodman, K. (1987). *Language and critical thinking in school: A whole language curriculum*. New York: Richard C. Owen.

Grumet, M. (1988). *Bitter milk*. Amherst, MA: University of Massachusetts Press.

Hall, N. (1987). *The emergence of literacy*. Portsmouth, NH: Heinemann.

Marx, K. (1984). *The 18th Brumaire of Louis Bonaparte*. New York: International Publishers.

Marx, K. (1988) *The German ideology*. New York: International Universities Press.

Marzano, R. J. (1990). Fostering thinking across the curriculum through knowledge restructuring. *Journal of Reading, 34*, 518–525.

Mills, H., & Clyde, J. A. (Eds.). (1990). *Portraits of whole language classrooms*. Portsmouth, NH: Heinemann.

Ollman, B. (1988). *Alienation* (2nd edition). Cambridge, England: Cambridge University Press.

Ribber, I., & G. L. Kittredge (Eds.). (1971). *The complete works of Shakespeare*. Waltham, MA: Xerox.

Shannon, P. (1990). *The struggle to continue*. Portsmouth, NH: Heinemann.

Smith, F. (1983). *Essays into literacy*. Portsmouth, NH: Heinemann.

Stuckey, J. E. (1990). *The violence of literacy*. Portsmouth, NH: Heinemann.

Wells, G. (1986). *The meaning makers: Children learning language and using language to learn*. Portsmouth, NH: Heinemann.

22

Bilingual Education

Robert E. Bahruth
Boise State University

In a recent visit to a "blue-ribbon school" in Texas, a Hispanic administrator paraded a fourth-grade student before a group of visitors to illustrate the success of his "bilingual education" program. When the child began school, he could not speak a word of English. For our benefit, the boy sat down in front of a computer and began working on a program in English, dealing with anatomy and the human skeletal system. He told us in English that he wanted to be a doctor.

When a series of questions were put to the boy in Spanish, his primary language, the interaction proved revealing and a cause for concern. The boy only responded in English. When asked whether he knew the names of the bones in Spanish, he replied, "Why would I want to?" It seems he had received the message that only English is of worth at school—to be successful and rewarded he must abandon his first language and culture. A brief look around the library in this 85% Hispanic school provided supporting evidence. The stacks were filled with books in English, except for a scant, low-quality selection of books on a shelf tucked away in the corner.

Can we call a program *bilingual* if the final interpretation of success affirms monolingualism? One might argue that the school is in compliance with the state law in Texas that emphasizes transition to English as soon as possible. One must inquire, Who makes the laws? Whose interests do these lawmakers represent? The child's? According to Romaine (1995), if transitional bilingual education produces unsatisfactory results, we blame it and its recipients rather than the mainstream that defines it, starves it, threatens it, and then blames it for not curing the problems that the mainstream is largely responsible for (p. 282). A best-case scenario will produce an English speaking doctor who will be unable to communicate with half the patients who might come to see him or her in this Spanish-dominant valley. The doctor may look like the locals but will not be able to understand them or meet their needs.

A worst-case scenario might be one which a student is not accepted to medical school because he or she does not have the strong roots that come from academic competence in a primary language. The root system is truncated below the soil, and the branch system of English cannot flourish. The person may end up confused and bitter as others have written about in their attempts to deal with a lack of wholeness for what has been systematically taken away. Worse yet, he or she may succeed in a White world while ashamed of his or her roots, heritage, and humble family. Will the educators who have participated in stripping away the vernacular language be around to pick up the pieces? Will the connections ever be clear between life in a White world and early educational experiences that mapped it out? Maybe this story will end happily ever after as it seems to have ended for the Hispanic educators who are charting a course for minority children with maps provided by legislators who ignore bilingual research.

NEOCOLONIALISM: DOMESTIC AND FOREIGN

In his conversations with Donaldo Macedo, Paulo Freire discussed the concept of neocolonialism in the former colonies of Portugal in Africa (Freire & Macedo, 1987). After several generations of having Portuguese as the official language during the colonial period, the upwardly mobile nationals became educated through and ideologically co-opted by the language of the colonizer. Once liberated, these same nationals became members of the ruling elite. When Freire recommended that their efforts to promote literacy throughout the infant nation be implemented using tribal languages, these same intellectuals insisted on using Portuguese as a national standard for their literacy project. In so doing, they became neocolonists of their own people and thwarted any promise of transforming their society and redefining themselves as a nation independent of Portugal.

Minority educators must understand their own colonization, hence liberatory pedagogy. To be effective in diversifying education, monolithic ideological politics must be exposed and challenged. Minority educators must come to understand the value of bilingual education as a pathway to empowerment for minority students. They must come to discover the water in which they swim not as stemming from one dominant river but the many tributaries of our pluralistic society.

Exploring and interrogating rhetoric and suppositions represents a critical first step toward understanding how power works through ideological monopolization and manipulation in schools and the wider society in ways that not only deny an equitable educational experience for nonmainstream populations but impoverish the educational experiences of the privileged. Monolithic educational practices, disguised behind the myth of neutrality, tend to reproduce privileged segments of our society who are monolingual, monocultural, paranoid, and suspicious of any other culture while they are also inept outside the comfort zones of their own groups. Critical pedagogues must deliberately work with the privileged to help them discover what was lacking in their own educations. It must help them to dispel the myth that getting an A and pleasing the teacher somehow represent learning and intelligence.

Other forms of rhetoric used to misrepresent or misinform demonstrate how the language of schools systematically skirts critical issues. The term "dropout" has been challenged in the educational reform literature with a variety of suggested substitutions to clarify the sources of the problem rather than blaming the victim while leaving the system uninterrogated, as the term does. Bahruth (1987) introduced the term "squeezed out" since it semantically begs the question of who does the squeezing. In fact, subtle, monolithic cultural practices in schools over time create cumulative conditions of manufactured failure and pedagogical wrongdoing to certain populations almost by zip codes. It is not surprising that the gradual wearing down of culturally different students over the years ends in their leaving school at the first legal window of opportunity. Giroux (1996) voices their dilemma:

> The convenience store and the basketball court have come to symbolize a future of ambivalence poised between dead-end labor, on the one hand, and the dream of gaining prosperity and fame as a professional athlete on the other. Neither of these positions, with their mix of despair and false hope, offers youth from subordinate groups much meaning in imagining a better future. Youth not only face the consequences of economic downsizing, they often find themselves being educated and regulated within institutions that have little relevance for their lives. This is expressed most strongly in schools. Strongly tied to the technology of print, located within a largely Eurocentric curriculum, and often resistant to analyzing how racial, class, and gender differences intersect in shaping that curriculum, schooling appears to many youth to be as irrelevant as it is boring. (p. 13)

As though the term "dropout" were not bad enough, further tweaking of language and statistics now has some schools reporting "retention rates." This may sound more positive, but often the problem still remains unaddressed, since the numbers are just reversed. For example, a district with a 45% "dropout" rate is now reporting 55% retention. Nothing has changed except the rhetorical shift to frame the report in a more positive light. Closer inspection of this particular situation has revealed that when all eligible students living within the district boundaries are included, the "dropout" rate is closer to 67%, in which case the district would hardly use the tactic of reporting a 33% retention rate.

In his discussion of "negatively charged words," Macedo (1994) addresses how certain societal issues become demonized as they are portrayed by media representatives of the status quo. Included in the list would be the concept of bilingual education. It has become an emotional topic and one about which almost every American has an opinion. Through the duping of America, many hold strong negative feelings about bilingual education without really understanding it. In conversations with lay Americans, it is often possible to "sell" the idea by describing a bilingual program without naming it. Most find it quite reasonable and desirable; a program from which they would like their own children to benefit. Only the most bigoted of Americans would continue to object. So why the negative propaganda?

GLOBAL ECONOMIZATION AND CULTURAL HOMOGENIZATION

It is only a few hundred of the world's 6 or 7 thousand languages that have any kind of official status, and it is only speakers of official languages who enjoy all linguistic human rights. Observing linguistic human rights implies on an individual level that everyone can identify positively with their vernacular language and have that identification respected by others, irrespective of whether their vernacular is a minority or a majority language (Skutnabb-Kangas, 1994).

It is no coincidence that official languages with full linguistic human rights in the world share an ideology of global economics. Nor is it coincidental that speakers of languages not enjoying full linguistic human rights share vernacular common ground in the sense that theirs are subsistence cultures with values that run counter to economization and development. Power reveals itself in the granting of official status to those speech communities of the world that have been colonized and ideologized into full participation in global economics. Cultural groups that have struggled tenaciously to preserve ancient traditions and epistemologies centered on survival rather than commodification are under siege. Although their traditions have provided a gestalt for millennia, their ways of knowing are counterproductive to the expansion of the global economy being forced on them.

Language policies reflect ideological controversies between world power brokers and subordinated cultural groups. Initiation of aggression is by those of the dominant ideology who apply increasing degrees of pressure on cultural groups outside the loop to conform with the expansion of global economics. Significant resistance is met with the most extreme application of pressure: genocide. Lesser degrees of coercion appear as economic subordination, linguistic imperialism during colonization, and, in an era of global high technology, the exportation of materialist values through cable television and computer networks. Links can be made between domestic and foreign policies that aim for conformity to the dominant ideology. Coexistence is not an option. Global economic expansion is bent on eradication of aboriginal cultures either through co-option or elimination.

Using Chomsky's concept of "the threat of a good example" in American foreign policy tendencies to disrupt any experiments which represent alternatives to capitalism in Latin America, Cummins (1994) draws a relationship between foreign policy and domestic educational policy. When school districts have established additive bilingual programs through federal grants, thereby demonstrating the strength of bilingual theory, Cummins reports a systematic tendency of federal decisions to defund these programs. Transitional programs that hurry students into English pose no threat of a good example and are richly rewarded by continuous funding. Conversely, consistent defunding has also been documented when effective, pedagogically sound dual-language programs, result in competence in two languages. Research on effectiveness of programs (Ramirez, Yuen, & Ramey, 1991), favors the latter, yet is ignored. In the words of Henry Giroux (1995), "The status quo has never been known to finance its own debacle" (personal communication). In fact, it works vehemently against nonconformity.

The argument returns to power. Spring (1991) defines power as "the ability to control the actions of other people and the ability to escape from the control of others." No reasonable American would suggest that American democracy is a blooming success. Carville (1996) demonstrates statistically how Americans are growing drastically apart economically since 1980. This by no means indicates a debacle for the status quo. A visit to inner cities across America provides strong indicators of the continued desperation of the human condition of underclass Americans of all ethnicities (Kozol, 1991).

The ideological power base of America is one of monolingualism and monoculturalism. As we approach the 21st century, mostly token gains based on gender and skin color rather than ideology have been made in the politics of representation; there still exists a paucity of representation of political diversity. That is to say, more and more ethnic diversity is represented across the hierarchy of professional, political, and social realities, but monolithic representation of politics continues to preserve and promote hegemony. In too many cases, ethnicity is represented biologically, not ideologically. This results from a reward system of moving up the ladder based on acting White (and male), rather than acting out.

In schools, intelligence is predicated on a definition that identifies knowledge, ideology, and abilities monopolized by the privileged class, which, as members, they "enjoy" de facto. Any outsiders who wish for recognition and mobility within the public education system must conform to the narrow definitions set forth to maintain a cornered market. Ironically, those outsiders who strive for academic success and recognition and achieve it pay no small price. They adopt the ideology of the privileged class, abandon their own first language and cultures, and become neocolonists of their own groups, often totally unaware of the price they have had to pay. Just as Bureau of Indian Affairs schools were designed to take the Indian out of the Indian, subtractive bilingual programs resulting from the great compromise (Crawford, 1991) to accept transitional bilingual education as a national policy—despite strong theoretical support for maintaining bilingual education—have provided the media with the data necessary to continue to bash bilingualism. To argue for bilingualism is perceived as "unAmerican."

Bilingualism threatens the very core of hegemony and power in the United States. American schools continue to predicate their mission of Americanizing of all citizens as fundamental to national identity (Giroux, 1996) and unity. What remains invisible throughout the effort is the racism and neocolonialism underlying national identity that pivots on the cultural capital of the privileged class. The yardstick that has been the standard by which all "Americans" are put to the litmus test continues to prove certain groups unacceptable, as it justifies their academic, social, and economic marginalization through goodness-of-fit standards. The "normal" curve represents statistically the impossibility of linear and chronological approaches to learning that attempt to educate all learners in cookie-cutter fashion. Where children fall on the "normal" curve seems to have more to do with goodness of fit in a one-size-fits-all educational system than it has to do with the innate ability of a student to learn. By the same token, "ready to learn" linguistically reflects an inflexible school system and might be more accurately stated as "ready to fit." As stated by Byrd (1996), "Many of us know firsthand how politically motivated testing, grading, and tracking policies have served to exclude and punish those of us who did not understand or wish to conform to education that continues to subject us to poverty and hopelessness" (p. 6).

When Macedo (1994) states "monolingualism is a curable disease," perhaps he named the cure for arrogant domination of vernacular cultures by capitalist power brokers. Bilingualism at least offers humans an opportunity to view the world from less ethnocentric positions through juxtaposition of cultures for the development of a critical reading of the world. Pedagogically, it provides opportunities to draw connections between affluence and poverty, language and ideology, and, hopefully, global economic expansion and the exploitation, dehumanization, and destruction of vernacular cultures around the world. Ultimately, an appreciation for vernacular cultural traditions might evolve that would provoke people to contemplate their roles as accomplices in the contamination and eradication of cultural groups that represent fundamental dimensions of our humanity.

REFERENCES

Bahruth, R. (1987). Dialogue journals and the acquisition of spelling in the bilingual classroom. *Dialogue, 4*(2) (J. Staton, J. Kreft Peyton, & S. Gutstein. (Eds). Washington, DC: Center for Applied Linguistics. P. 3.

Byrd, S. (1996). *Critical reflections on the educational experiences of a migrant student*. Unpublished manuscript. Boise, ID: Boise State University.

Carville, J. (1996). *We're right, they're wrong*. New York: Random House.

Crawford, J. (1991). *Bilingual education: History, politics, theory and practice* (2nd ed.). Los Angeles, CA: Bilingual Educational Services.

Cummins, J. (1994). The discourse of disinformation: The debate on bilingual education and language rights in the United States. In T. Skutnabb-Kangas & R. Phillipson (Eds.), *Linguistic human rights: Overcoming linguistic discrimination*. Berlin: Mouton de Gruyter.

Freire, P., & Macedo, D. (1987). *Literacy: Reading the word and the world*. South Hadley, MA: Bergin & Garvey.

Giroux, H. (1996). *Fugitive cultures: Race violence and youth*. New York: Routledge, Chapman & Hall.

Kozol, J. (1991). *Savage inequalities*. New York: Crown.

Macedo, D. (1994). *Literacies of power: What Americans are not allowed to know*. Boulder, CO: Westview Press.

Ramirez, J. D., Yuen, S. D., & Ramey, D. R. (1991). *Executive summary Final report: Longitudinal study of structured English immersion strategy, early exit and late-exit transitional bilingual education programs for language minority children*. (Contract No. 300–87–0156, submitted to the U.S. Department of Education). San Mateo: Aguirre International.

Romaine, S. (1995). *Bilingualism*, (2nd ed.). Oxford, England: Blackwell.

Skutnabb-Kangas, T. (1994). *Linguistic human rights: Overcoming linguistic discrimination*. T. Skutnabb-Kangas & R. Phillipson (Eds.), Berlin: Mouton de Gruyter.

Spring, J. (1991). Knowledge and power in research into politics of urban education. *Politics of Education Association Yearbook*, (45–56).

23

Cultural Literacy

Donaldo Macedo
University of Massachusetts

Although multicultural education is now very much in vogue in the United States, it often emphasizes the teaching of cultural tolerance so as to disarticulate multicultural pedagogy from a form of cultural politics. In my analysis in this chapter, multicultural education becomes a meaningful construct to the degree that it is viewed as a set of practices that function to either empower or disempower people. In the larger sense, multicultural education is analyzed according to whether it serves to reproduce existing social formations or serves as a set of cultural practices that promote democratic and emancipatory change. For this reason, I examine multicultural education in light of theories of cultural production and reproduction. I also argue more strongly for the deconstruction of the very language used in the multicultural debate as a prerequisite to the development of any meaningful multicultural pedagogy that purports to serve as the means to a critical appropriation of one's own culture and history.

Within the last decade, the issue of multicultural education has taken on a new importance among educators. Unfortunately, the debate that has emerged tends to recycle old assumptions and values regarding the meaning and usefulness of multicultural education. The notion that multicultural education is a matter of learning cultural characteristics about the "other" that will lead to cultural tolerance still informs that vast majority of multicultural programs and manifests its logic in the renewed emphasis on the management of the cultural "other." In other words, let us learn more about the cultural "other" so we can be more effective in dealing with "them." For example, there is a rapid growth of textbooks designed to teach racial and multicultural tolerance. What these texts do is hide the asymmetrical distribution of power and cultural capital through a form of paternalism that promises to the 'other' a dose of tolerance. That is, since we coexist and must find ways to get along, I will tolerate you. Missing from this posture is the ethical position that calls for mutual respect and even racial and cultural solidarity. As Susan Mendus succinctly argues, tolerance "presupposes that its object is morally repugnant, that it really needs to be reformed, that is, altered" (cited in Goldberg, 1993, p. 7). Accordingly, racial and cultural tolerance may be viewed as a process through which the different other is permitted to be with the idea, or at least the hope, that through tolerance the intolerant features that characterize the "other" will be eliminated or repressed.

I want to reiterate in this chapter that multicultural education cannot be viewed as simply the development of tolerance of other cultural groups. This view sustains a notion of ideology that systematically negates rather than makes meaningful the cultural experiences of the subordinate cultural groups who are, by and large, the objects of its policies. For the notion of multicultural education to become meaningful it has to be situated within a theory of cultural production and viewed as an integral part of the way in which people produce, transform, and reproduce meaning. Multicultural education must be seen as a medium that constitutes and affirms those historical and existential moments of lived experience that produce a subordinate or a lived culture. Hence, it is an eminently political phenomenon, and it must be analyzed within the context of a theory of power relations and an understanding of social and cultural reproduction and production. By "cultural reproduction" I mean collective experiences that function in the interest of the dominant groups rather than in the interest of the oppressed groups who are the objects of its policies. I use the term "cultural production" to refer to specific groups of people producing, mediating, and confirming the mutual ideological elements that emerge from and reaffirm their daily lived experiences. In this case, such experiences are rooted in the interests of individual and collective self-determination. By using these two theoretical constructs so as to facilitate my analysis, I do not want to give the impression of creating a false dichotomy between "cultural reproduction" and "cultural production." In reality, they represent interpenetrating realms of culture producing, in the different contexts, different results with varying consequences. That is, in "cultural reproduction" it is possible to also have cultural production, and vice versa. What is different is the context of production or reproduction and the power asymmetries they generate.

Finally, I analyze the role of language in the reproduction process that gives rise to insidious forms of racism. In fact, many multicultural educators prefer to reduce the complexity of cultural conflicts to an empty cliché of cultural diversity as a way to avoid struggling with the cruel reality of racism.

Many White Americans prefer not to be reminded of the appallingly oppressive and bloody history of racism that has characterized the very fabric of the society. In fact, many, if not most, White Americans would feel extremely uncomfortable if the curriculum in schools incorporated an antiracist pedagogy that asks, Mirror, mirror on the wall, is everyone welcome in the hall?

Sadly, not everyone is welcome in the hall. A report entitled "Muted Voices in The Newsroom," published by the National Association of Black Journalists, revealed that 32 percent of African American journalists fear that bringing up issues of race damages their chances for advancement (Jackson, 1993, p. 15). The same can be said of African American and other minority teachers. This condition of fear gives rise to a form of censorship that views the aggressive denouncement of racism as worse than the racist act itself.

As we approach the end of the century, some of the most pressing challenges facing educators in the United States is the issue of "ethnic and cultural war," which constitutes, in my view, a code word that engenders our society's licentiousness for racism. Although this chapter sheds light on the ideological mechanisms that shape and maintain our racist social order, I attempt to move my discussion beyond the reductionistic binarism of White versus Black racism. Not only do I avoid falling prey to a binaristic approach to race analysis, I differentiate ethnic and racial groups to avoid the facile interpretation of these ideological constructs. The fragmentation of ethnic and racial realities is part of the social organization of knowledge defined rigidly along disciplinary boundaries, that is, ethnic studies. This fragmentation not only represents a rupture with ethnic and racial relations, but it also hides behind an ideology that creates and sustains false dichotomies delineated by ethnic or race disciplinary boundaries. I believe that racism is an ideological construct that interpenetrates both ethnic and racial realities. In fact, what is important is not an isolated analysis of racism from other social organizations along the lines of ethnicity and culture. Only through a process through which the dominant White patriarchy is deconstructed can we begin to understand the intimate relationship of asymmetrical distribution of power and privilege along different ethnic groups, including lower-class ethnic Whites. In other words, we need to avoid the lumping of multiple identities into a monolithic entity such as race or ethnicity. Part of the deconstruction of dominant White ideology involves the understanding of how ethnicity and race interpenetrate each other, a concept that Pepi Leistyna (1998) refers to as "racethnicity, a process through which the ideological construction of race has a significant impact on ethnicity" (p.). We need to move beyond a discourse that views difference simply aesthetic or separate categories of analysis. What is important is to link difference to questions of power where whiteness and blackness, among other characteristics, are treated as political categories that do not exist in a power vacuum. These categories exist in relation to one another mediated always by asymmetrical power relationships. According to Stanley Aronowitz (1998):

> The concept of ethnicity with respect to education expresses two somewhat different characteristics of how issues of inequality are conventionally addressed in the literature. Recently, descriptively, the term has been employed to discuss issues of access and since we have no social scientifically acceptable discourse of class, ethnicity has become the displacement of this largely unacknowledged aspect of educational access and performance. (p. 193)

The challenge for educators is to interrogate the descriptive nature of the discourse on race, culture, and ethnicity to unveil the inherent ideology that hides how "ethnicity has become the displacement" of class. Educators need to also understand how "cultural differences are purged and social practices are reshaped around a racial identify [giving rise to] a hierarchy that subcategorizes while devaluing groups of people that are designated 'racial others,''ethnics,' 'outsiders.' "(Leistyna, 1998, p. 66).

Central to this ethnic and cultural war is the creation of an ideologically coded language that serves, at least, two fundamental functions. On the one hand, it veils the new racism that characterizes our society, and on the other hand, it insidiously perpetuates the functioning and devaluing of ethnic and racial identities. I want to argue that although the present ethnic and cultural war is characterized by a form of racism at the level of language, it is important to differentiate between language as racism and the experience of racism. For example, Pat Buchanan's call for the end of illegal immigration "even if it means putting the National Guard all along the Southern frontier" (cited in Rezendez, 1995, p. 1) constitutes a form of racism at the level of language that has had the effect of licensing institutional discrimination whereby both documented and undocumented immigrants materially experience the loss of their dignity, the denial of human citizenship, and in many cases, outright violence as evidenced by the cruel beatings of a Mexican man and woman by the border patrol not too long ago. I also believe that even though racism at the level of language is no less insidious, it hides the institutional racism that bears on the lived experiences of those who are victimized by institutionalized racism.

Language as racism constitutes what Bourdieu refers to as "'the hegemony of symbolic violence'" (cited in Giroux, 1992, p. 20). As educators, we need to fully understand the interrelationship between symbolic violence produced through language and the essence of experienced racism. Although the two are not mutually exclusive, "language also constitutes and mediates the multiple experiences of identity by both historicizing it and revealing its partiality and incompleteness, its limits are realized in the material nature of experience as it names the body through the specificity of place, space, and history (Giroux, in press). This is very much in line with John Fiske's (1994) notion that "there is a material experience of homelessness ... but the boundary between the two cannot be drawn sharply. Material conditions are inescapably saturated with culture and, equally, cultural conditions are inescapably experienced as material" (p. 13).

By deconstructing the cultural conditions that give rise to the present violent assault on undocumented immigrants, affirmative action, African Americans and other racial and ethnic groups, I attempt in this chapter to single out those ideological factors that enable even highly educated individuals to blindly embrace, for example, Rush Limbaugh's sexist and racist tirades designed to demonize and dehumanize other ethnic and cultural identities. I also discuss the psychological and political ramifications of fracturing cultural identities by pointing out that the racism and high level of xenophobia we are witnessing in our society today are not isolated acts of individuals such as Rush Limbaugh or David Duke. Rather, these individuals are representatives of an orchestrated effort by all segments of the dominant society to wage a war on the poor and on people, who, by virtue of their race, ethnicity, language, and class are reduced, at best, to half-citizens, and at worse, to a national enemy who is responsible for all the ills afflicting our society. We need to understand the cultural and historical context that gives rise to more than 20 million Rush Limbaugh "supporters" who tune in weekly to his radio and television programs. Only through a critical analysis of how racism and sexism have penetrated the deepest level of our cultural psyche can we begin to understand those ideological factors that enable seemingly educated individuals to blindly embrace sexist and racist tirades designed to demonize and dehumanize other cultural identities, as evidenced here:

- "Now I got something for you that's true— 1992, Tufts University, Boston. This is 24 years ago or 22 years ago. Three-year study of 5,000 coeds, and they used a benchmark of a bra size of 34C. They forward that—now wait! It's true. The larger the bra size, the smaller the IQ."
- "Feminism was established so that unattractive women could have easier access to mainstream society."
- "There are more American Indians alive today than there were when Columbus arrived or at any other time in history. Does that sound like a record of genocide?"
- "Taxpaying citizens are not being given access to these welfare and health services that they deserve and desire. But if you're an illegal immigrant and cross the border, you get everything you want." (Randall, Naureckus, & Cohen, 1995, pp. 47–54)

In addition to deconstructing the cultural conditions that foster Limbaugh's and others' sexist and racist tirades, we need also to understand those ideological elements that inform our policymakers and those individuals who shape public opinion by supporting and rewarding Limbaugh's unapologetic demonizing of other cultural subjects. For example, Ted Koppel considers him "very smart. He does his homework. He is well informed." George Will considers him the "fourth branch of government," and former Secretary of Education William Bennett—the virtue advocate—describes Limbaugh as "possibly our greatest living American" (Randall, Naureckus, & Cohen, 1995, p. 10). What remains incomprehensible is why highly educated individuals cannot see through Limbaugh's obvious distortions of history and falsification of reality. I posit that the inability to perceive distinctions and falsifications of reality is partly but not totally due to the hegemonic forces that promote an acritical education a the fragmentation of bodies of knowledge, which makes it very difficult for students to link historical events to gain a more critical understanding of reality.

Against cruel and racist cultural conditions, we can begin to understand that it is not a coincidence that Patrick Buchanan reiterated in his first presidential campaign platform that his fellow Americans should "wage a cultural revolution in the nineties as sweeping as the political revolution of the eighties" (cited in Giroux, 1992, p. 230). In fact, this cultural revolution is indeed moving forward with rapid speed, from the onslaught on cultural diversity and multicultural education to Patrick Buchanan's call to our national and patriotic sense to build a large wall to keep the "illegals" in Mexico. It is the same national and patriotic sense that allowed President Clinton not to be outdone by the extreme right forcing him to announce in his state of the union address that

> All Americans, not only in the states most heavily affected, but in every place in this country, are rightly disturbed by the large numbers of illegal aliens entering our country. The jobs they hold might otherwise be held by citizens or legal immigrants.
>
> The public services they use impose burdens on our taxpayers. That's why our administration has moved aggressively to secure our borders more by hiring a record number of new border guards, by deporting twice as many criminal aliens as ever before, by cracking down on illegal hiring, by barring welfare benefits to illegal aliens.
>
> In the budget I will present to you, we will try to do more to speed the deportation of illegal aliens who are arrested for crimes, to better identify illegal aliens in the workplace as recommended by the commission headed by former Congresswoman Barbara Jordan. (Clinton, 1995, p. 303)

An analysis of the far-right Republican attack on immigrants and cultural groups and our liberal democratic president's remarks during his state of the union address confirm what has been for decades the United States' best kept secret, that there is no critical ideological difference between the Republican and Democratic parties. Ideologically speaking, in the United States we have a one-party system of government represented by two branches with only cosmetic differences cloaked under the umbrellas of Republicans and Democrats.

If Patrick Buchanan's vicious attack on immigrants were to be interpreted in ways other than racist, how could we explain his unfortunate testament that: "I think God made all people good, but if we had to take a million immigrants in—say Zulus next year or Englishmen [why not Englishwomen?]—and put them in Virginia, what group would be easier to assimilate and would cause less problems for the people of Virginia?" (cited in Pertman, 1991, p. 15).

I believe that it is the same racist sentiment that enabled President Clinton to abandon the nomination of Lani Guenier to head the Justice Department's civil rights division just because she accurately demonstrated in her writings that the working-class poor, African Americans, and members of other minority cultural groups do not have representation in the present two-party system, within which the White, male-dominated capitalist ideology works aggressively against the interests of these groups. It is the same racist ideology that is forcing President Clinton to join the chorus in calling for an end to affirmative action policies, even though the benefactors of the real affirmative action since the birth of this country have been White males who continue to dominate all sectors of institutional and economic life in this society. For example, according to employment data on Boston banks from the Equal Employment Opportunity Commission "from 1990–1993, the industry added 4,116 jobs. While the percentage of white male officers and managers rose by 10 percent, the percentage of African-American officers and managers dropped by 25 percent. While the percentage of white female clerical workers went up 10 percent, the percentage of African-American clerical workers dropped 15 percent" (Jackson, 1995, p. 13).

Like multicultural education, affirmative action is also a code word that licenses the new racism that assuages the White working class' and middle class' fear as they steadily lose ground to the real affirmative action programs designed to further enrich the upper class and big business:

> When the Fed raises the interest rates, it helps big business at the expense of individual home owners. When politicians resist raising the minimum wage, it helps big business send off the working poor. When politicians want liability caps, they defend Big Oil, Ma Bell and her offspring and Detroit gas guzzlers over potential victims of defective products and pollution. As the Gingrich revolution slashes school lunches for the poor, corporations get $111 billion in tax breaks, according to Labor Secretary Robert Reich. (Jackson, 1995, p. 13)

We also know that even within the context of the present affirmative action policy, the real benefactors have been White women. Their convenient silence on the present assault on affirmative action, a program from which they have benefitted greatly, makes them complicit with the reproduction of the racist "myth that black people take jobs from white people, [which leads] one to conclude that African-Americans are not considered Americans. White men lose jobs to other white men who do not say, 'they gave my job to an inferior white man!' White male competency is assumed. African-Americans, regardless of achievement, are forever on trial" (Jackson, 1995, p. 13). In other words, Henry Louis Gates, Jr.'s, prominence as a scholar did not lessen the racism he had to face at Duke University when he taught there. Cornell West's status as a renowned public intellectual did little for him as he watched nine taxis go by and refuse to pick him up as a passenger in the streets of New York just because of the color of his skin. bell hooks' eminence as a major feminist scholar does not lessen the pain of racism coupled with the sexism she endures. Having written many highly acclaimed feminist books still does not provide her access to the media and magazines enjoyed by many White feminists. As hooks recently pointed out to Naomi Wolf:

> I have written eight feminist books. None of the magazines that have talked about your book, Naomi, have ever talked about my books at all. Now, that's not because there aren't ideas in my books that have universal appeal. It's because the issue that you raised in *The Beauty Myth* is still about beauty. We have to acknowledge that all of us do not have equal access. (hooks, Steinem, Urashi, & Wolf, 1993, p. 39)

hooks' statement denudes the myth created by the antiaffirmative action discourse that "pretends that we live in a color-blind society where individuals are treated according to [t]he American ethic [that] has always held that individual effort and achievement are valued and rewarded" (Jackson, 1995, p. 13). The separation of the individual from the group collective consciousness is part of the dominant White ideology's mechanism to fragment the reality so as to make it easier for individuals to accept living within a lie that proposes a raceless and color-blind society.

In conclusion, the real issue behind the present assault on multiculturalism and affirmative action is to never fall prey to a pedagogy of big lies. The fundamental challenge is to accept Derrick Bell's call for a "continuing quest for new directions in our struggle for racial justice, a struggle we must continue even if racism is an integral, permanent and indestructible component of this society" (Bell, 1992, p. xiii). A multicultural pedagogy not only needs to commit itself to a constant struggle for social justice, but it must also create conditions in which

> we will be able to embrace the other, enlarging our human possibility. People and their cultures perish in isolation, but they are born or reborn in contact with other men and women, with men and women of another culture, another creed, another race. If we do not recognize our humanity in others, we shall not recognize it in ourselves. (Fuentes, 1992, p. 411)

REFERENCES

Aronowitz, S. (1998). Between nationality and chaos. *Harvard Educational Review, 67*(2).

Baldwin, J. (1985). *The price of the ticket: Collected nonfiction*. New York: St. Martin's Press.

Bell, D. D. (1992). *Faces at the bottom of the well: The penance of racism*. New York: Basic Books.

Clinton, W. J. (1995, January 28). The state of the union, Clinton speech envisions local empowerment. For the Record. *Congressional Quarterly*, (January 28, 1995).

Fiske, J. (1994). *Power plays, power works*. London: Verso Press.

Fuentes, C. (1992, March 30). The mirror of the other. *The Nation*, Vol. 254(12), pp. 408–412.

Giroux, H. A. (1992). *Border crossings: Cultural workers and the politics of education*. New York: Routledge, Chapman & Hall.

Giroux, H. A. (in press). Transgression of difference. Series Introduction to *Culture and difference: Critical perspectives on bicultural experiences*. Westport, CT: Bergin & Garvey.

Goldberg, D. T. (1993). *Racist culture*. Oxford, England.

hooks, b., Steinem, G., Uruashi, V., & Wolf, N. (1993, September/October). Get real about feminism: The myths, the backlash, the movement, Ms. *Magazine*, p. 39.

Jackson, D. Z. (1993, September 2). Muted voices in the newsroom. *The Boston Globe*, p. 15.

Leistyna, P. (1998). Racethnicity: Whitewashing ethnicity. In D. Macedo (Ed.). *Tongue-tying multiculturalism*. Manuscript preparation.

Pertman, A. (1991, December 15). Buchanan announces presidential candidacy. *The Boston Globe* pp. 1.

Randall, S. Naureckus, J., & Cohen, J. (1995). *The way things ought to be: Rush Limbaugh's reign of error*. New York: New York Press.

Rezendez, M., (1995, March 21). Declaring "cultural war": Buchanan opens '96 run. *The Boston Globe*, pp. .

24

Multicultural Education

Etta R. Hollins
Wright State University

> The problem facing policymakers in Jefferson's time was how to dispossess Indians of large tracts of land without doing undue violence to their philanthropic ideals. Their ingenious solution to this dilemma was rooted in the conviction that it required much more land to support a nomadic hunting society than a like-sized population of sedentary farmers. Thus, the willingness of Indians to sell their land would be directly proportionate to their ability to acquire civilized ways. Moreover, in the civilizing process, they would be drawn inevitably into the White economy; they would come to hunger for the goods of Whites just as the White man hungered for Indian land. The pieces of the puzzle began to fall into place. (Adams, 1996, p. 49)

According to Adams (1996), the purpose and process of schooling for American Indians at the turn of this century were framed by an ideology based on Protestantism, capitalism, and Republicanism that, in practice, translated into Protestantism, individualization, and Americanization. This ideology was intended to replace core values of the Indian culture such as communalism, traditional beliefs, and the associated customs and rituals. In schools provided for the Americanization of Indian children, the Christian message was conveyed in the form of McGuffey readers, church services, prayer meetings, and religious clubs. Americanization included changing physical appearance and personal and group identity. In school, the children's hair was cut and they wore uniforms rather than their traditional clothing. Individualism was introduced as self-reliance, industrialism, perseverance, and personal accomplishment. Ultimately, the children were taught to view the European Americans as more civilized than Indians. Indian beliefs, customs, and rituals were considered savage. In essence, the children were taught the tools of assimilation (to speak, think, dress, and behave like European Americans); however, they were treated as outsiders.

Capitalism was at the heart of the dilemma faced by policymakers during Jefferson's time. The same is true today. In the contemporary economy, one aspect of the dilemma is an excess in the labor force resulting from both a global economy with cheap labor in underdeveloped countries that boosts corporate profits by replacing more expensive labor in the United States and from labor-saving technologies that have displaced workers in the United States. Under these conditions, policymakers still have the need to protect their philanthropic image and commitment to building a strong nation. One way of doing this is to emphasize the need to maintain the United States' role as a world leader in aide to underdeveloped countries while pointing to the inadequacy of schools as the primary factor in eroding this nation's position as an economic power.

The greatest excess in the labor market in the United States is among low-income and ethnic minority groups. Likewise, members of these groups tend to be underrepresented at the highest levels of educational attainment. Recent data provided by the U.S. Department of Labor (1997) shows an unemployment rate for European Americans to be 4.5% as compared to 11.3% for African Americans and 8.1% for Hispanic Americans. The U.S. Office of Education (1996) reports a college graduation rate (for persons 25 years or older) for European Americans of 24.0% compared to 13.2% for African Americans, and 9.3% for Hispanic Americans. According to the National Center for Educational Statistics (NCES, 1996a), European Americans comprise 73.5% of the college student population while the racial-ethnic minority comprises 23.8%. As in K–12 public schools, these students are generally taught by European American faculty.

Researchers and scholars have give considerable attention to explaining the low levels of academic achievement and performance among low-income and ethnic minority youngsters. Examples of the explanations tendered include low status within the society that influences beliefs in the efficacy of schooling (Ogbu, 1995), curriculum tracking and ability grouping (Braddock, 1995), and inadequate teacher preparation (Darling-Hammond, 1995).

Despite these explanations for the low levels of academic performance among many ethnic minority youngsters, the reality is that the purpose and practices of schooling for these groups today have much in common with that provided for Indian children at the turn of the century. Not much has changed in how we think about the principles undergirding the purpose and practices of schooling since the turn of this century. Youngsters are less likely to begin the school day by reciting the Pledge of Allegiance or Bible passages such as Psalms, Chapter 23. It is less likely today that authors of United States history textbooks for elementary and secondary schools will make the claim that Columbus discovered America. However, many textbook authors continue promoting an exclusively European American cultural perspective that supports the status quo. This includes particular cultural values such as the Protestant work ethic, individualism and self-reliance, competition, and materialism.

The question of whose culture should be represented in textbooks has fueled a debate between traditionalists and multiculturalists. Aspects of this debate are reminiscent of discussions about Indian education at the turn of the century. For example, the traditionalists such as Ravitch (1991/1992) argued that "it is not the role of public schools to teach children the customs and folkways of their ethnic and racial groups; that is, as it has always been, the role of the family, the church, and the local community. Nor is it the role of the public school to encapsulate children in the confines of their family's inherited culture" (p. 8). Ravitch further argued that "under no circumstances should the curriculum be patterned to stir ethnocentric pride or to make children feel that their self-worth as human beings is derived from their race or ethnic origin" (p. 11). At the turn of the century, Indian children were taught the customs and folkways of the European immigrants as part of the Americanization and assimilation process. In order to succeed in school, ethnic minority children are expected to adopt European American middle-class ways of thinking and behaving.

Lash (1979) described the preservation of European American culture through the schooling process in the following way:

> In dealing with their children, they insist not only on their own authority but on the authority of the past. Rich families invent historical legends about themselves, which the young internalize. In many ways the most important thing they give their children is the sense of generational continuity so rarely encountered elsewhere in American society. (p. 219)

Although Lash referred to rich families, this practice is apparent in the Eurocentric perspective presented in the school curriculum where there is limited inclusion of ethnic minorities. In contrast, Banks (1996), a multiculturalist, argued that:

> Education within a pluralistic society should affirm and help students understand their home and community cultures. However, it should also help free them from their cultural boundaries. To create and maintain a civic community that works for the common good, education in a democratic society should help students acquire the knowledge, attitudes, and skills they will need to participate in civic action to make society more equitable and just. (p. 75)

The central issue in the debate between the multiculturalists and the traditionalists is the purpose of schooling. It seems that both groups might agree on the central purpose of schooling as improving the quality of life on planet Earth. Using this general position as a point of departure might provide a basis for reframing school practices. In this instance, "quality of life" refers to the environmental, physiological, psychological, and sociological conditions under which humankind exists (Hollins, 1996). In this ideal schooling situation, all curriculum content (including mathematics, science, and social studies) would focus on these four aspects of human existence. In the debate between traditionalists and multiculturalists, the traditionalists seem to deny the importance of a healthy sense of ethnic identity to ones' psychological well being. If this factor were acknowledged, both groups might support a balance between particularistic and inclusive aspects of the school curriculum. In which case, both groups would support a curriculum in which youngsters simultaneously learn about their own ethnic origins and customs while learning to position themselves within a national and global society.

Building a learning community emphasizing collaborative inquiry and problem solving would support youngsters in identifying their life's work as committed to service, rather than to an individualistic, competitive pursuit of personal gain. Within this learning community each youngster would learn to use and expand her or his own learning strengths and preferences while appreciating and benefitting from those of others. In practice, this means providing equitable access to learning for all youngsters. One approach might be to divide the curriculum into two domains: *descriptive* and *expressive* (Hollins, 1996). The descriptive domain would present formal and procedural knowledge derived from empirical sources that can be quantified or verified. The expressive domain would present informal and impressionistic knowledge intentionally derived from intuitive, subjective, and qualitative sources and procedures. Youngsters could learn to use one domain to inform the other. It is the intersection of the two domains that represents a potentially complex state of knowing and understanding that supports constructing new knowledge.

Youngsters exposed to the process of schooling proposed here are likely to question traditional perspectives and core values. They might favor communalism over individualism, collaboration over competition, purpose in life over personal gain, and understanding and accepting others over fear and prejudice.

In conclusion, it is apparent that, over the past 100 years, the ideology undergirding schooling in the United States has remained stable. Some practices associated with Protestantism, such as Bible reading and prayer in schools have been eliminated; others, such as the work ethic, have become more subtle. The society has changed considerably. In this era of rapid technological advancement, some people have all the modern conveniences available, whereas others are victims of poverty, homelessness, and crime. These conditions, coupled with violence in schools and resistance to traditional practices, indicate that it is time to rethink the purpose and process of schooling. This rethinking musc include reexamining the supporting ideology.

REFERENCES

Adams, D. W. (1996). Fundamental considerations: The deep meaning of Native American schooling, 1880–1900. In E. R. Hollins (Ed.), *Transforming curriculum for a culturally diverse society* (pp. 27–57). Mahwah, NJ: Lawrence Erlbaum Associates.

Banks, J. A. (1996). Multicultural education: For freedom's sake. In E. R. Hollins (Ed.). *Transforming curriculum for a culturally diverse society* (pp. 75–82). Mahwah, NJ: Lawrence Erlbaum Associates.

Braddock, J. H. II. (1995). Tracking and school achievement: Implications for literacy development. In V. L Gadsden & D. A. Wagner (Eds.), *Literacy among African-American youth: Issues in learning, teaching, and schooling* (pp. 153–176). Cresskill, NJ: Hampton Press.

Darling-Hammond, L. (1995). Teacher knowledge and student learning: Implications for literacy development. In V. L. Gadsden & D. A. Wagner (Eds.), *Literacy among African-American youth: Issues in learning, teaching, and schooling* (pp. 177–200). Cresskill, NJ: Hampton Press.

Hollins, E. R. (Ed.). (1996). *Transforming curriculum for a culturally diverse society.* Mahwah, NJ: Lawrence Erlbaum Associates.

Lash, C. (1979). *The culture of narcissism: American life in an age of diminishing expectations.* New York: Norton.

National Center for Education Statistics (1996a). *Condition of education, 1996* (NCES indicator 45). Washington, DC: U.S. Government Printing Office.

National Center for Educational Statistics (1996b). *Fall staff in postsecondary institutions,* 1993 (NCES 96–323). Washington, DC: U.S. Government Printing Office.

Ogbu, J.U. (1995). Literacy and Black Americans: Comparative perspectives. In V. L Gadsden & D. A. Wagner (Eds.), *Literacy among African-American youth: Issues in learning, teaching, and schooling* (pp. 83–100). Cresskill, NJ: Hampton Press.

Ravitch, D. (1991/1992). A culture in common. *Educational Leadership,* 49(4), 8–11.

United States Department of Labor (1997). *The employment situation: Employment status of the civilian population by race, sex, age, and Hispanic origin* (USDL 97–74 Bureau of Labor Statistics). Washington, DC: Government Printing Office.

United States Office of Education (1996). *Current population survey: Educational attainment* (P20–489 CenStats). Washington, DC: Government Printing Office.

25

Cultural Studies

Crystal Bartolovich
Syracuse University

The story of "Cultural Studies" is often told something like this: in postwar British universities, the dominant understanding of "culture" was still an Arnoldian one—"the best that has been thought and known in the world"—a view that had been attached to a salvational pedagogical project by, most notably, F. R. Leavis and Q. D. Leavis and their "Scrutiny" group (organized around the journal of that name) in the years between the wars. From their (tenuous) base of operations at Cambridge, Scrutiny members argued that systematic study of the "best" culture, especially literature, would save a worthy core of English people from wallowing in the dubious pleasures of "commercial" entertainment: cinema, detective fiction, and so on. This fit few would enjoy fuller, richer lives themselves while protecting the national culture for everyone (cf. Leavis, 1932; Leavis & Thompson, 1933). The "best" culture was associated not only with particular forms (poetry rather than advertising, or "serious" novels rather than thrillers) but also—in Arnoldian fashion—with the redemptive social mission of a new "middle" class as opposed to both a dilettantish aristocracy (who accounted for much of the resistance to Leavisism at Cambridge) and a degraded proletariat.

Seeing a specifically English cultural tradition as the fabric that could bind a fragmenting nation together and as an elevating respite from existence in a dreary industrialized world, the Scrutiny group's fundamental concern was with what should be included in the domain of "high" culture, and how to disseminate its "civilizing" effects. In its moment of emergence, this project was in some respects radical—promoting hitherto unknown levels of discriminating and rigorous textual study in the universities and drawing widespread attention to the manipulations of advertising and the mediocrity of the popular press—but it was also idealist and elitist, offering intellectual and aesthetic compensations to help a few people endure impoverished industrial culture while assuming that existing social structures would remain largely intact (see Eagleton, 1983). Suspicious of this elitism and idealism, but retaining from Scrutiny a sense of the power of culture, "cultural studies" as an intellectual and interventionist project in postwar Britain attempted to understand its politics. In other words, it examined the ways that "culture" worked, by distinguishing "high" from "low" in order to help shore up social hierarchies and contain nondominant groups (this politics has been described and theorized at length in Stallybrass & White, 1986).

In the 1950s and 1960s, Richard Hoggart and Raymond Williams were especially prominent in the early moment of questioning extant understandings of "culture" in sociology and literary studies, moving them toward what would become "cultural studies." Both had been "scholarship boys" who grew up in working-class provincial families. Entering a university system that assumed that the working class had no culture, they resisted acceding to this view. Thus, although Hoggart's *Uses of Literacy* (1958) is in certain fundamental ways allied to Leavisite analysis, it also moves beyond it. In the Scrutiny tradition, it examines the threat to "traditional" British culture posed by the encroachment of "American" mass entertainment. However, its method—a quasi-ethnographic examination of the lifeworld of the working-class community in which Hoggart grew up—emphasizes understanding working class culture in all its complexity (as opposed to simply condemning it). In this way, it marks what is usually seen, in retrospect, as a first break with Leavisism (see Bennett, 1981).

Even more decisively for "cultural studies" as an institutional practice, Hoggart, following a period as an adult education instructor at Leeds, went on to establish in 1964 the Birmingham Centre for Contemporary Cultural Studies (CCCS), which, over the ensuing 2 decades, was to become the most prominent site for the development of the new cultural studies in Britain. Meanwhile, from his recently attained position at Cambridge, after a stint (like Hoggart) working in adult education, Raymond Williams provided the definition of "culture" that was to be formative in the British context, including at CCCS. In *Culture and Society* (1958) and *The Long Revolution* (1961), Williams develops his view of culture as an effect of "relations between elements in a whole way of life" (newspapers as well as poetry; sports as well as paintings; eating as well as reading) as people attempt to make sense of the conditions in which they find themselves (p. viii). This definition was immediately challenged and reworked in explicitly Marxist terms by the historian E. P. Thompson (1961) as "a whole way of conflict" (p. 33)—the form in which it was to have its broadest impact.

From its first moves away from a privileging of "high" culture, in favor of a more inclusive "anthropological" understanding of it, followed a host of innovations in the study of British culture and society. Since the existing disciplinary formations of the university were unaccommodating to the sorts of projects in which they engaged, the early practitioners of cultural studies called into question long-standing divisions of labor in knowledge production and refused to honor traditional boundaries. They experimented with ethnographic techniques, textual analysis, and collaborative composition. In addition to examining traditional subjects in new ways, they studied social forms, practices, and groups previously excluded from serious cultural analysis, such as film, television, popular magazines, clothing styles, sports, and youth. They asserted that culture was not a set of artifacts to be revered, but a site of struggle in the production of meaning (semiosis) and value. They emphasized the importance of the study of "everyday life" to any understanding of late capitalism; they critiqued behavioral models in sociology and argued for a return to a (significantly revised) version of the "speculative" or "ideological" approach associated with the Frankfurt School, especially in media studies (see Hall, 1982). Most important, they argued that questions of culture could not be addressed without at the same time addressing questions of power.

Education was an important part of this questioning and analysis, but it was by no means considered to be an end in itself, as had been the case with much Leavisism (see Giroux, 1992). As Richard Johnson (1987) asserts at the end of his influential essay "What Is Cultural Studies Anyway?": "We are talking not just of theoretical developments but about some of the conditions for effective political alliances as well" (p. 75). This emphasis on "praxis"—the union of theory and political practice—brought early British cultural studies into constant contact (and conflict) with the New Left, as well as with antisexist and antiracist struggles, in addition to other practical political movements in the 1960s and 1970s, all of which left their mark on its development.

While struggling to work out ways to pursue these new inquiries and struggles, practitioners of cultural studies began to experiment with continental theory. The earliest cultural studies work was relatively untheorized, and depended (at least in the case of Williams and Hoggart) on the techniques and assumptions of literary analysis brought to bear on other cultural forms and practices. Students and the small faculty at Birmingham, however, were soon caught up in reading and testing out the implications of mostly French structuralist (and later, poststructuralist) thought for their work, especially Althusserian Marxism. This turn caused a rupture in emergent cultural studies between the "structuralists" and the "culturalists" who differed largely in their understandings of subjectivity and human agency (see Hall, 1980). For the so-called "culturalists," such as E. P. Thompson, "experience" itself was the working classes' school in which they learned how to make their own history. To understand social relations in all their complexity, a historian need only seek out and provide an account of these working-class experiences, which had been neglected by bourgeois historiography. For "structuralists," on the other hand, the category of "experience" was more a problem than a solution, since they were suspicious of appeals to a sovereign subject of such experience, or the transparency of "reality" to his (or, later, her) grasp; seeing the "subject" and "reality" as irreducibly entangled in the very processes of signification through which they are described, structuralists emphasized the need for "experience" to be interrogated by an abstract, theoretical analysis to reveal its constructedness. The battle between these two views carried on at rather an impasse until the wider availability of Gramsci's (1971) work, and, thus, "hegemony" theory, shifted the terrain of the debate.

This itinerary can be tracked in the changing understanding of ideology over time in cultural studies. In the earliest work, "ideology," when it appears at all, is usually understood as a mystificatory formal system of ideas, as in Marx and Engels' polemical critique of antimaterialist philosophy in *The German Ideology*, especially in the rigid Internationalist interpretation of it. In such a view, ideas simply "reflect" specific material conditions; they have no effectivity of their own. Hence, class positions dictate specific ideological positions appropriate to a class, so that noncorrespondence between a class and the system of ideas appropriate to it (as in the working classes' accommodation to capitalism) can only be explained by "false consciousness"—being tricked into an "incorrect" understanding of "reality." Thompson (1966) emphasizes instead the conscious and active "making" of classes in their experience of relations to each other. For him the only "false consciousness" was to be found among the scholars who attributed it to the working class (or who simply did not consider the working class worthy of their attention at all), because their methodology and assumptions blinded them to the ongoing resistance of the working class to capital. Althusser (1971), alternatively, critiqued the "false consciousness" explanation of the accedence of the working class to capitalism by asserting that ideology performed most of its work by unconscious rather than conscious means. The irreducible realm of the ideological ("the imaginary relationship of individuals to their real conditions of existence") saw to it that capitalism could (and did) reproduce itself by means of ordinary "common sense" (as opposed to formal and systematic) views of the world—a "common sense" materialized in concrete institutions and practices (the family, religion, education) which positioned subjects via discursive mechanisms that operated largely at a preconscious level. In its emphasis on "reproduction" and unconscious conformity, however, Althusserian structuralism (at least in its cruder formulations) seemed to assume that parts of a system (e.g., subjects) developed in particular ways simply in order to promote the continued functioning of the whole, a view that seemed to allow little room for resistance or change.

It was to address this problem of "functionalism" that a Gramscian theory of "hegemony" was introduced to cultural studies. For Gramsci (1971), ideology is a terrain of struggle rather than a set of pregiven dispositions, whether conscious or unconscious. "Ruling" (and subordinated) ideas are an effect of struggles among competing groups, not their starting place. Ideology is the arena in which "consent" to rule is achieved, and consent from subordinated groups rarely comes on the terms that the ruling groups would have desired most. With its simultaneous attention to "struggle" and the influence of "common sense" as a crucial domain in the elaboration of specific social relations, Gramsci's "hegemony" theory addressed the concerns of—while it undermined—the positions of both "culturalists" and "structuralists." It moved away from a view of "class essentialism" with fixed, or "proper," ideological positions for each and offered a more flexible and nuanced model for understanding how change worked itself out in the details of everyday life as groups struggled among themselves for hegemony. In that process, the dominant bloc accommodates, necessarily, some of the positions and values of competing groups (both from within and outside the bloc), if it is actually to achieve consent for its rule. Of course, there can be dominance without hegemony if the ruling bloc fails in its attempt to secure ideological dominance and, thus, resorts predominantly to extraideological coercion (see Guha, 1989). However, where hegemony is sought and achieved, nonideological coercion is minimized, and ideology and representations do not "belong" to any one group but are precisely the site in which their relations are negotiated, consciously and unconsciously.

With this new emphasis on a state of constant ideological struggle, perhaps no Gramscian concept has seemed more attractive, or more elusive, for the various metropolitan practitioners of cultural studies than that of the "organic intellectual." For Gramsci, the "organic intellectual" is the ideologico-practical "leader" of a particular group who manages to organize its struggle for hegemony without disengaging from a continuous dialectic in this activity with the group as a whole. In other words, an "organic intellectual" is not "autonomous"—such as Lenin's vanguard who leads a group whose role is simply to follow—but rather he or she remains in constant contact with the group of organic alliance such that the directing activity is an embodiment of the group as much as of the "leader" (see Gramsci, 1971). The desire of cultural studies practitioners to ally themselves with progressive political projects and groups situated outside the university has often been described as an attempt to become "organic intellectuals" as opposed to "traditional intellectuals," who attempt to proclaim their independence from politics in their intellectual work. This desire is widely and variously expressed, as in Jameson's (1993) description of "cultural studies" in the United States as the university's staging area for the "new social movements." At the same time, the difficulties of engaging in such politics in the metropolitan university has generated continuous anxiety and disruption within cultural studies. In one of his influential accounts of the development of cultural studies in Britain, Stuart Hall (1992), who became the second director of the Birmingham Centre in 1968, observed, "We were organic intellectuals without any organic point of reference" (p. 281), suggesting (in this impossible formulation) both the power of the desire to fill such a role and the limits to that role encountered in the metropolitan university context.

The stakes of intellectual work have been perceived to be so high in cultural studies because these debates about "culture," "subjectivity," and political strategy were seen as a response to changes in the workings of capital as well as to dissatisfaction with Arnoldian conceptions. As outlined in David Harvey's *The Condition of Postmodernity* (1990), the Fordist reinscription of metropolitan "workers" as "consumers"—and therefore as important to capital in both roles—gave capital a vested interest in the "everyday" lives of workers in a far more intensive sense than ever before. Not only had capital managed to reorganize itself in ways that encouraged the recuperation of the metropolitan working class (or at least a significant fraction of it) but also how people spent their money outside the workplace became a matter of concern for capital along with how productive their labor was in it. With the development of the institutions of civil society and the intensification of mass cultural forms via the expansion and intensification of the media and other "culture industries," capital seemed to be entering the processes of direct social negotiation in an unprecedentedly explicit and intimate way. One of the fundamental assumptions of the Left's "turn to ideology" (so vehemently resisted by some Marxist theorists, such as Perry Anderson, 1976) was that when "everyday life" became a focus of capitalism—through a strengthening and enlarging of the advertising apparatus and the encroachment of capital into hitherto unsaturated areas of the planet and domains of social existence—"culture" itself becomes a more important battleground, a site of potential resistance to capital as well as an intensification of it. At the same time, the new social movements (feminism, ecology, civil rights, etc.) emerged, bringing fresh political energy to a field of struggle in which the labor movement had been losing ground. An alliance among these groups began to be seen as the most effective political strategy for the Left, both in recognition of the importance of concerns that had often gone un- or underaddressed in the old labor movement and in recognition that capital itself was changing its mode of operation in the metropolitan countries and, thus, that the new social movements offered more effective resistance to it (Laclau & Mouffe, 1985).

Since capital was undergoing rapid change in its mode of accumulation, it is not surprising that although left cultural studies engaged in its altered and expanded work of analysis and critique, corporate capital was developing its own version of cultural studies to assist in its globalization by training workers to be capable of functioning effectively in different cultural sites and by assimilating "multicultural" workforces (see Bartolovich, 1996; Watkins, 1995). With the infiltration of capital into the nooks and crannies of everyday life and its increased geographical saturation, corporations have shown themselves to be appreciative of the benefits of workers with linguistic skills and an understanding of cultural difference (including even critiques of ethnocentrism, which, after all, might impede business transactions in a global context). Although conducted in a quite different spirit and with far different interests, this corporate turn to an explicit study of "culture" nevertheless reinforces one of the central tenets of cultural studies—that "culture" has become a direct and explicit interest of capital in its current form.

In addition to pressures for a more corporate-oriented cultural studies from the business sector on the one hand and a more recognizable disciplinary practice from conservative colleagues and deans on the other left "cultural studies" has (as the preceding narrative indicates) come under fire from other Left positions as well. Most recently, standard narratives about its origins and content have begun to seem inadequate, indicating a struggle in and over the sign "cultural studies" itself as a "keyword" in Williams' (1976) sense: a word whose multiple meanings participate in the problems it is attempting to address. Especially prominent in the early moment of stock taking in left cultural studies have been Graeme Turner (e.g., 1992) and Meaghan Morris (e.g., Morris & Frow, 1993), who have tracked alternative itineraries for the development of cultural studies in the Australian (as opposed to British) context and resisted the assumption that it is solely, or even largely, a British import. Indicating the differences in local contexts of various Cultural Studies projects has forced what was once described in the United Kingdom simply as "cultural studies" to be specified as "British cultural studies" in recognition that it is not universal in its scope. Furthermore, the "nation-state" itself as a unit of analysis has seemed more and more problematical to many theorists, in and outside Britain, as the forces of globalizing capital as well as of migration and diaspora seem to demand more flexible spatial models. For example, tracking the various mechanisms through which "Englishness" has been constructed as a pure ethnicity from which blackness is categorically excluded has been foregrounded in much recent work in Britain, as has experimentation with alternative models for spatial analysis, such as the "Black Atlantic" proposed to study the arena of African diaspora by Paul Gilroy (1993).

These recent gestures of reassessment and reorganization have opened up the possibility of rethinking the disciplinary formation of cultural studies in terms of its exclusions as well as its inclusions (see Morley & Chen, 1996). Among the most pressing concerns of cultural studies at the current conjuncture is to assess the politics of its own formation as an institutional practice and to pursue a systematic study of the interrelations among "cultures" on the global as well as local terrain in which we all currently live and work. Postcolonial theory and historiography (see, e.g., Guha & Spivak, 1988) have indicated some directions that this work might take: investigations of the exclusion of colonialism and decolonization from early cultural studies in Britain, for example; or more systematic analysis of the various traditions that have fueled the various so-called 'national' cultural studies projects, explicitly or implicitly. A transnational cultural studies might also consider other trajectories, alternative "cultural studies," that have not usually been recognized as such: C. L. R. James' work, and that of his successors, for example, or Frantz Fanon's. In the decentering of the metropole from the history and contemporary practice of cultural studies, it might be possible to see how the forging of "organic intellectuals" is not (and has not been) so much a temporally foreclosed project as a geographically foreclosed one, opening up the possibility for metropolitan cultural studies to discover possibilities for praxis and resistance to oppressions in which it might even have been, unwittingly, complicitous in a global context.

When rethought on a global scale, such shifts in habits and practice in the metropolitan universities pose serious challenges for pedagogy at all levels as well as for scholarly research and political intervention. Gayatri Spivak (1993) has suggested that to bring Western cultural studies to a truly transnational perspective, it must

> negotiate between the national, the global, and the historical as well as the contemporary diasporic. We must both anthropologize the West, and study the various cultural systems of Africa, Asia, Asia-Pacific and the Americas as if peopled by historical agents. Only then can we begin to put together the story of the development of a cosmopolitanism that is global, gendered, and dynamic. (p. 278)

Such a project would differ from actually existing cultural studies in the metropolitan context in both its emphases and its methods. It would have to rekindle the political energy of cultural studies in its early British form but operate self-consciously within a larger, complex set of global relations. It would have to struggle against the tendency for metropolitan institutional recuperation, both academic and corporate, and pursue the challenges of "organic" affiliation with resistance movements on a broad scale. If the political hopes for social justice of early cultural studies in Britain are to be understood and realized in global as well as local terms, such changes are imperative.

REFERENCES

Althusser, L. (1971). *Lenin and philosophy*. B. Brewster (Trans.). New York and London: Monthly Review Press.

Anderson. P. (1976). *Considerations on western Marxism*. London: NLB.

Arnold, M. (1993). *Culture and anarchy*. In S. Collini (Ed.), *Culture and anarchy and other writings*. Cambridge: Cambridge University Press. (Originally published 1896).

Bartolovich, C. (1996). The work of cultural studies in the age of transnational production. *Minnesota Review, 45/46*, 117–146.

Bennett, T. (1981). *Popular culture: Themes and issues*. Milton Keynes, England: Open University Press.

Eagleton, T. (1983). *Literary theory: An introduction*. Minneapolis: University of Minnesota Press.
Gilroy, P. (1993). *The Black atlantic*. Cambridge, MA: Harvard University Press.
Giroux, H. (1992). Resisting difference: Cultural studies and the discourse of critical pedagogy. In L. Grossberg, C. Nelson, & P. Treichler (Eds.), *Cultural studies*. New York: Routledge.
Gramsci, A. (1971). *Selections from the prison notebooks*. Q. Hoare & G. N. Smith (Eds. & Trans.). New York: International Publishers.
Guha, R. (1989). Dominance without hegemony and its historiography. *Subaltern Studies, VI*, 210–309.
Guha, R., & Spivak, G. (Eds.). (1988). Selected subaltern studies. New York: Oxford University Press.
Hall, S. (1980). Cultural studies: Two paradigms. *Media, Culture, and Society, 2*, 57–72.
Hall, S. (1982). The rediscovery of ideology: Return of the repressed in media studies. M. Gurevitch, T. Bennett, J. Curran, & J. Woollacott (Eds.). *Culture, society and the media* (pp. 56–90). New York: Methuen.
Hall, S. (1992). Cultural studies and its theoretical legacies. In L. Grossberg, C. Nelson, & P. Treichler (Eds.), *Cultural studies* (pp. 277–294). New York: Routledge.
Hall, S., & Jacques, M. (1989). *New times: The changing face of politics in the 1990s*. London: Lawrence & Wishart.
Harvey, D. (1990). *The condition of postmodernity*. Cambridge, MA: Blackwell.
Hoggart, R. (1958). *The uses of literacy*. London: Penguin. (Originally published in 1957)
Jameson, F. (1993). On cultural studies. *Social Text, 34*, 17–52.
Johnson, R. (1987). What is cultural studies anyway? *Social Text, 16*, 38–80.
Laclau, E., & Mouffe, C. (1985). *Hegemony and socialist strategy*. London: Verso.
Leavis, F. R., & Thompson, D. (1933). *Culture and environment*.
Leavis, Q. D. (1932). *Fiction and the reading public*. London: Chatto & Windus.
Morley, D., & Chen, K. (1996). Introduction. In *Stuart Hall: Critical dialogues in cultural studies* (pp.1–22). New York: Routledge.
Morris, M., & Frow, J. (1993). Introduction. *Australian cultural studies: A reader*. Sydney: Allen & Unwin.
Spivak, G. (1993). *Outside in the teaching machine*. New York and London: Routledge.
Stallybrass, P., & White, A. (1986). *The politics and poetics of transgression*. Ithaca, NY: Cornell University Press.
Thompson, E. P. (1961). *The long revolution, I & II*. *New Left Review*, 9 & 10, 24–33; 34–39.
Thompson, E. (1966). *The making of the English working class*. New York: Vintage.
Turner, G. (1992). Of rocks and hard places: The colonized, the national and Australian cultural studies. *Cultural Studies*, 6.3, 424–432.
Watkins, E. (Ed.). (1995). *Social Text*, 44.
Williams, R. (1959). *Culture and society, 1780–1950*. London: Chatto & Windus.
Williams, R. (1961). *The long revolution*. London: Chatto & Windus.
Williams, R. (1983). *Keywords*. New York: Oxford University Press.

26

Social Studies Education

E. Wayne Ross
State University of New York at Binghamton

Social studies has had a relatively brief and contentious history as a school subject. The fundamental content of the social studies curriculum—the study of human enterprise across time and space—has always been at the core of education; however, there continues to be a lack of an agreed-on definition of social studies.

One of the earliest uses of the term "social studies" to refer to school subjects is attributed to Thomas Jesse Jones in an article that appeared in the *Southern Workman* in 1905 (Tabachnick, 1991). Jones expanded the article into a book, *Social Studies in the Hampton Curriculum*, in which he expressed his concern that young African Americans and Native Americans "would never be able to become integral members of the broader society unless they learned to understand that society, the social forces that operated within it, and ways to recognize and respond to social power" (Tabachnick, 1991, p. 725).

The roots of the contemporary social studies curriculum are found in the 1916 report of the Committee on Social Studies of the National Education Association's Commission on the Reorganization of Secondary Schools, which Jones chaired. The final report of the committee, *The Social Studies in Secondary Education*, illustrates the influence of previous National Education Association and American Historical Association committees regarding history in schools (e.g., Committee of Seven, 1899), but it also emphasized the development of students' citizenship values and established the pattern of course offerings in social studies that has been consistent for most of the 20th century.[1]

In 1992, Marker and Mehlinger's review of the social studies curriculum concluded that the apparent consensus that citizenship education is the primary purpose of social studies is "almost meaningless." Few social studies educators disagree that the purpose of social studies is "to prepare youth so that they possess the knowledge, values, and skills needed for active participation in society" (p. 832). Arguments have been made that students can develop "good citizenship" through the study of history (Whelan, 1997); through the examination of contemporary social issues (Evans & Saxe, 1996), or public policy (Oliver & Shaver, 1966), or social roles (Superka & Hawke, 1982), or social taboos (Hunt & Metcalf, 1955), or by becoming astute critics of society (Engle & Ochoa, 1988). The question, of course, is whether social studies should promote a brand of citizenship that is adaptive to the status quo and interests of the socially powerful or whether it should promote citizenship aimed at transforming and reconstructing society—a question that has fueled debates since Jones first employed the term "social studies" (see Barr, Barth, & Shermis, 1977; Hertzberg, 1981; Hursh & Ross, in press; Nelson, 1994; Ross, 1997; Shaver, 1977; Stanley & Nelson, 1994).

SOCIAL STUDIES, CULTURAL TRANSMISSION, AND SPECTATOR DEMOCRACY

It is within the context of the tensions between the relative emphasis on transmission of the cultural heritage of the dominant society and the development of critical thought that social studies education has had an inconsistent history, predominately conservative in its purposes but, at times, incorporating progressive and even radical purposes (Stanley & Nelson, 1994). Various schemes have been used to make sense of the wide ranging and conflicting purposes offered for social studies. Researchers essentially agree that social studies is used for three primary purposes: socialization into society's norms; transmission of facts, concepts, and generalizations from the academic disciplines; and the promotion of critical or reflective

[1]The dominant pattern of social studies course offerings and topics in the United States has remained largely unchanged since 1916: K—self, school, community, home; Grade 1—families; Grade 2—neighborhoods; Grade 3—communities; Grade 4—state history and geographic regions; Grade 5—United States history; Grade 6—world cultures, Western hemisphere; Grade 7—world geography or history; Grade 8—United States history; Grade 9—civics or world cultures; Grade 10—world history; Grade 11—United States history; and Grade 12—Government.

thinking (Barr, Barth, & Shermis, 1977; Morrissett, 1982). These researchers also agree that citizenship transmission, or conservative cultural continuity, is the dominant approach practiced in schools.

The dominant pattern of social studies instruction is characteristically text oriented, whole group, and teacher centered and aims toward the transmission of "factual" information. Although, many social studies educators have long advocated instructional approaches that include active learning and higher-order thinking within a curriculum that emphasizes gender equity, multiculturalism, environmentalism, and so forth, the dominant pattern has persisted. Giroux (1978) argues that social studies is characterized, in part, by a pedagogy that produces students who are either unable or afraid to think critically. This pedagogy results, in part, from socioeconomic realties beyond the direct control of teachers, which produces conditions such as classes with large numbers of students, a lack of planning time for teachers, the culture of teacher isolation, and a strong emphasis on standardized test scores as the only legitimate measure of educational achievement. The traditional pattern of social studies instruction however, also is sustained by the fact that it is easier for teachers to plan and to teach in accordance with a direct instruction approach that focuses on information transmission and content coverage which furthers teachers' low expectations of students.

Reinforcing these tendencies is the conservative restoration of the past 2 decades that has produced the "educational excellence" and "standards" movements, which have placed an emphasis on student recall and identification of social studies facts, persons, and events, thus diverting attention away from the ways in which the conditions of teaching and learning might be transformed to encourage critical, active, and democratic citizenship (Ross, 1996). Leming (1992) presents evidence that the majority of social studies teachers agree with the aims of the conservative approach to social studies education as opposed to the progressive critical position of college and university professors of education. Leming's "two cultures" argument represents "an academically oriented cultural ideology that is substantially at odds with the ideology and culture that pervades K–12 social studies classrooms" (Whitson & Stanley, 1994, p. 27).[2]

[2]Leming (1994) rejects critiques of the traditional pattern of social studies instruction (e.g., Apple, 1982; Cuban, 1991; Giroux, 1981, Newmann, 1991) because it "is the result of social studies teachers who have thought carefully about their approach to social studies instruction" (pp. 19–20). Leming also argues that this pattern of instruction is justified because it is ideally suited to the context of social studies teaching—the classroom. As for the content of the social studies curriculum, Leming endorses "memorization of factual information."

The difference between the two cultures, however, is not so great as Leming might have us believe. An "ideology of neutrality" has been internalized in the consciousness of both social studies researchers–teacher educators and classroom teachers. The linkages among political agendas, classroom pedagogy, and research on teaching have been blurred (Popkewitz, 1978). Many educational research studies accept objectives-based pedagogical program and seek to "explain" how the objectives were reached. For example, research on "effective teaching" extols the values of direct instruction over teaching that promotes student-to-student interaction, democratic pedagogy, and a learning milieu that values caring and individual students' self-esteem. The results of such research do not question the assumed conception of student achievement—efficient mastery of content as represented by test scores. Left unquestioned are such issues as the criteria of content selection, the resultant mystification and fragmentation of course content, linkages between improved test scores and national economic prosperity, and the ways in which the social conditions of schooling might unequally distribute knowledge. And, as another example, "critical thinking" in social studies most often focuses on procedural problem solving (e.g., distinguishing "facts" from "opinions") rather than on problem posing. Critical thinking approaches in social studies often stop short of equipping students to question, challenge, or take action to transform society and, as a result, serve to socialize students into accepting and reproducing the status quo (Giroux, 1978; Whitson & Stanley, 1994).

Another commonality of these "two cultures of social studies" is the conception of democracy and democratic society that students are being prepared to participate in. Throughout the 20th century, progressive intellectuals and media figures (e.g., Walter Lippmann, George Kennan, Reinhold Niebuhr, and many Deweyites) have promulgated spectator democracy, in which a specialized class of experts identify what our common interests are and then think and plan accordingly (Chomsky, 1997). The function of those outside the specialized class is to be "spectators," rather than participants in action. This theory of democracy asserts that common interests elude the general public and can only be understood and managed by an elite group. According to Lippmann, a properly running democracy is one in which the large majority of the population, whom Lippmann labeled "the bewildered herd" (cited in Chomsky, 1994, p. 85), is protected from itself by the specialized class' management of the political, economic, and ideological systems and in particular by the manufacturing of consent, for example, bringing about agreement on the part of the public for things that they do not want.

Spectator democracy is promoted in social studies classes through the traditional instructional patterns described here—which situate students outside the knowledge construction process as passive recipients of prepackaged information—as well as in the conceptions of democracy that dominate much of the content of social studies courses. For example, democracy is often equated with elections and voting. The procedure of allowing individuals to express a choice on a proposal, resolution, bill, or candidate is perhaps the most widely taught precept in the social studies curriculum. In this conception of citizenship, individual agency is construed primarily as one's vote, and voting procedures override all else with regard to what counts as democracy. Democracy, in this case, is not defined by outcomes but by application of procedures.

In social studies classes, "exercising your right to vote" is the primary manifestation of good citizenship; this, along with understanding the procedural aspects of government (e.g., how a bill becomes a law, the branches of government, separation of powers, etc.) becomes the primary focus of citizenship education. Democracy based on proceduralism leaves little room for individuals or groups to exercise direct political action; this is a function left to a specialized class of people such as elected representatives and experts who advise them. Yes, citizens can vote, lobby, exercise free speech and assembly rights, but as far as governing is concerned, they are primarily spectators. Active citizenship is most often taught under the banner of "rights and responsibilities." This framework tends to emphasize ways in which individuals can participate within established governmental procedures (e.g., voting, serving on a jury, writing a government representative, attending local government meetings, etc.) and does not encourage an examination of outcomes that may result from the application of "democratic" procedures (e.g., disproportionate numbers of African American males in prison or rich White men in government) or citizen action beyond a narrow set of activities.

Perhaps the apparent consensus on purpose of social studies as citizenship education is not, as Marker and Mehlinger (1992) suggested, meaningless. And, although there may be an "ideology gap" between social studies teachers and teacher educators, traditional liberal-democratic thinking—and the spectator democracy it engenders—has dominated the practice of both groups. Instead of a democratic society as one in which "the public has the means to participate in some meaningful way in the management of their own affairs and the means of information are open and free" (Chomsky 1997, p. 5), we have (sustained through much of what occurs under the auspices of social studies education) a spectator democracy, in which the public is barred from managing their own affairs and the means of information is kept narrowly and rigidly controlled.

TRANSFORMING SOCIAL STUDIES EDUCATION

Achieving a democratic society in which members of the public are meaningful participants in the management of their own affairs requires moving beyond a brand of citizenship that is adaptive to the status quo and interests of the socially powerful. Social studies education for citizenship aimed at transforming and reconstructing society requires both socialization and countersocialization (Engle & Ochoa, 1988). Accomplishing this vision within the context of hierarchical, bureaucratic institutions such as U.S. public schools, which reward passivity on the part of students and teachers, is no small challenge.

It should be no surprise that teachers are the key to transforming the aims and practices of social studies education. Students will never become meaningful participants (not mere spectators) in society unless they learn to understand society and the social forces that operate within it and learn how to recognize and *respond to social power in ways that are reconstructive of the old order, which privileges the rich and socially powerful*. Social studies education that is transformative and reconstructive can only be created by teachers who are practicing active, critical citizenship in their professional (and personal) lives. One way to bring active, critical citizenship in to the social studies classroom is for teachers, students, and community members to take democratic action to improve their schools.

The dialectical relationships among teachers' beliefs and actions and the contexts in which they work harbor a powerful, yet untapped, rejoinder to the top-down, centralized initiatives that have historically dominated our society and that currently dominate school reform efforts. One reason for this is that teachers and teacher educators have traditionally understood their power to affect change as stopping at the classroom door and not extending into schoolwide change or community-wide or national educational politics. True citizenship education (and educational reform), however, involves engaging policy debates and other struggles beyond the classroom. As teacher Stan Karp (1994) argues:

> If we recognize that effective education requires students to bring their real lives into the classrooms, and to take what they learn back to their homes and neighborhoods in the form of new understandings and new behavior, how can we not do the same? Critical teaching should not be merely an abstraction or academic formula for classroom "experimentation." It should be a strategy for educational organizing that changes lives, including our own. (p. 24)

There are many key educational issues determined in the larger context of community, state, and national politics (e.g., curriculum standards, voucher plans, privatization schemes). Teachers' efforts in the classroom are tied to broader endeavors to transform our society. If social studies educators (and others) truly want to transform schools and society, we must recognize and act on connections between classrooms and society. If we can find ways to link work for democratic reforms in both schools and society, both will be strengthened.

An alternative to top-down, state-centered educational and social change is the development of a democracy of community empowerment (Flacks, 1995). Building this kind of community power will require a combination of grassroots and governmental initiatives and resources that present fundamental dilemmas worth working through. In this alternative, schools must become part of broader self-determining communities with power to plan their own development and resources to fulfill those plans.

This is a vision of educational reform and social change in which the state is not the source of initiative or direction; instead it is the source of laws and capital that supports and nourishes local initiatives. One way to accomplish this is by taking advantage of the space for initiatives offered by the introduction of site-based management and shared decision-making reforms in schools. These reforms are not panaceas and bring with them many elements that may potentially further entrench hierarchical relations within schools and between schools and policy elites. Where site councils have real power and resources, teachers, students, parents, and community members can make significant decisions about the curriculum, instruction, and conditions of schools. Site-based restructuring is underway in many school districts, including large urban districts in Chicago and Philadelphia. These openings provide the opportunity to develop true grassroots, teacher-initiated reforms. Teachers in Milwaukee, for example, challenged the district's bureaucratic textbook adoption process and its heavy reliance on basal readers. Milwaukee teachers succeeded in winning support for a whole-language alternative to basal readers as well as resources to provide professional development and alternative materials. As a result, the number of teachers using whole language approaches rose dramatically.

Rather than increasing federal or state regulation of curriculum and teaching—which means more top-down bureaucracy and restrictive auditing measures (e.g., mandated, high-stakes tests)—this alternative provides the community voice in educational reform. The aim of community empowerment is to create a legal framework for participatory democracy, programs of comprehensive community power, rules for community voice, and resources to support community planning in all areas, not just in education (Flacks, 1995).

An integral part of building community power is enabling or indeed compelling all of the constituencies of a school to participate in the process of institutional change. A democratic strategy of response to budget cuts and increased external control of curriculum is not simply mobilizing resistance. The demand for increased voice of teachers, students, and community members in decisions affecting schools is not to privilege these groups, because exercising institutional voice is integrally connected with the need to take institutional responsibility. This implies a democratic restructuring of school life.

Even the best and most well-intentioned top-down educational reforms are easily corrupted or resisted by schools, and most bottom-up reforms have historically been frustrated by bureaucracy or lack of resources. Approaching educational (and social) reform from a community empowerment perspective is certainly not problem free, but this vision offers an opportunity for reforms to be responsive to contexts and needs of individual communities; avoids the problems of top-down reforms (such as doling out responsibility by restricting power and resources); and provides a way to integrate the educational reform activities with broader efforts aimed to promote democracy.

We need to imagine and to create modes of educational and social reform that cross boundaries, that are consciously multiperspective, that can encompass contradictory political and ideological tendencies, and at the same time that express the common human need for self-determination and voice. I can think of no better goal for social studies education.[3]

[3]This chapter draws on a series of columns I wrote for *Theory and Research in Social Education* in 1996 and 1997.

REFERENCES

Apple, M. (1982). *Education and power.* New York: Routledge, Chapman & Hall.

Barr, R. D., Barth, J. L., & Shermis, S. S. (1977). *Defining the social studies.* Washington, DC: National Council for the Social Studies.

Chomsky, N. (1994). *Manufacturing consent.* New York: Black Rose Books.

Chomsky, N. (1997). *Media control.* New York: Seven Stories Press.

Committee of Seven, American Historical Association. (1899). *The study of history in schools.* New York: Macmillan.

Committee on Social Studies, National Education Association. (1916). *The social studies in secondary education,* Bulletin No. 28. Washington, DC: Government Printing Office.

Cuban, L. (1991). History of teaching in social studies. In J. P. Shaver (Ed.), *Handbook of research on social studies teaching and learning,* (pp. 197–209). New York: Macmillan.

Engle, S., & Ochoa, A. (1988). *Education for democratic citizenship: Decision making in the social studies.* New York: Teachers College Press.

Evans, R. W., & Saxe, D. W. (Eds.). (1996). *Handbook on teaching social issues.* Washington, DC: National Council for the Social Studies.

Flacks, D. (1995). Taking ideology seriously: A route to progressive power. *Social Policy, 26*(2), 34–50.

Giroux, H. A. (1978). Writing and critical thinking in the social studies. *Curriculum Inquiry,* 8, 291–310.

Giroux, H. A. (1981). *Ideology, culture and the process of schooling.* Philadelphia: Temple University Press.

Hertzberg, H. W. (1981). *Reform in social studies, 1880–1980.* Boulder, CO: Social Science Education Consortium.

Hunt, M. P., & Metcalf, L. E. (1955). *Teaching high school social studies: Problems in reflective teaching and social understanding.* New York: Harper.

Hursh, D. W., & Ross, E. W. (Eds.). (in press). *Democratic social education.* New York: Garland.

Karp, S. (1994). Beyond the classroom. *Rethinking Schools,* 8,24.

Leming, J. S. (1992). Ideological perspectives within the social studies profession: An empirical examination of the two cultures thesis. *Theory and Research in Social Education, 20*(3), 293–312.

Leming, J. S. (1994). Past as prologue: A defense of traditional patterns of social studies instruction. In M. R. Nelson (Ed.), *The future of the social studies* (pp. 17–23). Boulder, CO: Social Science Education Consortium.

Marker, G., & Mehlinger, H. (1992). Social studies. In P. W. Jackson (Ed.), *Handbook of research on curriculum* (pp. 830–851). New York: Macmillan.

Morrissett, I. (1982). *The current state of social studies: A report of Project SPAN.* Boulder, CO: Social Science Education Consortium.

Nelson, M. R. (Ed.). (1994). *The future of the social studies.* Boulder, CO: Social Science Education Consortium.

Newmann, F. M. (1991). Classroom thoughtfulness and students' higher order thinking: Common indicators and diverse social studies courses. *Theory and Research in Social Education, 19,* 410–433.

Oliver, D. W., & Shaver, J. P. (1966). *Teaching public issues in the high school.* Boston: Houghton Mifflin.

Popkewitz, T. S. (1978). Educational research: Values and visions of social order. *Theory and Research in Social Education,* 6(4), 20–39.

Ross, E. W. (1996). Diverting democracy: The curriculum standards movement and social studies education. *International Journal of Social Education, 11*(1), 18–39.

Ross, E. W. (Ed.). (1997). *The social studies curriculum: Purposes, problems, and possibilities.* Albany: State University of New York Press.
Shaver, J. P. (1977). The task of rationale-building for citizenship education. In J. P. Shaver (Ed.), *Building rationales for citizenship education* (pp. 96–116). Arlington, VA: National Council for the Social Studies.
Stanley, W. B., & Nelson, J. (1994). The foundations of social education in historical context. In R. Martusewicz & W. Reynolds (Eds.), Inside/out: Contemporary critical perspectives in education (pp. 266–284). New York: St. Martin's Press.
Superka, D. P., & Hawke, S. (1982). *Social roles: A focus for social studies in the 1980s*. Boulder, CO: Social Science Education Consortium.
Tabachnick, B. R. (1991). Social studies: Elementary-school programs. In A. Lewy (Ed.), *International encyclopedia of curriculum* (pp. 725–731). Oxford, England: Pergamon.
Whelan, M. (1997). History as the core of social studies curriculum. In E. W. Ross (Ed.), *The social studies curriculum: Purposes, problems, and possibilities* (pp. 21–37). Albany: State University of New York Press.
Whitson, J. A., & Stanley, W. B. (1994). The future of critical thinking in the social studies. In M. R. Nelson (Ed.), *The future of the social studies* (pp. 25–33). Boulder, CO: Social Science Education Consortium.

27

Moral Education

David E. Purpel
University of North Carolina–Greensboro

The phrase "moral education" is a deceptively benign term, one that unfortunately has been used more as a rhetorical club than as a heuristic device. At its most innocent, the term can be used to describe the educational processes by which moral understandings and beliefs are taught and learned. In this virginal form, "moral" is meant to refer to preferred, idealized, or accepted modes of human relationships, that is, ways in which people should live with each other. This is only to speak to the obvious, namely, that all communities develop norms of acceptable social behavior as well as ways of imparting and enforcing them. Beyond this elemental level of meaning are, of course, issues of enormous import and controversy, since they involve conflicting views on some of the most important issues of human existence, indeed the kind of controversies that can and do engender bitter and even violent disputes.

Part of the controversy has to do with theories of the origin of moral frameworks—some insisting on them as originating in some form of divine revelation whereas others are equally sure that they represent purely human and social invention and construction. This difference goes far beyond the academic and the theoretical, as they also have enormous political significance not only as they generate the criteria for setting social policies but in influencing the question of who gets to shape and determine them. Obviously, these disputes are continuously contested in various social and cultural settings, with education being a particularly sensitive and critical area.

The history of education in the United States cannot be discussed without reference to the tremendous influence that religion has had on all our cultural and social institutions. We are a nation that was largely colonized and controlled by people driven to create a society based on sectarian Christian principles and practices and for whom education was simply another way to extend and deepen those Christian practices. The first community-sponsored schools in the Puritan colonies were clearly and totally directed at perpetuating deeply held religious and moral convictions through unambiguous didactic instruction. Clearly there were other forces operating in colonial America, but the force of religious (i.e., Christian) ideology persisted well into post-Revolutionary America and indeed into modern times.

This can be seen most clearly in the broad program of the common school movement in the 19th century that continues to shape the program and practices of the public schools in the present. The historian Carl Kaestle (1983) has interpreted this movement as a triumph of Anglo-Saxon Protestant ideology that emphasized the religious, cultural, and social values of the Puritan era, that is, affirmation of Christianity, hard work, and parental authority; delay of gratification; suspicion of sensual pleasure; and respect for property. The purpose of the state-controlled, tax-supported school systems was to integrate this ideology with the effort to create a unified, democratically oriented, industrialized, English-speaking American nation. There were to be Bible readings, flag salutes, anthem singings, Christmas celebrations, McGuffey readers, obedient, passive, hard-working students, and pious and morally correct teachers. The deliberately moral purposes of the schools were far from hidden; they were an explicit part of the public dialogue and debate. Indeed, Elizabeth Vallence (1973) contends that the discovery of the "hidden curriculum" in the 1960s testifies to the profound way in which our culture had so thoroughly assimilated the ideological agenda of the common school movement. Most Americans had so deeply internalized this orientation that they tacitly assumed that our patterns of schooling represented the only means of conducting public education.

If we can recognize that political and educational leaders have always intended the public schools to have an explicitly moral purpose, how do we then explain the emergence and vitality of a term that by itself would seem to be so redundant as to render it inane, if not meaningless? How do we account for the shift in educational discourse of the 19th century and its concern over which moral framework should govern the schools to the late-20th century concern over whether or not the curriculum should have *any* moral content?

One possible explanation has already been suggested, namely, that the moral content of school culture had been so deeply internalized that it had ceased to be debateable. Another reason may have to do with the growing secularization of the American schools such that its moral flavor became not only invisible out of its banality but also because the term "moral" had become outdated, if not obsolete. With the professionalization of the schools came the hope of rescuing them from the parochialism, provincialism, and pieties of religious discourse and corrupt politics and replacing these with the objectivity and detachment of rationality, science, and technology. Clearly, the language of morality and values was not compatible with the new positivism that took control of educational discourse. In addition, the courts had struck hard blows at the old ways as they continued to establish a sharper distinction between church by state by curtailing such well-intentioned practices as school prayer and Christmas pageants. More and more, the term "moral" became intertwined with either the language of religion or the remnants of old-fashioned and outdated pietism, or both.

The curriculum became more discipline-based as history, English, and science in the schools increasingly came to resemble history, English, and science at the college level, where analytic rigor and precision prevailed over superstition and ideology. Psychology, sociology, and analytical philosophy replaced theology and ethics as the language of educational criticism, which was also heavily influenced by pragmatism and, for some, Marxism. Those on the political Left tended to be extremely suspicious of moral and religious discourse because they identified it as central to the ideologies of the dominant socioeconomic classes in U.S. society. Those in the center tended to regard moral issues as marginal if not irrelevant, since they could not be rationally resolved and stood to interfere with the need for stability, order, and material progress.

Perhaps more significantly, the larger American culture had so dramatically shifted its concerns from the moral and spiritual to the economic and material that the connection between these realms had been seriously eroded, if not erased. Indeed, our culture has come to a place in which our moral orientation is driven by our economic policies rather than the other way around. The same holds true for our educational policies that are grounded not in a quest for goodness and virtue but in a drive for wealth and power. In addition, the emergence of the United States as a world power moved the culture into the amorality of *realpolitik*, in which moral concerns became a matter of posturing and expedience. The fundamental educational change was to transform the school from being primarily an explicitly moral and cultural institution to being primarily an explicitly economic and societal institution. Schools are now asked to feed the engines of a nation bent on dominating the global economy rather than on nourishing the vision of a Christian and democratic community. President Clinton made this point very clearly in his 1994 State of the Union address: [I support alternative forms of schooling] "as long as we measure every school by one high standard: Are our children learning what they need to know to compete and win in the global economy?"

In this context, educational discourse loses much of its moral character and takes on the instrumental quality of technology and applied psychology. The pervasive influence of positivism allowed for and demanded the notion of "value-free" education, which added intellectual respectability to the process of masking the inherent ideology. Limiting themselves to professional and technical concerns related to issues of school organization and instructional methodologies, initiatives carried out in the name of educational "reform" have avoided questions of the larger culture's basic values. Reduced to institutions for training "human resources," contemporary schools limit their sense of purpose to increasing the individual's value as an economic unit. Even the most "progressive" of reforms have aimed toward providing greater equality of educational opportunity under the assumption that this will facilitate greater equality of economic opportunity. The ever-rising inequalities between the rich and the poor, however, make it difficult to frame this vision of educational purpose in moral language. This vision can only express itself in terms of economic values. Consequently, individuals learn to value education only to the extent that it enhances their (or their children's) capacity to compete with others for various forms of economic advantage. At the same time, they learn to understand poverty in terms of individual educational and, hence, economic failure. This helps explain, in part, why the schools seem to remain in a constant state of reform, and it appears unlikely that any measure of educational reform alone will ever eliminate the problem of poverty, making the demands for future educational reforms that much more predictable. Furthermore, when cloaked in the language of value-neutrality, this educational vision makes it difficult for people to recognize the moral and political implications of teaching the nation's youth to understand human relationships as primarily economic and competitive in nature, as devoid of any collective responsibilities or concern for the common good.

A major consequence of the erosion of moral discourse and the persistence of the myth of value-free education was the emergence of a "new" field, one called "moral education," which I believe has, by and large, had a negative effect on the efforts to raise the level of education's moral discourse. The major problem with the term "moral education" is its reifying effect; that is, any validation of "moral education" as a distinct field of study and practice presupposes the existence of "other education"—education that is nonmoral. Though the idea of a nonmoral education is surely an oxymoron, it has benefitted the conservative movement's ability to launch and sustain a campaign to "return the schools to values." It also allows the public and the profession to get off the moral hook, since it frames moral education as a specialized field requiring special knowledge and expertise rather than as a central dimension of public policy. This formulation thus serves to change the fundamental question from, "Which moral orientation should ground our educational policies and practices?" to a very different question, namely, "*Should* we teach moral values in the schools?"

Such a question is disingenuous and mischievous at best, since it not only sets up a false polarity (between those who are interested in promoting morality and those who are opposed to a moral grounding) but it also distracts us from the profoundly important dialogue on what constitutes a valid moral framework for our schools. Because of the vacuum created by the reluctance and wariness of educational critics of the Center and the Left to deal with the moral dimensions of public education, the ground was left almost entirely to the forces of the Right. It is the political Right that has been able to seize the high ground of moral discourse and in so doing they have been able to blur their particular moral orientation with *any* moral orientation. In other words, in the current political code, the claim that "we must return to values" (an especially empty and inane phrase since by definition it is impossible to be without them) really means that "we must adopt the conservative moral orientation." All education inevitably has moral content, all forms of schooling have moral consequences, and all educational ideas can be morally analyzed. The notion that the political Right's moral agenda equals moral education is both intellectually moronic and politically cynical. However, we will continue to be vulnerable to such doublespeak as long as we have a formulation that sharply distinguishes moral education from education.

Perhaps some further clarification of terms is in order. This is unfortunately not an easy task, since the terms involved are used in a broad variety of ways and possess very intense emotional and political loadings. I shall try to limit myself to some very basic and simple distinctions, recognizing, of course, that the issues involved are immensely complex, controversial, and perplexing. For starters, the term "values" in its most elemental sense simply means preference. For example, when I say that I prefer chocolate to vanilla, I am informing my listener that I "value" chocolate more than I "value" vanilla. Obviously, there is a large arena of preferences, including aesthetic, political, interpersonal, psychological, and so on, as well as, of course, moral values. An extremely important aspect of the phenomena of values is the process of how one comes to make certain preferences (values) especially as this relates to another critical process, namely the question regarding the criteria for choosing values (preferences). Presumably we can be relaxed about whether a child likes chocolate better than vanilla. One the other hand, however, if one of these flavors has an added health benefit, the question of which choice is "better" and who gets to decide becomes stickier.

Moral values are those particular preferences and choices that relate to human interaction, social arrangements, and modes of human interaction—questions of how we are to live together. Such values serve to bind or divide both within and between communities and typically constitute a very important part of public dialogue, debate, controversy, and conflict. Clearly, a vital dimension of this struggle is education, that is, the process by which we transmit the community's views on moral issues. Simplistically, this can be equated to the society's transmitting its values, but in a complex and diverse society like ours, the process becomes not only much more problematic but infinitely more contentious and complicated. This adds to the soft pedaling of moral discourse by school administrators who exert an enormous amount of energy trying to respond to a multitude of often conflicting demands and pressures.

The impulse, then, for explicit moral education comes from several motivations and orientations. First, there are those who believe (and to my mind, naively) that the schools are not providing moral education but should. There are also those who believe that the schools *are* providing moral education but the wrong kind. In addition, there are people who believe that the schools are providing moral education but that it is incoherent and unsystematic and hence requires clarification. There are those who believe moral education is about training character through changing behaviors; others who are convinced that moral education is about rational and logical analysis of moral issues; there are those who believe that moral sophistication is an aspect of the maturation process that can be enhanced by appropriate stimulation; and there are those who believe that students need only to clarify and affirm their own values. There are educators who believe that moral education can be enhanced through existing curricular forms such as the teaching of history and literature, whereas others insist on the importance of specially developed curricula, and still others maintain that the real moral education comes through the hidden curriculum.

Nonetheless, regardless of the orientation, it is clear that education is inherently moral, and that education, however disguised and masked, is inevitably implicated in ideological matters. This is vividly demonstrated in the current case of the character education movement, which ostensibly is about promoting a number of consensual, if not universal, values such as honesty, courage, and perseverance, but which actually reflects an implicit and unacknowledged political and social agenda. The orientation of this movement resonates with the neoconservative concerns for social stability, the preservation of the conventional canons of schooling, and the restoration of the primacy of the old-fashioned bag of Puritan virtues of hard work, respect for authority, delay of gratification, and so on. It is also a moral consciousness that has contributed to our social and cultural problems by blindly refusing to go beyond superficial pieties to an examination of underlying values of hierarchy, privilege, competition, and success that pervade our culture and schools. Its refusal to provide a critical examination of the social, historical, political, and cultural contexts of its orientation mark it as less moral than moralistic and less intellectual than didactic. Unlike the Left, which tries to do political critique without moral discourse, the Right tries to get away with moralizing without political discourse.

Indeed, perhaps it is time to put the capitalized version of "Moral Education" to sleep since it operates to blur the inevitability of the moral component of education and at the same time to distract us from the necessity of engaging in a moral critique of education. The most truly moral analyses of education have not come from the ranks of capital M capital E moral educators but from people who have instead developed sensitive and penetrating moral critiques of the school–society–culture matrix. Critics and scholars like Maxine Greene, Paulo Freire, Henry Giroux, Michael Apple, and William Pinar are the truly moral educators in that they demand that the public and the profession confront our primary moral issues, those emerging from barriers to a life of justice, meaning, community, love, and joy for all.

What we need instead of "Moral Education" is much more moral discourse and analysis but not just that limited to the ethical implications of school life, for example, what to do when students cheat or steal. We also need to ground the intersection of moral beliefs and educational policies in such questions as the balance between individual autonomy and social responsibility, between the values of competition and cooperation. We need to confront the moral problematics of "excellence," testing, grading, and hierarchy. And we need to respond to these and other issues as critical *and* affirming educators. We do not need more moral education programs; we do need a moral code of analysis for education, but above all else we need something that is far more demanding and problematic than criticism, and that is a language of moral vision and commitment. Moral education without affirmation and commitment is a contradiction in terms, an evasion, and an act of irresponsibility. On the other hand, to seriously engage in the complexities and perplexities of a morally grounded education is surely the most important, profound, and dangerous of all responsibilities.

REFERENCES

Kaestle, C. (1983). *Pillars of the republic: Common schools and American society*. New York: Hill & Wang.

Vallence, E. (1973). Hiding the hidden curriculum. *Curriculum Theory Network, 4*, (1).

28

Service Learning

George Perreault
University of Nevada, Reno

One of the more noticeable trends in contemporary American education has been the growth of service learning activities in the public schools; indeed, nearly half the states now require some form of community service for high school graduation. Two important goals are cited to legitimate this expansion of the curriculum: "Learning and service are both vital outcomes in service learning, which narrows the gap between what students do in school and what they do after they leave school" (Follman, Watkins, & Wilkes, 1994, p. x). Rahima C. Wade (1994), a frequent publisher in the field, notes that students in such programs, "are developing firsthand knowledge about what it means to make a difference; at the same time they are learning valuable personal, social, and academic skills" (p. 1).

The inclusion of experiential community services to enhance student learning is not a new concept; Dewey (1900/1956), for one, believed in the value of critically assessing and responding to authentic problems, but the ideal of service learning has gained support recently both from within the educational community and from various agencies, public and private. Goodlad (1984) suggested community service as one of the ways to strengthen schools, a recommendation echoed by several others (Bryk & Driscoll, 1988; Lightfoot, 1983; Rutter, Mauglian, Mortimore, & Ouston, 1979). Boyer (1983) encouraged educators to require 120 hours of community service of students before graduation from high school, and Harrison (1987) supported that position by adding the weight of the Carengie Foundation (see also Carnegie's *Turning Points*, 1989). The William T. Grant Foundation's 1988 report on non-college-bound students, *The Forgotten Half*, urges the "creation of quality student service opportunities as central to the fundamental educational program of every public school" (p. 90). In the last decade and a half, enough books, articles, and reports have been added by advocates and by governmental and quasi-governmental agencies that the benefits of service learning have become "received wisdom," part of the terrain in which public education takes place (e.g., Council of Chief State School Officers, 1989; Education Commission of the States, 1985), even carrying with it special funding opportunities to induce schools to move in this direction (National and Community Service Act of 1990).

As is true of many programs that spring up in public schools, service learning means different things to different people, but the definition that is most often cited is that of the Commission on National and Community Service [CNCS] (1993):

A service learning program provides educational experiences:

- under which students learn and develop active participation in thoughtfully organized service experiences that meet actual community needs and that are coordinated in collaboration with school and community;
- that are integrated into the students' academic curriculum or provides [sic] time for a student to think, talk, or write about what the student did and saw during the actual service activity;
- that provide a student with opportunities to use newly-acquired skills and knowledge in real-life situations in their [sic] own communities; and
- that enhance what is taught in school by extending student learning beyond the classroom and into the community and helps [sic] to foster the development of a sense of caring for others. (p. 15)

A widely used guide for creating such programs was developed by the Johnson Foundation and published in its 1989 *Wingspread Special Report*. According to *Wingspread*, an effective program:

- Engages people in responsible and challenging actions for the common good.
- Provides structured opportunities for people to reflect critically on their service experience.
- Articulates clear service and learning goals for everyone involved.
- Allows for those with needs to define those needs.

- Clarifies the responsibilities of each person and organization involved.
- Matches service providers and service needs through a process that recognizes changing circumstances.
- Expects genuine, active, and sustained organizational commitment.
- Includes training, supervision, monitoring, support, recognition, and evaluations to meet service and learning goals.
- Insures that the time committed for service and learning is flexible, appropriate, and in the best interests of all involved.
- Is committed to program participation by and with diverse populations. (Honnett & Poulson, 1989, pp. 2–3)

Guidelines that exist on paper, however, do not always ensure effective implementation for particular programs, and it is important to ask if research bears out the attainment of the goals of enhanced academic performance and of social development that have been hypothesized for service learning. As with any program that is attempted in various sites, with varying approaches, and for various goals, the short answer is that results are unclear.

Academic Growth. When students work as tutors, they consistently show modest gains in the areas of reading and math achievement (Hedin, 1987; Houser, 1974). There also have been some gains found in social sciences learnings (Hamilton & Zeldin, 1987). Marcus, Howard, & King (1993) found significant classroom growth in their study of an undergraduate political science course. There is also some support for students involved in service programs becoming more open minded through participation (Wilson, 1974) and increasing their problem-solving skills (Conrad & Hedin, 1982). Several of the studies related to academic gains, however, suffer from methodological issues in such areas as instrument validity and sample size, and there need to be many more rigorous investigations before the purported academic benefits can be firmly established.

Social and Psychological Growth. The second area in which student gains have been claimed has been widely investigated. The study by Conrad and Hedin (1982) found students in experiential programs developed more favorable attitudes toward adults and toward the organizations and people with which they worked. A 1981 study by Luchs found gains in participants' sense of efficacy, self-esteem and attitudes toward others, and Calabrese and Schumer (1986) documented lower levels of isolation, alienation, and discipline problems among junior high students in a service program. Gains in ego and moral development have been noted by Cognetta and Sprinthall (1978). As with the results reported for academic growth, there are some methodological issues with the research, including small sample size, widely varying experiences within programs, and lack of strict controls. Given that, however, there seems to be some evidence that participation in service learning can strengthen students' self-concepts and have a positive effect on developing moral judgement (Gorman, Duffy, & Heffernan, 1994; Mosher, 1977).

Qualitative Findings. Many proponents of service learning argue that the strengths of such programs are not easily captured in standard quantitative ways. Conrad and Hedin (1982), for example, note that participants in experiential programs typically report that they have learned a great deal from their participation, with approximately 75% thinking they learned "more" or "much more" than in regular school activities. When these authors analyzed student journals in a later study (Hedin & Conrad, 1987), they noted such learning could be described as being different not so much in terms of its amount as in its significance—it became personally important and "owned" by the participants. It seems probable that when participants believe they have learned from an experience, they probably have, even if they cannot be precise about exact gains; therefore, these findings lend credence to the claims of benefits from service learning activities.

Concerns. This is not to say the growth in service learning programs is not without problematic aspects. There are two major intertwined areas that indicate caution should be taken with service learning; one of them is primarily programmatic and the other philosophical. First, it has been noted that reflection is an important aspect of service learning programs (CNCS, 1993; Honnett & Poulson, 1989), and research bears this out. Exum (1980) found that there were no noticeable student gains in experiential programs without a reflective seminar, and Gorman et al. (1994) reported significant differences in moral development between students who were involved in both fieldwork and reflection and those who experienced fieldwork alone. Given the burgeoning of programs, it should not be surprising, nevertheless, to find that service learning projects are sometimes implemented without reflective components or, when these are present, without students interacting with one another to examine their experiences in any depth. Furthermore, service learning is, in some cases, a "stand-alone" component in the curriculum and not effectively integrated with other planned experiences. To the extent that this is so, it can be expected that the effectiveness of such programs will be significantly weakened and beneficial potentials undermined.

The second concern, which is philosophical, is more than merely an extension of the first but is perhaps, in fact, the very reason the practice of reflection is often shortchanged. Open discussion of service learning within a larger social context leads to consideration of issues outside the scope of the typical school curriculum—to issues of social and political relationships and to consideration of how we and others define the common good. Rather than attempt this, practitioners have too often focused exclusively on what students will gain from the experience, and the suggestions, concerns, and benefits of other participants are simply ignored (Maybach, 1995). Certainly student learning is an important criterion for public schools, but failing to meaningfully involve others as full participants creates subtle yet powerful lessons that may go unnoticed. If, for example, students work in a shelter for battered women, and there is no analysis of the social conditions and cultural contexts that contribute to violence against women, can this lead to an unacknowledged acceptance of the status quo? Likewise, if there is no research conducted on the effectiveness of activities for service recipients, does this define them merely as a resource for students to use, as people for whom things "are done?" The potential for such an approach has been noted by Noddings (1992): "Human beings ... ought not to be used merely as means.... [yet] the people we are supposedly helping are rarely consulted about the means chosen" (p. 68).

One of the purported benefits of service learning is that it attempts to create a society that is more inclusive and exposes students to "others" with whom they might not normally interact. But the danger of superficial interactions with such "others" is that students come to define them merely as "the needy" without an attempt to "apprehend the reality of the other" and then to "struggle together" to better their conditions (Noddings, 1984, pp. 14–15). Students, therefore, might fail to realize the existence of "an unjust social order [which] is the permanent fount of ... [their own] 'generosity' [and] which is nourished by death, despair, and poverty" (Freire, 1970, p. 26). As a consequence, participation in service activities can lead to exactly the kinds of cynicism and exclusionary ideologies that service learning is, at its best, attempting to undermine.

One value of group reflection is that it can expose tendencies toward the sort of noblesse oblige reminiscent of Kipling (1889/1992) at his most jingoistic:

Take up the White Man's burden,
Send forth the best ye breed—
Go, bind your sons to exile
To serve your captives' needs.

Increasingly sophisticated reflection can be profitably guided by teachers who bear in mind Freire's (1970) observation that "pedagogy which begins with the egoistic interests of the oppressors (an egoism cloaked in false generosity of paternalism) and makes of the oppressed the objects of its humanitarianism, itself maintains and embodies oppression" (p. 36). The tendency toward surface busyness in experiential approaches has long been noted. For example, Hanna (1937) gave the example of students making Thanksgiving baskets for the needy and then noted, "Time and energy given to such superficial betterment could much more efficiently be spent in getting at the basic inhibiting influences which perpetuate a scarcity economy in the midst of abundance" (p. 187). False generosity or false charity does not challenge students at the fundamental level needed to recognize the other as a person in his or her own right and to move together toward what Freire (1970) calls *true generosity*:

> False charity constrains the fearful and subdues, the "rejects of life," to extend their trembling hands. True generosity lies in striving so that these hands—whether of individuals or entire peoples—need to be extended less and less in supplication, so that more and more they become human hands which work and, working, transform the word. (p. 27)

Wrestling with these issues in the classroom can be painful for students and teachers alike, because it can expose patterns of thinking that rarely see the light of day. It also draws on skills of critical analysis that students, and perhaps teachers, have not developed in their educational program. It asks teachers to reach out to the community in true partnerships that are focused less on their own role as experts and more on an evolving mutuality. Consequently, service learning is not something that can be prescribed like a lesson plan; it is about caring with and about service partners and not just for service recipients. As Noddings (1992) notes, "Caring is a way of being in a relation, not a specific set of behaviors" (p. 17).

If these things are not acknowledged and accomplished—and they are, given the circumstances of public education, very difficult tasks—service learning will fail to live up to its fullest potential. The hope is that it will *serve us rightly*: It will enable us to work across the lines of class and ethnicity that divide us from true community; it will enable us to name and struggle against the forces that impose fear and social injustice throughout the society; it will empower us to define and work for the common good as the good we pursue in common (McCann, 1987). If, on the other hand, we allow service learning to become no more than another tool for creating false charity and legitimating the marginalization of large numbers of people within our society, then *it serves us right.*

REFERENCES

Boyer, E. L. (1983). *High school: A report on secondary education in America.* New York: Harper & Row.

Bryk, A. S., & Driscoll, M. E. (1988). *The school as community: Theoretical foundations, contextual influences, and consequences for students and teachers.* Madison, WI: National Center on Effective Schools.

Calabrese, R., & Schumer, H. (1986). The effects of service activities on adolescent alienation. *Adolescence, 21,* 675–687.

Carnegie Task Force on Education of Young Adolescents. (1989). *Turning points: Preparing American youth for the 21st century.* New York: Carnegie Council on Adolescent Development of the Carnegie Corporation.

Cognetta, P. W., & Sprinthall, N. A. (1978). Students as teachers: Role taking as a means of promoting psychological and ethical development during adolescence. In N. A. Sprinthall & R. L. Mosher (Eds.), *Value development as the aim of education.* Schenectady, NY: Character Research Press.

Commission on National and Community Service. (1993). *What you can do for your country.* Washington, DC: Government Printing Office.

Conrad, D., & Hedin, D. (1982). The impact of experiential education on adolescent development. *Child and Youth Services, 4,* 57–76.

Council of Chief State School Officers. (1989). *Community service: Learning by doing.* Washington, DC: Author.

Dewey, J. (1956). *The school and society.* Chicago, IL: University of Chicago Press. (Originally published 1900)

Education Commission of the States. (1985). *Reconnecting youth: The next stage of reform.* Denver, CO: Author.

Exum, H. (1980). Ego development: Using curriculum to facilitate growth. *Character Potential: A Record of Research, 3,* 121–127.

Follman, J., Watkins, J., & Wilkes, D. (1994). *Learning by serving: 2,000 ideas for service-learning projects.* Greensboro, NC: Southeastern Regional Vision for Education.

Freire, P. (1970). *The pedagogy of the oppressed.* New York: Continuum.

Goodlad, J. I. (1984). *A place called school.* New York: McGraw-Hill.

Gorman, M., Duffy, J., & Heffernan, M. (1994). Service experience and the moral development of college students. *Religious Education, 89,*(3), 422–431.

Hamilton, S., & Zeldin, R. (1987). Learning civics in community. *Curriculum Inquiry,* 17, 407–420.

Hanna, P. (1937). *Youth serves the community.* New York: Appleton- Century.

Harrison, C. T. (1987). *Student service: The new Carnegie unit.* Princeton, NJ: Carnegie Foundation for the Advancement of Teaching.

Hedin, D., & Conrad, D. (1987). Service: A pathway to knowledge. *Community Education Journal, 15*, 10–14.

Honnett, E., & Poulson, S. (1989). *Wingspread special report: Principles of good practice for combining service and learning*. Racine, WI: Johnson Foundation.

Houser, V. (1974). *Effect of student-aide experiences on tutors' self-concept and reading skills*. Unpublished doctoral dissertation, Brigham Young University, UT.

Kipling, R. (1992). The white man's burden. In J. Kaplan, (Ed.), *Bartlett's familiar quotations* (16th ed., p. 593). Boston: Little, Brown. (Originally published 1889)

Lightfoot, S. L. (1983). *The good high school: Portraits of character and culture*. New York: Basic Books.

Luchs, K. (1981). *Selected changes in urban high school students after participation in community-based learning and service activities*. Unpublished doctoral dissertation, University of Maryland.

Marcus, G., Howard, J., & King, D. (1993). Integrating community service and classroom instruction enhances learning: Results from an experiment. *Educational Evaluation and Policy Analysis, 15*(4), 410–419.

Maybach, C. W. (1995). Redefining the service ethic: The need for a new understanding and inclusion of the service recipient. Paper presented at the meeting of the American Educational Research Association, San Francisco.

McCann, D. (1987). The good to be pursued in common. In O. F. Williams & J. W. Houck (Eds.), *The common good and U.S. capitalism* (pp. 158–178). New York: University Press of America.

Mosher, R. (1977). Theory and practice: A new E.R.A.? *Theory into Practice*, 16(2), 166–184.

National and Community Service Act of 1990. (P.L. 101–610), 42 U.S.C., Sec. 12651.

Noddings, N. (1984). *Caring: A feminine approach to ethics and moral education*. Berkeley, CA: University of California Press.

Noddings, N. (1992). *The challenge to care in schools: An alternative approach to education*. New York: Teachers College Press.

Rutter, M., Maughan, B., Mortimore, P., & Ouston, J. (1979). *Fifteen thousand hours: Secondary schools and their effects on children*. Cambridge, MA: Harvard University Press.

Wade, R. C. (1994). Community service-learning: Commitment through active citizenship. *Social Studies and the Young Learner*, 6(3), 1–4.

William T. Grant Foundation Commission on Work, Family and Citizenship. (1988). *The forgotten half: Pathways to success for America's youth and young families*. Washington, DC: William T. Grant Foundation.

Wilson, T. (1974). *An alternative community-based secondary school program and student political development*. Unpublished doctoral dissertation, University of Southern California.

29

Environmental Education

C. A. Bowers
Portland State University

The words "environmental education" carry layers of cultural baggage that severely limit our understanding of the radical implications these words should have for curriculum reform at all levels of education and especially in the areas of teacher education and graduate studies in education. The word "environment" still reproduces the dominant Western schemata that represents humans as separate from plants, animals, topsoil, and the rest of the biota. Learning about the environment too often becomes a matter of participating in the scientific gaze that illuminates changes occurring in natural systems. Studying the changes in the chemical properties of streams, observing the interactions between various natural systems, and, in the more systemic approaches to environmental education, investigating the source of toxic wastes represent both the mainstream approach to environmental education and the continuing influence of science as the dominant paradigm for understanding.

Although the scientific understanding of changes in natural systems is vitally important to all levels of environmental education, it nevertheless has a limiting influence that helps perpetuate the current double bind of accelerating global demands on the environment that, in turn, place even greater pressures on scientists to provide eco-management technologies. Science is an indispensable way of knowing, but it also contributes to the ecological crisis in ways that have been largely ignored by educators and, more generally, by the various groups that make up the environmental movement. Briefly, what is generally overlooked is that Western science provided the knowledge base for the Industrial Revolution, and it continues as the conceptual seedbed of the digital phase of this revolution that is now altering the scale and scope of the commodification process. Another aspect of the cultural baggage of Western science is that, in the name of enlightenment and progress, it continues to delegitimate the mythopoetic narratives that are (were) the basis of the moral norms in more ecologically centered cultures—cultures that scientists are now studying in order to patent (commodify) the vernacular knowledge of plants and animals. A third characteristic of Western science is that it is becoming more widely accepted as the cultural epistemology that provides a (supposedly) value-free metanarrative that explains the chemical origins and evolutionary dynamics of all forms of life. The different strands of this metanarrative further strengthen the mechanism and reductionism of sociobiology, with its emphasis on the primacy of genetic fitness as the basis of development. A fourth aspect of the cultural baggage that accompanies Western science that has a particularly powerful influence on environmental education classes is the way the scientific paradigm, in all of its specialized areas of inquiry, marginalizes the importance of culture. Because few environmental educators understand the culturally ladened nature of Western science, they help to reproduce in the next generation of students the limiting conceptual categories that previous generations of scientists have forged and are now representing as a culture-free epistemology. To state the double bind in the most straightforward way, students in science-based environmental education classes will not be given the language and theory necessary for illuminating the multiple relationships between science and the commodification process that is increasing the ecological destructiveness of the world's human population.

There is another problem connected with the dominant way of basing environmental education on a scientific way of understanding; it is also a problem that is present in many nonscientific approaches to environmental education, such as eco-art classes popular in elementary school and other educational efforts to raise consciousness about human–nature relationships. As long as public school teachers, regardless of subject area, are educated to think in ways that take for granted the liberal assumptions that are the basis of the high-status knowledge underlying the technology and commodified expressions of culture now being globalized, they will frame the content of their environmental education classes in terms of these same liberal assumptions. That is, environmental education, in its varied forms of expression, will be framed in terms of taken-for-granted assumptions that represent (1) the individual as the basic social unit; (2) intelligence, creativity, and the capacity for moral judgment as attributes of the autonomous individual; (3) change as the expression of social progress; (4) the pursuit of self and group interest (or what can be labeled as *anthropocentrism*) as an inevitable expression of the human condition; and (5) data as the basis of thought and individual empowerment. Again, this aspect of the double bind that still characterizes the thinking of most environmental educators leads to socializing students to think in the categories and assumptions that can be traced directly back to the origins of the transition to a modern, commodity oriented form of culture that has, over the last 300 years, changed the chemistry of life in ways that we are only now beginning to recognize.

A more adequate way of understanding environmental education is suggested in David Orr's (1992) observation "that all education" [is some form] of environmental education" (p. 90). This insight can easily be contextualized in every area of the curriculum, and at all levels of the educational process, by recognizing that the language processes mediated by the teacher encodes the cultural group's way of understanding not only the characteristics of the named world but also the moral norms that govern our relationship to it. That is, language is used to name (constitute) the relationships and attributes that make up the world we interact with; and as relationships always involve the moral question of how we should act in terms of the relationships and attributes that are culturally constituted (itself a process of moral judgment that is generally ignored) the language encodes the cultural group's moral understandings of these relationships. As the use of language is basic to every area of the curriculum, it reproduces not only the cultural group's understanding of relationships but also the moral norms that are to govern how we should act in terms of them. Thus, the linguist's insight that languages are about relationships corresponds to the insight that all education is some of environmental education. We can see this cultural encoding process in a patriarchically embedded language that both named the attributes of women and reproduced the moral norms that governed relationships in accordance with the culturally constituted attributes. Similarly, a cultural epistemology grounded in an anthropocentric view of human–nature relationships leads to a language that frames the attributes of the environment in terms of their economic value. Referring to the environment as a "natural resource" and identifying characteristics that can be commodified, while leaving unarticulated the attributes and relationships understood in more ecologically centered cultures, establishes what the moral relationships should be. At this level of environmental education, teachers and the experts who create the curriculum are seldom aware of the form of environmental education they are promoting in classes in history, literature, art, biology, and so on.

One of the great ironies today is that the liberal traditions of thought, which supposedly represent the most advanced expressions of enlightened thinking, prevent teachers from recognizing that language thinks us as we think within the conceptual and moral possibilities of the language. The cultural–ideological representation of rational thought as an attribute of a culturally autonomous individual, which is a keystone of modern liberalism, thus helps to hide from awareness how the cultural epistemology and moral norms are being reproduced in the language processes of the curriculum. If the teacher's taken-for-granted view of the world is that students, with guidance in how to become critical thinkers, will become more autonomous in thinking their *own* thoughts and reaching their *own* value judgments, they likely do not recognize that one form of emancipation is achieved by binding students to a set of cultural assumptions that are even more problematic. For example, reinforcing the authority of individual judgment and the cultural ontology that represents change as progressive also facilitates the current spread of the commodification of knowledge and relationships now transforming the different cultural expressions of the commons into the monoculture of the shopping mall. It also reinforces the anthropocentric view of human–nature relationships, which is a deeply encoded cultural view of relationships found in most areas of the curriculum.

The recognition of the teacher's mediating role in the language of the curriculum shifts the focus of environmental education in a way that makes the scientific understanding of natural systems supportive of a more broad based cultural approach to environmental education. Languages, in all their symbolic and relational constituting dimensions, are a primary aspect of human interaction and understanding, in the sciences as well as every other area of human endeavor that is educational. Indeed, the concerns raised earlier about the cultural baggage reproduced in the epistemology of science, including its metanarratives, forms of self-legitimation, and its delegitimation of the mythopoetic foundations of the moral systems of other cultures, was based on a recognition of the primacy of the encoding and reproductive processes essential to the transgenerational life of a cultural group. To restate Orr's (1992) point in a different way, all cultures encode in their language systems an expression of how human–nature relationships are to be understood, which has not always meant a form of environmental education that was ecologically sustainable or supportive of just and viable communities. That we cannot exist without participating in the cultural languages that sustain a particular understanding of human–nature relationships, and that we are equally dependent on the complex energy exchanges that sustain natural systems, suggest the direction that the reform of environmental education should take—That is, if we are to avoid basing our efforts to avoid overshooting the sustaining capacity of natural systems on the same deep cultural assumptions that were the basis of the earlier mechanical and now digital phase of the Industrial Revolution that is integrating the cultures of the world into the market place logic of production, consumption, and exploitation.

The recommendations for the reform of teacher education need to be extended into other areas of the university, but the starting place for reform must be in the cultural ecology that we participate most directly in. Although it is possible to identify a number of culturally based double binds that marginalize the significance of even the best approaches to environmental education, it should also be kept in mind that the forms of resistance, even from colleagues who are concerned about the future consequences of continuing to degrade the environment, will continually localize the process of reform. In many instances, "local" will mean using the content of the courses you teach to help students understand how teaching and learning are influenced by the language processes that teachers mediate, rather than collaborating with colleagues in the reform of an entire teacher education and graduate educational studies program. But even these more modest efforts can be compromised if the professor introduces a cultural–linguistic perspective on how the curriculum reproduces pre-ecological forms of intelligence as just one of many possible ways of understanding the challenges facing teachers. The liberal assumption that future teachers should be exposed to the widest possible number of choices (constructivism, systems thinking, behaviorism, computer-based learning, educational implications of brain research, and so forth) so that they can make up their own individual minds does not take account of the fact that changes in the chemistry of life systems caused by human greed and hubris is not a matter of choice. The smorgasbord approach to teacher education foregrounds the myth of freedom of choice that is basic to the consumer-oriented culture, and in leaving future teachers with only the most superficial understanding of the culture–language processes they mediate, they will continue to reinforce the cultural assumptions that are largely responsible for the current crisis.

As I have already written extensively on an ecologically and culturally based approach to reforming teacher education (Bowers, 1990, 1993a, 1993b, 1995, 1997), I identify here the more critically important changes that are needed. First, there is the need to provide students going into professional educational studies with an understanding of the cultural trends that are having the greatest impact on the environment. All teachers, for example, need to understand the origins, dynamics, and current expressions of the commodification process that is transforming community life and altering the genetic basis of natural systems. Instead of being exposed to educational theorists whose thinking is still based on modernizing cultural assumptions, they should read Karl Polanyi's (1957) *The Great Transformation*, Wolgang Sachs' (1992) *The Development Dictionary: A Guide to Knowledge as Power,* 1992), Vandana Shiva's (1993) *Monoculture of the Mind* (1993), Ivan Illich's (1978) *Toward a History of Needs,* and Alan Durning's (1992) *How Much is Enough?* 1992. Education students can obtain an overview of the nature and scope of the ecological crisis by reading *Our Stolen Future: Are We Threatening Our Fertility, Intelligence, and Survival?* by Theo Colborn, Dumanoski, & Myers (1996); Tom Athanasiou's (1996) *Divided Planet: The Ecology of Rich and Poor,* and the yearly publication of the World Watch Institute, *State of the World.*

These readings are essential to establishing why it is important for teachers to understand how the cultural assumptions that were the basis of the Industrial Revolution become part of the students' self-identity and natural attitude toward technology, progress, consumerism, and so forth. To understand how earlier forms of cultural intelligence are passed on from generation to generation, and how curriculum is part of this process of transgenerational communication, teachers need to understand the metaphorical nature of the language–thought encoding and reproduction process—in verbal and written language, in architecture, as well as in other material expressions of culture. Without this background understanding, teachers will be unable to help students consider the ecological implications of earlier metaphorical constructions that are given contemporary forms of expression, thus giving the impression that they are new and unencumbered by tradition. Nor will teachers be able to help students assess new and old technologies in terms of meeting ecological design criteria long established in vernacular cultures.

A cultural approach to environmental education is also dependent on teachers understanding the complex nature of tradition (which is really the historical aspect of the living present), the nature and extent of noncommodified aspects of community life in both minority cultures as well as in the dominant culture, and the nature of high-status knowledge and how it furthers the globalization of a commodity oriented culture. There are a number of other current liberal orthodoxies that contribute to a destructive form of environmental education. The increasing use of computers in the classroom reinforces the commodification of knowledge and socializes students to accept simulations and decontextualized thinking as more real than direct experience and knowledge of their bioregion. The assumption that intelligence is an attribute of the autonomous individual needs to be clarified in ways that enable teachers to understand the many ways in which students are nested in culture and culture is nested in natural systems. This radically different view of intelligence would enable teachers to recognize more easily how the language of the curriculum materials reinforces the dominant cultural schemata and to make more conscious judgments about when the schemata represents a preecological form of cultural intelligence. Similarly, creativity needs to be understood as a cultural construction that, in the modern sense of the metaphor, is tied directly to a commoditized system of values; and teachers need to understand the nature and role of creativity in ecologically centered cultures.

There are other dimensions of an ecologically and culturally centered approach to teacher education that also need to be introduced, such as a deep understanding of the cultural implications of scientifically based metanarratives, particularly the latest expressions of sociobiology. But the reforms suggested earlier will provide an initial basis for recognizing the form of environmental education that is implicit in the curriculum. These areas of conceptual awareness will also provide a basis for helping students recognize noncommodified traditions within their own communities, as well as in other cultures. This awareness is essential if the high-status forms of knowledge and values that underlie the current cycle of increased consumerism leading to an increased exposure of natural systems to toxic by-products is going to be challenged and alternative forms of community upheld.

REFERENCES

Athanasiou, T. (1996). *Divided planet: The ecology of rich and poor.* New York: Little, Brown.

Bowers, C. A., & Flinders, D. (1990). *Responsive teaching: An ecological approach to classroom patterns of language, culture, and thought.* New York: Teachers College Press.

Bowers, C. A. (1993a). *Education, cultural myths and the ecological crisis: Toward deep changes.* Albany, NY: State University of New York Press.

Bowers, C. A. (1993b). *Critical essays on education, modernity, and the recovery of the ecological imperative.* New York: Teachers College Press.

Bowers, C. A. (1995). *Educating for an ecologically sustainable culture: Rethinking moral education, creative, intelligence, and other modern orthodoxies*. Albany, NY: State University of New York Press.
Bowers, C. A. (1997). *The culture of denial: Why the environmental movement needs a strategy for reforming universities and public schools*. Albany: NY: State University of New York Press.
Colborn, T., Dumanoski, D., & Myers, J. P. (1996). *Our stolen future: Are we threatening our fertility, intelligence, and survival? A scientific detective story*. New York: Dutton.
Durning, A. (1992). *How much is enough?* New York: Norton.
Illich, I. (1978). *Toward a history of needs*. New York: Pantheon.
Orr, D. (1992). *Ecoliteracy: Education and the transition to a postmodern world*. Albany, NY: State University of New York Press.
Polanyi, K. (1957). *The great transformation*. Boston: Beacon Press.
Sachs, W. (1992). *The development dictionary: A guide to knowledge as power*. Atlantic Highlands, NJ: Zed Books.
Shiva, V. (1993). *Monocultures of the mind*. Penang, Malaysia: Third World Network.
Worldwatch Institute (yearly). *State of the world*. New York: Norton.

30

Global Education

Robin Good
Madhu Suri Prakash
The Pennsylvania State University

Global education, like global thinking and the global economy, is a western, modern concept, reflecting the paradigm of industrial society. Wolfgang Sachs (1992) calls the conceptual framework of modern industrialized societies the "development model of reality." He describes the "development discourse," the language that comprises the modern industrialized paradigm. The words, concepts, and terminologies of this language include the following key terms: development, global, market, nation-state, needs, production, profit, progress, resources, scarcity, science, standard of living, and technology. These words and concepts form the primary root assumptions of the modern industrialized paradigm. Global education promotes this paradigm in the classrooms of the world, stretching north, south, east, and west.

Foremost in the development model of reality is the elevation of economic activity to a central role in modern society. These economic assumptions have not only been absorbed, but many scholars contend that economics has become like a new religion, that is, economists are viewed as the ultimate authorities, and economic laws are viewed as the laws of the universe (Bowers, 1993; Esteva, 1992; Illich, 1978, 1992; Orr, 1992; Sachs, 1992a; Shiva, 1992).

Spend time in the American culture, and it is quickly evident that the shopping mall is a symbol of the primacy of economics and consumerism. It depicts the values and lifestyle of any industrialized nation: ease, convenience, multitudinous choices, unending desires, luxurious tastes. Modern industrialized societies have become obsessed with one idea above all—that through the production and consumption of material goods, the conditions for the "good life" can be created. It is the notion that humans, recast during the Enlightenment as creators, can forge their own path to material paradise (Orr, 1992; Sachs, 1992a; Shiva, 1992). This obsession with materialism has come to define meaning, identity, and purposeful activity for people in industrialized societies. *Homo economicus* or *economic man* is a term appropriate to this modern cultural orientation (Illich, 1992).

This path to material paradise can be forged, according to modernization dogma, through the alliance of hard work, scientific rationality, and technology, all factors controllable by human beings. Industrialism has been the outcome of such thinking. With the use of machines and scientific technology, modern humans have attempted to eliminate scarcity (what they see as a universal condition of social life), to liberate humanity from the "inhumane" universe of shortages, and instead, to create a "comfortable" standard of living for all (Lummis, 1992; Ullrich, 1992). In other words, individual materialistic "well-having" has come to define *well-being*. It is viewed as a universal right made attainable through the application of science and technology.

Underlying this notion of the right of all to a materialistic paradise is the concept of development. To modern cultures, development is viewed as a unilinear, singular pattern composed of a definitive one-way movement. It implies a favorable change, a step from the simple to the complex, from the inferior to the superior. "The word indicates that one is doing well because one is advancing in the sense of a necessary, ineluctable, universal law and toward a desirable goal" (Esteva, 1992, p.10). It is a concept of transformation that implies moving toward an ever more perfect form. Therefore, implicit in the concept of development is a linear view of time—that humanity's present material conditions greatly surpass any civilization's previous achievements. Furthermore, development also assumes that those conditions will continue to improve with economic growth and scientific and technological progress. Through the use of scientific technological production, a higher development of humanity is not only deemed possible; it is viewed as inevitable, universal and good.

Within this context of linear development and universal "well-having," industrialized societies have created two institutions that promote the ideal of the materialistic "good life": the market and the modern nation–state. An unfettered competitive market composed of producers and consumers of goods has been viewed, since Adam Smith's era, as the form of social organization best able to produce material wealth for all; it is through the nation–state that one can create, maintain, and regulate markets for economic growth. Together, these two forces—the market and the nation–state—have transformed cultures, first in the West and then elsewhere around the globe. Let us examine some of their ramifications.

THE CULTURAL CRISIS: NARROWING THE DEFINITION OF HUMANNESS

The cultural crisis stems from the inability of industrial production to satisfy the *full spectrum* of human needs. Dimensions of life, such as ties of affection with other people, self-esteem in society, and a sense of meaning, cannot be replaced effectively by material consumption. In addition, the accelerated time stress of modern activities oriented around speed, efficiency, and productivity leave little time and space for feelings, spirituality, creativity, or nonprofit activities. Modern industrial cultures, having suppressed—almost denied—emotional, spiritual, creative aspects of humanity while emphasizing the accumulation of material wealth, have fostered a definition of humanness that is narrow in scope. Furthermore, the emphasis on economics and industrialism has negated such values as cooperation, mutual aid, live and help live, and "ours for us"; instead, it fosters such values as narcissistic individualism, the supremacy of self-interest, immediate gratification, "mine for me," and "get-ahead-grab-and-keep" competition. In such a cultural environment, self-esteem and human dignity are easily injured as people continually jostle in the competitive workplace and treat one another as objects to be used to maximize production and profit. Oppression and exploitation, inhumane living and working conditions, suspicion, hostility, and violence become common in such an economically oriented atmosphere and have increasingly come to characterize the contemporary industrialized cultural experience. As such, the modern human experience can be described as often filled with frustration, stress, anxiety, exploitation, oppression, depression, dependency, disconnectedness, alienation, loneliness, and pressure—pressure to perform at a break-neck, mechanical speed. Is this truly the "good life?"

THE ENVIRONMENTAL CRISIS: HIDDEN COSTS

This modern developmental cultural framework not only allows for cultural activities that create and perpetuate cultural poverty and scarcity; it also creates and perpetuates biotic poverty and scarcity. The highly materialistic, consumptive lifestyle of modern industrialized societies, made possible by science and advanced technologies, undermines nature's power to renew and sustain life. It does so not only because of the vast quantities of natural resources that are necessary in order to satisfy the modern throw-away-get-another, planned obsolescence culture but because of the way in which modern production systems operate. Based on producing the largest quantity at the lowest monetary cost, modern systems of food, clothing, shelter, energy, transportation, waste disposal, and household and industrial products, transfer the costs of production onto the environment. For example, the modern production of food entails using large-scale monocropping, high rates of pesticides, fossil fuels, large farm equipment, irrigation, hybrid seeds, and antibiotics and hormones for animal production. Supermarket shelves are bulging with relatively low-cost food. To the modern eyes, this looks like success, progress. But, hidden are the environmental costs: massive soil erosion, contamination of wells and rivers due to fertilizer and pesticide run-off, more frequent and more lethal applications of pesticides due to insect resistance, salinization of soils due to irrigation....

The hidden costs reach far beyond the agricultural realm, however. An in-depth look at any other modern system—be it the modern methods in constructing buildings, disposing of waste, producing energy, or manufacturing clothing—would reveal biotic damage as well. In other words, this plundering of nature and the externalizing of costs is endemic to modernity's entire lifestyle. It is the large-scale productive and consumptive lifestyle that undermines nature's powers of renewability and sustainability of life. As this economic, consumptive, scientific, technological way of life mesmerizes more people, it creates a biotic sustainability crisis of major proportions and major impact. Industrialized technologies now have global impact—for example, alteration of weather patterns and ozone destruction due to combustion of fossil fuels. It is damage and destruction on a colossal scale, and it is damage and destruction that cannot be easily corrected, either by humans or by nature. What we are facing is the imminent decline of the ecological balance of the entire planet and with it, our own decline (Berry, 1990; Bowers, 1993; Orr, 1992; Sachs, 1992b).

THE HEGEMONY OF THE MODERN DEVELOPMENTAL PARADIGM: GLOBAL RAMIFICATIONS

As the modern developmental paradigm spreads globally, it has become the principle means for usurping people's rights to the domains of knowledge, for dismissing people's rights to participate in the creation of knowledge, and for diminishing their rights in matters affecting their own subsistence and survival. This paradigm dismisses natural processes as well as traditional nonscientific and nontechnological livelihoods as inferior and of marginal value. Thus, the very conception of what constitutes human normality has been redefined. As Claude Alvares (1992) states, "people [have] lost the right to claim that they could function as competent human beings unless they underwent the indoctrination required by modernity" (p. 227). It is the assumption that nonscientific, noneconomic people are deficient as human beings and have to be "remade." Thus, science–technology–economics—the modern developmental paradigm—is not a liberatory force, as the dominant myth proclaims; rather, it is part of the machinery of oppression, serving to colonize and control the direction of knowledge and, consequently, human behavior, within the confines of a straight and narrow scientific–technological–industrial configuration. Furthermore, this modern paradigm places humans in a predicament; in placing humans above and outside nature, the paradigm allows for cultural activities that create and perpetuate biotic scarcity and degradation. This scarcity and degradation make the long-term support and sustaining of life increasingly impossible.

EDUCATION: AS REPLICATOR AND TRANSMITTER

Education, like any other institution, is always embedded in a particular culture. As such, education's purposes, goals, and pedagogy are shaped by the root assumptions within that particular cultural context. One of education's primary functions is to replicate and transmit the cultural code of a particular society to the young people of that particular society (Bowers, 1993; Orr, 1992, 1993b). One can assert, then, that current educational systems operating in any industrialized nation (being embedded in and operating in a technological–developmental–industrial culture) reflect the technological–developmental–industrial paradigm of that culture. These educational systems mimic the values and structure of that culture and transmit (explicitly, but more often implicitly) these values and root assumptions to the next generation.

Rather than exposing, contesting, or offering an alternative to the destructive biotic and cultural nature of the modern paradigm, these educational systems serve to reinforce and perpetuate the biotic and cultural damage by teaching people to think reductionistically. David Orr (1993a) describes such people as "in-the-box thinkers"—individuals whose minds have been conditioned to fracture knowledge into bits and pieces, into isolated and boxed subjects. Their minds are not taught to transcend those boxes or to question how boxes fit with other boxes. Consequently, these "in-the-box thinkers" are unable to perceive the interconnected causes of degraded ecologies and persons.

Even if students are aware of the presence of environmental and social problems, their dualistic, mind-privileged-over-body culture and education frame the problems only in intellectual terms. By failing to join the intellect (mind) with affection and loyalty (heart) to the ecologies of particular places, modern education produces students who are unable to feel for the damage occurring to persons, flora, and fauna and are unmoved to take concrete corrective actions. Thinking in boxes not only prevents students from seeing and feeling the interconnected social and biotic damage of modernity but disconnects knowledge from the person. What one knows is assumed to have little or no bearing on what or who one is. Modern education (again reflecting the modern paradigm) views knowledge as primarily that information and those skills needed for the attainment and performance of a job and rarely as a unifying agent among the intellect, the emotions, and the competencies of the hands. This disciplinary divisiveness leaves students devoid of moral character and bereft of their social moorings.

Conditioned by modernity's characteristic tendency to fragment reality (mind from body, heart or ethics from actions, humans from the natural world, individuals from the collective group), the purpose of modern education has become narrowly defined as career preparation. This is especially true for those careers viewed as being the most valuable (e.g., scientists, technological researchers and developers, business people, bankers, lawyers, economists, engineers, financial managers, marketing professionals). Armed with diplomas and credentials, these newly minted "experts" join the throng of other professionals who strive for more economic growth and development, new and "better" technologies and products, increased sales of goods, and ways to decrease monetary (not hidden) costs of resources both human and natural. Whether working domestically or abroad, these experts perpetuate the culture of human and biotic domination and damage.

These highly valued "experts," however, are not solely responsible for the continuing human and biotic damage resulting from the mindset of domination for all modern students are educated to "fit" into the modern lifestyle, to embrace it and accept it and even be proud of it. Few, if any, are taught to question science, progress, development, technological advancement, production and consumption. Few, if any, are taught to see the links and connections between these concepts and values and the ongoing practices that damage our cultural and biotic communities. Few, if any, are taught to look for and create alternative paradigms that do not operate around exploitative relationships. Few, if any, are taught to imagine a "good life" that encompasses more than simply material wealth. Few, if any, are taught to develop an identity and purposeful activities that go beyond the shallowness of consumption. Few, if any, are taught to develop to their full human potential, to a depth of character and a richness of being that transcends the superficiality of consumerism.

As others around the globe are drawn to the seeming richness of the modern lifestyle and desire to become "modern" themselves, they, too, look to modern education with its reductionist knowledge and expert-proclaiming powers as the magical door to modernity. In going through that door, however, they may be bringing into their lives monsters rather than magic.

REFERENCES

Alvares, C. (1992). Science. In W. Sachs (Ed.), *The development dictionary: A guide to knowledge as power* (pp. 219– 232). Atlantic Highlands. NJ: Zed Books.

Berry, W. (1990). *What are people for?* San Francisco: North Point Press.

Bowers, C. A. (1991). Ecological literacy: Education for the twenty-first century. In R. Miller (Ed.), *New directions in education* (pp. 89– 96). Brandon, VT: Holistic Education Press.

Bowers, C. A. (1993). *Education, cultural myths, and the ecological crisis: Toward deep changes.* Albany, NY: State University of New York Press.

Esteva, G. (1992). Development. In W. Sachs (Ed.), *The development dictionary: A guide to knowledge and power* (pp. 6– 25). Atlantic Highlands, NJ: Zed Books.

Illich, I. (1978). *Towards a history of needs.* New York: Pantheon Books.

Illich, I. (1992). Needs. In W. Sachs (Ed.), *The development dictionary: A guide to knowledge as power* (pp. 88– 101). Atlantic Highlands, NJ: Zed Books.

Lummis, D. C. (1992). Equality. In W. Sachs (Ed.), *The development dictionary: A guide to knowledge as power* (pp. 38– 52). Atlantic Highlands, NJ: Zed Books.

Orr, D. (1992). *Ecological literacy: Education and the transition to a postmodern world.* Albany, NY: State University of New York Press.

Orr, D. (1993a). The problem of disciplines/the discipline of problems. *Holistic Education Review,* 6,(3), 4– 7.

Orr, D. (1993b). The dangers of education. In R. Miller (Ed.), *The renewal of meaning in education: Responses to the cultural and ecological crisis of our times* (pp. 25– 38) Brandon, VT: Holistic Education Press.

Sachs, W. (1992a). One world. In W. Sachs (Ed.), *The development dictionary: A guide to knowledge as power* (pp. 102– 115). Atlantic Highlands, NJ: Zed Books.

Sachs, W. (1992b). Environment. In W. Sachs (Ed.), *The development dictionary: A guide to knowledge as power* (pp. 26–37). Atlantic Highlands, NJ: Zed Books.

Shiva, V. (1992). Resources. In W. Sachs (Ed.), *The development dictionary: A guide to knowledge as power* (pp. 206– 218). Atlantic Highlands, NJ: Zed Books.

Ullrich, O. (1992). Technology. In W. Sachs (Ed.), *The development dictionary: A guide to knowledge as power (pp. 275– 287).* Atlantic Highlands, NJ: Zed Books.

31

SCIENCE EDUCATION

Helen Parke
Charles R. Coble
East Carolina University

C. P. Snow (1959) was among the first to warn of the perils of the two cultures developing in society, a small number of scientifically knowledgeable individuals within the larger scientifically illiterate society:

> It is dangerous to have two cultures which can't or don't communicate. In a time when science is determining much of our destiny, that is, whether we live or die, it is dangerous in the most practical terms. Scientists can give bad advice and decision-makers can't know whether it is good or bad. On the other hand, scientists in a divided culture provide a knowledge of some potentialities which is theirs alone. All this makes the political process more complex, and in some ways more dangerous, than we should be prepared to tolerate for long, either for the purposes of avoiding disasters, or for fulfilling—what is waiting as a challenge to our conscience and goodwill—a definable social hope. (p. 98)

Snow warned that when the two cultures grow apart, the society does not act out of wisdom. The rich living along side but essentially ignoring the existence of the poor, who need not be poor in a world with so much abundance. Aligned to the scarcity mentality and the greed that sustains material poverty is a growing separation of the "haves and have-nots" regarding knowledge, particularly scientific knowledge, that is becoming increasingly important to economic success in today's world.

It is a challenge for us to look at our education with new lenses. Indeed, there are multiple dangers to our future if we inadvertently cultivate only an elite scientifically literate group of people who understand the science inherent in issues that affect our entire society. The danger is not just that few understand but that so many do not understand the basic science behind such global issues as environmental pollution, deforestation, atmospheric warming, and nuclear radiation. Knowledge of basic science is also central to such personal issues as maintaining good health and understanding the influence of physical exercise good and nutrition.

Everyone is potentially victimized when the separation between those with basic scientific knowledge and those without such knowledge grows too large. A small elite group with knowledge and political power (or controlled by such power) can manage the destiny of a larger, less knowledgeable, and powerless society. If the decisions of the knowledgeable elite are "good," then everyone benefits. But, how can we be assured that the decisions will always be in the collective best interest? What if the decisions of the elite become more self-serving, such as funding research into the development of high cost medical treatments for the afflicted few who can benefit from such treatments because they have sufficient wealth or health care insurance to cover the cost? What if, instead, the decisions are to fund prevention-oriented health education and care programs that benefit everyone? Or what if an elite minority chooses to make certain trade-offs, such as building nuclear power generating stations close to major population centers instead of focusing resources on cogeneration and other energy saving technologies? What if this minority supports multibillion dollar military weapons research development in a nation in which 25% of the people live in poverty? When the less-educated majority lacks knowledge to take informed options, such scenarios could and do happen. Snow (1959) warns:

> Escaping the dangers of applied science is one thing. Doing the simple and manifest good which applied science has put in our power is another, more difficult, more demanding of human qualities, and in the long run far more enriching to us all. It will need energy, self-knowledge, new skills. It will need new perceptions into both closed and open politics. Changes in education will not, by themselves, solve our problems; but without those changes we shan't even realize what the problems are. (pp. 99–100)

It is no less dangerous for a scientifically illiterate majority with political power to ignore the warnings of the minority who understand the consequence of the majority's actions. Legislation allowing clear-cutting in national forests, blocking needle exchange programs for narcotic victims, and opposing the enactment of stronger emission controls on automobiles are all supported by the majority of the citizens of the United States. However, if the small scientifically literate elite are ultimately right about the consequence of clear-cutting forests, or allowing drug addicts to continue to spread disease with used needles, or the health risk that results from higher air pollution levels, then regardless of who has the political power, everyone will suffer the consequence for suppressing or ignoring the scientific knowledge associated with each of these and other issues.

These are not abstract notions. We can read recent newspaper accounts describing different groups of people taking polar opposite stands and attempting to force their will on others who have very different views on such issues as limiting automobile emissions, enforcing additional restrictions on pollutants in order to promote cleaner air, and reducing the rate of global warming. Different groups make counterclaims that there is no proven relationship between man-made emissions and increased pollution and changes in atmospheric temperatures. Certain groups strongly support measures to limit human population growth as a means of reducing the negative effects on the earth's natural resources, whereas some believe that the earth has an unlimited carrying capacity, meaning no controls on population growth are necessary.

Many of the arguments hinge on understanding the nature of scientific research and what constitutes "proof" in science as well as the mathematics of probability, statistics, and causality. These are largely theoretical ideas to most people. Thus, rational decision making in the face of possible negative economic consequence (which more people do understand) is difficult to achieve in a society increasingly characterized by the "two cultures."

Complicating the "two cultures" phenomena has been the post-modernist suspicion of science and the technology it has produced. There has been, since the late 1960s in the United States, a growing culture of disbelief which rejects the notion that technological spinoffs of scientific research will be universally beneficial. The growing loss of jobs in this country due to increased applications of technology in the workplace has only confirmed that belief. Another related postmodern concern, enhanced by the movie industry, is that science is the means of perverse control over people. Snow has written that one of the deepest problems in scientific history has been the complex dialectic between pure and applied science: "One is to understand the natural world, the other is to control it" (Snow, 1959, p. 67–68).

Recent research in science and technology has changed how the public perceives science as it is practiced, "how scientific knowledge emerges from social, natural, political, cultural, historical, and economic contingencies of scientific work. Many science educators agree that students should learn not only science but also *about* science" (Roth & McGinn, 1998, p. 213). Collaborations between science education and science and technology studies can inform educators about how individuals become competent in science.

In today's world, students participate in various forms of public science. However, when we examine how students learn science in our schools, we question the widespread use of cookbook science for understanding science conceptually or for understanding scientific habits of mind. This "pouring in" or indoctrination of science may be the result of teachers, administrators, schools, communities, policy makers, and business and industry entities who would have children only learn that which they personally think necessary for the good of the economy, a perspective that they have been programmed to believe. Bertrand Russell spoke to the antieducational effect of indoctrination:

> If the children themselves were considered, education would not aim at making them belong to this party or that, but at enabling them to choose intelligently between the parties; it would aim at making them able to think, not at making them think what their teachers think ... we should educate them so as to give them the knowledge and the mental habits required for forming independent opinions. (cited in Egner & Denonn, 1961, p. 401)

Consider the realist's perspective

> that science is a human creation, that it is bound by historical circumstances, that it changes over time, that its theories are underdetermined by empirical evidence, that its knowledge claims are not absolute, that its methods and methodology change over time, that it necessarily deals in abstractions and idealizations, that it involves certain metaphysical positions, that its research agendas are affected by social interests and ideology, that its learning requires that children be attentive and intellectually engaged, and so on. (Matthews, 1998, p. 166)

Mastering content knowledge, pedagogical content knowledge (Shulman, 1987) and the philosophy of science is no longer sufficient for science teachers. Teachers of science must also be able to recognize and to answer the challenges posed by critics such as those identifying with the postmodern perspective. The goal is not the possession of the belief but rather having adequate reasons for the beliefs one holds. Teachers of science may hold strong opinions on matters in the philosophy of science and yet still recognize that there are usually two, if not more, sides to most serious intellectual questions. This recognition needs to be intelligently and sensitively translated into classroom practice. Minimally, the strongest opposing case needs to be presented to students and their interest in alternatives needs to be encouraged (Matthews, 1998, p. 170).

One major national initiative to change the way the public and educators perceive science is being led by the National Research Council (NRC), a prestigious nongovernmental organization located in Washington, DC. With encouragement from the American Association for the Advancement of Science (AAAS), the National Science Teachers Association (NSTA), and many other groups, the NRC organized an effort that resulted in the identification and publication of national science education standards. These standards, for the fist time, provided a national benchmark for what students should know and be able to do at different levels of schooling, how science should be taught, how students should be assessed, what material conditions must exist in a school to support effective science instruction the needed teacher professional development, and the larger policies that must exist at the district level to assure sustained science education.

It is somewhat doubtful that science and mathematics literacy will soon be on the rise with students in the United States, for there is no agreed on mechanism at the national or state level which will assure that the initiatives accomplished by AAAS, NSTA, or NRC will impact local educational systems. Yet, as educators seek to establish partnerships among their members at the university, school, and community levels, these collaborations can investigate further how to educate a public in the knowledge, beliefs, and attitudes of science as contrasted with a methodology that dispenses knowledge to students. We need a citizenry who can reason, weigh assertions made by opposing camps, and make sensible decisions about science-related issues, issues that deal with personal health, environmental destruction, and information technologies.

So the question of whether we are able in education environments to teach our students science and about science so that the two-culture gap is lessened and societies seek to improve the human condition rather than use knowledge to protect the economic elite remains open for discussion. We challenge those who understand educational systems to speak in a collective voice to the possibilities of education that support the human spirit. There remains the hope and the challenge that education has the potential to exist as education, not as indoctrination or control.

REFERENCES

Egner, R. E., & Denonn, L. E. (Eds.). (1961). *The basic writings of Bertrand Russell*. London: Allen & Unwin.

Matthews, M. R. (1998). In defense of modest goals when teaching about the nature of science. *Journal of Research in Science Teaching, 35*, 161–174.

Roth, M. W., & McGinn, M. K. (1998). Knowing, researching and reporting science education: Lessons from science and technology studies. *Journal of Research in Science Teaching, 35*, 213–235.

Shulman, L. S. (1987). Knowledge and teaching: Foundations of the new reform. *Harvard Educational Review, 57*, 1–22.

Snow, C. P. (1959). *The two cultures: A second look*. New York: Cambridge University Press.

32

Math Education

Maggie McBride
Montana State University-Billings

Kathryn Ross Wayne
Western Washington University

Several questions guide us when we teach classes: How do I encourage a student culture that values responsibility toward the environment; what would the morality of such a responsibility be? How do I as a person who is concerned about the environment create lessons and teach classes? How can my teaching render explicit the cultural assumptions of our modern worldview and bring these assumptions under critical interrogation with our students? How is local knowledge and the notion of community displaced in lessons? In teaching, at any level, how is it that we highlight an ecocentered view of the world rather than a human-centered (*anthropocentric*) view of the world?

In asking these questions, we need to look critically at the context or culture in which we teach. With some few exceptions (at Bates College and Evergreen College, for example), students continue to behave in such a way as to put us on notice that we implicitly expect competition among them for the best grades. Further, our institutional culture dictates that our teaching perpetuate the belief that the most legitimate expression of learning is that which we can measure with our midterms, finals, pop quizzes, spelling tests, and multiple choice questions. Indeed, all these common examples require little else from a student than a good short-term memory. In those classes in which we do create group situations for learning, several students do not take this time seriously, since they can depend on the fact that most of their grade will come from their individual efforts on the aforementioned exams. We have had several conversations with colleagues who continue to believe that rigor disappears if individual students are not allowed to "think for themselves." Such beliefs articulate what C. A. Bowers (1987) identifies as some of the most basic assumptions within the modernist worldview—a view of the individual as an autonomous and self-creating being; a tendency to equate change with progress; a notion that language acts as a conduit, and last, an anthropocentric view of the world. In this chapter, we elaborate on the first assumption in and of itself and then, briefly, on its logical extension into the final assumption.

In *Habits of the Heart*, Robert Bellah and his colleagues identify four strands of individualism within the cultural fabric of modern America (civic, religious, utilitarian, and creative) each of which has received varying degrees of emphasis since Europeans first arrived on this continent (Bellah, Madsen, Sullivan, Swindler, & Tipton, 1985). In our contemporary society, Bellah et al. claim that we view anything that would violate our right to think and judge for ourselves both personally and professionally as morally wrong. That is, we cling to the myth that the highest aspirations for members of our society and the world directly link up to our individual stances. Even the notion of success, defined in *Habits of the Heart* as a conscious and calculated effort to acquire material betterment, appears to be an outcome of the consistent work of the individual, that is, individual achievement (p. 149). Individuals learn from an early age to measure themselves and their autonomous quest for achievement against others' incomes and lifestyles. This definition of "individualism"permeates the curriculum and the context in which we teach, teaching children, especially males, to recognize their success to be a result of their own hard work.

In much of our modern thinking, people share the notion that the individual takes precedence over the community and the environment. Bellah et al. (1985) challenges modern expressions of individualism—artistic and utilitarian—with their implicit assumptions of autonomy, their rejection of tradition, and their assumption that change is inherently progressive (read "good"), and he asks us to rethink the role of the modern individual as a civic and religious entity, a manifestation of the individual which tends to deemphasize personal autonomy. Bellah shares Bowers' (1993) concern for the cultural patterns that view the individual as autonomous and the contributions that those patterns have made toward devaluing the importance of context, relationship, and sense of community. Bowers, in particular, has long contended that such cultural tendencies rest at the core of the eco-crisis.

Like Bowers, Bellah and his colleagues claim that many of our most complex problems as a society, such as the eco-crisis, are linked to our sense of individualism and its partner, consumerism. These scholars illuminate a hidden dimension that has to do with our society's devaluing of tradition. That is, individuals are encouraged to rely on their own received authority in forming opinions and behavioral responses; in other words, to think for themselves without relying on advice or suggestions of others—especially elders.

If we consider a broad view of culture such as that advanced by people like Clifford Geertz (1973), Edward Hall (1976), and Ward Goodenough (1981), we can better understand the absurdity and the destructive effects of individualism. For Geertz, culture "denotes an historically transmitted pattern of meanings embodied in symbols, a system of inherited conceptions expressed in symbolic forms by means of which men communicate, perpetuate, and develop their knowledge about and attitudes toward life"(p. 89). For Hall, culture is "a series of situational models for behavior and thought ... it is not innate, but learned, the various facets of culture are interrelated—you touch a culture in one place and everything else is affected; it is shared and in effect defines the boundaries of different groups"(pp. 13, 16). With Goodenough, "culture, then, consists of standards for deciding *what is*, standards for deciding *what can be*, standards for deciding *how one feels about it*, standards for deciding *what to do about it*, and standards for deciding *how to go about doing it*"(p. 62, emphasis added). In addition, Goodenough emphasizes the importance of language as providing a set of forms that is a code for other cultural forms. ... To learn the language—that is, to learn to use its vocabulary acceptably—is indispensable for learning the cultural forms its vocabulary encodes"(pp. 65, 66).

What for students and ourselves constitutes knowledge in our classes is the result of the use of a certain language code. Classroom culture enforces the standards that students accept in order to define themselves within their culture within the larger society. For example, McBride's students often don't understand mathematics as a discipline of cooperative learning through which they can talk with one another and share ideas for solving problems. Often, when she hands out work in class, students work on their own even when she encourages them to talk with one another. What they understand and have come to expect as a standard for learning mathematics is the practice of working alone.

Meanwhile, as Bellah cautions us, at the same time that these inheritors of modernist consciousness learn to tacitly accept and reproduce the culture of individualism, should someone approach such students and suggest that their patterns of thought and action demonstrate a mode of existence that, if carried to its logical extension, steadily moves them in the direction of anomie and nihilism, they might scoff and send the intruders on their way. Concurrently and paradoxically, if we ask these same students about the necessity of breaking with the ideas of older people—especially parents—of establishing their own views about the world and self, and "finding themselves,"the majority will stress the ontological importance of such self-creation.

How, then, do we see this simultaneous denial and reinforcement of individualism affecting our teaching and our classes—in this case, most specifically, math? In our teaching, it is not just the individuals and information or the teacher and information that interact; another dimension of learning goes on in our classrooms that has to do with culture and relationships. For example, we acquire our understanding of mathematics concepts (generally thought to be neutral, culturally clean) through what Geertz 1973 call the hidden dimensions of "culture." The textbook McBride teaches from is a communication system though which she sends messages when she teaches. A problem, then, that exists with any of the mathematics textbooks she has used is that they are blind to culture. A solution is that she needs to teach the characteristics of culture within each concept she teaches and, in fact, complicate the taken-for-granted knowledge embedded in even the simplest of math story problems. For example, a problem asks students to figure out how many acres of trees are logged in a day if two acres are logged in 1 hour and 17 minutes. Rather than ignore the consumeristic implications embedded in such a problem, thus perpetuating ecological blindness, a math teacher could "critque" the problem and make explicit to students an awareness of how they, at a metalevel, need not experience math culture as neutral. How, for instance, do the following questions, even as they put into focus disturbing socioeconomic perspectives, still portray an anthropomorphic epistemology: Why are the trees being cut? What country stands to benefit and in what way? What problems might arise as a consequence of such logging? For whom? Perhaps a better question might be, How does the world experience math?

Most culture is learned and experienced at a taken-for-granted level. Cultural language or message systems are implicit; we cannot see them until our actions or patterns are interrupted. When we interact with students, so do we mediate culture. We do not act on our students nor do we act on our ideas. *Rather, we interact with student, idea, and text simultaneously and dynamically*. Even material culture is a message form, and to show its non-neutrality, we will use a more advanced math problem to further explore the perceived notion that math is neutral, to provide an example of how a lesson design sends a message about what the teacher intends to teach.

When McBride introduces the notion of exponential growth, she interacts with the ideas and teaching of exponential growth. Students learn through McBride's mind, through her vision and understanding of exponential growth. More specifically, students learn to understand about exponential growth of populations when she introduces the concept through her biases and interpretation of the concept. Students learn through her layers of cultural patterns and her control of the language she uses when she teaches. Sometimes McBride provides simple explanations, or she may present a complex vocabulary to explicate the complexity of the mathematical ideas. Her teaching may vary according to the amount of time available for class and according to the importance the textbook places on any particular concept. Generally, she completes teaching about exponential growth in a day's lecture and proceeds to the teaching of logarithmic functions and inverse functions. Textbooks always devote another lesson to some rather general applications of the exponential growth function, but these applications are not the focus of what McBride wants students to learn. She hopes students will learn more about the exponential growth function and will come to understand their community involvement with the social implications of this function when considering world population and sustainable growth for future generations.

Math and the sciences are the engines of the highly experimental culture in which we live. The question, then, becomes, how do I teach so I encourage student awareness of modernistic underpinnings that, in fact, perpetuate the ecocrisis? In teaching many concepts in mathematics, if McBride is not clear with her students when she puts into question modernistic notions that they take for granted (science and empirical evidence erase bias, the privileging of rationalism, decontextualization, language as neutral, linear approaches to problems, anthropocentrism, to name a few), anger and disorientation can result. That is, if McBride talks too much about viruses and AIDS when she introduces the concept of exponential growth, many students get quiet, fidget, and become obviously uncomfortable. Students believe that learning to manipulate exponential growth functions is somehow doing math, whereas learning about population dynamics or AIDS has little or nothing to do with math.

Often the message from students who study mathematics is, "Let's get on to the mathematics of exponential growth rather than the social implications (population growth or virus growth) of exponential growth, which is not math, anyway." If McBride does not visually perform the mathematical calculations of exponential growth but, instead, chooses to contextualize when and for what purposes such calculations may be applied, again, students likely will think they are not doing mathematics; they may, in fact, wonder why they are spending so much time doing research and writing rather than "figuring." She has had student responses that state, "after all, this isn't a writing class." We worry, given our current educational emphases that are deeply grounded in a modernistic view of the world, that students will fail to understand that doing mathematics does not infer studying alone and mastering calculations without any context in which to think about their results. Further, we can only begin to contemplate the moral and ecological complications of our students' continuing failure to understand that philosophy and cultural templates gird up the ways in which they understand the world and the metanarratives they then enact.

REFERENCES

Bellah, R. N., Madsen, R., Sullivan, W. M., Swindler, A., & Tipton, S. M. (1985). *Habits of the heart: Individualism and commitment in American life*. Berkeley, CA: University of California Press.

Bowers, C. A. (1987). *Elements of a post-liberal theory of education*. New York: Teachers College Press.

Bowers, C. A. (1993). *Education, cultural myths, and the ecological crisis: Toward deep changes*. New York: State University of New York.

Geertz, C. (1973). *The interpretation of cultures*. New York: Basic Books.

Goodenough, W. (1981). *Culture, language and society*. Menlo Park: Benjamin/Cummings.

Hall, E. (1976) *Beyond culture*. New York: Anchor Press.

33

Educational Computing

C. A. Bowers
Portland State University

In her acclaimed book *Life on the Screen: Identity in the Age of the Internet,* Sherry Turkle (1996) summarizes what appears to be a growing consensus among educators about the contribution that computers make to enhancing human life:

> I have argued that Internet experiences help us to develop models of psychological well-being that are in a meaningful sense postmodern: They admit multiplicity and flexibility. They acknowledge the constructed nature of reality, self, and other. The Internet is not alone in encouraging such models. There are many places in our culture that do so. What they have in common is that they all suggest the value of approaching one's "story" in several ways and with fluid access to one's different aspects. We are encouraged to think of ourselves as fluid, emergent, decentralized, multiplicitous, flexible, and ever in process. (pp. 263–264)

She is indeed correct about the academic disciplines that increasingly take for granted what she describes as the "fluid, emergent, ... multiplicitous, flexible, and ever in process" view of the person now being represented as the ideal citizen of the information age. Turkle can be faulted, however, for not including educators on her list. Even before the vocabulary of postmodernism swept through the academic community, educators were urging that this view of the individual be made the basis of classroom practice. The fact that what Turkle envisions as the emancipatory potential of computers to liberate the individual from the constraints of time, space, and cultural traditions had already been embraced by educators representing the subfields of their discipline may account for why they have asked so few critical questions about a technology that provides a new and more beguiling infrastructure for globalizing the digital phase of the Industrial Revolution.

In the 1980s, educational computing was heavily promoted in colleges of education with the argument that computer literacy was to be the future basis of citizenship. But most classroom teachers responded by relegating the computer to the back of the classroom, where its use became part of the reward system for students who completed their other assignments. This is no longer the situation. With the expenditure of over 9 billion dollars on educational technology, which resulted in over 5.8 million computers being placed in the nation's classrooms, state departments of education and local school districts are allocating significant amounts of their shrinking educational budgets to training teachers to make computer-based learning the central feature of every area of the curriculum. Universities are moving even more quickly to replace face-to-face communication as the basis of learning with computer-mediated thought and communication. Some university administrators are even beginning to question whether the "virtual university" made possible by the Internet will entirely replace traditional institutions of higher learning. With computers becoming an increasingly ubiquitous feature of classrooms and academic offices, educators at all levels may now have enough direct experience with the technology to recognize the need for serious reflection on whether the changes it is introducing in the world are as ameliorative as Turkle and other computer proponents claim.

Given the space restrictions of this chapter, I would like to identify three broad questions that can serve as a starting point for clarifying the nature of the cultural traditions that computers reinforce, as well as the implications of these traditions for the well-being of other cultures and ourselves. The questions will also help frame the direction that reform should take in the area of teacher education and graduate studies in education.

WHAT CULTURAL PATTERNS ARE PRIVILEGED BY COMPUTER-MEDIATED THOUGHT AND COMMUNICATIONS?

The development of computers, as well as their introduction into the classroom, has been supported by a number of assumptions widely shared within the academic community and by the public at large. Indeed, one of the difficulties in recognizing that computers, like other technologies, are not culturally neutral is that the cultural amplification characteristics that computers reinforce are the very ones that are taken for granted by their developers, promoters, and users. As these characteristics, and the assumptions they are based upon, serve as the schemata for understanding relationships, including the nature and uses of technology, their influence on the discourse of educational computing remains largely hidden. The cultural coding process amplified by computers can also be understood in terms of contributing to a particular form of subjectivity. Since I have written elsewhere on the cultural ways of knowing and subjectivity amplified by computers (Bowers, 1988, 1993, 1995, 1997), as well as on the dimensions of cultural experience that are marginalized or made to entirely disappear, I provide here only a brief summary. It should be kept in mind that the summary identifies what are, in fact, exceedingly complex issues that deserve chapter-length clarification.

- The cultural non-neutrality of computers can be seen in how they amplify only those forms of cultural knowledge that can be made explicit and in how they marginalize the existence and thus the importance of tacit, contextualized layers of cultural patterns and understandings.
- Second, computers amplify the cultural epistemology that represents thinking as based on data, while reducing the possibility of recognizing that thinking is actually based on the epistemic patterns encoded in the metaphorically based languages of the cultural group.
- Third, computers amplify the cultural assumptions that represent the individual as an autonomous and rational being and, thus, the basic social unit. Computer-mediated thought thus reduces the awareness of how much of our daily life is constituted and sustained by transgenerational communication.
- Fourth, computers amplify a conduit (sender/receiver) view of language and put out of focus how language reproduces, even in moments of critical reflection, the deepest metaphorical constructions of earlier periods of development in the cultural way of knowing.
- Fifth, computers amplify a print-based form of consciousness and pattern of relationship while marginalizing the more complex participatory and contextualized patterns experienced in face-to-face communication.
- Sixth, computers amplify the cultural orientation that represents relationships as instrumental and individually centered, while at the same time preventing the use of languages that represent humankind's relationships with nature as dependent and morally reciprocal.
- Seventh, computers amplify the cultural orientation of the technological and scientific elite who use metaphors derived from machines as a basis for representing the most basic characteristics of life; at the same time, computers marginalize the importance of languages that encode the moral guidelines laid down in the mythopoetic narratives of ecologically centered cultures. They also reduce the possibility of mainstream culture's developing a language of relationships that is not instrumental and human centered.

A summary of the cultural amplification characteristics of computers (explicit knowledge, individualism, a conduit view of language, representing data as the basis of thought, and so forth) also represents a summary of the taken-for-granted assumptions that underlie the high-status knowledge acquired in public schools and universities. Although the knowledge engineers who design computer technology are educated in highly specialized areas that are even further removed from the cultural patterns of everyday life, and especially from the deep epistemic and moral patterns of other cultures, their education, elite social status, and sense of hubris make questioning their guiding assumptions seem totally irrelevant. Unfortunately, the people who write the educational software programs such as SimCity, SimEarth, Myst, and Storybook Weaver as well as classroom teachers in general, have also learned these assumptions as the taken-for-granted foundation of their educational experience. Thus, at all levels of technological development and educational use, the culturally specific assumptions that served as the basis of the Industrial Revolution continue to be reproduced in the mediating characteristics of computers.

HOW DO THE CULTURAL ASSUMPTIONS AMPLIFIED BY COMPUTERS CONTRIBUTE TO THE ECOLOGICAL CRISIS?

If the differences in scale of ecological impact is taken into account, where Americans require 5.1 hectares of productive land to provide life sustaining resources and to assimilate the waste products, whereas the people of India require only .4 hectares, it is easy to recognize that differences in cultural ways of knowing (including approaches to technology) are a critical factor. Mathis Wackernagel and William Rees (1996) point out that it would take an additional two planets Earth to sustain all the cultures of the world if they were to adopt the consumer patterns and approaches to technology that characterize the dominant culture in America. The cultural dimensions of the ecological crisis can also be in seen in the spread of the Western technologically based consumer lifestyle to the more densely populated areas of the world and in the destruction of traditional cultures that have developed along more ecologically sustainable pathways. The impact of this lifestyle can be seen in the amount of toxins being spread over the environment and in the decline in the viability of natural systems. Underlying the spread of commodified knowledge and relationships are the deep cultural assumptions that continue to be reinforced through the use of computers.

The connection between the cultural epistemology amplified through computer-mediated thought and communication can be seen in the cultural patterns that cannot be digitally coded: ideological and epistemological orientations that can be described as cultural and bioconservative in orientation, mentor relationships and the knowledge of elders; mythopoetic narratives that represent humans and the natural world as part of the moral and spiritual whole; transgenerational knowledge that combines knowledge of biodiversity and moral reciprocity; a sense of time that assumes moral responsibility for the well-being of future generations; and metaphorical languages that do not represent humans as the only species with intelligence nor ascribe to humans the right to dominate "lower," less-evolved forms of life. The inability to program computers to reproduce these forms of cultural knowledge can further be seen in the fact that these aspects of cultural life are mostly communicated through face-to-face interaction and generally at the taken-for-granted level of background understanding.

One of the ironies is that even when computers are used for addressing environmental problems, as in environmental education classes or in modeling changes in natural system, they reinforce the cultural ideology and epistemology that coevolved with the development of the Industrial Revolution.

WHAT SPECIAL CHALLENGES DOES COMPUTER-MEDIATED LEARNING CREATE FOR TEACHERS?

Now that global warming, the destruction of fisheries and old-growth forests, and the widespread impact of chemicals on the reproductive patterns of natural systems (to cite just a few areas of ecological change) bring the Western myth of technologically based progress into question, it is hoped that educators will respond by taking seriously the need to understand the language systems that reproduce the deep cultural assumptions that equate technological change, consumerism, and greater individual autonomy with progress. This will mean understanding how the language process that reproduces earlier metaphorically constructed ways of representing reality are part of the process of primary socialization mediated by teachers as they introduce students to the symbolic representations of culture represented in the curriculum. It also means developing a deep understanding of the connections between the cultural patterns that are contributing to furthering the ecological crisis and the patterns reinforced when computers are used in the classroom.

In addition to helping students understand that data are processed on metaphorical constructions of a particular cultural group, and that forms of consciousness in the past may be radically different from how students interpret them to be, teachers also need to be able to help students understand the other cultural amplification and reduction characteristics of computers that were discussed earlier. Furthermore, teachers also need to help students recognize the culturally specific assumptions that are the basis of such programs as *The Oregon Trail*, *SimCity*, *SimEarth*, and *Environmental Toolbox*. In order to clarify the cultural assumptions underlying the thought patterns of the experts who are further contributing to the educational process by developing a seemingly endless flood of educational software, teachers will need to understand noncommodified forms of activities and relationships. And if students are to understand the differences in how noncommodified community relationships are valued and practiced by different cultural groups, as well as how these noncommodified patterns contribute to more ecologically sustainable communities, teachers will need to provide students with the language that legitimates learning about these noncommodified, low-status community activities.

In effect, the mechanical and social techniques for integrating computers into the curriculum are only marginally important. Rather, the cultural mediating characteristics of educational computing, particularly as they relate to the ecological crisis and to undermining culturally diverse noncommodified traditions of community life, should be the main focus of educating teachers to be computer literate. Unfortunately, most professors responsible for teacher education and graduate studies in education continue to take for granted the same cultural assumptions that are amplified by computers, which means they will continue to equate computer-mediated learning with progress. And if classroom teachers are unable to understand that educational computing is really a form of cultural coding, few students are likely to gain this understanding on their own, and thus the downward cycle is likely to continue.

REFERENCES

Bowers, C. A. (1988). *The cultural dimensions of educational computing: Understanding the non-neutrality of technology*. New York: Teachers College Press.

Bowers, C. A. (1993). *Critical essays on education, modernity, and the recovery of the ecological imperative*. New York: Teachers College Press.

Bowers, C. A. (1995). *Educating for an ecologically sustainable culture: Re-thinking moral education, creativity, intelligence, and other modern orthodoxies*. Albany, N.Y.: State University of New York Press.

Bowers, C. A. (1997). *The culture of denial: Why the environmental movement needs a strategy for reforming universities and public schools*. Albany, NY: State University of New York Press.

Turkle, S. (1996). *Life on the screen: Identity in the age of the internet*. New York: Simon & Schuster.

Wackernagel, M., & Rees, W. (1996). *Our ecological footprint: Reducing human impact on the earth*. Gabriola Island, British Columbia: New Society.

34

Educational Technology

Eugene F. Provenzo, Jr.
University of Miami, Coral Gables

Educational technologies have shaped the discourse of education and schooling from its earliest history. Yet we pay little attention to these technologies and their meaning. In large part, educational technologies are taken for granted—are assumed to be neutral, whether in the form of chalk and slate, manipulables such as building blocks or mathematical rods, textbooks and workbooks, or televisions and computers.

It is the argument of this chapter that educational technologies are not neutral but that they instead significantly shape and define what is discussed and how things are learned in our culture and schools. In pursuing this argument, I focus on one question: How do specific educational technologies shape and define the discourse of education and schooling? Education and schooling have always been shaped by the technologies used to teach and communicate information. During the Medieval period, the great scholastic universities such as Paris and Bologna developed their curriculums around the technology of the spoken word and the handwritten manuscript. Traveling scholars moved from one university to another as they sought the most knowledgeable experts in their field.

With the invention of moveable type during the late 15th century, the tradition of the wandering scholar gave way to the new educational technology of the book. With the introduction of relatively inexpensive and precisely reproducible print technology, it became possible to create definitive scientific and literary texts and to distribute them on a widespread basis. The student no longer needed to travel from university to university in order to obtain the wisdom of individual scholars. Instead, scholars' ideas could be transferred through the content of books housed in libraries and personal collections.

The educational technology of the printed book created a new type of discourse in European culture. Theorists such as Marshall McLuhan and Elizabeth Eisenstein remind us in their work of how relatively new this discourse is. Print technology as a discursive form, however, was not just limited to the university but also made its way into education at other levels as well—ones not always associated with schooling. (Eisenstein, 1983; McLuhan, 1962)

In the early phases of the Protestant Reformation, for example, Martin Luther not only printed illustrated Bibles but also developed catechisms for the use of adults and children. These texts represented important educational technologies used outside the traditional boundaries of schools. Significantly, catechisms led to the development of one of the most important and pervasive educational technologies of the modern era—the textbook. Modern textbooks, in the form of primers and spelling books, came into widespread use by the end of the 17th century. In the case of the American colonies, for example, textbooks such as *The New England Primer* made it possible to create a relatively uniform curriculum across different schools, a curriculum that could also be carefully scrutinized in terms of its political and social content.

New educational technologies brought with them new modes of discourse and new types of education. The medieval university, dependent on what could be remembered in a scholar's mind, emphasized repetition and memorization. In contrast, the modern text-based university has emphasized mastery of basic texts and reference sources. As Neil Postman (1984) argued, "Although culture is a creation of speech, it is recreated anew by every medium of communication—from painting to hieroglyphs to the alphabet to television. Each medium, like language itself, makes possible a unique mode of discourse by providing a new orientation for thought, for expression, for sensibility" (p. 10).

Textbooks, as the most significant educational technology of the early modern period, provided a new discursive space. Textbooks as a print-oriented medium emphasized the written over the spoken word. In doing so, the educational technology of the textbook was not only a vehicle of the curriculum but emphasized very specific ways of constructing and organizing knowledge. This is a key issue in terms of understanding the meaning of educational technology—that is, in terms of what it amplifies or reduces.

The idea of educational technologies amplifying or reducing specific ideas is a theme that has been developed by C. A. Bowers (1988) in his discussions of educational computing. Drawing on the work of Don Idhe and, in turn, Martin Heidigger, Bowers asks us to consider educational technologies such as the computer not only in a technical and procedural context but also in a larger cultural context—how they mediate and change our systems of knowledge and our ways of interpreting the world around us.

Bowers (1988) understands that computers and their software are types of educational technology that must be understood as "part of the much more complex symbolic world that makes up our culture" (p. 27). Although Bowers addresses issues in the context of computing, the question of what they amplify or reduce can also be asked of other types of educational technology, from textbooks, to chalkboards, to television. New educational technologies bring with them new ways of viewing the world and defining culture, ones that in turn change the nature of educational discourse. New educational technologies change not only the traditional discourse of education and schooling but where education takes place. Television, for example, has assumed much of the cultural and educational space traditionally assigned to the family and the schools. In doing so, it has profoundly redefined our understanding of knowledge and learning and even the very nature of our political and social discourse. The printed word no longer defines "the style of conducting politics, religion, business, education, law and other important social matters" (Postman, 1984, p. 92). Political arguments are increasingly made in the form of 30-second sound bites. As a result, our political discourse has changed, adapting itself to television as a medium.

If television changes the political and social discourse in our culture, then it also changes the knowledge students carry with them into school. As a result of television, children come to school with very different types of knowledge than they did 50 or 60 years ago. Every child who watches television knows about animals in other lands, about murder and violence, and about becoming consumers. As they watch their average 28 hours of television per week, they learn about a wide range of things traditionally unknown during childhood (Elkind, 1981; Postman 1982; Winn, 1983). Students learn to assimilate visual and auditory knowledge from television. Increasingly, we are moving toward a new model of education "based on the speed-of-light electronic image" (Postman, 1984, p. 145). Television as an educational technology has diminished the importance of the family and schools as purveyors of knowledge and cultural wisdom. In doing so, its role and the role of emerging technologies such as the Internet must be understand as shaping the type of discourse that takes place in our culture and more specifically in our schools. The introduction of an educational technology like the Internet, for example, brings a massive set of information resources into the classroom that have never been available before. Students can easily visit websites around the world—the Louvre in Paris, the Library of Congress in Washington, D.C., or the Victoria and Albert Museum in London. Students can have electronic pen pals in foreign countries, exchange scientific research data with other students across the country, and even talk to scientists by E-mail in remote locations of the world. They can also explore sexual materials normally prohibited from their view, masquerade as adults on sex oriented chat lines, and learn how to construct pipe bombs through information provided by various terrorist and hate groups.

Educational technologies such as the Internet change the authority of the teacher and the knowledge base of the student. Expert knowledge is less important in an era when information is more readily available to the user. Textbooks and other traditional sources become less authoritative as alternative sources of information become available. As a result, the nature of educational discourse, and ultimately the meaning of education and schooling, is changed. Richard Lanham (1993) made this point in reference to the use of hypertext and hypermedia. According to him, "Electronic text creates not only a new writing space but a new educational space as well. Not only the humanities curriculum, but school and university structures, administrative and physical, are affected at every point as of course is the whole cultural repository and information system we call a library" (p. 12).

What happens to writing when students have grammar and spell check systems readily available to them? Does learning how to diagram a sentence lose its importance in the general curriculum? Is there less need to have students drill and practice spelling words? What happens to writing when it can be combined with animations and video? Does it cause the type of writing that is created to be different? Do the illustrations become part of the actual process of writing? What happens when writing can be shared on a global basis? Do cultures and students become less insulated, less isolated? Is their perspective broader than that of their own community and culture? What happens when publishing becomes easier, almost universally available? Through technologies such as desktop publishing and the Internet, virtually everyone can publish their ideas.

What are the implications for equity and learning when a visually or learning disabled student can have a text read aloud to them by a computer? Are they literate, if words that they cannot read can be spoken for them? If new educational technologies change the nature of educational discourse—by actually enabling the process of discourse—then does having access to these technologies become an equity issue? If the new educational technologies, whether in the form of television or the Internet, change the nature of educational discourse, then there are serious questions that need to be raised about who has access to this technology and how different groups are portrayed through its use.

Considerable concern has been raised in recent years as to who has access to computing and the power associated with it. Our most widespread educational technology, television, is essentially available to anyone in the culture. This widespread availability, however, obscures the differentiated nature of the material that is available to different groups in the culture. Commercial television is more accessible to the poor and the young than the more specialized broadcasting provided through cable and satellite transmission. Advertising and its lessons of consumption are concentrated on those who can afford only commercial television. Access to computing is even less available to those who cannot afford expensive and complex equipment and services. Whether at home or school, the question of computer access and availability is an increasingly important issue, as computers in the form of multimedia learning systems and gateways to the Internet become increasingly important vehicles for the transmission of information and knowledge.

The question becomes one of who has access to computer-based educational technologies and what is the nature of that access? Simply having computers in a school or classroom is not enough. There is an enormous difference between the data access and knowledge available to a student who visits a computer lab for a couple of hours of activities per week and one who has several computers that are in regular use in the back of his or her classroom, or who has computer access at home. If educational technologies such as computers are going to provide the basis for new types of education and schooling—and in turn establish new models of discourse—then we need to ask questions such as, Who gets access to computers? Boys or girls? Rich or poor? Black? White? Brown? People with special needs versus the general population?

Are educational technologies such as computers actually reinforcing or discouraging desired patterns of access? As early as its 1988 report, the Office of Technology Assessment found that "in absolute terms, small schools have fewer computers than large ones, but smaller schools have proportionally more computers than large schools" (p. 35). Analyzing their data further, they observed that "because minority students are more likely to attend large urban schools, their access to computers has been worse than that of white students" (p. 35). Access has been related to acquisition policies and "wealthier schools have acquired technology more rapidly than schools with students of predominantly low socio-economic status" (p. 35). When poorer schools do have access to computing, is the emphasis on students' using programs that empower them by using the computer as a tool for inquiry and exploration or on rote drill and memorization? The organization and arrangement of computer access and the extent to which computers support existing models of teaching are factors that need to be examined, since they ultimately define the type of educational discourse that is possible as well as who can or cannot engage in the discourse.

CONCLUSION

Any educational technology, whether textbooks, television, or computers, ultimately shapes education and the experience of schooling. Contrary to popular belief, educational technologies are not neutral but represent specific ways of viewing and interpreting the world. As a result, educational technologies should be understood as being powerful tools in the definition of educational and cultural discourse. When combined with questions of who has access to educational technology and how that access can function to empower or disempower specific groups, the role of educational technologies, particularly emerging ones such as computers and the Internet, suggest that their importance in shaping educational and cultural discourse has been severely underestimated and requires much greater attention from both theorists and practitioners in the field.

REFERENCES

Bowers, C. A. (1988). *The cultural dimensions of educational computing: Understanding the non-neutrality of technology*. New York: Teachers College Press.

Eisenstein, E. (1983). *The printing revolution in early modern Europe*. New York: Cambridge University Press.

Elkind, D. (1981). *The hurried child*. Reading, MA: Addison-Wesley.

Lanham, R. A. (1993). *The electronic word: Democracy, technology and the arts*. Chicago: University of Chicago Press.

McLuhan, M. (1962). *The gutenberg galaxy: The making of typographic man*. Toronto, Canada: University of Toronto Press.

Postman, N. (1982). *The disappearance of childhood*. New York: Delacorte Press.

Postman, N., (1984). *Amusing ourselves to death: Public discourse in the age of show business*. New York: Viking.

Office of Technology Assessment (1988, September). *Power on! New tools for teaching and learning*, OTA–SET–379. Washington, DC: U.S. Government Printing Office.

Winn, M. (1983). *Children without childhood*. New York: Pantheon.

35

Technological Literacy

Mark D. Beatham
Plattsburgh State University College

> We must ... question the basic soundness of the current scientific and educational ideology, which is now pressing to shift the locus of human activity from the organic environment, the social group, and the human personality to the megamachine, considered as the ultimate expression of human intelligence—divorced from the limitations and qualifications of organic existence. (Mumford, 1972, p. 84)

Technology devotees consistently fail to notice that a technological culture favors mechanisms over humans and all other organic life. Neither are they able to recognize a logical relationship between the increasingly dehumanizing social scale (of cities, suburbs, bureaucracies, pop culture, and so forth), the maddening cultural pace, and the technical systems in which all are expected to interact daily. The technological culture escapes substantive criticism because of its symbolic, indeed mythic, quality. It symbolizes the most deeply held and cherished value of all "modern" cultures: the effort to control and manipulate all phenomena on the earth without moral consequences. This *remote control ethic* organizes all human and nonhuman elements into a super machine, a *megamachine*, that consumes all organic existence. Children born into the megamachine are taught the remote control ethic by living, working, and being schooled in a closed system of integrated technologies and techniques, increasingly disconnected from their own and other organic life. The system implicitly promises power without responsibility, for the price of organic integrity. The remote control ethic, which includes technology and the technique from which it springs, must be more deeply understood in order to confront the consequences of its dehumanizing and anti-ecological effects. It is important to begin by analyzing how the tools and techniques a technological culture creates and uses represent that culture's ethic. This analysis naturally leads to an investigation of the ideological foundation of these technologies: *technique*. Following this analysis, I discuss the consequences of the remote control ethic, paying particular attention to the dangers of abstraction. Finally, after speculating about the long-term consequences of this ethic's persistent growth, I will present several alternative criteria by which a culture should judge the appropriateness of its technological innovations.

TECHNOLOGY DEFINED

Technology materially represents the remote control ethic in its drive to control the forces of nature. It effectively orders relations with the world, determining what gets presented as problems and as tenable solutions. Most technology is antiecological, because it is produced to serve this end and thus serves to fragment experience and increase abstraction.

The ecologist, Jeremy Rifkin (1991), defines technology as "appendages of [human] limitations of time and space" (p. 27). Marshall MacLuhan (1964) defines it as "extensions," and said that "whether [they are] of skin, hand, or foot, [they] affect the whole psychic and social complex" (p. 4). These definitions encompass implements as simple as knives and as abstract and complex as fire and computers. Yet, as implied by both Rifkin and MacLuhan, technologies never *stand alone* as mere material elements. From the beginning, human implement making has been more a symbolic than a literal enterprise, involving the representation of dreams, hopes, and ideals.

Lewis Mumford (1972) spent much of his professional life exploring how human artifacts such as tools and buildings symbolize human beliefs and values about the world and their place in it. He claims that humans are "pre-eminently a mind-using, symbol-making, and self-mastering animal," and that the earliest human "technics," or extensions, were intended more "to bring order and meaning into every part of life," than to master the external environment (p. 81). These first extensions, which were mostly religious symbol making, were life centered, not work, power, or production centered. However, the majority of the current technologies express "a new stress upon the exploitation of physical energies, cosmic and human, apart from the process of growth and reproduction" (p. 81). The social context within which these technologies are made has shifted significantly. The roots of the current context are found in ancient times. Mumford claims that the original machine metaphors are found in ancient Egypt, nearly 5 thousand years before the metal marvels of the machine age. The first machines built the pyramids, roads, and dams, but they were principally composed of *human parts*. They were the highly organized human skills and physical energies, strapped as much to an ideology as to a yoke. Each human was an integral, often highly specialized, part of an elaborate hierarchical social organization, the first megamachine, which principally benefitted those at the top. In form and function, the first megamachine is identical to computers and telecommunications, as well as to corporate and governmental technologies. So, whereas self-flattering histories of progress are written by Westerners, pointing to grand technological achievements as evidence, Mumford shows that the culture is still mired in the same symbolic power paradigm as its Egyptian ancestors. Most modern technologies are merely extensions of the same ethic to efficiently dominate the world.

The works of Mumford, MacLuhan, and Riftkin help change the way that technology is viewed and evaluated: not in terms of isolated machines, or even in terms of all of the physical "extensions of humans" combined, but as integrated with and key facilitators of human symbolic ambitions. MacLuhan (1964) shows how the feudal system was a *social* extension of the stirrup from the eighth century and how the printed word burst the bonds of the monasteries and guilds, "creating extremist patterns of enterprise and monopoly" (p. 23). Mander (1991) demolishes the naive *individual machines only* perspective about technology with modern examples, such as how skyscrapers became possible with the invention of the telephone, and multinational corporations with the invention of the computer. Modern technologies integrate more and more "loose strands" of culture into one uniform pattern. A citizen in a technologically advanced (and thus, highly integrated) culture must learn to look at "right angles," in order to see the interlocking patterns and commitments one is automatically heir to. Suburbs are inextricably connected to cars and roads and supply stores, and Middle East politics, and concepts of time and distance. Mander talks about this modern technical integration and the paradox it has produced:

> While we walk on pavement, or drive on a freeway, or sit in a shopping mall, we are unaware that we are enveloped by a technological and commercial reality, or that we are moving at technological speed. We live our lives in reconstructed, human-created environments; we are *inside* manufactured goods.

There are significant costs to this envelopment, this integration, and especially to the ignorance of it. But before these are assessed, let us continue where we have been heading: to the sense-making ethic that connects the technologies to human consciousness.

TECHNOLOGY IS TECHNIQUE

> "Choices and ends are both based on beliefs, sociological presuppositions, and myths which are a function of the technological society." (Ellul, 1972, p. 86)

The philosopher Jacques Ellul (1965) claims that technique is what integrates the machine into society, what makes it *make sense*. He says, "It constructs the kind of world the machine needs.... It clarifies, arranges, and rationalizes; it does in the domain of the abstract what the machine did in the domain of labor" (p. 5). Technique is the "system logic" for the operation of technology.

Technique is the *logos* for the remote control ethic, the main ordering metaphor for the technological culture. Technique attempts to solve in advance all the problems that might possibly impede the functioning of an organization, not leaving it to chance, intelligence, inspiration, or ingenuity to find a solution at the moment the difficulty arises (Ellul, 1965). It has modified or replaced life-centered symbology and a pragmatic approach with an order that seeks to standardize and control all phenomena (Ellul, 1972). Thus, as Ellul (1972) argues, technique

> is the contrary of freedom, an operation of determinism and necessity. Technique is an ensemble of rational and efficient practices; a collection of orders, schemes, and mechanisms. All of this expresses very well a necessary order and a determinate process, but one into which freedom, unorthodoxy, and the sphere of the gratuitous and spontaneous cannot penetrate. (p. 91)

Because it focuses on "rational and efficient practices," and "orders, schemes, and mechanisms," technique encompasses all aspects of social, economic, and administrative life, all the technique-centered disciplines (religion, science, psychology, education, and so forth). We are a nation (and increasingly a world) obsessed with technique: the "How To Do It," as the ecologist John Livingston (1994) calls it (p. 11). And at the level of technique, there really is no substantive difference between political economies around the world. Socialism presupposes that the world is to be dominated and controlled by technical means. "The Russians have gone farthest [sic] in creating a 'religion' compatible with Technique by means of their transformation of Communism into religion" (Ellul, 1972, p. 88). The "New World Order" is not global capitalism; it's *global technique*, and everyone and everything is expected to conform.

THE EFFECTS OF AND RESPONSES TO THE TECHNIQUE MYTH

> It is only in the wild places that a man can sense the rarity of being a man. In the crowded places, he is more and more closed in by the feeling that he is ordinary—and that he is, on the average, expendable. You can best serve civilization by being against what usually passes for it. (Berry, 1972, p. 42)

The fragmentation, specialization, and abstraction on an enormous scale has many negative consequences. As living beings, humans have developed sophisticated and subtle patterns of relationships with the natural world, relying on nature for key ordering metaphors and essential, complex context for the development of imaginative plasticity (Cobb, 1959; Shepard, 1982). Living "inside manufactured goods" breaks these relationships, narrowing experience to a few discreet puffs of photons and the sensual banalities of concrete and plastic. The scale also mitigates against personal relevancy in the world, making it increasingly impossible to react as a human to the "live present."

A recent personal experience illustrates these *natural* frustrations. I was sitting in a restaurant in a large city when a "homeless person" came up to my table. He was carrying a stack of "street newspapers" and asked me if I would like to buy one. In the split second between his question and my programmed refusal, I realized something was different about him. But then my head was shaking and he was already on his way.

What was "different" was that this man, in appearance, manner, and style of question, instantly seemed like a real person in front of me, in real need. His humanity had surprised me. There was something disturbingly genuine about this early middle-aged man, something that broke right through my programmed defenses and to my emotions. I suddenly *felt* him alone and struggling underneath the heavy insensate machine on which I was still riding. And everything about his dress and manner suggested that he, too, had recently been a passenger on the same machine. What he, a suffering human, needed most from me was *my humanity*. What I had was a set of unwieldy abstractions, which couldn't account for him.

The ecologist, David Orr (1996) thinks that the enormous, abstract scale of our present socioeconomic life, founded upon high-energy use is responsible. This increasing abstraction discounts human senses and sense making, effectively rendering organismic responses irrelevant. Orr said, "A high-energy society undermines our sense of meaning and our belief that our lives can have meaning. It leads us to despair and to disparage the very possibility of intelligence" (p. 56). Orr is warning us of the inevitable consequences of a technical system that relies on so much power to get so much more power. Ellul (1972), argues that he, like this high-energy, technical society is not, and never was, about morality; it's about *power*. And sooner or latter, all nontechnical—that is, all organic—elements will be sacrificed. Morality, like democracy, requires a much smaller human scale in order to be sufficiently sensitive and responsive to real needs. Morality is in the details, not in abstractions and slogans.

THE "PSYCHIC ADVANTAGES" OF A TECHNICAL WORLD

So why would people, organic beings, continue to support a system that dehumanizes them, credits machines and predictability more than life, and discredits morality altogether? Except for *marginal* material benefits (for most, but a large one for those at the top of the social hierarchy), why would people consistently favor a system that requires such enslavement? The occasional benefits that spin from the reckless grinding of the technique juggernaut are incidental to its essential mission. Praising the incidentals is a little like feeling content with free cable in one's jail cell. Mander (1991) makes this point more ominously, pointing to the *logical* link between computers and the possibility of worldwide holocaust:

> Every military in the world has attached itself to computers, and all military strategies are now computer based. The programs are written, the computers are ready to act. In the face of this reality, to speak of computers helping you edit your copy or run your little business seems a bit absurd. (p. 74)

So what makes so many so willing to sacrifice to the megamachine? Perhaps, for Americans, it is because we are the ancestors of the war-weary ironists of the 1920s and 1940s, says the literary critic Andrew Delbanco (1995). We pretend with them that all of the problems of the past were attributable to religious and other social fanaticisms and that real progress could only be made through objective measures. Machines were and are worshipped as the totem of objectivity, and Westerners have an enormous psychological investment in keeping them socially and politically "clean."

Yet there is something more sinister lurking beneath the surface. As the social critic, Lionel Tiger (1991) says, "[The industrial system] provide[s] a uniquely efficient lubricant for moral evasiveness....Individuals with fully-fledged private moralities [are permitted] to conduct business without personal liability" (pp. 5 & 4). The inherent moral responsibilities of being "a distinct soul in the world" can be safely absorbed and diffused within the amoral machinery. The feminist Susan Griffin (1990) explains how easily Heinrich Himmler could avoid the likely moral devastation of having invented the gas chamber to murder millions by merely maintaining the pose of a good bureaucrat who *simply* wishes to solve a technical problem efficiently. Further, Delbanco (1995) shows how easily someone like General U.S.S. Grant could become an archetypal hero in the age of the machine and how he has become the model for the "modern, dead-eyed, murdering twentieth century man" (p. 139). Grant, he says, "was a man ... [with] no ground for faith ... [who was] at home in the mechanized world, thinking about men as bodies capable of obedient motion." He "doesn't think ... [he just] surrenders his spirit, grateful to have a function ... an alienation in the midst of action" (pp. 139–140). Grant is one on a growing list of spectacular examples of technique creating and using "heroes."

Technology is the material expression of the remote control ethic, a stupefying belief system underwritten by the desire to escape moral responsibility. By dehumanizing and desacralizing the world, the "machine man" successfully escapes the enormous obligations attendant on living with and relating to other living things. I was one of millions of Americans who grew up with the television show *Star Trek* helping to create my images of what the progressive future should be like. Although it purported to be about human adventures, we all knew that the use of powerful technologies was the key attraction. Push a button and food magically appears, free of concerns about soil, appropriate farming practices, the use of illegal immigrants, price supports, polluting transportation, rising cultural expectations of "exotic" foods from distant regions, and the ruthless forcing of nonindustrial countries into "cash crop" (versus self-sufficient) economies. Push another button and your body disintegrates and reintegrates in another place, with no responsibility for what lay in between.

Technique is necrophilic at its core, because its *logos* is to standardize and control. Fromm's (1941) definition of necrophilia fits with what Delbanco (1995) describes as a traditional view of sin: the failure to see humans as ends in themselves, not means; and, as the confusion of the self with the world; to impose the self onto the world. Delbanco arges that a literary tradition from Goethe to Melville and Dostoevsky to Conrad expounds evil as the capacity to render invisible another human consciousness. But now evil has been systematized, made banal, and spread across the globe. Satellites map "resources." Everything is being digitized. And the Puritan can't find the Devil anywhere.

The style of "modern evil" works by defter means. The psychologist Ernest Becker (1973) might argue that technology is an obvious spiritual convenience for overburdened humans. Becker argues that humans are "ontologically anxious," from being able to imagine the heavenly bliss of a starkly symbolic existence, while having to suffer the encumbrances and thousand, natural "bedevilments" of destiny." So, we'll frantically search for heroic projects to tie our fates to, machines and programs to diffuse the weight, in order to avoid the shock of recognition about our inevitable death. Lionel Trilling (1947) argues that the post-World War II suburbia boom was designed in every respect to "refuse knowledge of the evil and hardness of the world" (p. 86). In terms of the remote control ethic, the suburbs, "smart bombs," virtual reality, and the corporation are philosophically the same. They work with each other to control (and thus kill) the world from morally remote distances. All of these behavior characteristics and our irrational way of regarding technology—the willed ignorance, the unfounded belief in one's ability to be in control at any time, while constantly increasing one's dependency—fit the clinical definition of addiction, on a societal level (Glendinning, 1995).

ECOLOGICAL ALTERNATIVES

An existential bargain was made long ago. In a conspiracy designed to escape and rise above nature, and to clearly benefit a few at the expense of the many, a dangerous and far-reaching delusion was perpetrated. We and our ancestors have hitched our talents and fortunes together and have moved as an army against the forces of nature. The tacit expectation is that each person must ignore his or her natural heritage and potential wholeness and plug his or her special skill into the juggernaut. We are expected to do this every day, in countless ways, always without a formal argument.

This urge for power and agency has always been felt by humans but in proportion with other needs and desires. Mumford (1972) claims that power has only recently become the exclusive goal. He says:

> Our age has not yet overcome the peculiar utilitarian bias that regards technical invention as primary, and esthetic expression as secondary or even superfluous; and this means that we have still to acknowledge that, until our own period, technics derived from the whole man in his intercourse with every part of the environment, utilizing every aptitude in himself to make the most of his biological, ecological, and psychosocial potentials. (p. 80)

Mumford is hinting at an alternative that should be recovered. As long as humans continue to live in "a world of manufactured goods," constantly encountering and being reinforced by only the *remote control ethic*, they will further narrow their sensitivities and continue to erode any chance they might have of living as full beings, in "intercourse with every part of the environment, utilizing every aptitude ... to make the most of ... biological, ecological, and psychosocial potentials." And the megamachine will systematically eradicate all other organic existence.

The schooling system tacitly and formally supports the technical system, especially with its methods, testing, marketable skill, and technological literacy emphases. The schools are eagerly preparing children to become what Berry (1987) calls, "itinerant, professional vandals," roving, placeless, resource administrators who will sell their finely honed abstraction skills to the highest bidder, and willingly sacrifice any place for solely economic reasons (p. 54). The anthropologist and ecologist, David Abram (1996), also heaps scorn on what currently passes for knowledge in the United States saying, "A civilization that relentlessly destroys the living land it inhabits is not well acquainted with truth, regardless of how many supposed facts it has amassed regarding the calculable properties of the world" (p. 264). The very least that should be done in schools is to stop indoctrinating every young child in the necrophilic remote control ethic and to start indicating how this ethic, through technology and technique, is implicated in all that we see, think, and do.

Not all technologies and techniques are bad. The economist E. F. Schumacher (1973) discusses Buddhist standards for technology that fit ecological criteria. He describes two kinds of technologies: those that enhance a person's skill and those that replace essentially human qualities and make the individual a slave to the machine. Deep ecology alternatives complement Schummacher's first standard by favoring technologies and techniques that preserve and enhance the diversity of organic systems, enabling greater participation and integration. Wann (1996), Van der Ryn and Cowan (1996) provide many fine examples of this new ecological technology perspective.

What is needed, in order to help the sensate being wake up into his or her "live present" and the possibility and responsibility of wholeness are all of the experiences that most fully integrate the being into relationships with other beings. Abram (1996) says, "To *make sense* is to release the body from the constraints imposed by outworn ways of speaking, and hence to renew and rejuvenate one's felt awareness of the world. It is to make the senses wake up to where they are" (p. 265). Real progress in this direction requires a revolution of the spirit, not of "digitization" or any other allegedly more powerful and precise technique. Some ecologists (Berry, 1987; Bowers, 1993; Illich, 1969; Orr, 1994) have taken a long, hard look at how technical cultures and schools discourage "beingness" and have made some sound, life-affirming recommendations for change. The ecological legitimacy of their recommendations originates from their shared recognition that a shift from an ethic of power (remote control) to an ethic of care requires an individual's complete being in the world: mind, body, heart, and soul.

Ancient heroic tales of many different cultures are about whether one is going to live the life of the soul or to abdicate power and responsibility to the culture, the empire, the dogma, the bureaucracy, the system. The spiritual question for the potential hero (and in truth, for each of us) is, "Do you choose life and the song of the heart or your culture's conspiracy against it? Will you assume the humbling risks of being alive in the moment, or will you break off engagement in order to settle for the comfort of dogma?"

REFERENCES

Abram, D. (1996). *The spell of the sensuous: Perception and language in a more than human world.* New York: Pantheon.
Becker, E. (1973). *The denial of death.* New York: Free Press.
Berry, W. (1972). *A continuous harmony: Essays cultural & agricultural.* New York: Harcourt Brace Jovanovich.
Berry. W. (1987). *Home economics.* San Francisco: North Point.
Bowers, C. A. (1993). *Education, cultural myths, and the ecological crisis: Toward deep changes.* Albany, NY: State University of New York.
Cobb, E. (1959). *The ecology of imagination.* New York: Harcourt.
Delbanco, A. (1995). *The death of Satan: How Americans have lost the sense of evil.* New York: Farrar, Strauss, & Giroux.
Ellul, J. (1965). *The technological society.* New York: Knopf.
Ellul, J. (1972). The technological order. In C. Mitcham & R. Mackey (Eds.), *Philosophy and technology* (pp. 86-105). New York: Free Press.
Fromm, E. (1941). *Escape from freedom.* New York: Avon.
Glendinning, C. (1995). Technology, trauma, and the wild. In T. Rozsak, M. E. Gomes, & A. D. Kanner (Eds.), *Ecopsychology: Restoring the earth, healing the mind* (pp. 41-54). San Francisco: Sierra Books.
Griffin, S. (1990). Curves along the road. In I. Diamond & G. Orenstein (Eds.), *Reweaving the world: The emergence of ecofeminism* (pp. 87–99). San Francisco: Sierra Books.
Illich, I. (1969). *Deschooling society.* New York: Harper & Row.
Livingston, J. (1994). *Rogue primate: An exploration of human domestication.* Boulder CO: Roberts Rinehart.
MacLuhan, M. (1964). *Understanding media: The extensions of man.* New York: McGraw-Hill.

Mander, J. (1991). *In the absence of the sacred: The failure of technology and the survival of the Indian nations*. San Francisco: Sierra Books.
Mumford, L. (1972). Technics and the nature of man. In C. Mitcham & R. MacKey (Eds.), *Philosophy and technology* (pp. 77-85). New York: Free Press.
Orr, D. (1994). *Earth in mind: On education, environment, and the human prospect*. Washington, DC: Island Press.
Rifkin, J. (1991). *Biosphere politics: A new consciousness for a new century*. New York: Crown.
Schumacher, E. F. (1973). *Small is beautiful: Economics as if people mattered*. New York: Harper & Row.
Shepard, P. (1982). *Nature and madness*. San Francisco: Sierra Books.
Tiger, L. (1991). *The manufacture of evil*. New York: Marion Boyars.
Trilling, L. (1947). *The middle of the journey*. New York: Viking.
Van der Ryn, S., & Cowan, S. (1996). *Ecological design*. Washington, DC: Island Press.
Wann, D. (1996). *Deep design: Pathways to a livable future*. Washington, DC: Island Press.

36

Media Literacy

Daniel Kmitta
Miami University

David Barsamian once asked veteran media critic Noam Chomsky to assess the U.S. educational system as a potential source for providing students with the tools necessary for becoming media literate. Prefacing his response with a brief commentary on the history of state and corporate propaganda and its role in capitalist democracies such as the United States, Chomsky (1992) concludes that, "as to what the schools (presently) teach to defend people against this (propaganda), the answer is simple: zero. The schools," he contends, "are quite on the opposite side: they are part of the disinformation apparatus.... They are institutions for indoctrination, for imposing obedience, for blocking the possibility of independent thought, and they play an institutional role in a system of control and coercion" (pp. 61–62). In other words, the "institutional role" of the schools is nearly identical to the role that Chomsky is noted for attributing to the media. Given the similitary in their institutional roles, then, we should be cautious in our optimism for any government-mandated educational programs that would result in meaningful media literacy among students. "*Real* schools ought to provide people with techniques of self-defense," Chomsky argues, "but that would mean teaching the truth about the world and about the society, and schools couldn't survive very long if they did that" (1992, p. 62).

Supposing for a moment, however, that U.S. schools could successfully implement meaningful media literacy programs, an occasion that would require tremendous levels of sustained public activism, what sort of knowledge would a media literacy curriculum include? Though space prohibits an exhaustive account of the full spectrum of knowledges that such a curriculum could cover, I believe that minimum competency in media literacy requires, at least, some understanding of the political economy of the mass media. Toward this end, I believe that media literacy programs should assist students in coming to understand the following three basic traits of our current media system: the media have been monopolized under corporate control, the media function as major conduits of corporate propaganda, and corporate domination of the media precipitates the censorship of information and ideas considered hostile to corporate interests.

THE MEDIA MONOPOLY

Currently, most of the world's media, including television, radio, movies, books, magazines, newspapers, and ever more so the internet, are owned by just a few large multinational corporations. Ben Bagdikian notes in his book *The Media Monopoly* (1992) that over the past 2 decades "ownership of most of the major media has been consolidated in fewer and fewer corporate hands, from fifty national and multinational corporations at the time of the first edition, published in 1983, to twenty with this fourth edition" (pp. ix). Some would argue that Bagdikian is ignoring the fact that there are still thousands of small firms that are competing in today's global economy. We should bear in mind, however, that, whereas such small firms may have a "niche" in the market, their relative influence is still nominal.

Even with the passing of the Telecommunications Act of 1996, which allegedly was designed to open the doors for more competition within the industry, there has been unprecedented concentration of power through corporate mergers. In the past year, six corporate media giants merged (Time-Warner and Turner Broadcasting; Westinghouse and CBS; and Disney, Capitol Cities and ABC), creating less, not more competition.

One of the many dangers inherent within the corporate monopoly of the media is the creation of a *monoculture*. Since most of the large media giants are based in the United States, this means U.S. hegemony over the rest of the world. As with the subliminal messages revealed in the John Carpenter film *They Live*, the message emanating from the U.S. corporate monoculture is the myth that educational attainment improves one's economic choices and development, therefore, forget everything else, consume, and be happy.

Another operating assumption for the United States and its multinational corporations in defense of their monopoly is that the populations of developing countries are still relatively illiterate and that the United States can achieve domination over the world if the United States and the multinationals can control the content of information and literacy skills provided to the developing world (Chomsky, 1989). This allows for U.S. hegemony to go virtually unchecked among the people of the world.

When examining the flow of information, we find that it is unidirectional. That is, the world receives from the United States and the transnationals but from hardly anybody else. For example, the Associated Press, United Press International, American Federation of Papers, Reuters, and Tass combine to make up over 37 million words of newsprint each day for public consumption among the world's newspaper readers. By comparison, Inter-Press Service, Non-Aligned News, Pan African News, Caribbean, and Gulf News comprise only 300,000 words of newsprint for the worlds readers per day (Roach, 1993, p. 25).

Thus, the mechanism used by the mass media is not the free flow of information, which would allow true exchange and growth; rather, it is the use of monopolization of the media that leads to propaganda and censorship to control and exploit the vast market and resources of the world and her people.

PROPAGANDA

If one is to believe the media, there is an educational crisis of such dramatic proportions occurring in the United States that the ability of the United States to compete economically with the rest of the world is in serious peril. The media, of course, are only reporting the "facts." However, the evidence to support claims of an "education crisis" simply is not there—not there, at least, for most Americans. In a comprehensive review of the criticisms of the Sandia Report, Gerald Bracey (1997), provides substantive data demonstrating that the quality of education in the United States is second to none if you live in affluent suburban areas or can attend elite private schools. In addition, the crisis that is not mentioned, the miseducation of the our nation's poorest minority students, is one that may actually be serving the political agenda of the elite. There is an educational crisis in America, but it is not a general education crisis.

There are many who believe that the general education system is in crisis. Many of them are well educated themselves. Chomsky (1991) points out that

> one reason that propaganda often works better on the educated than on the uneducated is that educated people read more, so they receive more propaganda. Another is that they're the commissars. They have jobs as agents of propaganda, and they believe it. By and large, they're part of the privileged elite, and share their interests and perceptions (1988b, p. 708)

Of course we do often hear the refrain from the most educated segments of our society that education will improve the lives of the poorest. Former Secretary of Labor Robert Reich, himself a professor of economics at Harvard University, has espoused this belief during his tenure as the secretary of labor. According to Reich, the better educated will secure the better jobs. Ironically, Reich, an economist, knows that the United States government has artificially set the unemployment rate at above 5% so as to prevent inflation. This means that regardless of educational attainment, that at least 5% of the American workforce will have to be at one time unemployed in order for the elite in our country to enjoy high returns and less erosionary inflation on their stock market investments.

Obviously then, our education system is doing a fine job in keeping the economy running. If the education system was failing, the government would not have to set an artificial rate of unemployment. If we had a real education crisis whereby the educational institutions were unable to produce competent workers, then the unemployment rate would adjust, and only the unskilled and undereducated would be unemployed. As David C. Berliner (1996) notes the United States has already won the triple crown of productivity in the service, agricultural, and manufacturing industries and continues to do so. Instead of deprecating public schools, political and corporate elites should be throwing a party for the nation's educators.

CENSORSHIP

Censorship is becoming an increasingly difficult problem throughout the world. The publication "Index on Censorship: An International Magazine for Free Expression" (1993) monitors, documents, and then publishes international acts of censorship 10 times a year. It is clear in reading the index that censorship is as common in Albania, Britain, China, Greece, Malaysia, and Rwanda as it is in Russia and the United States. Scholars such as Chomsky (1989), Bagdikian (1992), and Parenti (1993) have all noted an increase in acts of censorship worldwide. Journalists such as Hugh Downs (1986), Bill Moyers (1990), and Molly Ivins (1993) have also noted extensive and pervasive censorship in the world today. In addition, media watchdog groups such as Project Censored, Fairness and Accuracy in Reporting (FAIR), Accuracy in Media (AIM), and the Center of Media and Public Affairs have also documented a global increase in the use of censorship.

According to Dr. Carl Jensen (1994), there are two kinds of censorship, prior restraint and information failure. *Prior restraint censorship* is the traditional definition of censorship; it is the censorship that allows for the rulers in society to prevent information from reaching the people. It is the classic "we know what is best for the masses and the people are better off without this information" argument. *Prior restraint censorship* is the kind of censorship that most totalitarian governments utilize, such as closing down presses or radio stations and preventing public speaking.

Information failure is a more insidious form of censorship in that it is assumed that the people are getting all the information when in fact the masses are only getting part of the story. Information failure is enhanced when the public sphere is flooded with trivial information such as advertising and public relation reports. It is the type of censorship most pervasive in allegedly free countries or that occurs where information is considered a commodity and thus can be privatized.

Contrary to public perception, the United States is playing a key role in censorship throughout the world. For example, Cook (1994) demonstrated that the United States raised the issue of censorship when the Sandinista government of Nicaragua closed down the opposition newspapers during the height of the Contra war. The United States expressed "moral outrage" at the closing of the opposition press throughout the 1980s. Yet the United States has actually supported the newly elected president of the Nicaragua's UNO party, Violeta Chammarro's, closing of the Sandinista newspaper Barricada and Radio Sandino four times in the last 3 years. Where was the U. S. outrage when the newly elected UNO coalition government closed down the Sandinista newspapers and radio stations immediately after the 1990 elections and again during the labor strife of 1991?

Another assumption that is operative is that information is a commodity, and the country or company that owns the information has every right to suppress that information. Davis (1993) argues that "competition breeds secrecy, and information not shared is information robbed of its potential (because of its synergistic "generative" effect of combing bits of information)" (p. 19). In other words, the competitive nature of the capitalist system that originated in the United States is best served if the information generated by the ruling power is kept secret. Yet the long term effects become detrimental to the developing countries and eventually to the United States and multinationals themselves. For it is an axiom that information sharing can unleash the creative spirits of the world's people, and who knows where the cure for AIDS or cancer will come if such information is censored.

Lyford (1994) demonstrates that the North American Free Trade Agreement (NAFTA) and the Global Agreement on Trades and Tariffs (GATT) are also two more negative by-products of global censorship. The U.S. citizenry was lead to believe through propaganda and censorship that the majority of the world citizens favored these agreements. The same is true for the citizens of other parts of the world, who were lead to believe that the majority of U.S. citizens favored both treaties.

TURNING THE TIDE

> The professed concern for freedom of the press in the West is not very persuasive in the light of ... the actual performance of the media in serving the powerful and privileged as an agency of manipulation, indoctrination, and control. A "democratic communications policy," in contrast, would seek to develop means of expression and interaction that reflect the interests and concerns of the general population, and to encourage their self-education and their individual and collective action. (Chomsky & Herman, 1988a)

I am not a media critic. I have had no formal training in media literacy or criticism. Perhaps like most of the audience for this book, all that I have learned about the media stems from involvement in grassroots activism. Whether environmental, feminist, labor, antiwar, antiracist, antihomophobia, or antiimperialist, organizations just getting involved forced me to question the information I was receiving from the popular press. It has been in the action of opposing injustice, those open festering sores manifested in the consolidation of monopolistic power, that I have become aware of how the media works.

Media literacy has to be critical and activist oriented—much along the lines of Paulo Freire's (1970) critical pedagogy. The self-education eluded to in Chomsky's comment cited previously is only possible if the flow of information is free and available to all. And with that information, people can act individually and collectively to pursue the life they prize.

There are valuable resources available to help on the journey. One resource that I prize is Jenson's *Project Censored Yearbook*, published by Four Walls Eight Windows (Jenson, 1993, 1994). The yearbook updates the lists of dozens of organizations committed to providing information and media literacy services throughout the world. In addition, the yearbook has an updated list of media outlets and key personnel to contact when one spots propaganda or censorship.

Another action that can be taken is to have activists file antitrust lawsuits against the major multinationals for violating antitrust law. This suggestion is a cornerstone for the folks at the Center for Media Education [(202) 628-2620]. Taking legal action—using the tools of the ruling elite—to dismantle the elite institutions is one option that certainly needs to be pursued.

Finally, let's quit being entertained and informed by the ruling class and get on with creating our own media. This is the theme sounded by the group Alliance for Community Media [(202) 393–2650].

REFERENCES

Bagdikian, B. H. (1992). *The media monopoly* (4th ed.). Boston, MA: Beacon Press.

Berliner, D. C. (1996, November). Uninvited comments from an uninvited guest. *Educational Researcher,* 25(8), 47–50.

Bracey, G. W. (1997, April). On comparing the incomparable: A response to Baker and Stedman. *Educational Research, 26*(3), 19–26.

Carpenter, J., (Director), & Blay, A., & Gordon, S. (Producer). (1988). *They live* [Film]. (Available from The Entertainment Connection, 100 Red Schoolhouse Road, Suite C5, Chestnut Ridge, NY 10977-7049)

Chomsky, N. (1988b) *Language and Politics*. New York: Black Rose Books.

Chomsky, N. (1989). *Necessary illusions*. Boston, MA: South End Press.

Chomsky, N. (1994, May). Foreign policy: Democracy enhancement 1. *Z Magazine*, 7(5), 21–33.

Chomsky, N. (1992). *Chronicles of dissent/Noam Chomsky; Interviews with David Barsamian*. Monroe, ME: Common Courage Press.

Chomsky , N., & Herman, E. S. (1988a). *Manufacturing consent: The political economy of the mass media.* New York: Pantheon.

Cook, M.. (1994, January–February). The La Penca bombing: Case closed or a rush to judgment. *EXTRA Magazine*, *7*(1), 24–26.

Cook, K., & Lehrer, D. (1994, January–February). Who will own the information highway? Reprinted in *UTNE Reader,* from (July 12, 1993) *The Nation*.

Davis, J. (1993). The incompatibility of capitalism and information. *Intertek information: Special issue on economic, social and technical aspects of information,* 3(4), 18–22.

Donmoyer, R. (1996, November). This issue: Talking "truth" to power. *Educational Researcher,* 25(8), 2, 9.

Downs, H. (1986). *On camera: My 10,000 hours on television*. New York: Putnam.

Forbes MediaCritic (1994, Winter). News plus: Recent stories of extra value. *Forbes Media Critic,*. 1(2), 6.

Freire, P. (1970). The pedagogy of the oppressed. New York: Continuum.

Index on Censorship (1993, September/October). Index index. *Index on Censorship*, *22* (8, 9), 33–41.

Ivins, M. (1993). *Nothin' but good times ahead*. New York: Random House.

Jenson, C. (1993). *Censored: The news that didn't make the news—and why. The 1993 Project Censored Yearbook*. New York: Four Walls and Eight Windows.

Jenson, C. (1994). *Censored: The news that didn't make the news—and why. The 1994 Project Censored Yearbook*. New York: Four Walls and Eight Windows.

Lyford, J., Jr. (1994, Spring). Trade Uber Alles: The propaganda & politics of NAFTA and GATT. *Propaganda Review, 11*, 22–27, 68–69.

Moyers, B. D. (1990). *Global dumping ground: The international traffic in hazardous waste*. Washington, DC: Seven Locks Press.

Parenti, M. (1993). *Inventing reality: The politics of news media*. New York: St. Martin's Press.

Roach, C. (1993). The movement for a new world information order. *Intertek information: Special issue on economic, social and technical aspects of information,* 3(4), 24–30.

37

Vocational Education

Joe L. Kincheloe
CUNY–Brooklyn College
The Pennsylvania State University

Too often the study of vocational education has focused on the practice and technique of teaching while ignoring the larger purposes of vocational programs. At the same time the field neglects this consideration of purpose, it also omits the examination of the social, political, and economic context in which vocational education takes place. The nature of the work, the workings of the economy, the social impact of technology, and the ethics of business are not central concerns of the vocational field. This social, political, and economic context is especially important at the end of the 20th century, a time when many Americans have concluded that the present organization of our economic life threatens the continued existence of our democratic way of life (Bellah, Madsen, Sullivan, Swindler, & Tipton, 1991; DeVore, 1983). I begin with the assumption that present economic organization is unhealthy on many fronts. Indeed, corporations have gained inordinate power in the process creating an atmosphere of unfairness that especially affects students who choose vocational career paths. Because of this reality, vocational teachers and students more than anyone else must gain the ability to expose such injustice. To protect their own self-interest, they must understand the way power works to undermine our way of life, our values, and our sense of right and wrong.

The vocational education I envision produces students who are aware of these threats to democracy, who understand the culture of work, and who can articulate a vision of what work should be. For example, workers with a vision do not passively accept hazardous workplaces that produce toxic products which not only affect the health of the employees who produce them but harm the environment as well. Vocational educators and workers who share such a vision can no longer confine their activities to schools alone; they must take part in a larger project that involves the workplace, government, and reform-oriented organizations. Vocational teachers and students have to realize that although vocational programs may help develop particular work skills of their students, such education cannot alter the reality of job scarcity—downsizing (Jonathan, 1990). The availability of jobs depends on both economic circumstance and political choice, and political choice can be affected by the political participation of vocational educators who are motivated by a vision of economic justice.

The American debate over the politics of work over the past 15 years has been reduced to a simplistic exercise in victim bashing. The reason individuals are un- or underemployed has little to do with economic conditions, the argument goes—it is a manifestation of their failure as individuals. Why develop vocational education programs or innovative antipoverty programs, many political leaders ask, when the cause of un- or underemployment involves the individual's moral inferiority or is the result of unsuccessful parenting. Family values are promoted as the "only way out" of the poor neighborhood or the degrading job. The problem with such arguments is that in many cases, family values have little effect on economic success, especially when one *lives* in an economic circumstance (an inner-city neighborhood) in which job opportunities are rare and informal networks through which openings are discovered are nonexistent (Coontz, 1992). If you live around people who are unemployed, typically you are the last to know when job opportunities are available. This is a bitter irony for those who seek a better life and economic mobility.

Pointing the finger of blame has become an art in the last couple of decades. Not only are the victims of economic injustice deemed culpable, but the schools have been found guilty of undermining our economy. In 1983, Ronald Reagan's National Commission on Excellence in Education (NCEE) set the parameters of the national conversation on schooling (Copa & Tebbenhoff, 1990). The commission convinced millions of Americans that schools were largely responsible for America's economic decline. The schools deserve much criticism, of course, but such an explanation was calculated and misleading. The economic problems America has suffered are very complex, and blame must be shared by a variety of institutions.

When corporate profits stagnated in Western economies in the early 1970s, corporations scrambled to cut costs. Managers realized that the quickest way to accomplish such a task involved lowering wages and taxes.

Not only were workers pitted against each other in the struggle for jobs, but local, state, and even national governments were forced into competition in the attempt to attract business and industry. The city of Greenville, South Carolina, for example, competed with Huntsville, Alabama, over which city would offer companies the lowest tax rates and the best infrastructures (roads, sewers, lax environmental regulations) in the race to attract companies and create jobs. The big winner in such competition, of course, was industrial management, because operating costs were cut, unions were undermined, labor was tamed, and executive salaries were raised. "What a great deal," corporate leaders exclaimed. As executive salaries increased, the trade deficit and the budget deficit grew, and managers focused more and more on short-term profits than on long-term stability (Pollin & Cockburn, 1991).

The shrinkage of America's manufacturing base that began in the early 1970s has continued into the 1990s; contrary to the pronouncements of the NCEE, this waning of manufacturing is not the fault of education in general or vocational education in particular (Chesnaux, 1992). One of the most important factors in the decline of American industry and economic institutions in general involved the reluctance of business and industrial leaders to reorganize the workplace in a way that eliminates low-skill positions and takes advantage of worker creativity and understanding of the specifics of the work process. This theme of workplace reorganization and worker empowerment, of course, is central to the study of vocational education at the end of the twentieth century. Make no mistake about it, vocational education should assume that the workers it produces should have significant input into the workplace decisions that are of concern to them.

Contemporary social and economic conditions demand a vision—a vision that will bring meaning to the lives of Americans dispossessed by the chaos that marks the end of the millennium. The two dominant economic visions of the 20th century are not working as proponents have hoped. Marxist–Leninist socialism has been a tragic failure; but (and this makes Americans very uncomfortable) multinational corporate capitalism has also manifested some fundamental flaws. In significantly different ways, the power elites that direct these systems escape the control of citizens. Indeed, their poisonous effect on the natural world and the social world undermine their viability as economic and social systems for the new millennium (Wirth, 1983). There has to be a humane third way to deal with these issues.

Vocational education and the everyday world of work do not contribute to the development of a coherent picture of the world. Indeed, such experiences tend to fragment our understandings of who we are and how our work fits into the larger society. We are isolated, shielded from many pieces of the social jigsaw puzzle, separated from a cognizance of the purpose of an operation. As a result, we become apathetic and withdrawn, released from responsibility for what ultimately happens in schools, workplaces, and other organizations to which we belong. A humane vision of a democratic society demands that vocation education confront this fragmentation of reality and its debilitation of the human spirit. A democratic vocational education struggles to empower future workers by helping them to see themselves as living systems within larger living systems. In other words, such an education induces students to ask, How does my work fit into the larger economy, the ecosystem, the historical tradition of professionals or crafts people in this field? Students and workers come to appreciate the fact that they are not Clint Eastwoodlike "high plains drifters," unconnected to anybody else, living and working in isolation. Workers are profoundly dependent on one another for the food we eat, the clothes we wear, and the homes we inhabit (Bellah et al., 1991; Ferguson, 1984; Wirth, 1983).

As we develop ways of acting on our democratic vision of worker empowerment, vocational educators must delineate what active popular participation means in the everyday life of economic and educational institutions. As we redefine our notion of individualism with its blindness to the ways the social context affects individual consciousness and performance, we must place the individual and his or her well-being at the beginning and the ending of any social and educational reform (Bluestone & Harrison, 1982). The enhancement of an individual's ability to participate in social and environmental movements is a centerpiece to our philosophy of vocational education.

The difference between the democratic vision of empowered, self-directed vocational students and workers presented here and the many other "visions" discussed daily involves one key concept: Our vision demands that we identify the social forces that impede its realization. No one in this society rejects outright the call for democratic institutions or smart empowered workers. Every expert guest on *Geraldo* or *Sally Jesse* proclaims that men and women should be self-directed, be their "own person." So what's the argument, you may ask, don't we all agree? Sure, we agree that democratic self-direction is a good thing until we get down to specifics. As we begin to identify the way power elites undermine self-direction, the way business managers with their scientific modes of administering subvert the empowerment of their workers, we start to see what happens when the rubber meets the road. The key to uncovering the difference between our vision of self-direction and the pop-psychologist on *Live With Regis and Kathy Lee* Show is that we name names, we identify the race, class, and gender oppression that undermines democracy. We finger from the witness stand the scientific conventions and the cult of experts that use their authority to prove the "deficiencies" of students and workers. We expose the mental models created by our interactions with school, media, and everyday life that insulate us from the consternation that learning entails.

To overcome the threats to empowerment, students and workers must act on their understanding of the forces that undermine their self-direction, their ability to participate in democratic communities. A democratic vocational education, unlike many technical programs of the present, helps students make sense of the way the world works, the economy operates, and the role of the everyday worker in these processes. Vocational educators with a democratic vision endeavor to graduate students as meaning-making young people who can get behind the surface, understand the social construction of their identities, and detect the fingerprints of power at various "crime scenes." As vocational detectives, these students display a socially grounded consciousness that allows them to reinterpret old evidence, reopening the cases in to order to expose the way the world actually works.

Why, for example, are workers treated with such disrespect at the local meat processing plant? The managers of the plant are not bad people; indeed, on a one-to-one basis they're quite friendly and compassionate. As empowered, analytical workers examine the crime scene (the social dynamics of the workplace) they uncover some startling evidence. The procedures for management used by the supervisors and the top managers are derived from the tradition of scientific management. Such procedures assume that workers are incapable of running a plant themselves and that they must be controlled and supervised at all times to guarantee productivity. Their job descriptions must be narrowly and precisely delineated so that they will know what to do at any particular moment. The company managers act as the science of their field dictates they act. They do not understand that the very principles on which their managerial training was based creates an inhumane and degrading work life for their employees. As vocational students and workers begin to understand these realities, they refuse to accept degrading work as simply a necessary evil in our daily lives. They reject political officials' explanation that poverty is permanent part of the human condition. Such visionary workers do not accept the notion that the violence and social pathology that accompany poverty is an inevitable reality (Coontz, 1992; Senge, 1990).

As demystifiers of the language of management and the public conversation about work, visionary students and workers challenge the legitimacy of the condescending cult of the expert (Kinchloe, 1995). Such a challenge confronts the very meaning of work in contemporary America. The democratic vision renders work less a technical and utilitarian act and more a calling. Interesting work that contributes to the good of others becomes its own reward. Our democratic vision moves students and workers to rethink the dogma that ensuring private profit is the only criterion for an industrial policy (Bellah et al., 1991). Instead, a reconceptualized industrial policy insists that a rising standard of living for working people becomes a primary goal. Such a policy would require that there be an adequate supply of useful goods and services whether or not they can be produced for profit. The model for democratic work becomes an ethos of art and craftsmanship that engages the spirit of the worker. Working men and women are regarded as sacred individuals whose thoughts, feelings, and insights are valuable resources to be protected at all costs (Wirth, 1983). In such a context, a democratic society demands that work become more hospitable, more engaging, less authoritarian, and safer. Our dedication to our sacred workers allows nothing less.

"WE DON'T GET NO RESPECT"—WORKERS AND VOCATIONAL EDUCATION

Workers, vocational education, and vocational students are the Rodney Dangerfields of the late 20th century. Often treated on TV as emotional dummies, workers understand all too well where they stand in the pecking order. We have no choice; our democratic principles demand that we respect workers. Such respect is especially important in the nation's attempt to increase economic productivity. Because American society fails to value the knowledge of job preparation, vocational students are often viewed as failures. Success in the academic curriculum has become a symbol not only of prestigious work but of virtue itself. Being academically schooled has become confused with the concept of being well-educated. It really doesn't matter what you know or what you can do; as long as you have the academic diplomas and high standardized test scores, you are deemed intelligent. The dirtying of one's hands is not an activity in which the "educated" man or woman engages. For employees who are not in management, thinking is an unnecessary activity (Copa & Tebbenhoff, 1990; Goodlad, 1992; Kolberg & Smith, 1992; Rehm, 1989).

To gain insight into the effects of this lack of respect for workers and vocational education, consider the fact that this nation financially subsidizes students who attend college seven times more than it does those who plan to enter the workforce as full-time workers (Hudelson, 1992). It's no wonder that such vocational students are often referred to as "the forgotten majority." In a democratic society with fundamental values demanding respect for workers and their work education, such disrespect and unfair funding could not take place. The renewal of this democratic respect is a necessity. But until certain attitudes change, such renewal will remain a dream. One of the most important themes I'm developing here involves the notion that it is the role of vocational educators to help in the larger effort to renew such democratic values. Here at the end of the twentieth century, many American leaders have come to believe that the restoration of our moral and economic strength depend on it (Wirth, 1983).

Powerful agencies such as the media and corporate management have portrayed workers as incompetent. If workers can be portrayed as lazy and inadequate, then managers can justify the disparity between their own salaries and workers' wages. Such a shallow portrayal allows managers greater freedom to design jobs that allow workers little input into how the workplace is administered or how particular tasks should be performed (Ferguson, 1984). It also releases corporate leaders from any responsibility for American economic decline—don't you understand, they tell the American people, workers today have little commitment to their jobs (Zunker, 1986). Can you believe their poor work habits? Many analysts make the argument that workers are treated like children in industrial and clerical factories. Despite all the rhetoric of workplace reforms that "empower" workers, still in the late-1990s only a small percentage of workplaces have joined such a movement. Working is still very similar to high school, workers reports. The principal turns into your general foreman and teachers mutate into your superintendents; constant surveillance based on distrust joins the workplace and schooling in an antidemocratic alliance. Such unproductive arrangements are perpetuated by "the great deception"—the argument that American workers are unable to take responsibility for the direction of their own lives. These excluded workers find it difficult to engage in their work with their hearts and their brains. How can you commit yourself when jobs require only minimal thinking? Workers execute plans they don't develop and that mean little to them. Rarely do workers know how their everyday tasks fit into the larger goals of the business or into the larger economy. When they do understand these concepts, they typically figure things out on their own—without the help of their superiors. Too often workers in America are seen as economic instruments, men and women estranged from not only their fellow workers but from meaning itself. The educational philosopher John Dewey argued years ago that workers often become no more than "industrial fodder" in a society controlled by money interests. Denied access to information and accumulated wisdom, workers are disempowered and removed from the realm of decision making. Such a reality holds dramatic implications for the health of a democratic society (Brosio, 1994).

When society views workers as clerical and industrial fodder, it loses respect for workers' bodies. America has allowed its workers to breathe asbestos, to endanger their eyes and ears, to develop cancers from exposure to carcinogens, and so on. The job insecurity that workers increasingly experience with its dramatic psychological and physiological effects is viewed by neoclassical economists as a positive trend. Too much security undermines work effort and productivity, they argue. In this way, worker security subverts the capital accumulation process, the conservatives conclude. How has such "logic" become the "common sense" of American economics? (Bluestone & Harrison, 1982; Copa & Tebbenhoff, 1990).

VOCATION, IDENTITY, AND A SENSE OF ETHICS

In studies of work and vocational education, the meaning of the word *vocation* is rarely addressed. In its best sense, vocation is a "calling" involving meaningful activity (Rehm, 1989, p. 119). As the American economy developed, fewer and fewer jobs carried with them this notion of vocation. For example, the sense of vocation understood by workers in the retail trades was undermined decades ago by the advent of corporations like McDonald's and their standardized selling strategies. In such a social and economic context, we have lost our ability to distinguish labor from work. The distinction, as obvious as the difference between Arrested Development and an Osmond Family concert, involves simply making a living (labor) and engaging the self in the production of products that enrich life (Wirth, 1983). Dewey expanded this definition of work, arguing that work in the vocational sense connects an individual's ability with the benefits of social service. Indeed, work in the Deweyan sense provides meaning to one's life as it transforms the world and human interaction (Litz & Bloomquist, 1980).

Vocation in a truly democratic society should never become a blind technical process—indeed it should be a form of self-creation. Once vocational education understands that work helps shape who we are, the field will have to change. Vocational educators will appreciate the fact that they're preparing not just workers but democratic citizens as well. Identity formation is constantly taking place in schools and workplaces. For example, when vocational students are placed as office workers and sheltered from discussions about an ethical and democratic workplace, their identities and self-perceptions are negatively affected (Rehm, 1989; Simon, Dippo, & Schenke, 1991; Valli, 1988).

The hidden message of such a vocational educational activity is that office workers are low-status laborers. Clerical workers are unconsciously taught to tell their bosses, in the words of Wayne and Garth, "We're not worthy!" As vocational teachers locate work with a moral context, such students and workers must be taught that they are indeed worthy. They must come to expect that in a progressive democratic society, all jobs, office work included, should encourage creative input and the exercise of judgement. When individuals argue that low-skill jobs constitute the reality young workers face, progressive vocational educators tell them that workers may face such a reality, but they don't have to accept it as inevitable. Workers can be empowered to imagine democratic forms of work and join in the struggle to make such visions a reality. Students in progressive vocational education programs learn that the way they see themselves as workers often reflects the way power elites want them to see their roles. When vocational education fails to challenge such domination, it plays into the hand of the dominant culture. It plays the social role of simply adapting vocational students to jobs that are unfair and undesirable (Kinchloe, 1998; Richmond, 1986).

WORK AND DEMOCRACY: PRODUCING MEANING IN AUTHORITARIAN WORKPLACES

Progressive vocational educators take democracy seriously. This means that they expect democratic values will shape the purposes and everyday activities of our social institutions. No democratic society can maintain its liberty if major discontinuities separate its professed values from its schools and workplaces (Wirth, 1983). But in America 2000, the blueprint for the future of American schooling released during the Bush administration, with great input from then Governor Clinton, and America 2000's successors, the guiding concept of democracy is dismissed. Indeed, social criticism or concern with the reality of democracy at the end of the twentieth century is viewed as impractical analysis, as a type of thinking that is too dangerous to pursue (Kinchloe, 1995). Such a perspective illustrates the crisis in contemporary American democracy. The crisis is also revealed by the pervading belief that democracy has little to do with the economic sphere of life (Brosio, 1994). Educators and economic analysts who speak of the inseparability of democratic precepts and the arrangements of workplaces are often met with silent stares from a public socialized to see no relationship between the two.

An important part of my vision for vocational education is grounded in the belief that the collision between democracy and the workplace should produce something called "economic democracy." This economic democracy would mandate that everyone who works gets a stake in the enterprise in which they work, while at the same time cushioning the harshness of the unrestricted labor market (Bellah et al., 1991). When workers gain a stake in their workplaces, they become participants in decision making. When workers become decision makers, private corporations become responsive to the needs of the public and more protective of the creative energies of their workers. In such an environment, workers no longer look at themselves as fellow cellmates on death row and their supervisors as wardens.

Supporters of democracy, in general, and economic democracy, in particular, know that democracy is incompatible with meaningless, deskilled jobs. John Dewey argued that one of the most important functions of school involved providing students information concerning the relationship between work and society and the role of industry in democratic society. In this context, I argue that one of the most important goals of vocational education is to address the political, social, and economic realities that shape work. Vocational education students must understand the underlying assumptions and values that shape their vocational education. In the spirit of John Dewey and other advocates of democracy, they must be able to discern between a truly democratic education and one that merely claims to be democratic (Lakes, 1985; Rehm, 1989).

REFERENCES

Bellah, R., Madsen, R., Sullivan, U. M., Swidlet, A. & Tipton, S. M. (1991). *The good society*. New York: Vintage Books.

Bluestone, B., & Harrison, B. (1982). *The deindustrialization of America: Plant closings, community abandonment, and the dismantling of basic industry*. New York: Basic Books.

Brosio, R. (1994). *A radical democratic critique of capitalist education*. New York: Peter Lang.

Chesneaux, J. (1992). *Brave modern world: The prospects for survival*. New York: Thames & Hudson.

Coontz, S. (1992). *The way we never were: American families and the nostalgia trap*. New York: Basic Books.

Copa, G., & Tebbenhoff, E. (1990). *Subject matter of vocational education: In pursuit of foundations*. Berkeley, CA: NCRVE.

DeVore, P. (1983). Research and industrial education searching for direction. Paper presented at the American Vocational Association Convention, Anaheim, CA.

Ferguson, K. (1984). *The feminist case against bureaucracy*. Philadelphia: Temple University Press.

Giroux, H. (1992). *Border crossings: Cultural workers and the politics of education*. New York: Routledge, Chapman & Hall.

Giroux, H. (1993). *Living dangerously: Multiculturalism and the politics of difference*. New York: Peter Lang.

Goodlad, J. (1992, February 19). Beyond half an education. *Education Week, 11*,(22), 34, 44.

Hudelson, D. (1992). Roots of reform: Tracing the path of "workforce education." *Vocational Education Journal*, 67,(7), 28–29, 69.

Jonathan, R. (1990, March–April). The curriculum and the new vocationalism. *Journal of Curriculum Studies, 22*,(2), 184–188.

Kinchloe, J. (1995). *Toil and trouble: Good work, smart workers, and the integration of academic and vocational education*. New York: Peter Lang.

Kinchloe, J. (1998). *How do we tell the workers? The socioeconomic foundations of work and vocational education*. Boulder, CO: Westview Press.

Kolberg, W., & Smith, F. (1992). *Rebuilding America's workforce: Business strategies to close the competitive gap*. Homewood, IL: Business One Irwin.

Lakes, R. (1985, Fall). John Dewey's theory of occupations: Vocational education envisioned. *Journal of Vocational and Technical Education*, 2,(1), 41–47.

Litz, C., & Bloomquist, B. (1980, April). Adult education: Resolution of the liberal–vocational debate. *Lifelong Learning in the Adult Years*, 12–15.

Pollin, R., & Cockburn, (1991, February). The world, the free market, and the left. *The Nation, 252*(7), 224–236.

Rehm, M. (1989). Emancipatory vocational education: Pedagogy for the work of individuals and society. *Journal of Education, 171*,(3), 109–123.

Richmond, S. (1986, December). The white paper, education, and the crafts: An assessment of values. *The Journal of Educational Thought, 20*,(3), 143–155.

Senge, P. (1990). *The fifth discipline: The art and practice of the learning organization*. New York: Doubleday.

Simon, R., Dippo, D., & Schenke, A. (1991). *Learning work: A critical pedagogy of work education*. Westport, CT: Bergin & Garvey.

Valli, L. (1988). Gender identity and the technology of office education. In L. Weis (Ed.), *Class, race, and gender in American education*. Albany, NY: State University of New York Press.

Wirth, A. (1983). *Productive work—in industry and schools: Becoming persons again*. Lanham, MD: University Press of America.

Zunker, V. (1986). *Career counseling: Applied concepts of life planning*. Monterey, CA: Brooks/Cole Publishing.

38

Adult and Continuing Education

Vivian Wilson Mott
East Carolina University

> Adult education's first concern will always be helping individual adults to learn, to grow, to increase their capacities, to attain a richer and fuller life in their own terms. What adults want to learn and are constrained to learn, however, is generated by the social milieu in which they live. (Hallenbeck, 1964)

Adult and continuing education is frequently viewed as a voluntary and hopeful activity, one in which autonomous adults are free to choose to participate for the purpose of achieving some personal sense of fulfillment, for bringing about improvement in their lives, or even for sake of leisure or recreation. Another lingering myth, derived from the legacy of our field, suggests that ours is a discipline committed to social service, if not transformation. We do have a long history, and there were—and are—educational efforts with profound and lasting effects, played out in response to significant social movements. Even before to the common usage of the term *adult education* and the official establishment of the discipline through the founding of the American Association of Adult Education in 1926, there were organized efforts focused on the education and training of adults: religious and civic education for new Americans in the 1600s; apprenticeship training for (primarily) young men in preparation for the industrial age; English language and citizenship training for immigrants in the early 1900s (Stubblefield & Keane, 1994). And the adult educators of those earlier periods genuinely "and apparently without question" perceived those offerings as an effective and advantageous means of acculturation and assimilation, progress and development in a developing nation. Now at the close of this

20th century, adult and continuing education efforts still echo those utilitarian and presumably beneficial goals in response to expressed and prescribed societal need. And today, as in our past, educators rarely question whose needs and interests are really being served.

Further, when we examine who participates in adult and continuing education activities and why, we then begin to understand that although large numbers of adults do engage regularly in adult and continuing education, that participation reflects a strong White, middle-class bias, markedly skewed toward those who are already better educated than most. Today's typical participant in adult and continuing education programs is likely to be White, between the ages of 28 and 40, with above average income, working full time at a white-collar job; currently there are only slightly more women participating than men. And where job training is concerned, those younger, male, married, and with higher levels of education are given the most frequent and substantial opportunities, whereas women and minorities, those in low-wage jobs or nearing retirement, are less likely to be trained at all and then only in areas that directly profit the organization (Mincer, 1989). Thus, in business and industrial settings, as in higher education, education and training opportunities are frequently made available to some at the expense of others, coerced for others if not mandated, and always orchestrated around economic and highly political agendas.

Educators readily agree that education at any level is a value-laden and highly political endeavor, carried out in a specific social milieu, a reflection of the economic values of the dominant cultural and political structure (see Cunningham, 1988, 1992; Foucault, 1972; Freire, 1985; Parsons, 1959; Welton, 1995). Cunningham 1988, in particular, argued that adult education is elitist in nature and an "apparatus for social control" (p. 133), which serves to preserve the status quo, maintaining society and its inequities as they are, rather than offering solutions for change. She also charged that claiming neutrality or an apolitical stance is

> one of the most political statements [an educator] can make. Because what one says when one declares neutrality (or objectivity) is that one is quite satisfied with the present organization of social relationships and the distribution of resources in the society. Those who "have" in society rarely see the need for change as clearly as those who "have not." (p. 136)

Two dichotomous sociological models—conflict paradigm and consensus paradigm—offer opposing interpretations of inequitable educational access in terms of societal structure. Although both the conflict and consensus paradigms acknowledge the inherent inequalities in society, the conflict paradigm views education as a vehicle of domination and one primary means by which existing power structures are reinforced and reproduced. Consensus paradigm, on the other hand, also sees education as an agent but that of appropriate and necessary selection, with any resulting inequality a reflection of the value systems in place (Collins, 1985; Lenski, 1966; Parsons, 1959). That these inequities seem right and normal to those who support the consensus paradigm, wrote Merriam and Caffarella (1991), "is a strategy of the ruling elite to maintain control" (p. 274) over those with less power and privilege.

The "why" of educational participation—that is, the purposes and functions of adult education—has also been of long-standing concern. The classification of the purposes, functions, and goals of adult education is also an expression of the political and economic agendas served by these functions. In 1936, for instance, Lyman Bryson cautioned us to recall that the "rapidly changing character of the [adult education] movement" (p. 29) was a reflection of "newly arising social needs." Bryson maintained that these emerging social needs were served through either remedial, occupational, relational, political, or liberal adult education. Half a century later, Jarvis (1985) broadened the typology by identifying six sets of functions, two of which he identified as maintenance of social structures and the reproduction of a cultural system. Although the transmission of knowledge is presumed to be neutral and innocuous, it is, in fact, those of the dominant culture who determine the kinds of knowledge transmitted and, therefore, which cultural values are protected and reinforced. Where academic preparation, continuing professional education, and training in business and industry are concerned, stratification of educational opportunity according to career or job classification—also a function of one's prescribed social role—is likewise evident. That is, those who are already privileged or better educated and paid participate in education that continues to promote social and economic mobility, whereas those in low-wage jobs commonly receive only mandatory types of training that does nothing to foster their own professional development but only serves to protect the competitive (economic) interests of the organization. Hence, Jarvis maintained that these forms of adult and continuing education do "no more than reproduce the existing social relations of production and the social structures remain unaltered" (p. 136).

Jarvis (1985) also mentioned leisure pursuits, individual advancement, legitimation, and personal liberation. He was quick to assert, however, that even in these functions, adult education "transmits the dominant culture and in the process reproduces the cultural system" (p. 139) rather than acting in the service of social change. The Elderhostel programs for seniors provide an excellent illustration. Elderhostel is a national program of leisure studies, generally offered through colleges and universities, with a broad curriculum, low tuition that typically includes lodging and meals as well as all instructional materials, and even scholarship assistance. Nonetheless, greater than 90% of the participants are White, middle to upper class, and well educated (Elderhostel Institute Network, 1996). Thus, the programs attract only those who already possess cultural capital (enhanced through previous education and economic sufficiency) as described by Bordieu (1977) and Freire (1985), thereby giving only the illusion of liberation.

Beder (1990) intended to simplify a classification scheme when he "collapsed [the various purposes] into four major categories: (1) to facilitate change in a dynamic society, (2) to support and maintain the good social order, (3) to promote productivity, and (4) to enhance personal growth" (p. 39). Others have altered the functional labels somewhat, depending on their philosophical and pragmatic orientations to education, to include assimilation, compensatory, cultivation of the intellect or personal growth, social improvement or the facilitation of societal change, among others. As Merriam and Caffarella (1991) suggested, "Common to most of the lists [of functions] is the ideal of a democratic society in which the individual can personally benefit through education and where access and opportunity are available to all" (p. 273). However, deconstruction of these stated functions and the "ideal" posits another, less optimistic and fulfilling scenario.

The question remains how adult and continuing education might serve a different agenda, one that supports people in their efforts to be self-determined and not tied to political and economic agendas which individuals are the victims of, rather than benefactors. Cunningham (1988) argued that it is the ethical responsibility of adult and continuing educators to consider the darker side of our practice and to "provide environments that allow people to examine critically" (p. 135) the hegemonic interests served by education. Cunningham (1992) maintained that ours is a discipline focused on "learning for earning," charging that the "engine that drives the adult education train is efficient and effective production" (p. 180). She suggested, however, that a return to our legacy of adult and continuing education as an instrument of social transformation is on the horizon. Cunningham urged a balancing of the now predominant technical orientation of preparation for new adult educators with more emphasis on action science wherein those affected by the subject of inquiry be among those engaged in its mediation; she also recommended a contextual, participatory, and empowering approach to program planning, such as outlined by Cervero and Wilson (1994), in place of the deficit model commonly in vogue.

With the urging of Cunningham and others like her, there are islands of promise—commitments toward a more egalitarian, holistic, and intersubjective educational interaction—scattered throughout the discipline, among its practitioners and professors, and in its literature. One such effort, founded by Myles Horton (1990), is the Highlander Research and Educational Center, situated unpretentiously on a farm in the hills of East Tennessee. There, until his death in 1990, Horton and those who shared his commitment worked toward empowerment and self-determination of those oppressed by dominant hegemonic structures and the pursuit of remedies to the southern labor struggles of the 1930s, the discrimination of the 1950s and 1960s, and environmental devastation of much of Appalachia by absentee industrial land owners of the 1980s and beyond.

In the adult and continuing education literature, five recent publications stand out as examples that hold promise for a reconstructed and more holistic model of human interaction through education. The first is bell hooks' (1994) *Teaching to Transgress,* a cogent, intellectual argument for education as engaged pedagogy or "praxis—action and reflection upon the world in order to change it" (p. 14). Drawing on her own experiences as a schoolgirl in the apartheid South and the works of critical theorists and activists such as Giroux, Freire, Booker T. Washington, and Martin Luther King, hooks maintained that "white supremacy, imperialism, sexism, and racism have so distorted education that it is no longer about the practice of freedom" (p. 29). One restorative approach that hooks suggested is the building of a teaching community through dialogue and border crossing, enabling us to understand and then appreciate the differences among us.

The second is Jerold Apps' (1996) *Teaching from the Heart* in which Apps described heartfelt teaching as an authentic and empowering endeavor and stresses the importance of emancipatory learning as a way of coming to know who we are. Apps also suggested that educators today suffer from an over-emphasis of the pragmatics of learning and teaching, a paradigm that he maintained is an artifact of the industrial age, but one that doesn't serve us well in a changing postmodern world. He added that a number of factors account for the preponderance of instrumentality in adult and continuing education, among them the "how-to" nature of our applied discipline and an overarching professional concern for being viewed as a contributor to human productivity. Instead, he said we need "new ways of thinking, new ways of incorporating mind, body, and spirit ... especially in our learning and in our teaching" (p. 8). One way, according to Apps, is teaching from the heart.

In Cervero and Wilson's (1994) *Planning Responsibly for Adult Education*, they maintained that planning educational programs is not merely a practical endeavor with ethical implications, but a social and political one that is "always conducted within a complex set of personal, organizational, and social relationships of power among people who may have ... conflicting sets of interests" (p. 4). Cervero and Wilson offered guidelines for substantively democratic program planning, by which they mean planning that is ethical, informed by an analysis of the political and organizational context, and includes the negotiation of interests of all individuals affected by the educational program.

A fourth resource is Kathleen Weiler's (1988) *Women Teaching for Change*, an insightful explanation of critical education theory and the forces of gender, race, and class in the classroom from the perspective of a feminist classroom teacher. Like other critical educators, Weiler advocated the examination of our classrooms and the recognition of "ways in which feminist teachers make existing social relationships problematic and make conscious sexist ideology and practices" (p. 144).

And finally, Welton (1995) is another who challenged that adult education "has abandoned its once vital role in fostering democratic social action" (p. 5). He suggested that much of adult education is seriously threatened by subtle and unexamined political and economic interests as well as our own over-emphasis on production. Welton charged that the "contemporary modern practice of adult education is governed by an instrumental rationality that works to the advantage of business, industry, and large-scale organizations [and is therefore] conceptually inadequate to serve the interests of the poor, oppressed, and disenfranchised" (p. 5). In his edited text *In Defense of the Lifeworld*, Welton and his contributors suggested a return to adult education practice as a critically reflective, intersubjective, and communicative interaction—a lifeworld orientation, according to Habermas—grounded both philosophically and sociologically and with expectations of learner autonomy, self-determination, and liberation.

According to Flannery (1994), a critical postmodern approach to adult and continuing education such as these educators prescribe "offers hope to a democratic ideal, a process that accepts and empathizes with differences, continues to deconstruct existing meanings, and seeks also to understand common elements in peoples' lives and struggles against oppression and exclusion ... where power is transformed from the domination of a few into collection action" (pp. 151–152).

As Rachal (1990) reminded us, knowledge gained through adult and continuing education or otherwise is "indeed power—especially when some have it and others are intentionally deprived and education is a potent force for either distributing or perpetuating power" (p. 13). So, although ours remains a pragmatic discipline, one grounded in process and (perhaps necessarily) instrumental rationality, there are those among us who strive to promote recognition and nurturance of autonomy, self-determination, and individual power, as well as places such as the Highlander Research and Educational Center that are committed to emancipatory education practice. These and the foregoing examples are among those in adult and continuing education today that strive to redistribute the power of knowledge in an economic and political world. Our challenge today, as it has been throughout our history, is to critically question who is called to the table in needs assessment, program planning, and instruction and to reflect critically on whose interests are ultimately served by our educational efforts.

REFERENCES

Apps, J. W. (1996). *Teaching from the heart*. Malabar, FL: Krieger.

Beder, H. (1990). Purposes and philosophies of adult education. In S. B. Merriam & P. M. Cunningham (Eds.), *Handbook of adult and continuing education* (pp. 37–50). San Francisco: Jossey-Bass.

Bordieu, P. (1977). Cultural reproduction and social reproduction. In J. Karabel & F. Halsey (Eds.), *Power and ideology in education* (pp. 487–511). New York: Oxford University Press.

Bryson, L. (1936). *Adult education*. New York: American Books.

Cervero, R. M., & Wilson, A. L. (1994). *Planning responsibly for adult education: A guide to negotiating power and interests*. San Francisco: Jossey-Bass.

Collins, R. (1985). *Three sociological traditions*. New York: Oxford University Press.

Cunningham, P. M. (1988). The adult educator and social responsibility. In R. G. Brockett (Ed.), *Ethical issues in adult education* (pp. 133–145). New York: Teachers College Press.

Cunningham, P. M. (1992). From Freire to feminism: The North American experience with critical pedagogy. *Adult Education Quarterly, 42*(3), 180–191.

Elderhostel Institute Network. (1996). *Network News*. Durham, NH.

Flannery, D. D. (1994). Adult education and the politics of the theoretical text. In P. McLaren & C. Sleeter (Eds.), *Critical multiculturalism* (pp. 149–163). London: Sage.

Foucault, M. (1972). *The archaeology of knowledge and the discourse on language*. New York: Pantheon.

Freire, P. (1985). *The politics of education: Culture, power, and liberation*. Granby, MA: Bergin & Garvey.

Hallenbeck, W. (1964). The role of adult education in society. In G. Jensen, A. A. Liveright, & W. Hallenbeck (Eds.), *Adult education: Outlines of an emerging field of university study* (pp. 5–25). Washington, DC: Adult Education Association of the USA.

hooks, b. (1994). *Teaching to transgress: Education as the practice of freedom*. New York: Routledge, Chapman & Hall.

Horton, M. (1990). *The long haul: An autobiography*. New York: Doubleday.

Jarvis, P. (1985). *The sociology of adult and continuing education*. London: Croom Helm.
Lenski, G. (1966). *Power and privilege: A theory of social stratification*. New York: McGraw-Hill.
Merriam, S. B., & Caffarella, R. S. (1991). *Learning in adulthood*. San Francisco: Jossey-Bass.
Mincer, J. (1989). Human capital and the labor market: A review of current research. *Educational Researcher, 18*(4), 27–34.
Parsons, T. (1959). The school class as a social system: Some of its functions in American society. *Harvard Educational Review, 29*(3), 297–318.
Rachal, J. R. (1990). The social context of adult and continuing education. In S. B. Merriam & P. M. Cunningham (Eds.), *Handbook of adult and continuing education* (pp. 3–14). San Francisco: Jossey-Bass.
Stubblefield, H. W., & Keane, P. (1994). *Adult education in the American experience*. San Francisco: Jossey-Bass.
Weiler, K. (1988). *Women teaching for change: Gender, class and power*. New York: Bergin & Garvey.
Welton, M. R. (Ed.). (1995). *In defense of the lifeworld: Critical perspectives on adult learning*. Albany, NY: State University of New York Press.

III

Terms of Resistance

39

Critical Pedagogy*

Peter McLaren
University of California at Los Angeles

Critical pedagogy is a way of thinking about, negotiating, and transforming the relationships among classroom teaching, the production of knowledge, the institutional structures of the school, and the social and material relations of the wider community, society, and nation-state. Developed by progressive teachers attempting to eliminate inequalities on the basis of social class, it has sparked a wide array of antisexist, antiracist, and antihomophobic classroom-based curricula and policy initiatives. Critical pedagogy has grown out of a number of theoretical developments such as Latin American philosophies of liberation; the pedagogy of Brazilian educator Paulo Freire; the social reconstructionists in the 1930s United States; the sociology of knowledge; the Frankfurt school of critical theory; feminist theory; and neo-Marxist cultural criticism. In more recent years, it has been taken up by educators influenced by Derridean deconstruction and poststructuralism. Yet at the level of classroom life, critical pedagogy is often seen as synonymous with whole language instruction, adult literacy programs, and new "constructivist" approaches to teaching and learning based on Vygotsky's work. Although critics of critical pedagogy often decry this educational approach for its idealist multiculturalism, its supporters, including Freire, have complained that critical pedagogy has often been domesticated and reduced to student-directed learning approaches devoid of social critique.

It is painfully evident that critical pedagogy and its political partner, multicultural education, no longer serve as an adequate social or pedagogical platform from which to mount a serious challenge to the current social division of

*An expanded version of this chapter is forthcoming in *Educational Technology*.

labor and its effects on the socially reproductive function of schooling in late capitalist society. In fact, critical pedagogy no longer enjoys its status as a redoubtable herald for democracy, as a clarion call for revolutionary praxis, as a language of critique and possibility in the service of a radical democratic imaginary which it promised in the late 1970s and early 1980s.

A nagging question has resurfaced: Can a renewed and revivified critical pedagogy serve as a point of departure for a politics of resistance and counterhegemonic struggle in the 21st century? On the surface, there are certain reasons to be optimistic. Critical pedagogy has, after all, joined antiracist and feminist struggles to articulate a democratic social order built around the imperatives of diversity, tolerance, and equal access to material resources. But surely such a role, although commendable as far as it goes, has seen critical pedagogy severely compromise an earlier, more radical commitment to class struggle and tactfully demur to its erstwhile socialist beginnings.

Once considered by the faint-hearted guardians of the American dream as a term of opprobrium, critical pedagogy appears to have lost its compass. It has become so completely psychologized, so liberally humanized, so technologized, and so conceptually postmodernized that its current relationship to broader liberation struggles seems severely attenuated if not fatally terminated. The conceptual net known as critical pedagogy has been cast so wide and at times so cavalierly that it has come to be associated with anything dragged up out of the troubled waters of educational practice, from classroom furniture organized in a "dialogue friendly" circle to "feel-good" curricula designed to improve students' self-image. Its multicultural equivalent can be linked to a politics of diversity that includes "respecting difference" through the celebration of "ethnic" holidays and themes such as "Black history month" and "Cinco de Mayo." If the term "critical pedagogy" is refracted onto the stage of current educational debates, we have to judge it as having been domesticated almost beyond all recognition such that it has not redounded sufficiently to the benefit of the oppressed and has imparted ballast to the very conditions that it has historically challenged.

Most educationalists who are committed to critical pedagogy and multicultural education propagate versions of it that identify with their own bourgeois class interests. One doesn't have to question the integrity or competence of these educators or dismiss their work as disingenuous—for the most part it is not—to conclude that their articulations of critical pedagogy and multicultural education have been accommodated to mainstream versions of liberal humanism and progressivism. Whereas early exponents of critical pedagogy were denounced for their polemical excesses and radical political trajectories, a new generation of critical educators have since that time emerged who have largely adopted a pluralist approach to social antagonisms. Their work celebrates the "end of ideology," and the critique of global capitalism is rarely, if ever, brought into the debate.

The reasons for the domestication of critical pedagogy are various, but space permits me to essay only a rudimentary sketch of a few of them. There has been a strong movement among many critical educators infatuated by postmodern and poststructuralist perspectives to neglect or ignore profound changes in the structural nature and dynamics of U.S. late capitalism. This infatuation has occurred alongside a more general shift among many North American critical educators from earlier Marxist perspectives to liberal, social-democratic, neoliberal, and even right-wing perspectives. We have seen on the theoretical front the conscription of some Marxist writers, such as Antonio Gramsci, into the service of a neoliberal political agenda. In all, we have witnessed the evisceration of Marxist politics in current education debates and the accommodation of some of its positions into the capitalist state apparatus. Discussions of political and ideological relations and formations are being engaged by many North American leftist educators as if these arenas of social power exist in antiseptic isolation from class struggle. It is clear that a renewed agenda for critical pedagogy must include more than the postmodernist goals of troubling fixed notions of identity and difference or an unsettling notion of a bounded, pregiven or essential "self."

Why should global political economy be a concern to educators in this era of post-Marxist sympathies and multiple social antagonisms? Precisely because we are living at a particular historical juncture of doctrinaire unregulated capitalism with overwhelming income reconcentration at the top. There are currently 70 transnational corporations with revenues greater than Cuba's—70 privately owned economic nations! Millions are unemployed in First World economic communities and millions more in Third World communities. Three quarters of the new jobs in the capitalist world are temporary, low paid, low skill, and carry few, if any, benefits. Latin American countries are in the thrall of a decade-long crisis. In the United States the top 1% earned more collectively than the bottom 40%. As Charles Handy (1996) surmised in the case of England, although the government recently stated that 82% of all workers are in "permanent" employment, in fact 24% of the labor force are part-time, 13% are self-employed, 6% are temporary, and 8% are unemployed, making a total of 51% who are not in a full-time job. Further, the length of a full-time job is approximately 5.8 years. So capitalism is really about employability, not employment

(Handy, 1996). Overconsumption—the political subsidization of a sub-bourgeois, mass sector of managers, entrepreneurs, and professionals—continues unabated at the same time that we witness an obscene redistribution of wealth from the poor to the rich as corporations are benefitting from massive tax cuts and reorientation of consumption toward the new middle class. This is also accompanied by a general retreat of the labor movement (Callinicos, 1990). Moreover, this latest phase in the globalization of capital has unleashed new practices of social control and forms of internaitonalized class domination. This is not to suggest, however, that certain cultural forms and institutions do not mediate the economic or that there exist relative decommodified zones.

REVOLUTIONARY MULTICULTURALISM FOR THE NEW MILLENNIUM

Critical pedagogy has become closely allied with multicultural education (McLaren, 1995; Sleeter & McLaren, 1995). However, just as we have witnessed in the project of critical pedagogy an avoidance of issues related to class and the social relations of production, so too have we witnessed in multicultural education an absence of discussions linking the practice of racism to capitalist social relations. Consequently, both critical pedagogy and multicultural education need to address themselves to the adaptive persistence of capitalism and to issues of capitalist imperialism and its specific manifestation of accumulative capacities through conquest (which we know as colonialism). In other words, critical pedagogy needs to establish a project of emancipation centered around the transformation of property relations and the creation of a just system of appropriation and distribution of social wealth. The domestication of critical pedagogy has not infirmed its revolutionary potential.

Neo-Marxist accounts have clearly identified imperialist practices in recent movements toward global capital accumulation based on corporate monopoly capital and the international division of labor. The West has seen a progressive shift in its development that some liberals would champion as the rise of individuality, the rule of law, and the autonomy of civil society. Yet from a Marxist perspective, these putative developments toward democracy can be seen, in effect, as "new forms of exploitation and domination, (the constitutive 'power from below' is, after all, the power of lordship), new relations of personal dependence and bondage, the privatization of surplus extraction and the transfer of ancient oppressions from the state to 'society'—that is, a transfer of power relations and domination from the state to private property" (Wood, 1995, p. 252). Since the triumph of European capitalism in the 17th century, the bourgeoisie have acquired the legal, political, and military power to destroy virtually most of society in its quest for accumulation (Petras & Morely, 1992).

Capitalism in advanced Western countries must be dismantled if extraeconomic inequalities—such as racism and sexism—are to be challenged successfully. Although it is true that people have identities other than class identities that shape their experiences in crucial and important ways, anticapitalist struggle is the best means to inform educators as to how identities can be conceived and rearticulated with the construction of a radical socialist project. As Ellen Meiksins Wood (1995) notes:

> Capitalism is constituted by class exploitation, but capitalism is more than just a system of class oppression. It is a ruthless totalizing process which shapes our lives in every conceivable aspect, and everywhere, not just in the relative opulence of the capitalist North. Among other things, and even leaving aside the direct power wielded by capitalist wealth both in the economy and in the political sphere, it subjects all social life to the abstract requirements of the market, through the commodification of life in all its aspects, determining the allocation of labor, leisure, resources, patterns of production, consumption and the disposition of time. This makes a mockery of all our aspirations to autonomy, freedom of choice, and democratic self-government. (pp. 262–263)

Critical educators need to consider how racism in its present incarnations developed out of the dominant mode of global production during the 17th and 18th centuries of colonial plantations in the "New World." They, along with multicultural educators, also need to better understand and more forcefully address the process by which the immigrant working class has been historically divided along racial lines. How, for instance, does racism give White workers a particular identity that unites them with White capitalists (Callinios, 1992)?

The issue of whether a culturalist or an economist perspective prevails today in critical pedagogy is a nagging one, but essentially presents us with a false dichotomy. Individuals and groups live class relations through difference (i.e., raced and gendered experiences), and live difference through class relations. Identity, difference, and class are mutually informing relations. Class relations embody all kinds of differences that have been historically organized and structurally determined by imperialist and colonialist economies of privilege. The question is: How are differences mediated through the social contradictions of class formations and vice versa? This suggests that we examine the institutional and structural aspects of difference as they have been produced historically out of the contradictions of capitalist social practices. We can do this only if we examine how the production of gendered and racialized identities are shaped by the totality of social relations of production. That is, how can we read off in a dialectical manner particular formations and expressions of difference against the overarching and complex organization, networks, and mutually informing relationships that, at different levels and in different modalities, constitute global capitalist relations?

Critical pedagogy as a partner with multicultural education needs to deepen its reach of cultural theory and political economy and expand its participation in social–empirical analysis in order to address more critically the formation of intellectuals and institutions within the current forms of motion of history (San Juan, 1996). Critical pedagogy and multicultural education need more than good intentions to achieve their goal. They require a revolutionary movement of educators informed by a principled ethics of compassion and social justice, a socialist ethos based on solidarity and social independence, and a language of critique that is capable of grasping objective historical conditions. Given current U.S. educational policy with its goal of serving the interests of the corporate world economy—one that effectively serves a de facto world government made up of the IMF, World Bank, G–7, GATT, and other structures—it is imperative that critical and multicultural educators renew their commitment to the struggle against exploitation on all fronts (Gabbard, 1995). In emphasizing one such front, that of class struggle, I want to emphasize that the renewed Marxist approach to critical pedagogy that I envision does not conceptualize race and gender antagonism as a static, structural outcome of capitalist social relations of advantage and disadvantage but rather locates such antagonism within a theory of agency that acknowledges the importance of cultural politics and social difference. Far from deactivating the sphere of culture by seeing it only or mainly in the service of capital accumulation, critical pedagogy and multicultural education need to acknowledge the specificity of local struggles around the micropolitics of race, class, gender, and sexual formation. A critical pedagogy based on class struggle that does not confront racism, sexism, and homophobia will not be able to eliminate the destructive proliferation of capital.

Critical pedagogy must assume a position of transmodernity. Enrique Dussel (1993) describes transmodernity as one

> in which both modernity and its negated alterity (the victims) co-realize themselves in a process of mutual creative fertilization. Trans-modernity (as a project of political, economic, ecological, erotic, pedagogical, and religious liberation) is the co-realization of that which is impossible for modernity to accomplish by itself: that is, of an *incorporative* solidarity which I have called analectic, between center/periphery, man/woman, different races, different

> ethnic roups, different classes, civilization/nature, Western culture/Third World cultures, et cetera. For this to happen, however, the negated and victimized "other-face" of modernity—the colonial periphery, the Indian, the slave, the woman, the child, the subalternized popular cultures—must in the first place discover itself an innocent, as the "innocent victim" of a ritual sacrifice, who, in the process of discovering itself as innocent may now judge modernity as guilty of an originary, constitutive, and irrational violence. (p. 76)

The critical pedagogy to which I am referring needs to be made less informative and more performative, less a pedagogy directed toward the interrogation of written texts than a corporeal pedagogy grounded in the lived experiences of students. Critical pedagogy, as I am re-visioning it, is a pedagogy that brushes against the grain of textual foundationalism, ocular fetishism, and the monumentalist abstraction of theory that characterizes most critical practice within multicultural classrooms. I am calling for a pedagogy in which multicultural ethics is performed rather than simply reduced to the practice of reading texts. Teachers need to displace the textual politics that dominates most multicultural classrooms and engage in a politics of bodily and affective investment. A critical pedagogy for multicultural education should quicken the affective sensibilities of students as well as provide them with a language of social analysis and cultural critique. Opportunities must be made for students to work in communities in which they can spend time with ethnically diverse populations in the context of community activism and participation in progressive social movements that have an international reach and commitment.

Students need to move beyond simply knowing about criticalist multiculturalist practice. They must also move toward an embodied and corporeal understanding of such practice and an affective investment in such practice at the level of everyday life such that it is able to deflect the invasive power of capital.

Critical educators must possess those qualities of the intellectual about which Edward W. Said (1996) has written so eloquently. According to Said, the intellectual must possess an "unbudgeable conviction in a concept of justice and fairness that allows for differences between nations and individuals, without at the same time assigning them to hidden hierarchies, preferences, evaluations" (p. 94). Further, Said notes that "intellectuals possess an alternative and more principled stand that enables them in effect to speak the truth to power" (p. 97).

"Yes, the intellectual's voice is lonely," Said (1996) goes on to say, "but it has resonance only because it associates itself freely with the reality of a movement, the aspirations of a people, the common pursuit of a shared ideal" (p. 102). In other words, this is more than a question of intellectual probity, rather, it's an issue of critical self-reflexivity. It is in this sense that critical educators need to adopt the distinction made by Said between the professional and amateur intellectual:

> The professional claims detachment on the basis of a profession and pretends to objectivity, whereas the amateur is moved neither by rewards nor by the fulfillment of an immediate career plan but by a committed engagement with ideas and values in the public sphere. The intellectual over time naturally turns toward the political world, partly because, unlike the academy or laboratory, that world is animated by considerations of power and interest writ large that drive a whole society or nation, that, as Marx so fatefully said, take the intellectual from relatively discrete questions of interpretation to much more significant ones of social change and transformation.... [T]he intellectual who claims to write only for him or herself, or for the sake of pure learning, or abstract science is not to be, and must not be believed. (p. 110)

I would argue that we even need to exceed this model outlined by Said and operate within the compass of Gramsci's organic intellectual who employs a pedagogical and agitational role, is aware of uneven capitalist development, and incorporates the needs and demands of the oppressed into its national-popular program of action. The organic intellectual is not content to participate in the low-intensity democracy of Western neo-liberal regimes but is singularly focused on the high-intensity democracy that only a socialist policy can hasten forth (San Juan, 1998).What I have attempted to underscore in such a short space is quite simple but none the less urgent: that the struggle over our schools is fundamentally linked to struggles in the larger theatre of social and political life. The struggle that occupies and exercises us as school activists and educational researchers needs to entertain global and local perspectives in terms of the way in which capitalist relations and the international division of labor are produced and reproduced. Although I am largely sympathetic to attempts to reform school practices at the level of policy, curriculum, and classroom pedagogy, such attempts need be seen from the overall perspectives of the worldwide struggle against capitalist social relations.

REFERENCES

Callinicos, A. (1990). *Against postmodernism: A Marxist critique*. New York: St. Martin's Press.
Callinicos, A. (1992) *Race and class*. London: Bookmarks.

Dussel, E. (1993). Eurocentrism and modernity (Introduction to the Frankfurt lectures). *Boundary 2*, 20, 3, 65–76

Gabbard, D. A. (1995, Fall). NAFTA, GATT, and goals 2000: Reading the political culture of post-industrial America. *Taboo*, II pp. 184–199.

Handy, C. (1996). What's it all for? Reiventing capitalism for the next century. *RSA Journal, CXLIV* (5475), 33–40.

McLaren, P. (1995). *Critical pedagogy and predatory culture*. London: Routledge.

McLaren, P. (1997). *Revolutionary Multiculturalism: Pedagogies of dissent for the new millenium*. Boulder, CO: Westview Press.

Petras, J., & Morley, M. (1992). *Latin America in the time of cholera: Electoral politics, market economies, and permanent crisis*. New York & London: Routledge.

Said, E. W. (1996). *Representations of the intellectual*. New York: Vintage Books.

San Juan, E., Jr. (1996). *Mediations: From a Filipino perspective*. Pasig City, Philippines: Anvil.Sleeter, C., & McLaren, P. (1995). *Multicultural education, critical pedagogy, & the politics of difference*. Albany, NY: State University of New York Press.

San Juan, E., Jr. (1998). The Limits of postcolonial criticism: The discourse of Edward Said. *Against the Current, 77*, 28–32.

Wood, E. (1995). *Democracy against capitalism: Renewing historical materialism*. Cambridge: Cambridge University Press.

40

Postcolonialism

Bernardo P. Gallegos
University of Chicago, Illinois

Excitement resonated throughout Los Angeles County as thousands of enraged Latino high school and junior high school students, mainly Mexican, stormed out of their classrooms and took to the streets waving Mexican flags, chanting, "We didn't cross the border, the border crossed us." It was the fall of 1994, and the upcoming elections included a vote on the controversial and racist Proposition 187 (which has since passed). Proposition 187 threatened the "undocumented" with penalties and loss of invaluable services including medical care and education for youth. Just days earlier, Aztec dancers, also waving Mexican flags, led upward of 100 thousand marchers from east Los Angeles to downtown. The events, well publicized in the media with a barrage of front page photos of brown bodies waving Mexican flags, left the voting public (mainly European Americans) bewildered as to why these immigrants would wave Mexican flags while protesting the proposition within the United States. Several letters to the editor in the *Los Angeles Times* expressed great disapproval at the waving of Mexican flags on "American" soil. A European American policeman (a helicopter pilot) who worked surveillance from the air during the student demonstrations actually suggested to me that it was the waving of the Mexican flags that ensured the passage of the proposition and furthermore recommended that "we" (a point I will discuss later) had better learn to control our kids.

What was apparently incomprehensible to the voters and letter writers was the depth of the rage of the protesters, including me. How dare these Europeans now residing on the American continent attempt to restrict the movements of the descendants of the native peoples? Have they forgotten that just over 150 years ago, the United States, in the name of White supremacist dogma they call "Manifest Destiny," invaded and occupied the northern half of Mexico, an action not unlike the event that brought the wrath of the United States on the population of Iraq? Have they forgotten the Alamo? Do they not notice the Indian faces of those they are naming illegal aliens? Can they actually believe that "we" have completely forgotten the past?

What transpired in those days, the walkouts, protests, editorial letters, as well as my interpretation, all inextricably connected, captures the essence of postcoloniality, which signifies both a condition and an analysis. More important, postcoloniality as a theoretical space rejects the distinction between context and interpretation for, "with colonization, and consequently with the "post colonial," we are irrevocably within a power-knowledge field of force." It is a refusal of the "false and disabling distinction between colonization as a system of rule, of power and exploitation, and colonization as a system of knowledge and representation" (Hall, 1996, p. 253). Thus, whereas the walkouts, the Mexican flags, the chant represented a historical moment, they also constituted an articulation of categories and narratives that were situated outside the official hegomonic story of how the world works, an alternative narration of the arrangement of social space. The United States is reduced from a fixed category and field of power to a temporary condition, one of many ways of telling a story, albeit one that is intimately connected to the differentiated right of peoples to occupy space and social locations.

In the public transcript, the official narrative, Los Angeles is the United States, and many Mexicans and Central Americans are here illegally, having crossed the border imposed after the United States' invasion during the mid 19th century. In the story, the United States did not "invade" the Southwest but instead "annexed" it. However, among the Native American/Mexican population of the Southwest, alternative stories circulate that contradict the official discourse and, thus, open spaces for a theoretical remapping of territory. In the 10 years that I worked as a professor in Los Angeles, I heard countless student accounts of their parents' urging them not to ever feel that they don't have a right to be here, because California is Mexico. During the days before the elections, my mechanic, originally from Mexico City, asked me what I thought of Proposition 187 and then proceeded to tell me that its proponents were crazy, that Los Angeles was Mexico. This narrative, however, although articulated from a location of resistance, merely replaces one narration (United States) with another

(Mexico) and leaves itself open to the critique of Mexico as a colonial project. More to the point, it does not interrogate "Mexico" as a disabling narration that functions to erase indigenous identities, thus limiting the possibilities from which to situate a theoretical analysis from a Native American or subaltern position.

A less common but more theoretically potent and postcolonial reading of the chant, "We didn't cross the border, the border crossed us" *would discursively problematize nation* and locate both Mexico and the United States as agents of the Western imperialist project, ultimately resulting in European occupation of Native American territory and the subjugation of its peoples. Although an enormous amount of energy has been invested by historians and educators in the erasure of the United States' imperialist past, it is a story that lingers in the memory of the conquered. In one of the most atrocious and brutal campaigns of conquest, the Europeans conducted the massacre of millions of native peoples to appropriate land and transplant European culture.

The chant of the protesters challenges the official narrative and exposes the imperialist project that we name the United States, for by simply making reference to imposed borders, they remapped the territory and created potential space from which to transform relations of power. The students became counterhegemonic agents, rearticulating the United States as a colonial narrative and thus positioned themselves in an anticolonial discourse and challenged current power relations. For although colonialism refers to a historical moment, it is also a way of explaining how the world works, a way of "staging or narrating a history," always from a specific theoretical location (Hall, 1996, p. 254). The post in the postcolonial then, not only refers to the rearrangement of social relations that mark the moment in which we live but also signifies a displacement of the distinction between power and knowledge that marks the colonial. In this, the inextricable link between the postcolonial and postmodern is made clear (Foucault, 1972).

The stories of the subaltern are also located in discourses that emerge in particular temporal contexts and in particular social locations marked by relations of power. Thus the counterhegemonic narrative of the protesters was as much a challenge to a current social arrangement as it was a rejection of a story. The economic and social arrangements that characterize the present, connected in large part but not limited to the emergence of the global economy, have radically altered colonial relations and opened spaces from which to critique but, more important to transform relations of power. The geographical boundaries that once characterized the colonial relations are rapidly dissolving, spawning a powerful racist backlash in the metropolises of Europe, as many Europeans are not accustomed to the presence of the colonial subject in what they consider their spaces. This is articulated in several forms ranging from the emergence of racists skinhead and neo-Nazi movements in Europe to Proposition 187 in California. The globalization of the economy has all but eliminated the privileged, highly paid European worker all over the world. Companies scrambling to make profits now have a world market for labor and essentially are renting the cheapest bodies that money can buy to produce their goods. In this economic context then, the distinction between the colonial subject and the European worker has been significantly altered, opening up yet another potential space from which to rearticulate power relations.

My description of the events surrounding Proposition 187 emerges from discursive locations forged from a configuration of memories, dominant narratives, and relations of power that characterize the postcolonial condition in which I find myself. Colonialism has created a major crisis of location for the subaltern writer–scholar, for at the moment of articulation, contradictory narratives that remove and inhabit the writer–scholar–teacher must be framed within the dominant Western academic discourse, which remains situated in colonial relations of power (Prakash, 1994). Locating oneself outside this knowledge or power field is no easy task, for we must piece together narratives from vestiges of resistance memories and frame them in a discourse we are ultimately attempting to deconstruct.

Considering the immense labor invested in creating colonial conditions, the problem of situating a postcolonial analysis is comprehensible. Spain's 300 year rule over its colonial subjects for example, characterized by the replacement of cultural elements, erasures of native concepts and categories, and the transplantation of new sets of schemata, radically altered the mental world of the native population of its dominions (Gallegos, 1992). The result was the emergence of new social subjects born discursively within colonial relations, hybrid identities forged within the negotiation of power between the colonizer and colonized.

The emergence of the modern Mexican nation in 1821 after a war of independence from Spain only exasberbated the problem of location and identity for native peoples, for "nationalist" narratives are themselves constructed from the "cannibalized remains of other collective loyalties; [thus] to speak the national subject is to silence another" (Luykx, 1996, p. 243). The problem, then, for the subaltern is that once we are narrated into a nationalist discourse, we are theoretically restricted, for we are limited to those categories of identity that exist within that particular narrative. Ultimately, we are left with no place to theorize from that is not bound up in the hybrid identities that were formed from our appropriation into colonialist discourses. As Bhabha (1990) states, "The other is never outside or beyond us; it emerges forcefully within cultural discourse when we think we speak most intimately and indigenously." The subaltern then must construct discourses and alternative identities form which to write from within the very colonial locations and national identities that we are rejecting and attempting to transform .

Aside from the devastating economic and social arrangements, colonialism has left the subaltern with undeniable and damaging psychological conditions (Fanon, 1969). Among these are the problems surrounding the construction and performance of identities, made painfully clear in the following recollection by Stuart Hall:

> When I look at the snapshots of myself in childhood and early adolescence, I see a picture of a depressed person. I don't want to be who they want me to be, but I don't know how to be somebody else ... Gradually, I came to recognize I was a black West Indian, just like everybody else, I could relate to that, I could write from and out of that position. It has taken me a very long time, really to be able to write in that way, personally. Previously, I was only able to write about it analytically. In that sense it has taken me fifty years to come home. It wasn't so much that I had anything to conceal. It was the space I couldn't occupy, a space I had to learn to occupy. (Cited in Morley & Chen, 1996, pp. 488–489)

Hall's recollection speaks poignantly to my own adolescence, a troubled time, a time when I attempted to wash the brown off of my skin with Comet bleach powder. Recently my younger brother and his in-laws visited me from New Mexico, and I was reminded of the discomfort as they kept referring to me as "Ben," a name I have since come to despise. I was discursively located in a space that I have since transcended, an identity I cannot perform, a narrative I can no longer occupy. For me, "Ben" constitutes an acceptance of a colonial location; it signifies, a national identity. The choice between "Bernardo" and "Ben," then, is ultimately a political one, just as is my decision to speak in English or Spanish. In the problematics of discursive location, we cannot separate the personal from the political, for identity is an "intersubjective, performative act that refuses the division of public/private, psyche/social" (Bhabha, 1996, p. 206). It is from within the myriad of colonial power relations and narrations that we construct self, "not a 'self' given to consciousness, but a "coming-to-consciousness" of the self through the realm of symbolic otherness—language, the social system (Bhabha, 1996, p. 206)."

Counternarratives, stories constructed from fragments of memory, emerging from subaltern locations are crucial in the reconstitution of identities. The postcolonial condition is itself marked by the construction of new identities, a "recomposing of the self, by [the] re-proposing [of] texts and paths that are strictly linked to urban hardship and discontent" (Triulzi, 1996, p. 83). These are texts that recast the world, that reconfigure the social landscape, that emerge from the subaltern experience. In Los Angeles, Mexican Corridos function in this way, making heroes of people opposing the law, singing the exploits of border crossing and symbolically leading the audience across discursive borders, giving voice to the people's stories that are silenced in the dominant discourses, and naming injustices from subaltern locations. In these narratives, new folk-saints emerge, such as "Malverde," patron of persons who function outside of the law, one of the most popular deities in botanicas across the Southwest.

This brings me to the heart of this essay, the relationship between "Memory" and "location" and its significance for this Native American scholar/teacher. Location, the place from which I theorize, informed by a myriad of events, memories, conditions, and stories, continues to be painfully elusive. One of the most difficult problems I struggle with is the realization that the narratives I inherited and that inhabit me are most often in stark contradiction to the narratives that exist in the academic world in which I work. The stories about how the world works that I heard and learned growing up are so radically different from explanations I learned in institutions that they are almost irreconcilable, making writing incredibly painful. It is as though I am forced to write from a space that has no textual legitimacy. I am compelled to compose from a location that does not yet exist, which I have to invent from reconstituted fragments of memory and stories.

Central to this painful conjecture of identity is my relationship with my maternal grandmother, Libradita Aragon, who I lived with from birth until I went away to college at the age of 17. Libradita was a poor woman, a mixed blood Indian whose father split wood for people in the neighborhood to feed his family. Libradita however, was a proud woman who didn't want to be poor nor to think of herself as poor. Accordingly, she always tried to buy the most expensive clothes and furniture she could, but most often couldn't. I can recall an ivory colored vinyl couch she bought, which she covered with plastic and never let anybody sit on.

She told stories, lots of them, but one in particular had great importance in my struggle with location. The story was my introduction to America. "As it were," my grandmother explained, "we were not always poor. My great-great-grandfather was a rich and powerful man who had so much money he used to light his cigars with 20 dollar bills. He had a blanket quilted with 100 dollar bills, and had hundreds of peons and servants. When the Americanos came, everyone gathered what belongings they could and fled to the mountains for safety. On returning to their home, her family discovered that all the gold they had buried in their yards had been stolen, "probably by the neighbors" the story goes, and from this point on we were no longer rich.

Although the purpose of her story was to justify her poverty and situate us outside a subordinate space at least discursively, the unintended outcome was to locate me in an antiimperialist discourse in my adult life and in my scholarly work. More specifically, I was permanently narrated into a colonial relationship with America. Americans to me are invaders, responsible for much misery, shamelessly speaking of this territory as if it belonged to them and naming other peoples, who like me occupy Native American bodies, "illegal aliens." To me, the United States is a European imperialist project. Furthermore, Europeans residing on the American continent, no matter for how many generations, have absolutely no right (other than that won by brute military power) to impose borders on native peoples of America. So unwittingly, Grandma Libradita situated me in an anticolonial space, outside the dominant discourse. Because of her influence, in my work, I engage myself in the process of decentering the West, which ultimately means not placing the West in the center but attempting instead to seize a space outside it from which to theorize, to write, and to lecture.

As I have attempted to lay out in this chapter, postcolonial analysis, for Native Americans/Mexicans, especially nontribal peoples, is potent in the construction of enabling locations from which to theorize. For Mexican peoples in the Southwest, the emergence of Proposition 187 brought about a critical problem of identity. For it problematized the constitution of "we," or more to the point, the categorical void within the narrative "American." Because the proposition was characterized by the "othering" of peoples outside the United States' geographical border, it subsequently located Mexicans and other Latinos residing in the United States outside the discursive borders surrounding national identity. It forced Mexicans who are United States citizens to choose between "family" and "nation," as the two fictive kinship systems were rendered irreconcilable. That is, for many Mexicans living in the Southwest, the "we" does not end at the San Diego–Tijuana border. The imagined communities that we occupy exist outside the discursive boundaries of the United States, constituting a crisis that is indicative of the postcolonial moment in which we live.

REFERENCES

Bhabha, H. (Ed.). (1990). *Nation and narration*. New York: Routledge, Chapman & Hall.

Bhabha, H. (1996). Unpacking my library ... again. In I. Chambers & L. Curti (Eds.), *The post colonial question: Common skies, divided horizons* (pp. 199–211). New York: Routledge, Chapman & Hall.

Chen, K., (1996). The formation of a diasporic intellectual: An interview with Stuart Hall. In D. Morley & K. Chen (Eds.), *Stuart Hall: Critical dialogues in cultural studies* (pp.484–503). New York: Routledge, Chapman & Hall.

Fanon, F. (1969). *The wretched of the earth*. Harmonsdworth, England: Penguin.

Foucault, M. (1972). *The archeology of knowledge*. London: Tavisteck Press.

Gallegos, B. (1992). *Literacy, education, and society in New Mexico, 1693–1821*. Albuquerque: University of New Mexico Press.

Hall, S. (1996). When was "the post-colonial"? Thinking at the limit. In I. Chambers & L. Curti (Eds.), *The post colonial question: Common skies, divided horizons* (pp. 242–260). New York: Routledge, Chapman & Hall.

Luykx, A. (1996). From indios to profesionales: Stereotypes and student resistance in Bolivian teacher training. In B. A. Levinson, D. E. Foley, & D. C. Holland (Eds.), *The cultural production of the educated person* (pp. 239–272). Albany: State University of New York Press.

Prakash, G. (1994, December). Subaltern studies as postcolonial criticism. *American Historical Review*, 1475–1490.

Triulzi, A. (1996). African cities, historical memory and street buzz. In I. Chambers & L. Curti (Eds.), The post colonial question: Common skies, divided horizons (pp. 199–211). New York: Routledge, Chapman & Hall.

41

Critical Race Theory*

Gloria Ladson Billings
University of Wisconsin, Madison

According to Delgado (1995), "Critical Race Theory sprang up in the mid-1970s with the early work of Derrick Bell and Alan Freeman, both of whom were deeply distressed over the slow pace of racial reform in the United States" (p. xiii). They argued that the traditional approaches of filing amicus briefs, protests, marching, and appealing to the moral sensibilities of decent citizens produced smaller and fewer gains than in previous times. Before long they were being joined by other legal scholars who shared their frustration with traditional civil rights strategies.

Critical race theory (CRT) is both an outgrowth of and a separate entity from an earlier legal movement called critical legal studies (CLS). Critical legal studies is a leftist legal movement that challenged the traditional legal scholarship that focused on doctrinal and policy analysis (Gordon, 1990) in favor of a form of law that spoke to the specificity of individuals and groups in social and cultural contexts. Critical legal studies scholars also challenged the notion that the civil rights struggle represents a long, steady march toward social transformation" (Crenshaw, 1988, p. 1334).

According to Crenshaw (1988), "Critical [legal] scholars have attempted to analyze legal ideology and discourse as a social artifact which operates to recreate and legitimate American society" (p. 1350). Scholars in the CLS movement decipher legal doctrine to expose both its internal and external inconsistencies and reveal the ways that "legal ideology has helped

*This chapter is adapted from a manuscript written by the author entitled, "Just what is critical race theory and what's it doing in a nice field like education" which is currently under review for publication.

create, support, and legitimate America's present class structure" (p. 1350). The contribution of CLS to legal discourse is in its analysis of legitimating structures in the society. Much of the CLS ideology emanates from the work of Gramsci (1971) and depends on the Gramscian notion of "hegemony" to describe the continued legitimacy of oppressive structures in American society. However, CLS fails to provide pragmatic strategies for material social transformation. CLS scholars critiqued mainstream legal ideology for its portrayal of U.S. society as a meritocracy but failed to include racism in its critique. Thus, CRT became a logical outgrowth of the discontent of legal scholars of color with CLS.

CRT begins with the notion that racism is "normal, not aberrant, in American society" (Delgado, 1995, p. xiv.), and because it is so enmeshed in the fabric of our social order, it appears both normal and natural to people in this culture. Indeed, Bell's (1992) major premise in *Faces at the Bottom of the Well* is that racism is a permanent fixture of American life. Thus, the task of resistance is exposing and unmasking racism in its various forms.

Second, CRT departs from mainstream legal scholarship by sometimes employing storytelling to "analyze the myths, presuppositions, and received wisdom's that make up the common culture about race and that invariably render blacks and other minorities one-down" (Delgado, 1995, p. xiv). According to Barnes (1990), "Critical race theorists ... integrate their experiential knowledge, drawn from a shared history as 'other,' with their ongoing struggles to transform a world deteriorating under the albatross of racial hegemony" (pp. 1864–1865). The primary reason that storytelling is considered important among CRT scholars is that a story adds the necessary contextual contours to the seeming "objectivity" of positivist perspectives.

A third quality of CRT is an insistence on a critique of liberalism. Crenshaw (1988) argues that the liberal perspective of civil rights as steady but incremental progress is flawed, because it fails to understand the limits of current legal paradigms to serve as catalysts for social change. CRT argues that racism requires sweeping changes, but liberalism has no mechanism for such cataclysmic change. Liberal legal practices support the slow process of arguing legal precedence to gain citizen rights for people of color.

Fourth, CRT scholars argue that Whites have been the primary beneficiaries of civil rights legislation. Although under attack throughout the nation, affirmative action has benefitted Whites. The major recipients of affirmative action hiring policies have been White women. One might argue that the majority of these White women have incomes that support households in which other Whites live—men, women, and children. Bell

(1980) argues that the only way for African Americans to benefit from the privileges that Whites accrue from civil rights legislation is through his notion of "interest-convergence." Interest-convergence occurs when the interests of Whites and people of color intersect. For example, school desegregation is said to have "worked" when Whites agree to participate because of the special programmatic benefits (specialty schools, after school programs, etc.) and African Americans or other children of color are bused out of their neighborhood schools.

In a recent compilation of CRT key writings, Crenshaw, Gotanda, Peller, & Thomas (1995) point out that there is no "canonical set of doctrines or methodologies to which [CRT scholars] all subscribe" (p. xiii). But, these scholars are united by two common interests–to understand how a "regime of white supremacy and its subordination of people of color have been created and maintained in America" (p. xiii) and to break the bond that continues to exist between law and racial power.

The use of "voice" or "naming your reality" is a way that CRT links form and substance in scholarship. CRT scholars use parables, chronicles, stories, counterstories, poetry, fiction, and revisionist histories to illustrate the false necessity and irony of much current civil rights doctrine. Delgado (1989) suggests that there are at least three reasons for "naming one's own reality" in legal discourse:

1. Much of "reality" is socially constructed.
2. Stories provide members of outgroups a vehicle for psychic self-preservation.
3. The exchange of stories from teller to listener can help overcome ethnocentrism and the dysconscious (King, 1992) conviction of viewing the world in one way.

The first reason for naming one's own reality involves how political and moral analysis is conducted in legal scholarship. Many mainstream legal scholars embrace universalism over particularity. According to Williams (1991), "theoretical legal understanding" is characterized in Anglo-American jurisprudence by the acceptance of transcendent, contextual, universal legal truths or procedures.

In contrast, CRT scholars argue political and moral analysis is situational—"truths only exist for this person in this predicament at this time in history" (Delgado, 1991). For the critical race theorist, social reality is constructed by the formulation and the exchange of stories about individual situations (see, for example, Matsuda, 1989). These stories serve as interpretive structures by which we impose order on experience and it on us (Delgado, 1989).

A second reason for naming one's own reality is the psychic preservation of marginalized groups. A factor contributing to the demoralization of marginalized groups is self-condemnation. Members of minority groups internalize the stereotypic images that certain elements of society have constructed in order to maintain their power. Storytelling has been a kind of soothing balm to heal wounds caused by racial oppression. The stories help individuals realize how they came to be oppressed and subjugated and allow them to stop inflicting mental violence on themselves.

Third, naming one's reality with stories can affect the oppressor. Most oppression does not seem like oppression to the perpetrator (Lawrence, 1987). Delgado (1989) argues that the dominant group justifies its power with stories, stock explanations, that construct reality in ways to maintain their privilege. Thus, oppression is rationalized, causing self-examination by the oppressor. Stories by people of color can initiate the necessary cognitive conflict to jar dysconscious racism.

In conclusion, several of the legal scholars who have been in the forefront of this movement reject the "prevailing orthodoxy that scholarship should be or could be 'neutral' and 'objective' " (Crenshaw et al., 1995, p. xv). Rather, they believe that all legal scholarship in this country is subjective, particularly when the legal issue is race. These scholars credit Derrick Bell with the vision, foresight, and experience to confront legal issues revolving around race in new and exciting ways. Two pivotal moments—a boycott by Harvard law students and the critical legal studies conference of the 1980s formed the institutional and ideological antecedents of CRT. By the mid-1980s, law students and scholars interested in new conceptions of race-related law began to gather in small groups following larger law school conferences and conventions. These small groups contributed to the founding of the Critical Race Theory Workshop. The major organizers of this workshop were Kimberle Crenshaw, Neil Gotanda, and Stephanie Phillips, who called together about 35 law scholars "who responded to a call to synthesize a theory that, while grounded in critical theory, was responsive to the realities of racial politics in America" (Crenshaw et al., 1995, p. xxvii).

REFERENCES

Barnes, R. (1990). Race consciousness: The thematic content of racial distinctiveness in critical race scholarship. *Harvard Law Review, 103*, 1864–1871.

Bell, D. (1980). Brown and the interest-convergence dilemma. In D. Bell (Ed.), *Shades of brown: New perspective on school desegregation* (pp. 90–106). New York: Teachers College Press.

Bell, D. (1992). *Faces at the bottom of the well.* New York: Basic Books.

Crenshaw, K. (1988). Race, reform, and retrenchment: Transformation and legitimation in antidiscrimination law. *Harvard Law Review, 101*, 1331–1387.

Crenshaw, K., Gotanda, N., Peller, G., & Thomas, K. (Eds.), *Critical race theory: The key writings that forced the moment*. New York: Free Press.

Delgado, R. (1989). Symposium. Legal storytelling. *Michigan Law Review, 87*, 2073.

Delgado, R. (1991). Brewer's plea: Critical thoughts on common cause. *Vanderbilt Law Review, 44*, 1–14.

Delgado, R. (1995). *Critical race theory: The cutting edge*. Philadelphia: Temple University Press.

Gordon, R. (1990). New developments in legal theory. In D. Kairys (Ed.), *The politics of law: A progressive critique* (pp. 413–425). New York: Pantheon.

Gramsci, A. (1971). Selections from the prison notebooks. In Q. Hoare & G. N. Smith (Eds. and Trans.). New York: International Publishers.

King, J. (1992). Diaspora literacy and consciousness in the struggle against miseducation in the Black community. *The Journal of Negro Education, 61*, 317–340.

Lawrence C., (1987). The id, the ego, and equal protection: Reckoning with unconscious racism. *Stanford Law Review, 39*, 317–388).

Lawrence, C. (1995). The word and the river: Pedagogy as scholarship and struggle. In K. Crenshaw, N. Gotanda, G. Peller, & K. Thomas, (Eds.), *Critical race theory: The key writings that formed the movement* (pp. 336–351). New York: The Free Press.

Matsuda, M. (1989). Public response to racist speech: Considering the victim's story. *Michigan Law Review, 87*, 2320–2381.

Williams, P. (1991). *The alchemy of race and rights: Diary of a law professor.* Cambridge, MA: Harvard University Press.

42

Critical Feminist Pedagogy

Jeanne F. Brady
The Pennsylvania State University

Feminist theory has radically evolved over the past 30 years. Feminism today, in its political, practical, and theoretical realms, represents divergent interpretations to many people. More recently a postmodern feminist theory has provided space to embrace multiple positions so as not to define feminism as one conception or to create binarisms by placing one position in opposition to another. It allows for multiple positions of difference and diversity while at the same time supports an overarching feminist philosophy that challenges us to think and act in particular ways. More specifically, it links the cultural politics of difference and identity with the social politics of justice and equality. In this sense, postmodern feminism represents a politics in which people actively participate in the shaping of theories and practices of liberation by acknowledging both diversity and unity and at the same time focusing on the lives of the people who work and live in a multiracial and multicultural society.

Historically, the U.S. feminist debate was formulated in an attempt to identify and describe women's oppression, to theorize its foundations and effects, and to conceive ways to generate strategies for women's liberation. It is no less important today that we acknowledge and challenge the specific gendered realities of oppression and exploitation. Yet, it is worth noting that focusing on shared forms of oppression is neither unproblematic nor is it the only basis on which feminists can develop a politics of solidarity. Rather, I would emphasize that women should question their shared victimage as the essential location of injustice, since this reflects male supremacist thinking that to be female is to be victim. Instead, women should organize around their shared commonalities and their ability for self-determination and communal agency. Extending this point, I want to emphasize that a politics of solidarity that allows for multiple positions of difference and diversity should also include men who are in opposition to logocentric and hierarchical values within the hegemonic patriarchal system. This is not to suggest that women should not represent themselves as much as it is to maintain that feminist politics is not limited to a specific gender.

One does not need to look too deeply to realize that institutions, and in this case schooling, do not address diversity and difference but rather allow for discrepancies based on gender as well as on race identity, class location, ethnicity, and other forms of difference to continue. As we know, traditional educational theory, even defined in terms of a gender equitable one, does not promote the multiple spaces for all children to learn. Instead, it adheres to a dominant conception of schooling that supports a White, middle-class definition of knowledge. Children need to assimilate to be successful in this game by denying their own cultural identity. In this sense, schooling is not connected to the larger multicultural society. Rather than point to the larger social structures that explain gender, race, and class inequities in schooling, such as patriarchy, the sexual division of labor, and the economy, we can locate the problems within the institution of schooling itself—believing that education can be the "great equalizer" capable of reforming society.

This is not to deny that much has been done over the past 2 decades that encourages gender equity in education. Nevertheless, education is not equal in both subtle and not so subtle ways. Operating under the assumption that girls do not receive an equal education to boys, research has provided us with evidence of the various ways in which girls are disadvantaged. Several areas that point to gender inequity in education include academic achievement; classroom interactions between teacher and student; student and student; sex stereotyping; and gender bias in curricular materials. Many sensitive educators have provided nonsexist alternatives to assure that all children—that is, both boys and girls—receive a quality and equal educational experience. This work is important and has brought the discussion of gender equity to the forefront in schooling debates. I do not wish to refute or challenge the notion that gender equity exists or is absent in classroom practices but believe that we need to explore the narrow scope of analysis that is provided by this liberal feminist framework. In this sense, gender is treated as an isolated category of analysis. Gender, as well as other forms of difference, set in isolation, gives an important but inadequate reading of complex issues that coexist within cultural and economic realms. Taken alone, these elements (e.g., a liberal feminist pedagogy) are important but limited in their awareness of the multiplicity of injustices that persist.

CRITICAL FEMINIST PEDAGOGY

As an educator, I am interested in the relationship among postmodern feminist theory and the politics of a critical pedagogy. A feminist critical pedagogy intersects a postmodern feminism with critical praxis understood within the context of economic, political, and cultural constructs. Developing one's role as a critical feminist educator involves asking oneself questions about the nature of every theory and practice that determines the conditions of our environment. In this sense, theory as a form of both self and cultural criticism is concerned with the issue of who speaks, for whom, under what conditions, and for what purpose. Theory in this case is not innocent. The bridging of these philosophies into a critical feminist pedagogy not only offers students and teachers the opportunity for raising questions about how the categories of race, class, and gender and other forms of oppression and privilege are shaped within the margins and centers of power, but it also provides a new way of reading history as a way of reclaiming power and identity. Moreover, a critical feminist pedagogy provides students and teachers with the opportunity to acknowledge the relevance and importance of different literacies, narratives, and experiences as part of a broader attempt to negotiate and transform the world in which they live. A critical feminist perspective, which incorporates multiple ways of knowing and understanding based on difference, can transform teaching and especially the interaction of knowledge, agency, and cultural identity that have been male biased and prescribed by White, middle-class values.

GUIDING PRINCIPLES OF A CRITICAL FEMINIST PEDAGOGY

To embrace the project of a critical feminist pedagogy, I call for six guiding principles. This is not to define a methodology of feminist practice but rather to encourage a discussion of key concepts that could disrupt the political agenda of traditional educational theory and bring about the possibility of change.

First, a critical feminist pedagogy should engage in students' experience as central to teaching and learning. This means that educators need to accept that the learner is an active participant in the construction of knowledge in contrast to the traditional educational view in which the learner is the receiver of knowledge. In this sense, a critical feminist pedagogy understands knowledge as something to be analyzed and understood by students and informed by their own experiences.

Second, students should be offered both the knowledge and skills that allow them to reclaim their voice and their history so as to enable them to name new identities. By affirming students' experience and providing a safe space from which to speak of their own historical and cultural place, we present students with the opportunity to assume ownership and become active agents in their lives. This position, however, should not oversimplify the notion of student voice or refuse its contradictions.

Third, students should be provided the opportunity to rewrite the relations between centers and margins as part of an effort to understand power and agency. Exploring the complexity of difference within power relations provides the opportunity to understand how these relations enable or silence different students who come from diverse backgrounds.

Fourth, students should be given the opportunity to understand and reconstruct cultural differences, economic inequities, and social identities so as to produce knowledge and democratic practices. It is not enough to say that there will be unity with diversity, that students will respect one another; rather, a critical feminist pedagogy needs to allow for the creation of new forms of knowledge by breaking down old boundaries and allowing for new connections that both legitimate and produce democratic social relations free of sexism, bigotry and domination.

Fifth, students should be presented with a language of critique and possibility. In particular, we need to develop a language that challenges sexist and racist assumptions and calls into question taken for granted definitions of gender and other forms of domination. Furthermore, it should allow for the creation of imaginary possibilities to re-vision classroom praxis.

Finally, all this must take place within the realm of teachers as engaged intellectuals who call into question educators' subject positions and recognize the limits underlying their own views. To embrace the guiding principles of a critical feminist pedagogy in an attempt to include all children, educators need to acknowledge that their styles of teaching and interacting may need to change. This is not to say that educators are not well meaning or truly committed to quality education for all. But educators will need to shift paradigms from "banking education," which reduces learning to the dynamics of transmission and opposition, to the acknowledgment that there are multiple ways of knowing and to create a space for constructive confrontation and critical interrogation of that knowledge. This challenges the assumption that knowledge flows in only one direction from teacher to student as though it were one dimensional. This assumption comes from the content knowledge that teachers possess and hold over students, which creates a power imbalance used to exercise and justify control. Belief in this one-way flow of knowledge reflects the attitude that teachers cannot, or need not, learn from their students. When knowledge becomes more than information—that is, when it goes beyond the notion of banking education—it becomes connected to how one lives, behaves, and acts. Critical feminist pedagogy recognizes the power relationships that exist in the educational system whether those relationships exist between student and teacher, teacher and principal, or other. This recognition allows authority to be unmasked and renegotiated if need be, and within this framework the pedagogy becomes the means to empower the learner. It is within this realm that schools become a place to reinvent oneself and the world—from kindergarten through higher education. Schools can also become sites of contention and conflict, and at times these ideas of reinvention might run counter to the values and beliefs one learns at home. It also can place one's self at risk, challenging conformity and striving to disrupt domination. In this sense, knowledge and practice become political.

Classrooms need to reflect a democratic setting, one that builds a community of difference that is safe—a zone of equality—which enhances intellectual rigor and intellectual development. Furthermore, knowledge needs to be rooted in the respect for multiculturalism and difference. Knowledge and information must be made relevant so that it not only strengthens intellectual development but makes the connection between knowledge and the everyday to expand our capacity to live more fully in the world.

CONCLUSION

Real-world thinking is a messy, multifaceted enterprise. What a critical feminist pedagogy does is offer a different approach to educational theory and practice that calls for a revision of schooling so as to embrace a future that is more just. Included in these multiple cultures are gender, race, ethnicity, sexual orientation, age, class, and a wide range of subcultures. A critical feminist pedagogy not only offers students and teachers the opportunity to raise questions about how these categories are shaped within the margins and centers of power, it also provides them with a new way of reading and working as a way of reclaiming power and identity. Moreover, a critical feminist pedagogy provides students and teachers with the opportunity to acknowledge the relevance and importance of different experiences as part of a broader attempt to critically negotiate and transform the world in which they live.

Critical feminist pedagogy aims for education as the practice of freedom and moves toward a postpatriarchal discourse and social practice. It is a philosophy of schooling directed at restructuring the relations of power in ways that enable all children to speak and act as subjects within democratic social relations. Its purpose is to end oppression while challenging the politics of domination. Difference and gender discourses provide not only new analyses for understanding how subject positions are constructed; they also reclaim the importance of linking the personal with the political. As I try to describe or define critical feminist pedagogy, I also recognize its ever-changing nature but, nevertheless, engage in the endeavor in order to have an impact on the present and future of educational theory and practice.

43

Biocentric Education

Robin Good
Madhu Suri Prakash
Pennsylvania State University

> Where we are, we stand in relationship to others [and the natural world], part of a dialogue, fibers of an intricate web that spins itself into the fabric. (Krall, 1994)

Becoming dwellers on the human scale involves a shift in paradigm from the modern developmental framework to a postmodern constructive biocentric model of reality. The assumptions of a biocentric framework rest on the primacy of nurturing and sustaining life. Words such as *interconnectedness*, *interdependence*, *interdisciplinary*, *interactive*, *holistic*, *dynamic*, and *dialectical* comprise the fundamental discourse of the humanity-through-nature paradigm. In contrast to the humanity-over-nature paradigm, which likens the universe to a knowable and predictable machine, the holistic paradigm emphasizes a systems view of life. The biocentric approach looks at the world in terms of relationships and integration. These relationships are perceived as dynamic, interactive, and dialectical, providing both context and meaning to the human experience (Gang, 1989).

In this holistic construct, humans view themselves as part of a dynamic pattern that interconnects people and the biotic community. From this interconnection arises well-being; the health of the whole is contingent upon the health of the parts, and the health of the parts is contingent upon the health of the whole. This mutuality and reciprocity call for a moral code that strives to preserve and nurture the integrity of those relationships. This requires living on the human scale, rediscovering and reestablishing sustainable communities: communities whose residents have relearned how to be dwellers of the land and have rediscovered the meaning of rootedness; communities governed by a biotic ethic rather than by the violence of economic expediency. What this requires is adaptation of people to a particular place—that is, acquisition of knowledge of specific places and their particular traits of soil, microclimate, wildlife, and vegetation and the adoption of cultural practices that are environmentally suited for that particular location (Orr, 1992). This type of knowledge is traditional, indigenous knowledge that has been arrived at through a coevolutionary process between a specific social and ecological system.

Rooted knowledge is not separated, as it is in the modern world, from the multiple tasks of living well in a specific place over a long period of time. There is a union among knowledge, livelihood, and living. It is a shift from the modern notion of "livelihood"—which has broken this union using knowledge for one purpose only, increasing productivity, thereby opening the door to exploitation, neglect, and damage of the human and ecological kind—to a multi-faceted notion of livelihood. Survival, or "making a living" would be only one facet; others would include political activity, spirituality, cultural celebrations, creativity, artistic expressions, and maintaining family, friend, and community relationships. All of these aspects—physical, intellectual, political, creative, spiritual, and emotional well-being—are components of livelihood. All are components of what Wendell Berry (1990) describes as the art of living well in a particular place. It is the affirmation of the multidimensional aspect of human potential and human experience. It is living within and across multicontexts so as to nourish human wholeness. It is creating meaning from the deepest sources. Ultimately, it measures wealth in terms of experiences of well-being rather than in commodities of "well-having," a notion arising from a new definition of development that is organic rather than mechanistic in nature. It is the on-going process of unfolding, of "flowering," of becoming more fully human (Freire, 1970; Hanh, 1996; Lipschutz, 1996; Macy, 1990; Orr, 1992).

Reestablishing local communities entails reestablishing local economies. A local economy depends on itself for many of its essential needs and is thus shaped from the inside, unlike most modern industrialized populations that depend on purchases produced in distant places and are thus shaped from the outside by the purposes and influence of salespeople and profit-driven corporations. This, in turn, suggests bioregionalism: the creation of regionally appropriate means of living and livelihood. This requires decentralization and the rebuilding of local communities based on the reinvention of policies at the ecosystems level. It is a disengagement from the modern concept of national and global economies; it is also a disengagement from the modern concept of growth economics. It will be a lifestyle that, by conscious choice, design, and consistency with the biocentric paradigm, will be more frugal and simplistic. It is based on the realization that nature is limited. It leads to the notion of enoughness, but enoughness only in the sense of limiting the production and consumption of material "things," not in the limiting of human compassion, character, and potential (Orr, 1992; Sachs, 1992; Shiva, 1992).

EDUCATING FOR SUSTAINABILITY

> Reform does not require a master plan before it begins; but it needs to be guided by a clear sense of the direction in which we must move, and the full awareness of the consequences if we fail. (Bowers, 1993a)

Educational institutions can be leverage points for the transition to sustainability. It requires an educational system, however, that is different from the current system. Foremost, it demands an uncompromising commitment to life and its preservation, a commitment to health, harmony, balance, wholeness, and diversity as these pertain to both human and natural systems. It requires a deep sense of the sacredness of life expressed as love, nurture, creativity, wonder, faith, and justice. Anything less is seen as morally indefensible.

Such a commitment does not describe a specific agenda so much as it does an ethos or a direction. As Orr (1992) states, it is "more than an attitude[;] it signifies a motivating and energizing force underlying education ... [that] transcend[s] narrow concerns of professional acclaim, career advancement, and institutional aggrandizement" (p. 133). The purpose of sustainable education is fourfold: first is helping students to understand current reality as defined by the modern developmental paradigm; second is helping students to develop a different framework for understanding the world, one based on the interconnectedness of life; third is helping them to become whole persons (that is, clear in thought, compassionate in heart, and competent in hands); and fourth is helping them to become active, participatory citizens. Many holistic–ecological scholars have addressed the issue of sustainable education and clarified what they perceive as necessary shifts in purpose, pedagogy, and curriculum. David Orr has probably been both the most elaborative and concrete in his description of a new educational model based on sustainability.

Awareness is the first step toward change. A shift to sustainable root metaphors requires Paulo Freire's concept of conscientization: awareness of current self and society, critical reflection, and positive action to change and heal those aspects of the modern paradigm that have been individually, societally, and biotically damaging. This awareness and critical reflection require persons of wide understanding and of greater philosophical depth and perspective. This implies a broad-based study of subjects and critical analysis and discussion of the assumptions comprising the development model of reality.

Orr (1992) contends that students must become whole, balanced persons. Wholeness of the individual implies the Gandhian notion of head, heart, and hands: "the integration of the personhood of the student, the analytic mind with feelings, the intellect with manual competence" (p. 101). The current industrial educational system produces thinkers who cannot do and doers who cannot think. In both cases, the third aspect of wholeness is neglected—the heart. Virtues such as a sense of justice, equality, empathy, compassion, and care are minimally addressed, thus perpetuating the graduation of persons with little moral sense.

Awareness and moral sense must then lead to action. Students must be taught to be healers, to think in terms of possibility, to become transformative citizens who summon up the courage to imagine a different and more just world and to struggle for it. This requires the ability to make wise public and private choices about environmental and human issues that, in turn, depend largely on the extent and breadth of public and private knowledge. To reorganize local or household systems supplying energy, water, food, resources, and economic support that minimize environmental and human damage requires people who know a great deal about such things as solar design, horticulture, recycling, composting, greenhouses, intensive gardening, food preservation, household economics, and on-site energy systems. These, in turn, require mastery of biology, chemistry, physics, engineering, architecture, community dynamics, and economics—all of which, Orr maintains, should be part of a sustainable educational curriculum.

Orr proposes a "connective" pedagogy and curriculum. This entails a pedagogy that is interdisciplinary in approach, one that strives to situate knowledge within a more profound experience of the natural world while simultaneously making it more relevant to the great quandaries of our time. It is a pedagogy that teaches students to seek out connections, and it is based on the Deweyan concept of theory and praxis (Orr, 1992; 1993). This requires restructuring the learning environment in order to overcome the centripetal effects of academic specialization and the split between intellect and experience that is ingrained in the current educational system.

What kind of learning environment rejoins intellect and experience, grounds students in the knowledge of the natural world, and addresses the quandaries of our time? It could be described as "campus-based" learning. Applying Freirean pedagogy, teachers as well as learners systematically examine their own oppressor–oppressed roles as members of a particular unsustainable community and culture: their own high school or college campus. Orr's curriculum and pedagogy suggest how faculty and students can begin to engage in critical studies of their own concrete reality. They begin by studying the various systems of their campus—food, water, heating and cooling, incoming and outgoing school materials, waste disposal, energy usage, architectural maintenance and design—and proceed by asking questions. For example, in the case of food, according to Orr (1993), we could ask the following sorts of questions:

- Where does the food come from?
- How is the food produced and at what ecological and human cost?
- How much energy does food production consume?
- What hidden costs does this food production system impose on the environment? Is it possible to design an agricultural system that repays those costs by being net energy exporters and, if not, are there other ways to balance ecological accounts?
- What in our ethical code justifies producing and eating food that degrades ecosystems, jeopardizes other species, or risks human lives and health?
- Where these costs are deemed unavoidable to accomplish a larger good, how can we balance ethical accounts?

In the process of answering these questions, students will be answering another set of questions: What will people need to know to live responsibly in a finite world? What skills, abilities, values, and character traits will be useful and necessary for the transition ahead? What does sustainability imply for technology? Politics? Community design? Social structures? Economics? Values? What does consideration of these issues imply for the substance and process of education? What does the dawning awareness of planetary limits and interrelatedness of all life have to do with the way we define, direct, and transmit knowledge? What does it have to do with living a "good life"—a life of riches that go far beyond the material kind?

Education can play a major role in determining whether a culture acts in a life-damaging or in a life-enhancing way. Learning competencies of head, heart, and hands, it is possible that students can act as active agents, as healers and nurturers transforming modernity's paradigm of destruction to a postmodern paradigm of life-centered sustainability.

REFERENCES

Berry, W. (1990). *What are people for?* San Francisco: North Point.
Bowers, C. A. (1991). Ecological literacy: Education for the twenty-first century. In R. Miller (Ed.), *New directions in education* (pp. 89–96. Brandon, VT: Holistic Education.
Bowers, C. A. (1993a). Implications of the ecological crisis for the reformation of teacher education. In R. Miller (Ed.), *The renewal of meaning in education: Responses to the cultural and ecological crisis of our times* (pp. 38–52). Brandon, VT: Holistic Education.
Bowers, C. A. (1993b). *Education, cultural myths, and the ecological crisis: Toward deep changes*. Albany, NY: State University of New York Press.
Freire, P. (1970). *Pedagogy of the oppressed*. New York: Continuum.
Gang, P. (1989). *Rethinking education: A new look at educational philosophy in the context of cultural change*. Chamblee, GA: Dagaz.
Hanh, T. (1996). *Cultivating the mind of love: The practice of looking deeply in the Mahayana Buddhist Tradition*. Berkeley, CA: Parallax.
Krall, F. (1994). *Ecotone: Wayfaring on the margins*. Albany, NY: State University of New York Press.
Lipschutz, R. (1996). *Global civil society and global environmental governance: The politics of nature from place to planet*. Albany, NY: State University of New York Press.
Macy, J. (1990). The greening of the self. In A. Badiner (Ed.), *Dharma Gaia: A harvest of essays in Buddhism and ecology* (pp. 38–52). Atlantic Highlands, NJ: Zed Books.
Orr, D. (1992). Ecological literacy: Education and the transition to a postmodern world. Albany, NY: State University of New York Press.
Orr, D. (1993). The problem of disciplines/the discipline of problems. *Holistic Education Review, 6*(3), 4–7.
Sachs, W. (1992). One world. In W. Sachs (Ed.), *The development dictionary: A guide to knowledge as power* (pp. 102–115). Atlantic Highlands, NJ: Zed Books.
Shiva, V. (1992). Resources. In W. Sachs (Ed.), *The development dictionary: A guide to knowledge as power* (pp. 206–218). Atlantic Highlands, NJ: Zed Books.

44

Situated Cognition

David Kirshner
Louisiana State University

James A. Whitson
University of Delaware

Part of what makes a book like this viable is the systemic nature of the pervasive tendency to interpret education in the terms of economic development. This is not a unitary project of sly conspirators but a consequence of a certain worldview, deeply entrenched in Western culture, and pervading all aspects of our social and intellectual life. And so too must the resistances to economization share certain connections or linkages—notwithstanding differences of purpose or method. Thus, the delights of this book are bound to include a cascade of unanticipated connections forming among the diverse topics encountered.

This chapter takes as its explicit challenge to facilitate such connections by presenting situated cognition theory against the backdrop of our culture's common sense that uncritically embraces a view of knowledge as information (a commodity to be transferred or bartered), learning as accumulating knowledge, and thinking as the transformation or processing of information.

In this view, education is not just being interpreted as metaphorically comparable to market economics; it is being viewed (and, increasingly, managed) as just another instance of market economics—with knowledge, learning, and thinking taken, respectively, as examples of marketable commodities, their acquisition, and their value-added processing (Lave, 1991). In keeping with this view, efforts to reform or improve education increasingly take the form of market-style management, which by the very nature of its accounting system, is incapable of accounting for what's lost when education is reduced to the production of commodified market values.

A good illustration of this commodification of knowledge comes from the recent history of mathematics education.[1] A decade or two ago, the National Council of Teachers of Mathematics (NCTM, 1980) produced an influential document recommending that "problem solving be the focus of school mathematics" (p. 1). In large part, the problem-solving focus was stimulated by the work of the mathematician George Polya (1957) describing the heuristics that accomplished mathematical problem solvers use to approach nontrivial problems. What was so powerful about Polya's exposition was his understanding of heuristics as methods in motion. He took great pains to describe the covert, subliminal role that a teacher must play, recommending certain questions to the student as useful heuristic questions to ask oneself *in the context of an ongoing problem-solving process*. The student learns, not from didactic instruction but from acculturation to the teacher's mathematical ways of being. Textbooks are designed to systematically instruct Polya's heuristic methods, using problems specially contrived to illustrate each one (Stanic & Kilpatrick, 1988). In effect, heuristics were subverted from problem-solving process into curricular commodity.

The discomfort of the textbook authors with process goals for education is symptomatic of the commodified view of knowledge: Being able to perform means having the specified units of knowledge that underlie the performance. Thus, "know-how" can be packaged and delivered in curricular modules. The alternative is to recognize that activities and know-how are cultural products, built up not from objective facts or instructions but from ongoing patterns of social interaction. Becoming competent in a domain is a matter of acculturating to ways of doing, valuing, interacting, and thinking, not just acquiring and following decontextualized instructions.

For the most part, the psychological sciences support the textbook author's impulse to reduce knowledge and know-how to discrete decontextualized units. Information-processing psychology, which now

---

[1]Commodification is used by Marx in *Das Kapital* to signify the process in capitalist economies whereby producers are shorn from personal associations with the goods and services they produce, which then have exchange value but not use value. In a similar way, we argue that schooling conceived in economic terms tends to disassociate students from their personal use of knowledge, reducing it to a commodity to barter for grades and other social capital.

dominates in educational theorizing, views the mind according to the model of the serial digital computer. Indeed, computers do solve problems in much the way that the textbook authors presumed students do: Symbolically encode problem situations, then manipulate the symbolic terms to arrive at a desired goal state. Heuristics are a procedural tool for selecting promising routes through the problem space (Newell & Simon, 1972).

So deeply entrenched is this point of view that our introspections about our own thinking are likely to conform to it. Sequential planning, rehearsing, and executing of actions are highly valued cognitive activities in our culture. Indeed, it was the intellectual legacy of the great mathematician and philosopher René Descartes (1596–1650) to position such processes as the basis for all secure knowledge. In his famous *Meditations on First Philosophy*, Descartes (1979/1641) sought systematically to eliminate every vestige of uncertain knowledge from the foundations of his philosophy. What remained as unshakable was the introspective self reference of introspection itself: "I think, therefore I am."

It is a powerful irony of conscious rational thought that it is blind to all other forms of cognitive engagement, and so can believe itself alone in the mental landscape. Harré's (1984) social theory offers a refreshing alternative account of rationality as justification of actions—a social function—rather than as the cognitive basis of actions. In situated cognition theory, action is born of *activity*, understood as culturally organized engagements that persist and evolve over time.

In Kirshner and Whitson (1997), we identified two trajectories of situated cognition research. The first comes form a tradition of critical anthropology (e.g., Lave, 1988) in which cognition is studied in everyday contexts of activity. Actually getting out and observing the enmeshment of cognition and context in everyday practices like shopping, cooking, and working provides a base from which alternative conceptions of cognition can be derived.

One area of anthropological investigation that has been particularly suggestive for education is apprenticeship learning (Lave & Wenger, 1991). In apprenticeships, the social foundations of learning are apparent. The apprentice learns from the master craftsperson and from other apprentices, not in a didactic exchange of information but in the context of an ongoing production of goods and services. The setting for the apprenticeship is not a neutral collection of physical artifacts to be mastered analytically but a repository of valued, felt, and lived resources within which patterns of activity have evolved and continue to coevolve. Furthermore, development is not just cognitive, but transformative of personal identity. Experts aren't just knowledgeable novices, they also are more central social actors of the community of practice into which the novice gradually is drawn (Lave & Wenger, 1991).

When structured effectively, apprenticeships seem not to result in the inert knowledge, negative self-images, and high failure rates characteristic of schooling (Lave, 1991). This observation inspired Brown, Collins, and Duguid (1989) to introduce *cognitive apprenticeship* in an effort to apply part of what is effective in apprenticeship learning to the classroom. Cognitive apprenticeship positions the teacher as a coparticipant in the students' learning rather than as a dispenser of knowledge. In this new role, the teacher is concerned with *modelling* skillful performance, *coaching* students as they attempt to assume a more central role in the activity, and then *fading* from the scene as the student moves toward independent functioning (Collins, Brown, & Newman, 1989). (See Anderson, Reder, & Simon, 1996, for an information processing critique and Greeno, 1997, for a rebuttal.)

These ideas from the anthropological tradition are consistent with *sociocultural theory*, the second approach that situated cognitivists have relied on. Based on the work of the Soviet psychologist Lev Vygotsky, his colleagues, and students, sociocultural theory is fundamentally concerned with the educational processes of internalization, or "appropriation" (Leont'ev, 1981). Appropriation is like Piaget's biological notion of assimilation, but it recognizes the essential role of the social milieu (Newman, Griffin, & Cole, 1989):

> For Leont'ev, the objects in the child's world have a social history and functions that are not discovered through the child's unaided explorations. The function of a hammer, for example, is not understood by exploring the hammer itself (although the child may discover some facts about weight and balance). The child's appropriation of culturally devised "tools" comes about through involvement in culturally organized activities in which the tool plays a role. (pp. 62–63)

From the sociocultural perspective, learning takes place in the zone of *proximal development* (ZPD)

> which is an interactive system within which people work on a problem which at least one of them could not, alone, work on effectively. Cognitive change takes place within this zone, where the zone is considered both in terms of an individual's developmental history and in terms of the support structure created by the other people and cultural tools in the setting. (p. 61)

The desire to account for cognition in terms that are both social and individual is central to situated cognition theory, distinguishing it from social psychology. It also is the source of greatest challenge for situated cognitionists. It seems that one can develop a coherent individualist account or a coherent social account of learning; but developing a truly integrative, dialectical union must be more than just a juxtaposition of the two theories. As Lave (1988) put it, dialectical relation is more than a declaration of reciprocal effects of two terms upon one another … "A dialectical relation exists when its component elements are created, are brought into being, only in conjunction with one another" (p. 146).

Kirshner and Whitson (1997) identified limitations in the anthropological and sociocultural approaches to situated cognition theory with respect to a true dialectical integration of individual and social perspectives. Both approaches tend to reify the social aspects of cognition, making the autonomy of the individual more difficult to apprehend. In educational terms, this means that situated cognition theories have been better able to account for cognition within a closed community of practice (say the classroom) than for cognitive continuity across diverse practices.

Lave (1988) gave a compelling critique of the psychological investigation of *transfer of training*, which is the usual way in which the problem of cognitive continuity is framed. Through the past century, psychologists have been struggling with how learning in one context can be transferred to applications within another. Current theories point to abstraction as the most powerful vehicle for transfer: If knowledge can be sufficiently decontextualized, it can be lifted out of its domain of learning to be applied in diverse settings. This rationale serves as the usual justification for schools, understood as sites for the development of decontextualized knowledge (Simon, 1980). Lave's (1988) contribution was to show that psychologists have been far less successful in finding evidence for transfer than they like to tell themselves: People just don't seem to transfer knowledge as often or as successfully as transfer theories predict.

But retreating from problems of continuity across contexts to studies of unitary contexts seems an inadequate strategy. We believe that situated cognition theory needs to take on a fundamental reconceptualization of humans as, at once, both individual and social beings: "No theoretical reconfiguration of the social world or of social practices can compensate for an individual cast in the dualist tradition [of Descartes]. This reformulation probes the physiological, psychoanalytic, and semiotic constitution of persons" (Kirshner & Whitson, 1997).

A variety of theoretical tools are being brought to bear in reconceiving the individual in terms that resist Cartesian dualism. St. Julien (1997) focuses on the neurological substrate of cognition. He notes that the metaphor of a serial processor breaks down when one considers how the brain actually is wired. Cognition is massively parallel, not serial. Computers excel at serial-reasoning tasks such as mathematical calculation, which humans are relatively poor at; but they have tremendous difficulty with the simplest human abilities to identify letters in different fonts, or one's mother from different angles. The serial digital computer tries to perform such feats by calculating what Mom would look like from different angles. But the brain seems not to operate like that. Rather, cognition is realized as patterns of neural activation that flow through the synapses. A new branch of psychology called *connectionism* (see Salomon, 1993) posits pattern matching, not calculation, to be the fundamental cognitive activity. St. Julien argued that our situated activities in the world serve to establish patterns, not rules, that form the basis of our cognitive competencies.

Walkerdine (1990, 1997) brings the tools of psychoanalysis and semiotics (Lacan, 1977) together with Foucault's social theory to understanding the social production of subjectivities ("woman," "the child," "the good student," etc.). For Walkerdine (1990), subjectivities evolve in discursive practices operating in schools and other social institutions. More specifically, they evolve in the conflicting spaces between discursive practices—for instance, a female child playing house positions herself as mother with relative power over other participants, who consequently opt for other discursive practices; or young boys introduce a sexist discourse from home in opposition to their female teacher's preference for a more schoolish discourse. Such cognitive functions as mathematical thinking are analyzed semiotically as a chaining of signifiers, in which illusions of omnipotence accompany discursive repositioning. In Walkerdine's work, we begin to see an account of the interrelatedness of contexts not through transfer but through the intersection of discursive practices as realized in semiosis.

We could continue with further examples, but the central points of this chapter already are touched on. The understanding of knowledge and know-how as commodities that can be delivered through curriculum is central to the modern organization of schooling. These understandings are part of our culture's common sense about the nature of mind and being, deeply rooted in the philosophical tradition. Situated cognition theory struggles against this commodification of knowledge by (re)establishing life experience and mind as dialectically related. In the most current scholarship, this points toward a far reaching and exciting reformulation of the individual as social.

REFERENCES

Anderson, J. R., Reder, L. M., & Simon, H. A. (1996). Situated learning and education. *Educational Researcher, 25*(4), 5–11.

Brown, J. S., Collins, A., & Duguid, P. (1989). Situated cognition and the culture of learning. *Educational Researcher, 18* (1), 32–42.

Descartes, R. (1979). *Meditations on first philosophy in which the existence of God and the distinction of the soul from the body are demonstrated* (D. A. Cress, Trans.). Indianapolis, IN: Hackett. (Original work published 1641)

Greeno, J. G. (1997). On claims that answer the wrong question. *Educational Researcher, 26*(1), 5–17.

Harré, R. (1984). *Personal being: A theory for individual psychology*. Cambridge, MA: Harvard University Press.

Kirshner, D., & Whitson, J. (1997). *Editors' Introduction*. In D. Kirshner & J. Whitson (Eds.), *Situated cognition: Social, semiotic, and psychological perspectives*. Mahwah, NJ: Lawrence Erlbaum Associates.

Lacan, J. (1977). *Ecrits: A selection*. London: Tavistock.

Lave, J. (1988). *Cognition in practice*. Cambridge, UK: Cambridge University Press.

Lave, J. (1991). Situated learning in communities of practice. In L. B. Resnick, J. M. Levine, & S. D. Teasley (Eds.), *Perspectives on socially shared cognition* (pp. 63–82), Washington, DC: American Psychological Association.

Lave, J., & Wenger, E. (1981). *Situated learning: Legitimate peripheral participation*. Cambridge, England: Cambridge University Press.

Leont'ev, A. N. (1981). *Problems in the development of mind*. Moscow: Progress.

NCTM. (1980). *An agenda for action: Recommendations for school mathematics for the 1980s*. Preston, VA: National Council of Teachers of Mathematics.

Newell, A., & Simon, H. A. (1972). *Human problam solving*. Englewood Cliffs, NJ: Prentice-Hall.

Newman, D., Griffin, P., & Cole, M. (1989). *The construction zone*. Cambridge, UK: Cambridge University Press.

Polya, G. (1957). *How to solve it: A new aspect of mathematical method*. Princeton, NJ: Princeton University Press.

Salomon, G. (Ed.). (1993). *Distributed cognitions: Psychological and educational considerations*. Cambridge, England: Cambridge University Press.

St. Julien, J. (1997). Explaining learning: The research trajectory of situated cognition and the implications of connectionism. In D. Kirshner & J. Whitson (Eds.), *Situated cognition: Social, semiotic, and psychological perspectives*. Mahwah, NJ: Lawrence Erlbaum Associates.

Stanic, G. M. A., & Kilpatrick, J. (1988). Historical perspectives on problem solving in the mathematics curriculum. In R. I. Charles & E. A. Silver (Eds.), *The teaching and assessing of mathematical problem solving* (pp. 1–22). Hillsdale, NJ: Lawrence Erlbaum Associates.

Walkerdine, V. (1990). *Schoolgirl fictions*. London: Verso.

Walkerdine, V. (1997). Redefining the subject in situated cognition theory. In D. Kirshner & J. Whitson (Eds.), *Situated cognition: Social, semiotic, and psychological perspectives*. Mahwah, NJ: Lawrence Erlbaum Associates.

45

Individualization

Leslie A. Sassone
Northern Illinois University

The notion that individualization should be a primary educational goal is distinctively modern and romantic. Jean-Jacques Rousseau's *Emile*, the first work in educational philosophy that makes individualization an educational aim, is founded on the distinction between two forms of self-love—*amour propre* and *amor de soi*. *Amour propre* is based on comparative judgments of inferiority and superiority and is a fully socialized concept, whereas *amour de soi* is a primary love of one's own life and capacities and a will to express those capacities. Rousseau's (1974) pedagogy in *Emile* attempts to allow an individual to emerge who has not been trained to base his self-estimation on prevailing social standards, but instead on his own personal development. *Amour de soi* is the kernel of individualization.

Through the 19th century, educators and educational theorists associated with romanticism developed and applied Rousseau's paradigm. Henri Pestalozzi adapted the emphasis on individualized development to the school setting. Max Stirner radicalized *amour de soi* into a pedagogy based on individual expressivity. The second half of the 19th century and the early decades of the 20th would later bring the educational implications of individualization of Friedrich Nietzsche and John Dewey to their modern(ist) fruition.

In Nietzsche's (1967) hands, individualization is a complex term. It refers to a being in-and-for-oneself, who with reflective awareness realizes his or her particular virtues that paradoxically, often come to be only from departing from what the self already is. Nietzsche's concept of individualization (and that itself may be a paradoxical expression) can be understood by putting it in terms of the figures of Dionysus and Apollo. The Dionysian tendency breaks through limits and runs to excess over any form, whereas the Apollonian tendency stresses the intensification of life within the limits of specific forms. Individualization for Nietzsche is neither wholly Dionysian nor wholly Apollonian but is a never ceasing, unachievable balance between those two tendencies.

Individualization in Nietzsche's writing is the other side of the coin from his notion of self-overcoming. In the language of Dewey (1938), it is the provisional and always-changing consummation of moments of self-overcoming in which "individuals" break with their pasts and become other to themselves, yet still retain some continuity with the past.

Throughout its usages in romantic educational discourse, individualization refers to the particularity of each person and to a life process that, although according to most of its adherents contains rational components, is on the whole nonrational. Neither the particular individual nor the life process can, in the romantic discourse of individualization, be reduced to any concept.

The fact that the background assumptions of individualization emphasize the nonrationality of being does not mean that pedagogical practices are antithetical to its achievement. Both Nietzsche and Dewey are clear that the development of the individual self to the point of self-direction and self-enjoyment takes place within a social setting and can be encouraged by discursive practices. For Dewey, the scientific method, understood as a general and flexible logic of inquiry, is the basic means to achieving individuality in a democratic setting. That method can be taught, according to Dewey, in the context of a democratic schooling. Nietzsche, who was far more dubious than Dewey about the possibilities for educational reconstruction, also respectfully emphasizes that undertaking disciplines that strengthen the self by enhancing vital capacities is an essential means to individualization. For Nietzsche, education is an unknowing experiment that could, with benefit, become more reflexive. Discipline is the Apollonian moment of individualization, the provision of form in which the individual's life can become more refined, intense, and configured.

Romantic educational theorists, though they recommend individualizing disciplines, usually stand against the kinds of disciplines that characterize modern educational institutions, which they believe are repressive rather than liberatory of individuality. To get at that distinction the contemporary notion of disciplinization is useful. For Michel Foucault (1988), contemporary organizations exert control over individuals through practices of disciplinization that produce docile bodies rather than self-directing and self-enjoying individuals. Although Foucault distances himself from romanticism, he is a partisan of an attenuated form of individualization that subverts organizational controls through strategies of shifting identity. In his later writings, he advocated practices of self-care as disciplines that might produce states of being akin to those promoted by Dewey and Nietzsche. However, Foucault, like most contemporary critical theorists, was far more contained about the promise of individualization in a society of disciplinizing organizations than was Dewey or even Nietzsche, both of whom wrote before the tendency toward disciplinization become hegemonic.

Since the fall of the Soviet Union, disciplinization, which is the antithesis of individualization, has been carried out in the context of global capitalism and, therefore, has taken on a predominately economistic cast. It is appropriate to speak of a deindividualizing emphasis in contemporary education that goes beyond the familiar modern forms by which individuality is suppressed. Under hegemonic capitalism, education becomes thoroughly economistic, subordinating every other aim that characterized modern education to mobilizing functionaries to take part in global economic competition.

Whereas in the period of consumer capitalism, which was termed "late capitalism" by many critical theorists, debased forms of individuality centered on consumer lifestyles (the consumption of "culture") were permitted or even encouraged; under a pan-capitalism (Kroker & Weinstein, 1994) that plays out in conditions of a global competition and the fiscal crisis of the state, education is totally subordinated to interpellating producers. Even more than in immediately preceding decades, in the 1990s Louis Althusser's (1986) notion that capitalism is productionism—a system that produces *both* producers and consumers through interpellation—is an appropriate descriptor.

The deindividualizing economistic drive of educational institutions under pan-capitalism manifests itself ubiquitously. The justification of every disciplinizing measure is invariably its contribution to increased competitiveness. In the United States, the obsession with national standards; moves to abolish tenure and diminish the power of teacher's unions; school uniforms; aggressive drug enforcement; student courts; the cutting back on "peripheral" programs like arts, music, and physical education; the intrusion of corporations into the schools; the vogue of privatizing education through choice, charter schools, and religious schools all converge on disciplinization to bring students up to levels of performance that will make them docile bodies in the global capitalist system.

In the current rhetorical and policy environment, the last vestiges of educational progressivism, which at least paid lip service to individuality as a goal of education, are disappearing. In the place of progressivism has not come its traditional rival, essentialism, but adaptation to the requirements of technological systems that are deployed, for the most part, by capitalist enterprises.

Within an environment of increasing disciplinization, prospects for the actualization of educational practices that foster individualization are dim. It is a long way from Rousseau's confident proclamation of *amour de soi* to Foucault's tentative embrace of self-care, and the change can be marked by the growing dominance of organizational technologies in the constitution of life under capitalism.

The contemporary practice of individualizing education is a matter of interstitial resistance, of opening up transient spaces for experimentation with self-direction and self-enjoyment within institutions that are mainly bent on repressing their possibility. Radical educational reformers of the post-World War II period have grasped the timeliness of resistance in suggestive phrases such as Neil Postman's "loving technological resistance fighting," Jonathan Kozol's "informed irreverence" and "disobedience instruction" to educate "intellectual guerrillas," and Ivan Illich's "disciplined dissidence." Continuing the romantic tradition of individualization, Illich (1970) poses the possibility of personal growth "which cannot be measured against any rod, or any curriculum, not compared to someone else's achievement" (p. 57). The ideals of Rousseau are still alive, but they take temporary root in the shadows of the techno-corporate structure.

REFERENCES

Althusser, L. (1986). Ideology and ideological state apparatuses. In *Lenin and philosophy* (Ben Brewster, Trans.). New York: Monthly Review Press.

Dewey, J. (1938). *Experience and education*. New York: Collier Books.

Illich, I. (1970). *Deschooling society*. New York: Harper.

Foucault, M. (1988). The ethic of care for the self as a practice of freedom. In J. Bernauer & D. Rasmussen (Eds.), *The final Foucault* (pp. 1–20). Cambridge, MA: MIT Press. (J. D. Gauther, Trans.)

Nietzsche, F. (1967). The birth of tragedy. In *The birth of tragedy/The case of Wagner* (W. Kauffman, Trans.). New York: Vintage.

Kroker, A., & Weinstein, M. A. (1994). *Data trash*. New York: St. Martin's.

Rousseau, J. J. (1974). *Emile* (Barbara Foxley, Trans.). Rutland, VT: Everyman's Library.

46

Dialogue

Nicholas C. Burbules
University of Illinois at Urbana-Champaign

Dialogue is not just another term for talk. In the Western tradition of educational thought, dialogue has served as a prescriptive ideal pointing to a particular type of communicative interaction thought to have special, even unique, educational potential. We see one account of dialogue in the work of Plato, another in the work of Paulo Freire. These two accounts differ in many respects—their views of knowledge, of the aims of education, and certainly of the merits of democracy: Freire is a radical democrat, Plato extremely suspicious of democracy. But they share the idea that there is something intrinsic to the dialogical process, the process of questioning, doubting, reexamining assumptions, clarifying meanings, and so forth that joins partners in a teaching–learning relation in which, together, they can unlearn the falsehoods they might be burdened with and reconstruct a truer, fuller understanding of their worlds. For both Plato and Freire, this relation has emancipatory potential.

Elsewhere, I have suggested that this dialogical relation can take at least four distinct forms (Burbules, 1993). These forms depend on certain assumptions about (1) the nature of the investigation at hand (whether discussion should *converge* on a single answer, solution, or compromise, or *diverge* into a range of possibilities and points of view, all potentially of value) and (2) the nature of the relation among the dialogue's participants (whether *critical* discussion is thought likely to cull unacceptable alternatives from consideration through skeptical questions, or whether a more *inclusive* dialogue is favored, as a way of drawing in participants who might otherwise be alienated or intimidated by a more aggressive mode of interaction). These two pairs yield four combinations, which I called *dialogue as conversation*, an inclusive and divergent process of exploring interpersonal understanding; *dialogue as inquiry*, an inclusive and convergent process of co-investigating a problem in order to find an answer, solution, or compromise; *dialogue as instruction*, a critical and convergent process of drawing one or more participants, through a sequence of leading questions, to a conclusion that another participant (teacher) already has in mind; and *dialogue as debate*, a critical and divergent process in which agreement is not an expected aim but in which the vigorous confrontation of alternative views is thought to inform all participants. These are quite different forms of communicative interaction.

Now, each of these kinds of dialogue can have a distinct educational benefit, I believe, and each can take forms that are aimless and educationally counterproductive. A good teacher, such as a Socrates or a Freire, will learn how to use any of these in appropriate moments, with different students or different subject matters. In short, dialogue is not just one type of communicative relation but a family of related kinds. Thinking about dialogue in this way alerts us to the question of which kinds are suitable to different learning circumstances; and, most important for my purposes here, it alerts us to an important issue—the very different types of students one encounters in teaching–learning situations and the very different forms of verbal interaction with which they are likely to be at ease and to which they are likely to respond.

One of the chief features of the present world is an increased awareness of such *difference*—difference along a spectrum of dimensions, including sex, race, class, ethnicity, gender, nationality, religion, sexual orientation, and so on (see Burbules, 1997). Theorists from feminist, poststructuralist, queer, and postcolonial perspectives have all challenged the presumptions of commonality and unity underlying modern social and political arrangements, including educational arrangements, even in ostensibly pluralist democracies. New social movements organized around previously marginalized or publicly invisible aspects of identity and group solidarity—such as gay, lesbian, and bisexual movements—have directly challenged prevailing notions about what is "normal" and what is "deviant," and have made society more aware of the presumptions about normalcy and conformity that are hidden in arrangements society has fallen into the habit of regarding as universal or natural. New conditions in an increasingly globalized world—including rapid travel, international media, transnational capitalism, the rise of global organizations and institutions that work beyond the confines of particular nation–states, and worldwide communication and information sharing via the Internet—all have brought people from very different cultural contexts into closer real (or virtual) proximity, in which they have increasingly had to confront the difficulties of establishing consensus, or even just mutual understanding, across their differences. Such conditions have reinforced the more theoretical analyses of "difference" and have pushed the issue of difference beyond merely "tolerance for diversity."

As Homi Bhabha (1995) has argued, "difference" is not the same thing as "diversity." Difference represents a more profound challenge to the very categories and principles with which modern societies operate. Difference reveals continuities and blurred boundaries where tradition assumes sharp distinctions; questions the arbitrariness of many demarcations that have been taken as natural or given; alerts society to hybrids and creoles, internally complex and conflicted identities, where society prefers easily classifiable instantiations of general types; inverts the valuation of mainstream and marginalized norms or practices; and challenges the dynamics of power that invest certain standards with a significance that is more about the preservation of privilege for certain groups than the freeing up of human freedom and possibility. Diversity suggests the limits of tolerance and inclusion *within* a set of norms that are largely taken for granted; difference poses a critical challenge to those norms themselves and the ways in which they may be *inherently* exclusionary.

The account of dialogue posed earlier is not protected from such challenges. As Elizabeth Ellsworth (1989) and others have argued, the prescriptive ideal of dialogue often masks factors that are in fact exclusionary or silencing for many prospective participants. When the ideal of dialogue assumes a singular homogeneous model of communication, it frequently can have a contradictory effect: constraining communicative possibilities rather than opening them up. I believe that this objection can be met, in part, by pointing out the multiplicity of forms dialogue can take, not all of which are governed by the same standards of practice, and some of which, as I said, will be more accommodating of certain individuals and groups than of others. But this objection also makes us consider the contexts and circumstances under which dialogue operates: the prejudices, power relations, or histories of harm that close people out of a dialogue or leave them silent within it. Yet those objections, it must be noted, are not a challenge to the ideal of dialogue but a challenge to the conditions that make it difficult, threatening, or impossible; and that challenge, in fact, implicitly endorses the value of dialogue, since it is criticizing the factors that inhibit it.

None of this is meant to deny that there are contexts in which dialogue, in any of its senses, is neither a possible nor an entirely desirable option in social or political discourse. Dewey, in one way, and Habermas, in another, may exaggerate the possibilities of orienting all public discourse around such a dialogical model. Plato and Freire, similarly, may exaggerate the possibilities of orienting all educational discourse in the same way. But their aspirations to do so are far from empty or simply oblivious to the dynamics of unequal power and of ideology.

For democratic theorists, such as Dewey and Habermas, the desire to balance a tolerance for multiple perspectives within an imperative for fostering reasoned public deliberation means seeking a mode of discourse that is flexible enough to accommodate diverse voices, but self-regulating enough that threats to the fabric of public deliberation (such as lying) can be rejected as out of bounds. Dialogue, as a dynamic that encourages participation and reciprocity, holds promise as such a mode of discourse, since it seems to maximize the opportunities for questioning and critically reexamining alternative points of view, so that agreement—when it can be achieved—is based on a mutually respectful deliberative process, not on monolingual pronouncements that cannot be questioned. This mode of discourse is a direct assault on certain kinds of power and ideologies, at least.

Similarly, for Plato and Freire, education through dialogue seeks to allow for the broadest possible exploration of belief. This mode of education is emancipatory, they would say, both because it encourages the critical reexamination of taken-for-granted assumptions, mistaken ideas, or illusory ideologies and because it highlights the collective development of, and responsibility for, new beliefs and understandings. Both contrast dialogue with more didactic or monological modes of teaching, which they reject on the basis of both pedagogical efficacy and concerns about the abuses of power to which such forms of authority are subject.

Therefore, it is far from trivial to acknowledge the profound *critique of power and ideology* essential to the accounts of dialogue proposed by these theorists. A respect for diversity, a desire for inclusion within a democratic conversation, and an ideal built on a mutually respectful, reciprocal, open-ended form of pedagogical communication remain well beyond the attainments of modern society, and before one hastens to abandon such ideals as compromised, outmoded, or superseded by new theory, one ought to pause and reflect seriously on how much better off society would be if we succeeded at least that far.

As I mentioned before, there is a reflexive sense in which radical critiques of dialogue are sometimes patently self-undermining, serving more to buttress the value of dialogue than to challenge it. Critiques that point out barriers to dialogue or conditions that make it practically unattainable in present circumstances are actually endorsements of dialogue, in some sense, as an ideal. Even further, such attempts to argue for or against certain norms, perhaps *especially* educational norms, do expect to be heard, taken seriously, and responded to—but toward what end, if a person truly did not believe in dialogue? Many critiques of dialogue are therefore caught up in what Karl-Otto Apel calls a "performative contradiction."

Having said that, however, I think there is something else, deeper and more interesting, at stake here. Dialogue, where it exists, can only be enacted by real people, with their actual characteristics, under the specific circumstances in which they come together. What functions do ideals such as dialogue have, in these situations? They can have a regulatory function, helping to adjudicate disagreements or misunderstandings, *when* people actually share them and can talk about them together. For example, given my discussion of four types of dialogue, previously, it may sometimes happen that some participants think they are having one kind of dialogue—a debate, perhaps—when others want and expect a different kind of dialogue—a more open-ended conversation. Pointing out these different expectations may help to illuminate the issues at stake; but it will not alter the situation that participants want or feel comfortable with different forms of interaction, nor will it, alone, make them capable of engaging in alternative forms effectively. Similarly, in a political context, different groups or individuals may want to participate in reasoned public deliberation about their conflicting interests, but such dialogues will not change the fact of conflicting interests. And here is the point: Shifting the focus away from an examination of such conflicts, where they come from, and who they benefit or harm toward a proclamation of dialogue as a panacea for conflicts and misunderstandings can have the effect of keeping those conflicts unexamined and in place, rather than questioning them. Prescriptive ideals, such as dialogue, may set admirable goals; but the function of such ideals, in social contexts, may be paradoxically to engender resentment and resistance among those who do not see their issues as addressed by such ideals.

Furthermore, dialogue, even if it is "successful," may not succeed in providing agreement or understanding across differences—one kind of "success" may be in *heightening* an awareness of differences and an appreciation of how difficult it can be to bridge them without other changes, which are beyond the scope of dialogue, having more to do with sacrifices of power and privilege that people may be unwilling or unable to make. This point is fairly clear, I hope, in the context of pluralist democracies, but it bears upon educational discourses as well, because different systems of belief, inquiry, and communication are intrinsically wrapped up with larger social and cultural dynamics, as the recent "Ebonics" debate made excruciatingly clear.

As a result, we need to go beyond simple arguments about whether dialogue is a "good thing" or not. We need to be reflective about what dialogue can and cannot be expected to accomplish, and we need to be sensitive to when a focus on dialogue as a prescriptive ideal can become a distraction away from a more encompassing, critical understanding of *when* and *how* dialogue can be expected to thrive. There are contexts in which the conditions we try to create to promote dialogue may actually have the effect of inhibiting it for some prospective participants. For example, taking turns speaking in a group may be a practice intended to encourage more participation, but it may not be experienced that way—people may feel pressured, and hence *less* willing to speak up; or they may feel that this procedure frustrates the easy sort of to-and-fro among conversants they feel most comfortable with. This "tragic" perspective, in which the very efforts we make to broaden a conversation actually impede it, is rarely acknowledged, and is especially pointed in contexts of *difference*, where seemingly neutral or objective procedural conditions come to be seen as actually biased and exclusionary in effect.

Hence, procedural models of education, or of democratic deliberation, which place primary significance on the means and methods of pursuing consensus, can only be partially helpful as we try to imagine the personal characteristics and capabilities that enable participants to engage in these procedures effectively and the social arrangements that foster the development and exercise of those capabilities, or inhibit them. Purely procedural norms, such as dialogue, are empty without an examination of the conditions that make them practicable. Freire, for example, places great emphasis on the conditions of "intransitive consciousness" and self-contempt that can demoralize prospective participants to critical dialogue; elements which require interventions that are not themselves necessarily "dialogical" in nature. There is a limit to what forms of pedagogy alone can provide (particularly in terms of creating the conditions that make those forms of pedagogy practicable and meaningful). So it is ironic to reflect on the shift in educational thought that has placed a focus on issues of pedagogy per se as the site of radical educational practice. As Jennifer Gore (in press) has argued, for both critical pedagogy and feminist pedagogy authors, it is sometimes assumed that there is something *intrinsic* about certain pedagogical methods, such as dialogue, that gives them progressive or emancipatory efficacy.

Democratic societies and their educational institutions aspire to create contexts that make dialogue a real possibility. But often, I have argued, the very attempt to create such conditions has paradoxical, counterproductive effects. Seeking to create such contexts while having people who are unwilling or unable to participate, or who are discouraged from doing so, is a thin achievement. A good argument can be made that modern democracies tend to *limit* dialogue by setting explicit or implicit conditions for participation that exclude broad categories of prospective participants. Others argue that democratic practices can *create* and *foster* the capacity for dialogue and democratic deliberation. Yet, ironically, the condition of democracy that allows majorities to ignore or override the will of minority or marginalized groups raises the question again of whether the exercise of procedural norms, especially but not only those pertaining to dialogue and public deliberation, can in fact "bootstrap" the capacities to engage in them effectively. Drawing those at greater risk of vulnerability into certain topics of discussions, or certain types of discussion, is not always a way of *actually* including them.

Hence I have two concerns about the role dialogue has played in educational and democratic theory: One is its *proceduralism*, which elevates issues of pedagogy over an examination of the broader factors that do or do not make dialogue possible; the other is its *prescriptivism*, which despite good intents at accommodating diversity may be actually counterproductive in contexts of difference.

A major limitation in fostering dialogue is a population that cannot acknowledge difference, or that is threatened by it, or that does not see the possibility of difference as an occasion for rethinking its own presuppositions. This becomes a constraint on the possibilities of dialogue and a major factor discouraging or dismissing certain prospective participants from even entering into it. Addressing this issue is a central problem, a central *educational* problem, for democracies today.

REFERENCES

Bhabha, H. K. (1995). Cultural diversity and cultural difference. In B. Ashcroft, G. Griffiths, & H. Tiffin (Eds.), *The post-colonial studies reader* (pp. 206–209). New York: Routledge, Chapman & Hall.

Burbules, N. C. (1993). *Dialogue in teaching: Theory and practice*. New York: Teachers College Press.

Burbules, N. C. (1997). A grammar of difference: Some ways of rethinking difference and diversity as educational topics. *Australian Education Researcher*, 24,1, 97–116.

Ellsworth, E. (1989). Why doesn't this feel empowering? Working through the repressive myths of critical pedagogy. *Harvard Educational Review*, 59, 291–324.

Gore, J. (in press). On the limit to empowerment through critical and feminist pedagogies. In D. Corlson and M. Apple (Eds.), *Critical theory in unsettling times*. Minneapolis: Universityof Minnesota Press.

47

Public Franchise

Jeffrey Williams
University of Missouri

A couple of years ago, at the faculty convocation inaugurating the school year, the dean of arts and sciences at the public university where I then taught urged us to go thence and seek grants, to "market the college to alumni and friends of the university," and to forge "partnerships" with local business (e.g., Glaxo/Wellcome, which very profitably manufactures AZT in Greenville, and the like). While I usually slouch in the back and whisper to my friends—such events bring out my adolescent defiance, like misbehaving in church—I sat up and took notice. The year before the theme had been "excellence," in scholarship and teaching, the kind of predictable if fatuous motivational rhetoric one expects at such events, particularly since university administrators have started going to management seminars. But this was different and announced a more concrete imperative. The dean had previously been an enthusiastic defender of the humanities and the values of traditional scholarship, extolling us to publish more to boost our "bibliographies" and hence our "national reputation"—his cheerleading toward the vague vista of "excellence" fit consistently with this—whereas now he seemed to be advising us to get out of our library carrels and start hawking our wares, trading vita lines for a more tangible bottomline, and afterward he instituted a policy that we now receive publication credit on our yearly evaluations for grants submitted, four grants equaling an article.

The dean's speech prompted one of my colleagues to suggest that rather than our being the indirect and occasional conduits of grants and donations we streamline the process and simply stop, say, every half hour in class and give a 1 minute pitch for the local McDonald's, or Wendy's, or Hardee's, or Burger King, which line the perimeter of campus. We proceeded to draw out the all-too-viable possibilities for this new form of academic fundraising, but fortunately my friend has no aspirations to be in administration. Although this might seem farfetched, it's not entirely a joke, as witnessed by the advent of Channel One in many public high schools, including those in Greenville, NC, that daily feeds students with 10 minutes of Entertainment Tonight-style news mixed with 5 minutes of commercials for Coke, corn chips, and Clearasil (see Kleinfeld, 1991).

Though this is admittedly anecdotal, I think it typifies the looming trend in university funding from being publicly funded to a new and unabashed imperative to be corporate sponsored. I could provide hard evidence for this—for instance, drastic and disproportionate cuts in the University of California and SUNY systems and the ensuing pressure for private funding (see Lauter, 1995)—but my interest here is its rise and trenchance as a cultural dominant, as an accepted and appropriate model by which universities should operate to bring them "into the twenty-first century" (for a college dean's rationale for the benefits of public–private partnerships in funding, see Breneman, 1997). And I think that the shift in this dominant prescription for public education is succinctly represented by the concept of "franchise" and its two senses: its historically celebrated sense as attaining a vote and in general a purchase in the public sphere and its more contemporary colloquial sense as a licensed storefront for name-brand corporations. Universities are now being conscripted as the latter kind of franchise, directly as training grounds for the corporate workforce (even the less "practical" humanities, as Evan Watkins, 1996 shows)—in fact, many corporations have been getting into the education business for themselves (see Bartolovich, 1995)—and as serving corporate agendas, while the traditional view of the university as offering a liberal education, presumably enfranchising citizens of the republic, not to mention more radical views, has been evacuated without much of a fight.

One can surmise the tacit expression of this new cultural dominant in two recent films, *The Nutty Professor* (Shadyac, 1996) and *Chain Reaction* (Davis, 1996). Both were, of course, relatively run-of-the-mill vehicles for their respective stars, Eddie Murphy and Keanu Reaves, and predictably popular summer releases (especially *The Nutty Professor*, hailed as Murphy's "comeback"). Without rehearsing their plots, assuming most folks have seen them, what I find striking about them, as an inveterate university watcher, is their image of and assumed rationale for university work. If you recall, in *The Nutty Professor*, Professor Klump teaches—inattentively and irresponsibly, missing classes after his transformation to Buddy Love—but his real work is his research into genetic manipulation for the sake of weight loss. In other words, not only is teaching peripheral, but his research is not for the advance of scientific knowledge per se. His professional prospect is essentially product development for a techno-miraculous diet drink, which would obviously have extraordinary market potential. That this transformation of professional prospect goes without saying in the film demonstrates how deeply the corporate–cultural norm has been naturalized in the popular imagination. We've come a long way from Mr. Chips.

Further, the portrait of the dean marks a precipitous shift in the popular image and expectation of the academy. The dean is uptight, condescending, and sneaky, alternately cajoling and bullying, parodying the stereotype of a White, male, white-collar manager and carrying on a long line of film satires of college life. However, previous portraits of deans, most famously in *Animal House*, show their job as that of a stuffed-shirt headmaster, worrying about behavior codes and keeping fraternities in check. The dean in *The Nutty Professor* has only one interest: to garner a donation from a local businessman, and his job is coded not as dealing with students but in managing—coaxingly or threateningly—faculty toward the goal of dollar signs. Though bullying, he is remarkably complacent on discovering Professor Klump has missed a class, delivering an ultimatum about his research, that his job, and in fact his life, depends on his success in procuring the grant. This characterization of the dean testifies to the blatant shift in university rationale for work that directly generates funds and synechochally represents the reconfiguration of administration as managing faculty, pressing the mandate on faculty to "produce," in common parlance. Although my dean is polished and decorous, the administrative protocol is one and the same; that *The Nutty Professor* is a satire I think especially shows the cultural assumption of these protocols, commonplace enough to be able to be satirized.

Chain Reaction, to a less concerted extent, since it follows the conventions of an action movie rather than that of an academic satire (we see Keanu Reaves speeding around on a motorcycle, dodging bullets, saving the woman, etc.), entirely evacuates a university setting for a lab, or rather reconfigures a university setting as a research and development (R&D) lab (Keanu Reaves is spared grading CHEM 101 papers), the end goal of which is to generate energy from water, again a techno-miracle with boundless market potential. The film broaches the question of the ends of research, posing the utopian prospect of free energy (from the presumably uncommodified raw material of water) and its free dispersal (the forces of evil blow up the lab a split second before the data of the experiment are released on the egalitarian Web), against its sinister control by conspiratorial forces. However, it finally effaces that utopian prospect—as the Morgan Freeman character argues, the idealistic distribution of energy would have catastrophic global effects, destabilizing current economies—and recodes the tension as one between proper management and rogue management, thus reaffirming the protocols of the market economy and its state protection and the need for pragmatic management of impractical academics who don't quite understand real-world consequences. Rather than the academic as a kind of freelance entrepreneur as in *The Nutty Professor*, *Chain Reaction* projects academic research as directly serving and tied to state interests. I would also add that Eddie Vassilitch, the Keanu Reaves character, redefines the role of students, or at least graduate students, as incorporated as apprentice labor in the new university of profitable results.

Overall, I would distinguish three dimensions to the present cultural reimagination and material reconfiguration of the university. First, there is the codification of administrators as managers, overseeing and pressuring faculty to generate revenue. As Stanley Aronowitz (1995) points out, there are two senses of academic freedom:

> We understand and generally support the right of an individual faculty member to speak and write free of legal or administrative sanction and according to the dictates of her own conscience.... But the second dimension of academic freedom, the rights of the faculty as a collectivity to retain sovereignty over the educational process, has been buried with the restructuring. Matters such as the establishment, expansion, retention, or elimination of departments and programs; the hiring and dismissal of faculty; the assignment of positions to programs and departments; and workload and class size are only a few of the crucial decisions that were traditionally addressed by faculty and have been gradually assumed by administration and boards of trustees. (p. 91)

In short, faculty have progressively been disenfranchised from having any determinate political power in the university. And, in the configuration of the corporate university, administrative jobs, rather than being service positions that fell to those tired of teaching or retired from research, have become preeminent, constituted as "winner-take-all" jobs, as it's put in the new corporate lingo, and administrations now account for a substantial portion of university budgets. In times of budget crises, you never hear of cuts in administration.

Second, the recoding of faculty not only as researchers but as research and development workers, directly to develop marketable and corporately approved products. Even in traditional terms as teachers, faculty have been placed in the position of service workers, required to process more "product," as students are now called in fiscal reports and the assessment of Full Time Equivalencies (FTEs). In this sense, faculty have been disenfranchised as independent intellectuals, taking up a direct service position to those "who pay their salaries," whether students or grantors.

The third dimension, less visibly in the films I've mentioned, is in seeing students as consumers, as shoppers at the store of education, buying a career-enhancing service. This commodification of students' interests manifests itself ideologically, in seeing the university as a necessary accreditation for entry into the professional–managerial class; but it also occurs in a different way, materially, in the wildly disproportionate rise in college costs and the ensuing restructuring of financial aid. As David Lipsky and Alexander Abrams (1994) explain, tuition rose exponentially from the 1970s, at more than twice the rate of inflation despite relatively stagnant wages, and to pay for it there has been a massive increase in programs like the GSL. About the GSL, Lipsky and Abrams note, "In 1978, after thirteen years of the program, a little more than $10 billion had been loaned to students....By the early nineties, more than 62 million student loans had been made through the federal government"—bear in mind that this doesn't include private or other forms of loans—"ten times as many as the 6 million loans in the GSL's first decade. There had been more than $100 billion borrowed," more than $15 billion a year in the nineties (p. 119).

In other words, higher education has become a substantial banking franchise, effectively indenturing students for 10 to 20 years after graduation and intractably funneling them into the corporate workforce to pay their loans. As the staid *U.S. News and World Report* observed with some shock in 1993: "Nearly 8,000 banks, savings and loans, credit unions and other lenders will make an estimated $18 billion in new federally backed student loans in fiscal year 1993" (p. 56). In this way, students have progressively become more disenfranchised, literally kept out of colleges they can't afford, and objects of usurious profit in the new pyramid scheme of the franchising of higher education.

In the face of these circumstances, it's hard not to be resigned, taking the current changes to be inevitable. But that is precisely the power of ideology, that we take these conditions as necessary and inevitable. They're not. On the level of ideology—and as intellectuals, we are ideologists, both in critiquing the complacent if not pernicious ideologies we live by and in posing new vistas of the way the world and social relations might be—I think that we have to reclaim the ground of a public rather than private interest, and to reimagine the rationale for education as serving that public interest, enfranchising citizens and bringing them into a more convivial society, rather than as simply fostering profit-driven job-training. In contrast to the extant representation of the university I've detailed, I offer the counterexample of a film like *Higher Education*, which, although schematically representing issues such as women's rights, race rights, and the profusion of identity politics, sees the university as a realm of an expressly political education—an education in citizenship, in collectivity, and in voice. We need to reclaim this prospect for education, to reimagine its role as enabling a genuinely public franchise, declaiming the corporate takeover not only of the management but of the imperatives of the university, for students and faculty alike.

We need to reassert the sense of franchise as empowering citizens, unrelentingly, to deans, to administrators, to students, and to the larger public. We need to recoup the root concept of franchise as offering, as the OED defines its, freedom, immunity, and privilege to our students—constituents not customers. And we need to make the point that corporations by definition are private, to produce profit (that is, to extract the surplus labor of the other 90 percent of us who don't own the means of production) and therefore not necessarily, if at all, in the public good. (To cite another film, *The Farmer's Daughter*, it depends on if you're receiving it or if you're paying it what you think is a living wage.) One might imagine a different form of life than the commodity, a different form of profession than grant-supplicant, a different form of education than job training, and a different form of franchise that allows people to seek an education, rather than a source of monetary profit.

REFERENCES

Aronowitz, S. (1995). Higher education: The turn of the screw. *Found Object, 6*, 89–99.

Breneman, D. W. (1997, March). The "Privatization" of public universities: A mistake or a model for the future. *Chronicle of Higher Education, 7*, B4–B5.

Davis, A. (Director). (1996). *Chain reaction* [film].

Kleinfield, N. R. (1991, May 19). What is Chris Whittle teaching our children? *New York Times Magazine*, p. 79.

Lauter, P. (1995). Political correctness and the attack on American colleges." In Newfield & Strickland (Eds.), *After political correctness: The humanities and society in the 1990s* (pp. 212–225). Boulder, CO: Westview.

Lipsky, D., & Abrams, A. (1994). *Late bloomers: Coming of age in today's America: The right place at the wrong time*. New York: Times Books.

Shadyac T. (Director). *The nutty professor* [film].

Watkins, E. (1996). The educational politics of human resources: Humanities teachers as resource managers. *The Minnesota Review*, 45: 147–166.

Author Index

L

M

Subject Index

E

N

DATE DUE

MY 15 '04			
AP 05 '07			